Macintosh™
Programming Techniques

Microsoft® BASIC 2.0

Macintosh™
Programming Techniques

Microsoft® BASIC 2.0

David C. Willen

Howard W. Sams & Co., Inc.
A Subsidiary of Macmillan, Inc.
4300 West 62nd Street, Indianapolis, Indiana 46268 U.S.A.

FIRST EDITION
FIRST PRINTING — 1985

International Standard Book Number: 0-672-22411-9
Library of Congress Catalog Card Number: 84-51275

Printed in the United States of America

Macintosh, MacPaint, MacWrite are trademarks of Apple Computer, Inc.
Multiplan is a trademark of Microsoft Corp.
American People/Link is a division of American Home Network, Inc.
Compuserve refers to the Compuserve Information Service.
Dow Jones is a trademark of Dow Jones and Company, Inc.
The Source is a trademark of Source Telecomputing, Inc.

Contents

Preface

Apple's Macintosh is unique in the history of microcomputers. It is the first machine designed to be easily used by the novice. Apple achieved this by incorporating several special devices and concepts. Programs and data files are represented pictorially, and they are selected and manipulated through use of the Macintosh mouse.

Apple defined standard procedures for the user to accomplish such basic computer activities as selecting data, modifying data, and invoking program functions. Because these procedures are standardized, most Macintosh applications programs can incorporate them, and anyone familiar with Macintosh operations can easily use almost any applications program on the machine. Therein lies the true power of Macintosh. Those long and unwieldy manuals, a different one for each applications program, can finally be eliminated.

The Macintosh user interface, although comfortable and easy to use, represents an extra burden for software developers: it is very difficult to program with. This book is intended to help simplify that task and clear up many of the mysteries surrounding the way the Macintosh works. It discusses such Macintosh techniques as

- **windowing**
- **dialog boxes**
- **pull-down menus**
- **using the mouse**
- **graphics**

and incorporates many sample programs.

This book will show you how to write Macintosh applications using Microsoft's BASIC programming language. This is an excellent language with which to begin your study of the Macintosh. The fundamental components of the language are simple to learn and use. More important, the language does a fine job of providing programming structures that allow access to the Macintosh user interface mechanisms. Thus, while learning this language, you will automatically be learning how Mac works.

This book is not a reference work; it is a tutorial. I see no point in filling a book with hundreds of pages that list each BASIC keyword in alphabetical order when Microsoft's manual provides the same information in that very format. Rather, what I have done here is to separate the various features of the language by function. Thus, each chapter of this book concentrates on a different aspect of the overall language. When you read about a particular language feature, all of the statements and functions pertinent to that feature are also presented. This makes the book a lot easier to work with and enjoy. Once you have gained experience with the language, you can use the many tables and figures in this book for reference. You can then use the Microsoft manual to look up a specific keyword or statement alphabetically.

If you are new to the BASIC language, do not panic. There is detailed information on the fundamental concepts of this popular language in Chapter 2. (The experienced BASIC programmer may want to skim over this chapter.) In Chapter 3, I cover language extensions that help give structure to your programs. Interrupt and error processing techniques are also covered here. Chapter 4 deals with various techniques for accessing data files, the serial communications port, and the Macintosh Clipboard. Chapter 5 is about graphics and focuses on those statements in Microsoft BASIC that can be used on other computers as well as the Macintosh. In Chapter 6, you will learn how to deal with the Macintosh's ubiquitous mouse. Graphics are revisited in Chapter 7, where you will discover the many powerful graphics functions that are unique to the Macintosh. Text fonts and type styles, filled graphics shapes and patterns, and line drawing techniques are all covered in this chapter. Chapter 8 is about windows and dialog boxes — how to create and use them. You will learn how to build custom dialog boxes to make your programs look just like professional Macintosh applications. Finally, Chapter 9 covers pull-down menus. Here you will learn how to add your own menus to the menu bar and how to remove existing ones.

Throughout the book I have included a great many sample programs. These start out simple and get more and more complex as the book progresses. I return to many of the simpler programs in later chapters, continually refining them and making them more powerful as new language features are added. This closely follows the way programs are written by professional programmers. Such programs usually start out representing nothing more than a basic idea that might work nicely on a computer. Through continual refinement and the adding of new features, the program eventually becomes a full-fledged application useable by you or other microcomputer owners.

David C. Willen

Acknowledgments

I would like to thank Peter Mann for his generous and invaluable assistance during the development of this book. Thanks go also to James V. McCusker for his many Macintosh insights.

Most important, I must thank the Howard W. Sams Company for their tireless dedication to accuracy and quality. They have made this book possible.

Chapter 1

Introduction

Apple's Macintosh ("Mac") is a remarkable microcomputer. Take it out of the box, turn it on, and insert a disk—you can use it immediately! By placing very sophisticated software inside the machine, Apple provides a friendly user interface that is easy to learn. Because of the Apple-defined standards for this interface, most application programs that run on the Mac can be operated by the user in a short period of time. This does away with a multitude of complicated manuals, and that means more people can and will want to use the Mac. Of course, any powerful application program requires experience to master. Commands and functions have to be read about in the documentation which should always be present for any serious program, but for many common program functions there is a "way of doing it" that is unique to the Macintosh.

Shortly after Apple unveiled the Mac, Microsoft released a BASIC interpreter for the machine. Microsoft has written many BASIC interpreters that are well-known and well-regarded by microcomputer users. Microsoft's initial BASIC interpreter for the Mac was not particularly different from those that run on other popular machines. In this regard, it has been disappointing to Macintosh users, because who wants to write a computer program that runs on the Mac just as it runs on another machine? On the Macintosh, one would surely want to take advantage of the powerful user interfaces that Apple provides.

Fortunately, Microsoft has since released Version 2.0 of their Macintosh BASIC interpreter. In this version, Microsoft gives the BASIC programmer the tools necessary to write application programs that take full advantage of the Macintosh user interface. That is precisely what this book is about.

In this chapter, I show you how to use the Microsoft BASIC program itself. The following chapters cover the various features of the language and how to use them. There are many example programs, and I encourage you to try them out as you read through the book. You should also experiment with your own variations on the basic ideas that I present.

What You Will Need

To follow the experiments and run the programs in this book, you need a Macintosh computer and Microsoft BASIC Version 2.0. Some of the programs require the Imagewriter printer. It is a good idea to have a printer in any case, since you may want to make listings of your longer programs. For the communications programs and experiments, you need a modem and a cable (I show you how to wire the cable if you choose to build it yourself). A second disk drive is not required but is strongly recommended. Without the second drive, copying data from one disk to another and making disk backups become truly arduous tasks. In a one-drive system, the machine will prompt you to switch disks quite often, and this can easily discourage one from pursuing more complex functions and programs.

As of this writing, the Macintosh is available in two basic models. The models differ only in the amount of memory they contain. There is the original Mac, with 128K of memory, and the so-called "fat" Mac, with 512K. Although it is possible to run BASIC and many of the programs in this book with the 128K machine, I strongly advise the use of the 512K model. The extra memory gives you the freedom to write larger and more complex programs. It also enables the machine to run faster and perform fewer disk accesses.

I also assume that you, the reader, have some experience in working with the Macintosh. I do not go into detail about how to use the mouse or some of the other basic Macintosh functions. If you are new to the Mac, however, do not be discouraged. These basic concepts are easily learned.

Starting Up BASIC

To begin, turn on your Macintosh and insert the Microsoft BASIC disk. The contents of the disk should look something like Figure 1-1. The two icons on the left represent two versions of the BASIC interpreter application itself. The *Sample Programs* folder contains a number of sample BASIC programs that are provided with the software package from Microsoft. The *System Folder* contains the standard Macintosh operating system. To start the BASIC interpreter, you must open either of the two application icons appearing on the left of the screen in Figure 1-1.

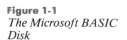
Figure 1-1
The Microsoft BASIC Disk

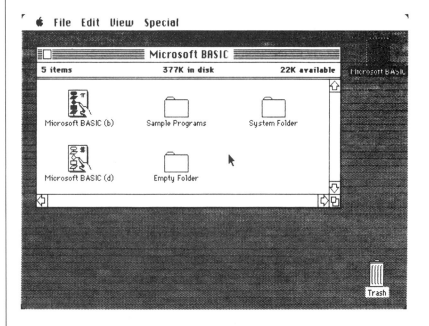

The two icons represent two different versions of the same program. They differ only in the way they process numeric data. The version titled *Microsoft BASIC (b)* processes all numeric data in the binary number system, while the *Microsoft BASIC (d)* version uses the decimal number system. The binary version operates somewhat faster, and it is the version I have used for all of the examples in this book. In some cases, however, this version could produce round-off errors, causing a value in a financial application to be off by one cent. This is why the decimal version is provided.

The Three Windows

When you open the BASIC application icon, your screen will set up as shown in Figure 1-2. As you can see, the BASIC screen layout contains three windows. These windows are summarized in Table 1-1. The currently active window is called the *List* window. The text of the BASIC program that the interpreter is currently working with can be viewed and/or modified in this window. You may also enter a program by typing it into this window. Behind this window, and dominating most of the screen, is the *Output* window. In Figure 1-1, it is labeled *Untitled*. All of the visual results produced by your program will appear in the Output window. The narrow window at the bottom of the screen is the *Command* window. When this window is active, you can use it to enter various commands that will be read and acted upon immediately by the interpreter. Some of these commands duplicate functions that may be exercised by pulling down menus from the menu bar.

As long as a program is not actually executing, you can move from one window to the next, using the mouse to click on the

Figure 1-2
The Three Windows

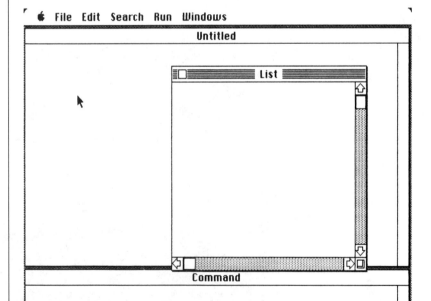

Table 1-1
BASIC's Three Windows

List Window	Displays the text of the current program in memory. Use this window to view, enter, and/or modify the program.
Output Window	The visible output produced when the program runs appears here. This window is automatically made active when the program begins.
Command Window	Use this window to manually enter BASIC commands such as RUN, LLIST, NEW, etc. You must make this window active manually before it can be used.

window that you wish to activate. The active window is indicated by highlighting within its title bar. You can also use the mouse to move the windows about, to resize them, or to remove them altogether.

If you double-click the mouse on the title bar of a window, it will immediately expand to fill the entire screen. Double-click again to shrink the window back to its original size. This is a feature most often used on the List window. Whenever you are viewing the text of a program, entering a program, or modifying a program, it is nice to have a full size List window. Of course, when the program is actually executing you will be viewing the Output window. When you start a program, the Output window automatically becomes active and is moved in front of all other windows. When the program ends, the List window is automatically made active. For this reason, it is best not to leave the List window at full screen size before starting a program. If you do so, when the program ends the List window will be moved in front of the Output window and obliterate any results produced by the program.

With the List window active, you can enter a program by typing it in on the keyboard. In Figure 1-3, I have entered a small sample program into the List window (more details on this program appear in the next chapter). When entering text in the List window, the standard Macintosh editing techniques are available. You can therefore use the mouse to set the insertion point or select some text. You can delete selected text with the <Backspace> key. You can use the **Cut, Copy,** and **Paste** functions in the Edit menu just as you would in MacWrite. (Since I am assuming that you are familiar with the Macintosh itself, I will spare you any further details on how to edit with the mouse and the Edit menu.)

Running a Program

Once a program is entered, you will want to run it. The fastest way to accomplish this is to hold down the <Command> key and press

Figure 1-3
Entering a Program

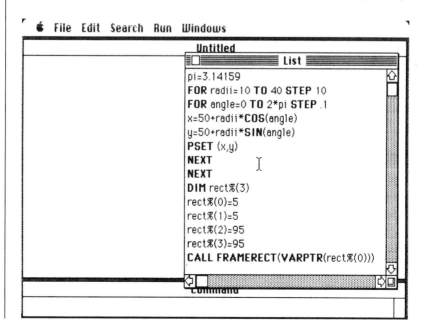

the <R> key. In Figure 1-4, I have done this. The program has executed, and the output it produced can be seen in the Output window.

Figure 1-4
Running the Program

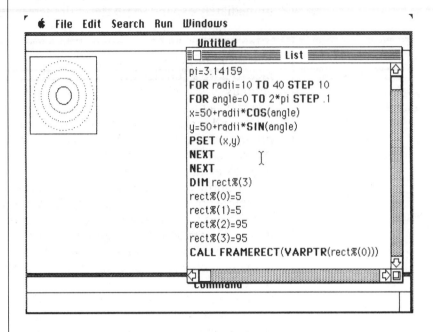

Since the program has ended, the List window is active once again. While the program was actually running, the Output window was active. To stop a program while it is running, hold down the <Command> key and press the <.> key.

The Run menu can also be used to start and stop the execution of programs. When you pull down this menu, you will see the functions **Start** and **Stop.** The <Command> key equivalents for these functions are displayed in the menu.

Maintaining Program Files

You will want to save programs as files on your disks. By doing this, you need not type them in every time you want to use them. The File menu has an **Open** function that you can use to load in programs that already exist on your disk. It works just like the **Open** function of MacWrite and MacPaint. Of course, only BASIC program files will appear in the Open Document window in this case. The file menu has save options you can use to save your programs. If you already know the name of the disk file that contains your program, you can type in the command

```
LOAD "filename"
```

into the command window, where "filename" is the name of the desired file. This will immediately load the file specified, and will save time by bypassing the Open Document dialog box.

To save a program in a disk file, select the **Save** function from the File menu. Figure 1-5 shows the dialog box produced when this function is invoked. For the most part, this dialog box is the same as that used by MacWrite and MacPaint. You specify the name of the file, and press <Return> or click the Save control button with the mouse. I am bringing it to your attention here because of the three additional control buttons that you will see near the bottom of the box. These buttons allow you to select one of three possible file formats. You can save your BASIC program either as a *Text* file, a *Compressed* file, or a *Protected* file. These file formats are summarized in Table 1-2.

For the most part, you will use the compressed format. This format can be processed fastest and uses the least amount of disk space. Why the other formats then? Well, the text format is one that is readable by many other application programs, including word processors such as MacWrite. Use this format to process your program text with other software. The protected format should be

Figure 1-5
Saving a Program

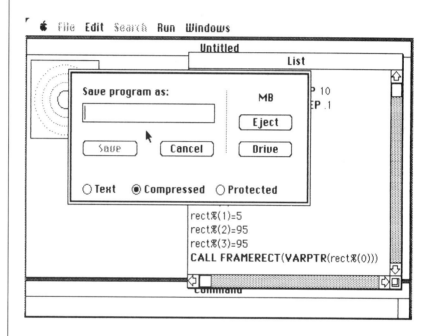

Table 1-2
BASIC File Formats

Text Format	The file contains the complete BASIC program listing in a format that is compatible with other applications programs such as word processors. The program can be run, listed, and modified in this format.
Compressed Format	The file contains the complete BASIC program listing in a format that uses the least amount of disk space and that can be processed in the least amount of time. The program can be run, listed, and modified in this format.
Protected Format	Similar to Compressed Format, except the program can only be run. In this format, it is not possible to list or modify the program listing.

used with extreme caution. A program saved in this format can be loaded and run by the BASIC interpreter, but it cannot be listed or modified. This format should only be used after you have completed a program and intend to give it to someone who must not be allowed to see or change the program code. Always save your programs in one of the other formats before using the protected format. Otherwise, you will not be able to view or change your own program!

An alternate way to save a program is to activate the Command window and type in the command

```
SAVE "filename"
```

where "filename" is the name desired for the file which will hold the program. The command automatically uses the compressed format, but you can force use of the text format as follows

```
SAVE "filename",A
```

The protected format can be specified via

```
SAVE "filename",P
```

Listing Programs

The fastest way to get a printed listing of a program is to activate the Command window and type in the command

```
LLIST
```

This sends the contents of the List window to the printer as a stream of characters. Any conventional microcomputer printer can be attached to the Macintosh and used to produce program listings with this approach. If Apple's Imagewriter printer is used, this approach will result in the quickest print time. Unfortunately, this technique does not enable the printer to display text in various fonts and type styles. The listing therefore appears as just plain text. As you can see from Figure 1-3, a BASIC program contains text in both standard and boldface type styles. This aspect of the program listing will be lost when the LLIST command is used.

The alternative approach is to select the **Print** function from the File menu. This will permit you to print the program listing in graphics mode, and thus greater detail will be provided. In this case, you must use the Imagewriter; an ordinary printer will not suffice. The **Print** function will present you with a dialog box, as in Figure 1-6, that will allow you to specify the quality of the printout to be produced. Higher quality printouts take longer. For long program listings, I recommend using the Standard Quality setting. This preserves the graphic detail of the listing, but does not take an inordinate amount of time.

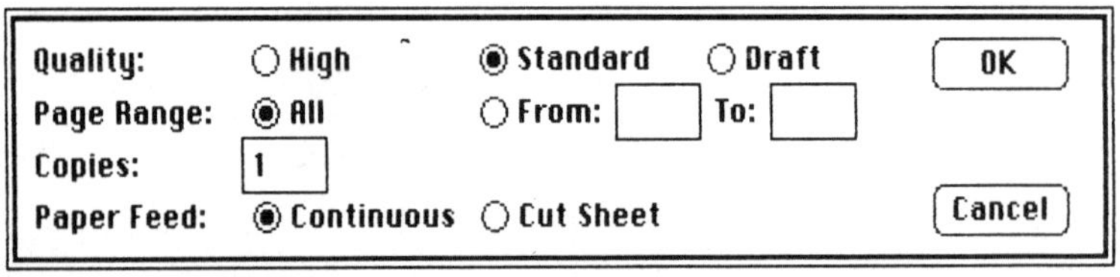

Figure 1-6
Print Dialog Box

Quality:	○ High	⦿ Standard	○ Draft		OK
Page Range:	⦿ All	○ From: [ ]	To: [ ]		
Copies:	[1]				
Paper Feed:	⦿ Continuous	○ Cut Sheet			Cancel

Other Menu Functions

The **New** function in the File menu is used to erase the current program in memory. Use it in preparation for entering a new program from scratch. The same function can be achieved by using the command

```
NEW
```

in the Command window. The **Quit** function of the File menu is, of course, used to exit from the BASIC interpreter back to the Finder, which is the visual part of the Macintosh's operating system. This action can also be achieved by entering the command

```
SYSTEM
```

in the Command window.

The Windows menu has four functions within it. They are

```
Show Command
Show List
Show Second List
Show Output
```

Three of these functions are used to simply bring back a window once it has been removed from the screen (recall that a window can be removed by clicking its close box). For example, the **Show Command** function will display the Command window on the screen and make it the active window.

The **Show Second List** function is very interesting. It can be used to display a secondary List window. Both List windows will display the same program text. However, each window can be scrolled to a different portion of that text. This is useful when working with very large programs because it enables you to view two discontinuous sections of the program at the same time. For example, see Figure 1-7. For small-sized to medium-sized programs, the second list

Figure 1-7
Using Two List Windows

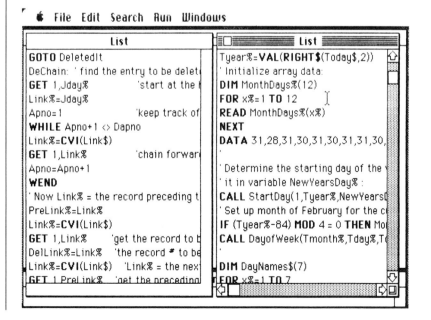

window is not recommended. It consumes main memory and clutters the screen.

The **Find** function of the Search menu can be used to search the program text for a specific sequence of characters. When invoked, it presents a dialog box in which you specify what you are searching for. This feature is useful in locating particular items in a long program listing. The function will scroll through the program listing and stop when it reaches the requested text. That text will then appear highlighted in the List window. To search for a subsequent occurrence of the same text, hold down the <Command> key and press the <N> key. In Figure 1-8, I have invoked the Find function and have entered the word "pset" to be searched for. Figure 1-9 shows the result of this operation. Note that the word is found and highlighted in the List window. The Search menu also contains a **Replace** function that can be used to replace each occurrence of a specified character sequence with an alternate sequence. The **Replace** function dialog box is shown in Figure 1-10.

Figure 1-8
The Find Function

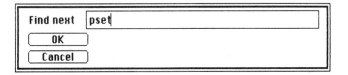

```
Find next    pset|
        [    OK    ]
        [  Cancel  ]
```

Figure 1-9
Found "pset"

```
▤☐▤▤▤▤▤▤▤▤▤▤▤ List ▤▤▤▤▤▤▤▤
pi=3.14159                                    ⇧
FOR radii=10 TO 40 STEP 10
FOR angle=0 TO 2*pi STEP .1
x=50+radii*COS(angle)
y=50+radii*SIN(angle)
PSET (x,y)
NEXT
NEXT
DIM rect%(3)
rect%(0)=5
rect%(1)=5
rect%(2)=95
rect%(3)=95
CALL FRAMERECT(VARPTR(rect%(0)))            ⇩
⇦ ☐ ▒▒▒▒▒▒▒▒▒▒▒▒▒▒▒▒▒▒▒▒▒▒▒ ⇨☐
```

Figure 1-10
The Replace Function

```
Find next     [                          ]
Replace with  [                          ]
[    OK    ]    ☐ Verify before replacing
[  Cancel  ]    ☐ Replace all occurrences
```

Onward

Now that you know how to operate the BASIC application program itself, you can proceed to learn about the language that it supports. As you read through the following chapters of this book, you can enter the accompanying program listings and try them out. I also encourage you to try out your own ideas as you develop them. Do not be afraid to experiment, as this is the best way to gain a deeper understanding of how things work. Above all, enjoy programming in BASIC with the Macintosh computer.

Chapter 2

BASIC Program Structure

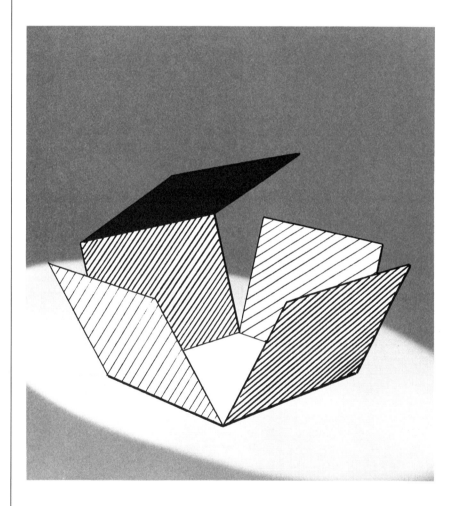

In this chapter, you will learn about the various elements that make up a Macintosh BASIC program. A solid understanding of these fundamental concepts will be crucial to your success in future programming endeavors. This will be true regardless of the specific applications you decide to tackle.

Even if you are an experienced BASIC programmer, you should at least skim through this chapter to note the unique aspects of Macintosh BASIC.

Basic Statements

A sample BASIC program is shown in Listing 2-1. Here you can see the different components that make up a BASIC program. All BASIC programs are composed of a series of BASIC *statements*.

Listing 2-1
*Sample Macintosh
BASIC Program*

```
' This program uses the trig functions to
' plot circles of various radii. It then draws
' a box around the circles using a Macintosh
' ROM routine.
pi=3.14159
FOR radii=10 TO 40 STEP 10
FOR angle=0 TO 2*pi STEP .1
x=50+radii*COS(angle)
y=50+radii*SIN(angle)
PSET (x,y)
NEXT
NEXT
DIM rect%(3)
rect%(0)=5
rect%(1)=5
rect%(2)=95
rect%(3)=95
CALL FRAMERECT(VARPTR(rect%(0)))
```

Each statement appears on a single line in the List window, and represents a single function for the computer to perform. The order in which the statements appear is very important. In general, BASIC programs are executed one statement at a time in the order in which the statements appear. This straightforward, sequential order of execution can be altered, as you shall see shortly. Note, that unlike most other versions of BASIC, Microsoft's BASIC 2.0 for the Macintosh does not require that each statement be numbered.

There are various different types of BASIC statements—each one represents a different function that BASIC can perform. Several of the more common statement types are illustrated in Listing 2-1. There is the *comment* statement, which begins with the single quote, ', character. Comment statements are not actually executed—when the program is executed they are simply skipped. Comment statements serve as a method whereby the programmer can insert descriptive information into a program. Because programs can grow to become quite complex and difficult to understand, it is always a good idea to add descriptive and explanatory comments. In this way, if you return to a program you wrote some time ago, you will have some help in understanding how it operates.

Keywords

Most statement types can be identified by the specific *keywords* found in the statement. Keywords are special, reserved words that have a predefined meaning in the BASIC language. In the List window, keywords are always easy to identify because they appear in bold face type. The keywords in Listing 2-1 are FOR, TO, STEP, COS, SIN, PSET, NEXT, DIM, CALL, FRAMERECT, and VARPTR. Keywords do not have to be entered in capital letters. In spite of this, they will be capitalized when they appear in the text of this book, to make it easier for you to identify them.

The first keyword to appear in a statement usually defines the function of the statement, and gives the statement its name. In Listing 2-1 you can find two FOR statements, two NEXT statements, and a PSET statement, among others. The FOR and NEXT statements are used to set up *program loops* (explained later), while the PSET statement is used to plot a graphics point in the output window (also explained later).

One very important statement type that does not begin with a keyword is the *assignment* statement. Before I look at this statement in greater detail, I will cover some other elements of the BASIC language.

Variables

Virtually all meaningful BASIC programs will contain *variables*. A variable represents a place in memory in which program data can be stored. The variables used in Listing 2-1 are named *pi*, *radii*, *angle*, *x*, *y*, and *rect%*. They are used to store the mathematical value pi, the radius of the circle being drawn, the angle of the point being plotted, the x and y coordinates of the point, and the coordinates of the box, respectively.

When writing a program, define the variables used by giving them names. A variable name can consist of any combination of letters and numbers, but it must begin with a letter. Do not use reserved words for variable names. This could cause BASIC to become confused as to the intent of your statements.

Variable names can be as many as 40 characters long, although you should keep them relatively short so that your programs do not become too verbose and hard to read. Choose variable names that are descriptive of the data that they will contain, as was done in Listing 2-1. If you want to convey several thoughts in a single variable name, you can do so by embedding a period, ., character in the name. For example, an invoicing program might use variable names such as

```
sales.tax, net.price, gross.price, and
total09
```

As with keywords, BASIC does not distinguish between uppercase and lowercase letters in variable names. Thus the names *sales.tax*, *SALES.TAX*, and *Sales.TAX* will all refer to the same variable.

Constants

When writing a program, you will often find the need to place fixed data values into the program text itself. Such fixed values are called *constants*. Another term that is often used to describe some constants is *literals*. As this word implies, these are values that are meant to be read *literally* when the program is executed. In the program of Listing 2-1, the constants used are

3.14159, 10, 40, 0, 2, .1, 50, 3, 5, and 95

Because BASIC supports different types of data, there are different types of constants that can be used. For example, if you are working with *character strings* (to be described shortly) then you might want to use a *character string constant*, such as

"HI THERE"

These concepts will be explained more fully later in this chapter, in the section on data types.

The Assignment Statement and Expressions

The *assignment* statement is the single most important statement in the BASIC language. It can be used to move information from one variable to another, as well as to perform calculations. The assignment statement has the general form

variable name = expression

The variable specified at the left of the equals symbol is said to be the *target*, or recipient, of the statement. When the statement is executed, the expression at the right of the equals symbol is evaluated, and the value produced is stored in the target variable. The expression can be a simple constant, another variable, or a more complex formulation. A simple example of an assignment statement might be

gamma = 38

In this statement, the target variable is named *gamma*, and the expression consists of the constant value 38. When executed, this statement will cause the contents of variable *gamma* to be set to the value 38. It is very important to realize that this statement should not be interpreted according to the standard rules of algebra. In that science, the statement

gamma = 38

would be called an *equation*, and would suggest that the variable gamma is always equal to 38. Beginners are often confused by this, since the BASIC assignment statement and the algebraic equation are written in an identical fashion. The distinction is that the BASIC statement is a statement defining an action that is to take place, while the algebraic statement is a statement of known fact. In BASIC, when you write the statement

```
gamma = 38
```

you are requesting that action be taken to set variable *gamma* to 38; at some later time *gamma* may be set to another value. By contrast, once the same algebraic statement is made, it would not be possible for *gamma* to take on any other value.

Moving Data

Another simple form of the assignment statement sets the contents of a variable to the contents of another variable. An example of this might be

```
gamma = beta
```

In this case, the variable *gamma* is being set to the current contents of the variable *beta*. This is a simple and straightforward way of moving data from one variable to another in your programs.

More Complex Expressions

The real power of the assignment statement becomes evident when more complex expressions are used to the right of the equals symbol. Such expressions are formed by combining variables with other variables and constants, through use of *operators*. The most commonly used operators represent familiar arithmetic operations as addition, **+**, subtraction, **-**, multiplication, *****, and division **/**. As an example, consider the statement

```
x = y + 3
```

This statement is interpreted as "set the contents of variable *x* to the current contents of variable *y*, plus three." A more complex example is

```
tax = .3 * sales + 500
```

This statement is interpreted as, "set the contents of variable *tax* to .3 times the current contents of variable *sales*, plus 500."

Using Parentheses in Expressions

In the last example, the expression was evaluated from left to right, in the same manner in which it was written. This straightforward, left to right evaluation of expressions is not the general rule, however. For example, the expression

```
3 + 4 * 5
```

would be evaluated by multiplying four by five, and then adding three; the result will be 23. The expression will be evaluated in that order because the multiplication operator has a higher *precedence* than the addition operator. When expressions are evaluated, operations of higher precedence are always performed before those of lower precedence. When several operations of the same precedence are encountered, they are evaluated in left to right order. The numeric operators are listed in Table 2-1 in ascending precedence order. Note that the operations which are of higher precedence have a lower precedence number in Table 2-1. This is because the precedence number shows the order the operations should be executed. We will look at them more closely in a moment.

When it is necessary to override the order of evaluation imposed by the precedence system, parentheses can be used to group specific operations together. For example, the expression

```
(3 + 4) * 5
```

would be evaluated by adding three plus four, and then multiplying by five; the result will be 35. Parenthetic expressions may be *nested* if necessary, to yield large and complex expressions. For example

```
delta = 58 + (y * (4 - alpha) + (8 * (qs / 5)))
```

When writing such expressions, care must be taken to insure that all of the opening (left) parentheses are properly matched by closing (right) parentheses.

Table 2-1

Arithmetic Operators (in order of Precedence)

Precedence Level	Symbol	Operation	Example
1	^	Exponentiation	x^3 x cubed
2	–	Negation	–x negative x
3	*	Multiplication	a*b a times b
3	/	Division	a / b a divided by b
4	\	Integer Division	a \ b a divided by b, whole portion of result only
5	MOD	Modulo	a MOD b a divided by b, remainder of result only
6	+	Addition	a + b a plus b
6	–	Subtraction	a – b a minus b

The Arithmetic Operators

As already mentioned, the arithmetic operators available in BASIC are listed in Table 2-1. Here you will find the four common arithmetic operations, addition, subtraction, multiplication, and division. In addition, there are several other, less well known, operators.

The *exponentiation* operator, represented by the symbol ^, is used to raise values to a power. For example, the expression

```
alpha^3
```

represents "alpha cubed." This operator can also be used to extract roots, as follows

```
x^.5 = "square root of x"
x^(1/4) = "fourth root of x"
```

Another interesting operator is the *integer division* operator, represented by the symbol \ . Unlike the standard division operator /, the integer division operator divides one value into another and returns only the integer, or whole portion of the result. For example

```
4/3 = 1.33333
4/3 = 1.0
```

A companion to the integer division operator is the *modulo* operator, represented by the keyword MOD. This operator also performs a division operation, but it returns only the remainder of that operation. For example

```
6 MOD 3 = 0
7 MOD 3 = 1
2 MOD 3 = 2
```

Current and Next Values

Since assignment statements are not bound by the rules of algebra, you can use the same variable name on both sides of the equals symbol. For example, consider the statement

```
x = x + 1
```

It is important to realize that the variable name x represents a different value in its two appearances in this statement. The x to the right of the equals symbol represents the current value of variable x at the time the statement is executed. The x to the left of the equals symbol represents the new value of variable x, to be effective at the completion of the statement's execution. Thus, the effect of the statement is to cause the contents of variable x to be increased by one. If x contains the value 3 before this statement is reached, then it will contain 4 after the statement has been executed.

Data Types

Up to this point, you have been concerned with *numeric data* (i.e. numbers) only. One of the nice features of Microsoft BASIC for the Macintosh is its ability to deal with different types of data. The primary alternative to numeric data is *character string* data. Character string data is made up of sequences of alphabetic, numeric, and other characters. To deal with this type of data, you can use *string variables* and *string constants*; there is even a *string operator* that may be employed to create *string expressions*. Thus you can see that the concepts and techniques that you have already developed may be applied in general to the different data types that are available.

The two basic data types that you will be dealing with are numeric and string. To make matters more complex, however, the numeric data type can be further subdivided. There are actually three different numeric data types; they are called *integer, single precision,* and *double precision*.

BASIC recognizes two other data types, although these appear to be simply numeric data. These special data types are called *logical* and *pointer*. These will be described shortly.

Variable Name Suffixes

To identify the data type of a variable, a special suffix character is appended to the end of the variable's name. If no suffix is used, the variable will assume a *default* type, which depends upon the version of BASIC you are using. In each version, the default represents a general purpose numeric type; this is the type I have used in the program examples up to this point.

Table 2-2 indicates the suffix to be used for each data type. For example, character string variables are identified by appending the dollar sign symbol, $, to their names. Thus the variable names

```
a$, address$, id$, and nak.code$
```

all represent character string variables.

Two variable names that are identical except for their suffix represent two distinct data storage areas. Thus, for example, the two variables *ALPHA* and *ALPHA$* can be used in the same program. The first will refer to a numeric variable and the second will refer to an independent character string variable. While it is possible to do this, it is not recommended because the similarity between the names can lead to programmer errors.

Numeric Data Types

Table 2-2 shows which numeric data type will be used as the default data type if no variable name suffix is used. This will depend upon whether you are using the *binary* or *decimal* versions of the Microsoft BASIC program. In many applications, this default data type will be adequate for numeric data. There are times, however, when it is useful to be able to specify that numeric data be stored using one or more of the other numeric formats that are available. Using the other formats can produce savings in computation time and/or memory requirements, at a cost of numeric accuracy.

The three numeric data types can be divided into two general categories, real numbers and integer numbers. Real numbers are more flexible than integers because they can have fractional parts. Integer numbers can be positive or negative, but they must be *whole numbers*—i.e., they cannot represent fractions. The values

```
0      5     28      -3      200028       -150
```

can be stored as either real or integer numbers, but the values

```
28.75      -.05   ·    98.6        -0.000825
```

can only be stored as real numbers.

Calculations can be performed faster with integers than with reals. For this reason, you should always use the integer data type

Table 2-2
Data Types

Data Type	Variable Name Suffix	Bytes Required	Used to Store
Integer	%	2	Values in the range −32768 through +32767, no fractional parts allowed.
Single Precision	! or none for binary version of BASIC	4	In binary version, positive or negative values as small as 1.18×10^{-38} and as large as $3.3 \times 10^{+38}$ with up to 7 significant digits. In decimal version, positive or negative values as small as 10^{-64} and as large as 10^{+63} with up to 6 significant digits.
Double Precision	# or none for decimal version of BASIC	8	In binary version, positive or negative values as small as 2.23×10^{-308} and as large as $1.78 \times 10^{+308}$ with up to 15 significant digits. In decimal version, positive or negative values as small as 10^{-64} and as large as 10^{+63} with up to 14 significant digits.
String	$	5 + # of characters	Strings of characters (can be up to 32767 characters long).

when your application will not require numbers that have fractional parts. For example, if you are writing a program that will calculate the number of days between two given dates, the variable that will hold the result will certainly be an integer variable—it will not be possible to come up with a fractional result. On the other hand, suppose you are writing a program to calculate development times for photographic film. If one of your input values is the temperature of the developer solution, then you will probably need a real variable for that value—temperature measurements often have a fractional part.

There are some applications that will require you to use real variables even though your data does not have fractional parts. This is because reals have another advantage over integers—they can be used to store numbers that are very large, while integers cannot. The integer data type can be processed with the greatest speed and uses the least amount of memory, but if you use it, your values are limited to the range −32768 through +32767. You might want to use an integer variable, say *CLASS%*, to count the number of students in your geometry class. If, however, you wanted to count the total number of geometry students in the United States, the number would be too large to be held in an integer variable. For that application, you could use a single precision variable (i.e., *STUDENTS!*).

Both single and double precision variables, which are reals, can hold very large numbers by using a scheme called *scientific notation*. Using this notation, each number is expressed in two parts, called the *mantissa* and the *exponent*.

The mantissa is always between 0 and 10, and contains the *significant digits* of the value. The exponent represents a power of ten; it indicates how far and in what direction to move the decimal point of the mantissa to obtain the true value being expressed. For example, the number 5000 would be expressed in scientific notation with a mantissa of 5.0 and an exponent of 3, thus

```
5000 = 5.0 × 10^3
```

To express a value in scientific notation as a numeric constant in BASIC, you write the mantissa, followed by the letter "E" and then the exponent, thus

```
5.0E3
```

This same method can be employed to represent numbers that are extremely small. For example, your Macintosh computer processes data in fundamental time units, each of which is approximately 128 nanoseconds (.000000128 seconds) long. By simply using a negative exponent, we can express this number in scientific notation

```
.000000128 = 1.28 × 10^-7 = 1.28E-7
```

Real numbers in BASIC are stored and processed using the scientific notation principle. The precision of a real variable determines the number of significant digits in the mantissa. Single precision reals have up to six significant digits in the binary version of BASIC (BASIC(b)), and up to seven significant digits in the decimal version (BASIC(d)).

Double precision reals have up to fifteen significant digits in BASIC(b), and fourteen significant digits in BASIC(d). The choice as to which to use depends upon the precision required for your application, but must be tempered with the knowledge that higher precision requires more memory and more processing time.

Logical Data

When writing programs in BASIC, you will often find yourself dealing with a special type of data called *logical* or *boolean* data. Logical data can at any time be in one of two different states. These two states are referred to as true and false, although you may also think of them as 1 and 0. Logical data is stored using conventional numeric data types. The false state is stored as the value 0, and the true state is stored as the value −1 (although any nonzero value will represent true).

Logical data is most often used as the object of a BASIC statement that conditionally performs some action. The most common statement of this type is the *IF . . . THEN* statement which is described in more detail later. In these applications, the logical data often represents the outcome of a test on some other data type. For example, a statement used to test whether or not numeric variable x contains 0 might be written as follows

```
IF x = 0 THEN . . .
```

In the above statement, a logical value of either true or false is generated from two numeric values—the numeric variable x and the numeric constant 0. If variable x contains 0, then the logical value will be true, otherwise it will be false. The logical value is created as a result of the use of a *relational* operator.

Relational operators are used to create a logical data value that represents the outcome of a test between two other data values. In our case, the relational operator was equals $=$. Table 2-3 lists all of the relational operators that are available and describes their action.

Symbol	Operation
<	less than
=	equal to
>	greater than
< =	less than or equal to
> =	greater than or equal to
< >	not equal to

It is important to realize that whenever a relational operator is used, the result will be either the value 0 or the value −1. For example, consider the statement:

```
test = x < y
```

This statement sets the variable test to either the value −1 (true) or 0 (false). If variable x is less than variable y, then test will be set to -1, otherwise it will be set to 0. It is also possible to use relational operators to compare character string data; this will be illustrated later in this chapter.

Two or more logical evaluations may be combined by use of logical operators. Although there are several logical operators, the most commonly used ones are *AND* and *OR*. The AND operator will produce a result of true only if both of its operands are true. The OR operator will produce a result of true if either of its operands are true. The logical operators are listed, in order of precedence, in Table 2-4. Here are some examples of how they might be used

```
IF (x < y) AND (z < t) THEN . . .
IF (x = 0) OR (y = 0) THEN . . .
```

Pointer Data

In certain cases, the general purpose numeric data type can be used to store a special kind of data called *pointer data*. Although pointer data is not needed for many programming applications, it does have some important uses.

Table 2-4
Logical Operators

Operator	Example	Result
NOT	NOT x	True if x is False False if x is True
AND	x AND y	True only if both x and y are True.
OR	x OR y	True if either x or y is True.
XOR	x XOR y	True if either x or y is True, but False if both x and y are True.

A pointer data item represents an actual memory address within the Macintosh. Some of the Macintosh's built-in routines, as well as other machine language routines that you can call from your BASIC program, will require that information be passed in the form of memory addresses. Such memory addresses are usually obtained by using the BASIC function **VARPTR**. This function will return the address of the variable presented to it. For example, the statement

```
x = VARPTR(y)
```

will set variable x equal to the address at which variable y is currently being held. In a 128K Macintosh, memory addresses go as high as 131071. In a 512K Mac, they go as high as 524287. Numbers this large cannot be held in an integer variable, so you should always use a variable of at least single precision when manipulating pointer data.

Caution must always be exercised when using pointer data. Many commonly used Macintosh functions can cause the contents of memory to be rearranged. For this reason, you should always use VARPTR to obtain the address of a variable just before you are about to use that address. If you obtain the address, store it, and then go off and do some other things, when you actually use the address it may no longer be correct. Some of the other operations you performed may have caused your variable to be moved to another area of memory. An example of the use of VARPTR can be found in the sample program of Listing 2-1.

Character String Data

String data can consist of any combination of letters, numbers, and other special characters. String constants must be enclosed in quotes, for example:

```
"This is a string constant"
"SO IS THIS. . . ."
"XYZ 1298"
"@#$&*"
```

As shown in Table 2-2, string variables end with the $ symbol, and can store strings up to 32767 characters long. The length of a string variable at any time is the number of characters held in that variable. This is a value that can range from 0 to 32767. When a string variable contains no characters, its length is said to be 0. A character string of length 0 is referred to as a *null string*. A null string constant can be specified by writing two consecutive quote symbols, with nothing between them, thus

```
" "
```

Values may be assigned to string variables in the same manner they are assigned to numeric variables, for example:

```
a$ = "Hi There!"
address$ = "23 ST. JOHNS ROAD"
null$ = " "
```

String Expressions

String expressions can be formed by combining two or more string values with a *string operator*. There is only one string operator; it is called *concatenation*, and is represented by the + symbol. This operation acts between two string values by simply combining them. Thus, for example, if

```
a$ = "Good" and
b$ = "Bye" then
a$ + b$ = "GoodBye"
```

The concatenation operator can be used to build a composite string by repeatedly adding new string data to the composite. Using this technique, the composite string $c\$$ is initialized to the null string:

```
c$ = " "
```

Once this is done, each time some new string data $new\$$ is obtained, it is concatenated to the end of $c\$$

```
c$ = c$ + new$
```

An example that uses this technique will be shown later in this chapter.

String values may also be combined using the relational operators of Table 2-3. This results in a string comparison, which produces a logical data result of either true or false. For example, the expression

```
a$ = "HELLO"
```

will produce a result of true only if string variable $a\$$ contains the exact string "HELLO".

Suppose we use the expression

```
a$ < "HELLO"
```

We were able to understand what it meant for two strings to be
equal, but what does it mean for one string to be less than another?
To understand the answer to this question, I must explain how
character string information is stored within the Macintosh
computer.

The ASCII Standard

Within the computer, each string character is stored in a single byte
of memory. A byte can hold any one of 256 different values, from 0
through 255. Some time ago, a standard was developed that maps
the first 128 of these values to a complete set of printable symbols.
These symbols include the alphabet from A to Z, in both uppercase
and lowercase, as well as the digits 0 through 9, and a compre-
hensive array of other special characters. The standard is known as
the *American Standard Code for Information Interchange*, or
ASCII for short. It is shown in Table 2-5.

Table 2-5
*The American Standard
Code for Information
Interchange (ASCII)*

Control Codes as used on
Macintosh:

3	Enter Key	60	<	94	^
7	Beep (Command-G)	61	=	95	—
8	Backspace Key	62	>	96	`
9	Tab Key	63	?	97	a
10	Line Feed	64	@	98	b
12	Form Feed (Imagewriter)	65	A	99	c
13	Return Key	66	B	100	d
32	Spacebar	67	C	101	e
33	!	68	D	102	f
34	"	69	E	103	g
35	#	70	F	104	h
36	$	71	G	105	i
37	½	72	H	106	j
38	&	73	I	107	k
39	'	74	J	108	l
40	(	75	K	109	m
41	)	76	L	110	n
42	*	77	M	111	o
43	+	78	N	112	p
44	,	79	O	113	q
45	-	80	P	114	r
46	.	81	Q	115	s
47	/	82	R	116	t
48	0	83	S	117	u
49	1	84	T	118	v
50	2	85	U	119	w
51	3	86	V	120	x
52	4	87	W	121	y
53	5	88	X	122	z
54	6	89	Y	123	R
55	7	90	Z	124	/
56	8	91	[	125	T
57	9	92	/	126	
58	:	93	]	127	DEL,Rubout
59	;				

When studying Table 2-5, note that the first 32 ASCII codes have been reserved for special control codes and do not represent printable characters. The most commonly used control codes correspond to values 7, 8, 9, 10, and 13. Code 7 is called BELL; you can cause the Macintosh to sound an audible beep if you "print" this character. To give it a try, enter and execute the statement

```
PRINT CHR$(7)
```

Code 8 is called BKSP and represents the Backspace key on your keyboard. Code 9 is called TAB and represents the Tab key. Code 10 is called LF and can be used to produce a line feed (i.e., new line) on either the display or printer. Code 13 is called CR and represents the Return key on your keyboard. One additional code, unique to the Macintosh, is code 3, which represents the Enter key on your keyboard.

Looking at the rest of Table 2-5, you can see that the letters of the alphabet appear in the expected order, first in uppercase, and then again in lowercase. This gives us a hint as to how string comparisons such as

```
a$ < "HELLO"
```

are made. BASIC compares two strings one character at a time, working from left to right. For each character position, the ASCII code values are compared. If they do not match, then the string with the lower ASCII code value is said to be smaller. If the characters in the position being compared are the same, then the test continues with the next position to the right. If each character position matches, but one string is shorter than the other, then the shorter string is said to be smaller. Thus, if *a$* contained the value "HELP" as in our above example, then the expression would evaluate to false, because

```
"HELP" > "HELLO"
```

In a similar fashion, you can see that

```
"Delta" < "Echo"
"Handy" > "Handyman"
```

Note that, although

```
"XRAY" = "XRAY"
"XRAY" < > "XRAY "
```

this is because the extra blank space in the latter example is considered significant.

Note that the ASCII scheme combined with BASIC's relational operators makes it possible for you to sort various strings of data into alphabetical order. More techniques for dealing with strings will appear later in this chapter.

Array Variables

Variables in BASIC can be used to represent two kinds of data structures. These are the *scalar* and the *array*. In all of the examples up to this point, we have used scalar variables. A scalar variable is capable of storing one data value (of the appropriate data type, of course). Thus, for example, the scalar numeric variable *xyz* might be used to store the numeric value 289. The scalar string variable *addr$* might be used to store the string value "BANK ST." In each case, a single data value is held by the variable named.

In contrast, an array variable may be used to store multiple data values under a single variable name. Such variables are useful for storing collections of data values, as in a list or table.

All arrays must be defined as such before you can use them in your programs. This is accomplished by the *dimension* statement, which begins with the identifying keyword, DIM. The dimension statement allows you to name an array variable and simultaneously define the number of dimensions and the size of each dimension. For example, the statement

`DIM array1(9)`

names variable *array1* as a one-dimensional array with ten elements. Such an array is illustrated in Figure 2-1. Each element of the array acts just like a scalar variable—it can be used to store a single data value. To access the individual elements of an array, you specify the array name followed by a subscript value in parenthesis. Thus, for example, the third element of our sample array would be accessed as

`array1(2)`

As shown in Figure 2-1, this array element contains the value 29. So a statement such as

`x = array1(2)`

would set variable *x* to 29. On the other hand, a statement such as

`array1(2)=0`

would set the third element of the array to 0. The point being made here is that an array variable with a subscript specified is no different from a scalar variable. The real power of arrays becomes evident when we specify the subscript by using another variable (or an expression). For example, consider the statement

Figure 2-1
A One-Dimensional Array

```
DIM array1(9)

array1(0) = [        ]
array1(1) = [        ]
array1(2) = [   29   ]
array1(3) = [        ]
array1(4) = [        ]
array1(5) = [        ]
array1(6) = [        ]
array1(7) = [        ]
array1(8) = [        ]
array1(9) = [        ]
```

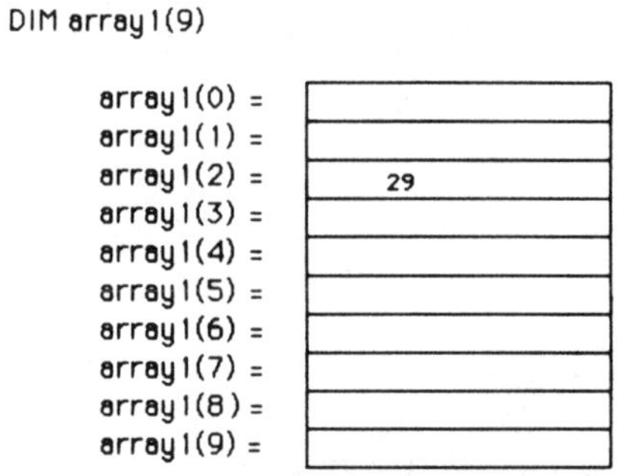

```
x = array1(i)
```

What value will the above statement place into variable *x*? The answer depends upon the value of variable *i* at the time the statement is executed. The statement thus allows us to dynamically select a single value from a list of values, with the selection being made at the time the program is executed.

Subscript Ranges

All arrays have a default lower subscript bound of 0. The upper bound of an array subscript is specified in the dimension statement that defines the array. In this manner, the total number of elements in the array are defined. Note, because the subscript range starts with 0, the actual number of elements is one more than the number specified in the dimension statement. Thus, in our previous example, array1 was defined with an upper subscript bound of nine, yielding a total of ten elements. In many applications, it is desirable to number the elements of an array starting with the number one. In these cases, it is best to simply ignore the element with subscript zero. Thus, you might define an array as

```
DIM array2(10)
```

and use the ten elements array2(1) through array2(10), ignoring element array2(0). The amount of memory wasted is minimal, since only a single array element is not being used. If the idea of wasting this element bothers you, Microsoft provides a special statement. By placing the statement

```
OPTION BASE 1
```

at the beginning of your program, all arrays dimensioned will begin with subscript 1, not 0.

Multidimensional Arrays

The array shown in Figure 2-1 is called a *one-dimensional* array, and is useful for representing a simple list of values. To represent more complex structures, *multidimensional* arrays can be defined. For example, a two-dimensional array can be used to effectively represent a table of data, as shown in Figure 2-2. In this figure, an array named grades is used to hold the exam grades for each of the ten students in a class. The array holds a total of five exam grades for each student. The ten students are represented by subscript values of one through ten in the first dimension, while the five different exams are represented by subscript values of one through five in the second dimension. The array would be defined using the statement

```
DIM grades(10,5)
```

To access the third exam grade for the second student, we would access array element grades(2,3). To obtain the class average for the fourth exam, we would hold the second dimension subscript constant at four, while allowing the first dimension subscript to vary from one to ten, thus accessing all elements in the fourth column of the table. An array reference such as

```
grades(i,4)
```

could be used for this purpose. To obtain the grade average for the fifth student, we would hold the first dimension subscript constant at five, while allowing the second dimension subscript to range from one to five, thus accessing all elements in the fifth row of the table. An array reference such as

```
grades(5,i)
```

could be used for this purpose. Note the amount of flexibility we have, once we store data using this kind of structure.

Figure 2-2
A Two-Dimensional Array

DIM grades(10,5)

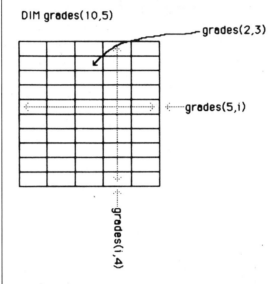

Arrays are not limited to just two dimensions. Figure 2-3 shows what a three-dimensional array, defined using the statement

```
DIM array3(8,5,3)
```

might look like. Although they cannot be easily represented on paper, arrays with more than three dimensions can be defined as well. In fact, you can define an array with up to 255 dimensions! In actual practice, however, one rarely uses more than three dimensions. This is usually enough to represent the data structures that you will be working with.

Data Types in Arrays

Arrays can be used to store any of the data types already discussed. Thus, for example, an array declared as

```
DIM alpha%(5,5)
```

could be used to store a matrix of integers, while an array declared as

```
DIM beta#(100)
```

could be used to store a list of double precision values.

In a similar fashion, you can declare an array of strings using a statement such as

```
DIM names$(20)
```

Each element of a string array has all of the properties of a scalar string variable. This means that each element can contain as many as 32767 characters, or as few as none. Each element of a string array has its own length.

Figure 2-3
A Three-Dimensional Array

```
DIM array3(8,5,3)
```

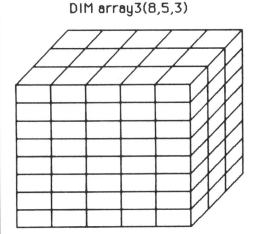

Statement Labels

Much of the power of the BASIC language comes from the ability to execute sections of a program repeatedly, and to execute different sections of a program under different conditions. There are various different statements that you can use to direct program flow to a particular section in a program. To identify a specific program section so that you can direct program flow to it, you use *statement labels*.

Most BASIC language implementations require that each statement have a label which is a number. These numbers define the order of the statements in the program, and the normal order in which the program will be executed. On the Macintosh, this requirement has been removed. It is therefore only necessary to label those statements that you specifically need to call out from other points in the program. The order of statements in a Macintosh BASIC program is defined by their order of appearance in the listing window. This is also the normal order in which the program will be executed.

Statement labels in Macintosh BASIC can be either numbers, names, or a combination of both. Statement labels always appear at the very beginning of a statement, and should be followed immediately by a colon, :. For example, consider

```
ASSIGNMENT: x=0
```

The statement shown above, which assigns the value zero to variable *x*, has been given the label ASSIGNMENT. As another example, consider

```
101 PRINT "hello there"
```

This statement, which displays the text "hello there" in the output window, has been given the statement number 101. Note that statement labels must always be followed by a colon, while statement numbers are not.

Once a statement has been labelled, it can be referenced by other parts of the same program. The simplest form of a statement reference is the *GOTO* statement. This statement has the form

```
GOTO label
```

where label is any statement label in the program. It has the effect of diverting program execution to the specified point in the program.

Listing 2-2 shows a simple example of a program that uses a statement label "Again" as well as the GOTO statement. Try entering and running this program. It will produce output that looks like that shown in Figure 2-4. Note that this program will never end, since it continually executes the same sequence of statements over and over again. These statements form what is known as an *infinite loop*. To stop the program, use the mouse to pull down the Run Menu and select the Stop option.

Listing 2-2
Demo of Statement Labels and the GOTO Statement

```
x=1
Again: PRINT "Hello, x=";x
x=x+1
GOTO Again
```

Figure 2-4
Output of Listing 2-2

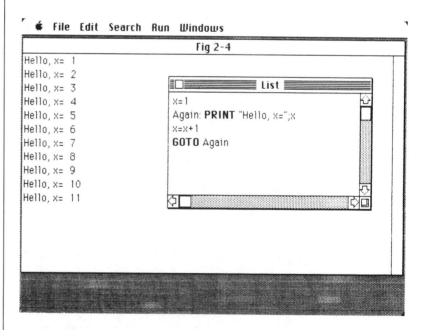

To increase program readability, statement labels may also be placed alone on a line. In this case, they apply to the line immediately following. This is illustrated in Listing 2-3.

Listing 2-3
*Statement Label on
Separate Line*

```
x=1
Again:
PRINT "Hello, x=";x
x=x+1
GOTO Again
```

Simple Input and Output

BASIC on the Macintosh provides the same simple input and
output commands used in most versions of BASIC. I have already
used the PRINT statement, which can be used to display results in
the Output window. The simplest form of this statement is as
follows

```
PRINT expression
```

The expression following the keyword PRINT may be a constant,
variable, or more complex formulation. The following are all valid
PRINT statements

```
PRINT x+5
PRINT name$
PRINT "Welcome Aboard!"
```

A single PRINT statement may be used to display more than one
item. In this case, two or more items are placed after the keyword
PRINT, and separated from each other by either commas or
semicolons. If separated by commas, the items will be spaced out
when displayed in the Output window. If separated by semicolons,
the items will be placed directly adjacent to one another. This is
illustrated in Figure 2-5.

Figure 2-5
*PRINT Statement
Separators*

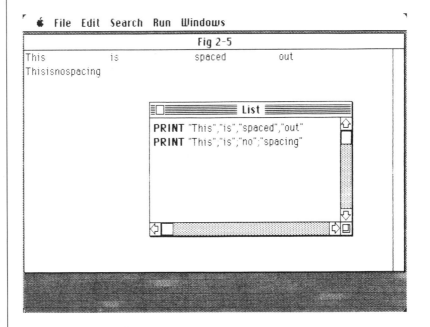

Normally, each PRINT statement begins producing its output on a new line in the Output window. If, however, you place a semicolon at the end of a PRINT statement, then the subsequent PRINT statement will begin producing output exactly where the previous one left off. This is illustrated in Figure 2-6.

Figure 2-6
PRINT Statement with Semicolon

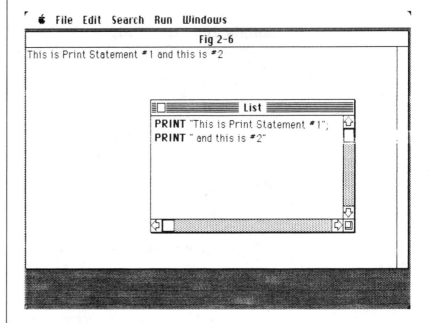

Print Using

The PRINT statement alone offers very little control over the way numeric results are displayed. It is fine to use if you just need to display a single value at some point, and are not concerned with how it appears in the Output window. If, however, you are producing a detailed report or table of output, then you will need more control over the appearance of numeric output. This additional control is provided by a modified version of the PRINT statement, called the *PRINT USING* statement.

The PRINT USING statement has the following general form

```
PRINT USING fstring; expression
```

This statement will display the value of the expression specified, but it will do so using the formatting information provided in *fstring*— a format string. The format string can be either a string variable or constant; its job is to define exactly how the programmer wants the data specified by *expression* to be displayed. The format string must contain one or more format specifier characters, chosen from the list shown in Table 2-6.

The # character specifies that one digit position be reserved on the display line for the numeric result. A series of # characters can be used to reserve a specific number of digit positions. For example, the statement

```
PRINT USING "###"; x
```

will reserve three digit positions for the value of variable *x*. this will allow us to display values of *x* in the range 0 to 999. Larger values would not fit in the three digit field created by our format specifier.

Table 2-6
PRINT USING Format Specifiers

Format Specifier Character	Effect
#	Reserves a digit position. Example: PRINT USING "###";5 will produce: 5
.	Forces positioning and display of the decimal point. Examples: PRINT USING "##.##";3.5 will produce: 3.50
+	Displays the sign (+ or −) of the value at position specified. Must be at beginning or end of specifier. Example: PRINT USING " + ##";28,−33 will produce: + 28 −33
−	If the value being printed is negative, then this specifier will display "−" at position specified. Must be at end of specifier. Example: PRINT USING "###.##−";−150 produces: 150.00−
**	Reserves two digit positions for the value being printed; and causes any leading spaces in the field to be filled with asterisks. Example: PRINT USING "**####.##";35.40 produces: ****35.40
$$	Reserves two digit positions for the value being printed; and causes "$" to be displayed immediately to the left of the value. Example: PRINT USING "$$##.##";25 produces: $25.00
**$	Reserves three digit positions; causes any leading spaces to be filled with asterisks; *and* causes "$" to be displayed to the left of the result. Example: PRINT USING "**$###.##";9.9 will produce: ****$9.90
,	Reserves a digit position and causes a comma to be inserted to the left of every third digit. Example: PRINT USING "#########,.#";1300000 produces: 1,300,000.0
^ ^ ^ ^	Causes the value to be displayed using scientific notation and reserves 4 positions for the exponent. Example: PRINT USING "#.###^^^^";.0000235 produces: 2.350E−05

If the value of *x* were negative, then we could only display values in the range −1 through −99. This is because one of the digit positions must be reserved for the minus sign character which indicates that the number is negative. The PRINT USING format specifier thus defines how many positions on the display line can be occupied by the value to be displayed.

By inserting a decimal point into the format specifier, you can define exactly where the decimal point should appear in the displayed result. You can also specify how many digits should be displayed to the right of the decimal point. This is extremely useful when displaying values that represent dollars and cents. Left to itself, the PRINT statement will only print digits that are significant. Thus, a value representing three dollars and fifty cents would appear as 3.5. Using the format specifier, you can get it to appear as 3.50 (see examples in Table 2-6). Other special characters that can be used in format specifiers allow you to insert a dollar sign, **$**, into the result, place positive or negative-signs, **+** and **-**, and produce other effects. Table 2-6 contains examples of each.

Positioning Results within the Output Window

A sequence of PRINT statements will, in general, tend to fill the Output window from top to bottom. When the window is full, it will begin to scroll. Old information will be moved up in the window, and new data to be PRINTed will appear at the bottom. You can see this effect for yourself if you run the program in Listing 2-2.

There are several techniques that you can use to gain better control of where results produced by the PRINT statement will appear on your screen. Within the PRINT statement itself, you can specify the exact column position on the current line for display. This is accomplished by inserting the TAB function in the PRINT item list. For example, the statement

```
PRINT "Value of x = "; TAB(50); x
```

will display the text "Value of x = " at the beginning of the current line; it will then tab over to column 50 on that line before actually displaying the value of *x*. This technique is useful for producing tabular output; an example is shown in Figure 2-7.

Figure 2-7
The TAB Function

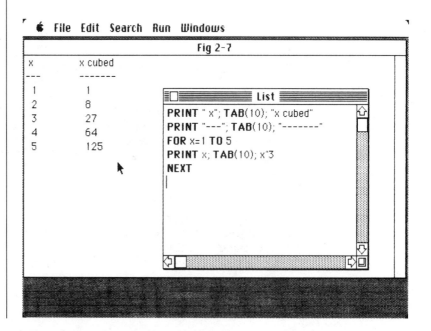

A more flexible technique for positioning displayed results in the Output window is available through use of the *LOCATE* statement. When you code the LOCATE statement, you give it two values that specify the row and column position within the Output window for the next data to be displayed. For example, the statement

```
LOCATE 5,10
```

would cause the next PRINT statement to begin displaying results in row 5, column 10. The top row in the Output window is considered row 1, and the leftmost column, column 1. An example is shown in Figure 2-8. For added flexibility, variables and expressions may be used in place of constants in the LOCATE statement.

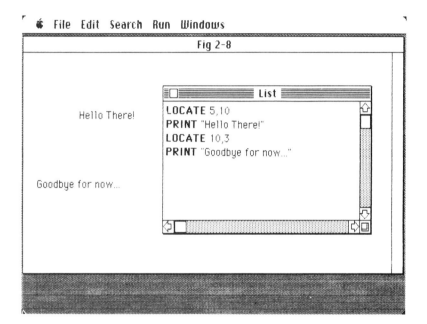

Output to the Printer

If you have a printer connected to your Macintosh, you can use the *LPRINT* statement to print results on paper. The LPRINT statement works exactly the same as the PRINT statement, except the results are displayed by the printer and not on the Output window. All of the options and techniques discussed so far for the PRINT statement will work with the LPRINT statement (comma, semicolon, USING, TAB, etc.).

The only exception is the LOCATE statement, which has no effect on printed output. An example of the LPRINT statement might be

```
LPRINT x,y,z
```

This statement would cause your printer to display the contents of variables *x*, *y*, and *z*.

Input from the Keyboard

While your program is running, it can request and obtain information from the user at the keyboard through use of the *INPUT* statement. The simplest form of the INPUT statement looks like this

```
INPUT variablename
```

The variable name specified in the INPUT statement will receive the data supplied by the user at the keyboard. When the INPUT statement is reached, the program pauses and displays a question mark, **?**, in the Output window, followed by a flashing "insertion point" cursor. The user types in the information requested and the program assigns that data to the variable in the INPUT statement. Program execution then continues.

To make a program more "user-friendly," it is often helpful to add a prompt string that describes what information is being requested. This prompt string can be placed in the INPUT statement itself; it will then be displayed when the statement is executed, just before pausing to wait for the user's reply. An example is shown in Figure 2-9.

Figure 2-9
The INPUT Statement

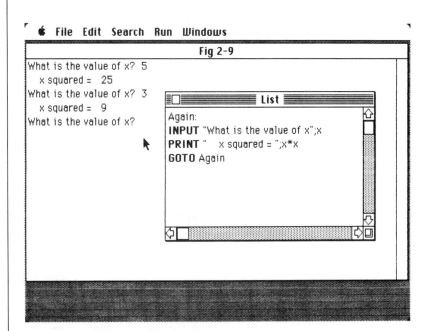

The LINE INPUT Statement

While the INPUT statement is easy to use, it does have some drawbacks. When you type in a reply to an INPUT statement, BASIC checks to make sure that your reply matches the type of the variable in the statement. Thus, for example, if the statement was attempting to input into a numeric variable, and you accidentally entered some character string data (e.g., "ABC"), your program would be aborted with an error message. Another drawback to the INPUT statement is that it always displays a question mark before waiting for input. There may be times when you do not wish to have this question mark appear. In these cases, you can use the *LINE INPUT* statement.

The LINE INPUT statement is coded exactly like the INPUT statement I have already shown you. The variable specified, however, must be a string variable. An example of the LINE INPUT statement might be

```
LINE INPUT "Please enter your name:
";name$
```

The statement acts exactly like the regular INPUT statement, with two exceptions. First, no question mark is displayed prior to waiting for the user reply. Second, any reply will be considered valid and will be input into the string variable specified. It will therefore be impossible to accidentally stop the program due to an error in input. Of course, this puts an added responsibility on the program to perform careful error checking of the reply.

The INKEY$ Function

Both of the input techniques I have just introduced will automatically echo the user's reply on the Output window as it is typed in. Both techniques also require that the user press the <Return> key before the input is accepted. There are some applications where you might want to get keyboard input from the user and act on it immediately, without any echo to the Macintosh screen. This can be accomplished through use of the **INKEY$** function. It will be described later in this chapter.

Decision Making

The ability to make decisions is crucial to any useful computer program. The fundamental decision-making statement in BASIC is the *IF-THEN* statement. Its form is as follows

```
IF expression THEN clause
```

Note the placement of the two identifying keywords IF and THEN in this statement. The *expression* that appears between them will always be interpreted as representing logical data, as explained earlier in this chapter. If the expression evaluates as logically *true*, then the clause part of the statement will be executed. Otherwise, if the expression is evaluated as *false*, then the clause will not be executed. The clause can be any other BASIC statement, or a series of statements separated by colons. For example, consider the following

```
IF x=0 THEN PRINT "ZERO!"
```

The above statement will display the message "ZERO!" on the Output window if variable x contains 0 when it is executed. If x is not 0, then the clause will not be executed; in either case, execution always resumes with the next sequential program statement.

The decision-making power of the IF-THEN statement can be increased by adding an *ELSE* clause. The ELSE clause allows you to specify a separate action to be taken if the IF-THEN expression evaluates as false. For example

```
IF x=0 THEN PRINT "ZERO!" ELSE PRINT
"NON-ZERO!"
```

Notice that the ELSE clause always follows the THEN clause of the statement and is indicated by the keyword ELSE. The ELSE keyword can then be followed by one or more BASIC statements. The statements in the ELSE clause are only executed when the expression is false. After the statements in the ELSE clause are executed, execution will continue with the next sequential program statement (unless, of course, the clause contained a GOTO statement).

By combining relational operators (Table 2-3) with logical operators (Table 2-4), the IF-THEN expression can be made as complex as is necessary to accomplish your task. For example, consider the following rather complex statement

```
IF ((x=0) AND (y=0)) OR (z<>0) THEN . . .
ELSE . . .
```

The above expression will be evaluated as true if both variables *x* and *y* are 0, or if variable *z* is not 0 at the time of its execution.

Program Loops

Everyone knows that computers are great for performing repetitive tasks. In programming, the process of repeating a task over and over again is called *iteration*. The programming structure that allows one to perform iteration is called a *loop*. You have already seen how a GOTO statement that is directed to a previous statement can be used to create a never ending "infinite" loop (see Listing 2-2). By making the GOTO statement in this program conditional, you create a better behaved loop that is not infinite. This has been done in Listing 2-4. Study this listing, and note how the IF-THEN statement only allows the loop to be executed ten times (with values of *x* ranging from 1 to 10).

Listing 2-4
A Fixed Duration Loop

```
x=1
Again:
PRINT "Hello, x=";x
x=x+1
IF x<11 THEN GOTO Again
```

BASIC provides an alternative means of creating loops which, like this one, iterate over a fixed range of values. This alternate technique is called the *FOR-NEXT* loop. The FOR-NEXT loop always begins with a *FOR* statement and always ends with a *NEXT* statement. Between these two statements lie the statements that comprise the body of the loop. The statements in the loop body will be executed repeatedly for the entire range of loop values. The structure of the FOR statement is as follows

```
FOR loop-control-variable = start-value
TO stop-value
```

The statement must always begin with the keyword FOR and must always contain the keyword TO, as well as the special "equal sign" character. The loop control variable may be specified as any numeric variable desired. This is the variable that will take on an ever increasing or decreasing value as each loop iteration is made. The start-value and stop-value specified in the FOR statement define the range of values that the loop control variable will take on. In so doing, they also define the total number of iterations that will be made by the loop. For example, the statement

```
FOR x = 1 TO 10
```

would request a total of ten loop iterations, with x ranging in value from 1 to 10. The statement

```
FOR x = 5 TO 25
```

would request a total of twenty-one loop iterations, with x ranging in value from 5 to 25.

The FOR statement is followed immediately by the statements that make up the body of the loop. These are then followed by the NEXT statement which denotes the end of the loop body. The NEXT statement may consist simply of the keyword NEXT. Listing 2-5 shows a complete example of a FOR-NEXT loop; its function is the same as that of Listing 2-4. Notice that in this case, the loop body consists of a single statement, a PRINT statement.

Note also how I specifically declared the loop control variable in Listing 2-5 to be an integer, $x\%$. This is a good idea when loops are being used to simply count out a whole number of iterations, because calculations with integers are much faster than with real numbers. Since the variable is used only to keep count of the number of iterations, it has no need for a fractional part.

```
FOR x% = 1 TO 10
PRINT "Hello, x=";x%
NEXT
```

The STEP Clause

By adding a STEP clause to the FOR statement, you can cause the loop control variable to be incremented in steps other than one. The STEP clause consists of the keyword STEP, followed by a step-value. The FOR statement with a STEP clause looks like this

```
FOR loop-control-var = start-val TO
stop-val STEP step-value
```

The step-value is the amount that will be added to the loop control variable upon the completion of each loop iteration. When not specified, this value is, of course, 1. As an example, consider the statement

```
FOR x% = 2 TO 10 STEP 2
```

This statement will set up a loop that will cause variable x% to take on the values 2, 4, 6, 8, and 10. Suppose we used the statement

```
FOR x% = 1 TO 10 STEP 2
```

What would happen in this case? Well, the loop would be executed for values of $x\%$ equal to 1, 3, 5, 7, and 9. After the iteration with $x\% = 9$, the variable would be incremented by 2, to 11. But since this value exceeds the stop-value (10), no loop iteration would be made for $x\% = 11$. Program execution would therefore continue with the first statement following the NEXT statement, and variable $x\%$ would have a value of 11.

The STEP clause can also be used to create loops in which the loop control variable is stepped by fractional amounts on each iteration. An example of this can be found in Listing 2-1. Of course, when this is done, the loop control variable cannot be an integer.

Using a Negative Step Value

By specifying a step value that is negative, you can cause the loop control variable to decrease in value on each iteration. When a negative step-value is used, the loop will terminate once the loop control value is *less than* the stop-value (as opposed to when it is greater than the stop-value, as in the previous examples). As an example, consider the statement

```
FOR x% = 5 TO 1 STEP −1
```

This statement will set up a loop in which the control variable, $x\%$, will take on the values 5, 4, 3, 2, and 1, in that order.

Nesting Loops

FOR-NEXT loops may be nested—that is, one may be placed entirely within another. When this is done, the inner loop control variable will go through all of its values once for each value taken on by the outer loop control variable. This technique is useful in applications where you have two or more independent variables and you need to generate all combinations of the values that each variable can take on. For example, suppose you have a two-dimensional array and want to display the value of each of its elements. This could be accomplished using the statements shown in Listing 2-6.

Listing 2-6
Nested FOR-NEXT Loops

```
DIM array(5,10)
'  ...
' ... fill array with data ...
'  ...
' Display array contents:
FOR x=1 TO 5
FOR y=1 TO 10
PRINT "Array(";x;",";y;") = ",array(x,y)
NEXT
NEXT
```

When loops are nested in this fashion, the order in which the array elements are accessed is determined by the order of the nesting. In the example shown, the first dimension subscript of array is set and then all elements in the second dimension are accessed. Only after all subscript values in the second dimension have been used will the first dimension subscript be changed.

A graphic illustration of this concept can be seen by running the program shown in Listing 2-7. This program simulates the elements of a 10 by 10 array in ten rows and ten columns of the Output window. It uses the LOCATE statement to access the appropriate row-column position, as determined by the loop control variables. Watch closely as you run the program. Notice how, when the column variable is in the inner loop, the array is accessed by columns. When the row variable is in the inner loop, the array is accessed by rows.

Listing 2-7
Nested Loop Ordering

```
' Visualize the print positions in the
' output window rows 2 - 11, columns 1 - 10
' as the elements of a 10 x 10 array:
PRINT "Access in column-major order:"
FOR row = 2 TO 11
FOR column = 1 TO 10
LOCATE row,column
PRINT "X";
NEXT
NEXT
LOCATE 12,1
LINE INPUT "Press Return Key to continue";a$
LOCATE 1,1
PRINT "Access in row-major order:
FOR column = 1 TO 10
FOR row = 2 TO 11
LOCATE row,column
PRINT "Y";
NEXT
NEXT
```

Storing Data within a Program

BASIC provides a technique for storing a set of data values (either numeric or string) within the program itself. These data values may then be accessed as needed by the program when it is executed. The facility is provided by the two BASIC statements *READ* and *DATA*.

Of the two statements, the READ statement actually performs an action, whereas the DATA statement provides the place where the information will be held. A DATA statement consists of the keyword DATA, followed by one or more data values, separated by commas. For example

```
DATA 3,28,19
```

DATA statements may be placed anywhere in a program, as they are not executed. If a DATA statement is encountered while a program is being run, it is simply skipped over and the next statement after it is executed.

To access the information placed in DATA statements, you use a READ statement. This statement begins with the keyword READ, which is then followed by one or more variable names, separated by commas. For example

```
READ x,y,z
```

When the READ statement is executed, BASIC searches the program for the first DATA statement, reads the information contained therein, and places it into the variables specified. Thus, the example above would cause the values 3, 28, and 19 to be placed into variables x, y, and z, respectively. Information is "read" from DATA statements starting with the first DATA statement encountered in the program, and continuing on in a sequential fashion. Thus, the order in which DATA statements are placed in the program is very important. Once information is read from DATA statements, it cannot be accessed again until special action is taken. When all the information in the DATA statements is used up and another READ is executed, an error will occur. To enable the information in the DATA statements to be accessed again, a *RESTORE* statement must be executed.

An example of how READ and DATA statements might be used is shown in Listing 2-8. This listing contains a short program that will fill the Output window with title information, in preparation for displaying a screenful of data. The program is made general purpose by using DATA statements to hold the actual text to be displayed, along with the location of each text item on the screen.

Listing 2-8
Use of READ/DATA Statements

```
' The set of screen messages is defined in
' DATA statements in the format:
' DATA row, column, string$
' where row,column = start location to
' display string$ at.
' The end of the data is denoted by row=0.
Screen.Display:
READ row%,column%,message$
IF row%=0 THEN END
LOCATE row%,column%
PRINT message$;
GOTO Screen.Display
DATA 1,7,"DRAPER COMPANY - INVOICE DISPLAY"
DATA 3,3,"Invoice #"
DATA 3,35,"Date"
DATA 5,3,"To"
DATA 6,31,"Cust Code"
DATA 9,3,"Item"
DATA 9,29,"| Unit |"
DATA 9,35,"Quan |"
DATA 9,40,"Totl"
DATA 10,3,"-------------------------------------------"
DATA 16,3,"-------------------------------------------"
DATA 17,18,"TOTAL--->"
DATA 18,3,"Ship Wgt"
DATA 0,0,0
```

For the sample data shown in the listing, the results will appear as shown in Figure 2-10. The nice feature of this approach is that if you need to change the screen layout, you can do so without having to make a change in the program itself. You only need to change the information in the DATA statements.

Notice that this program uses the keyword *END*, in the IF-THEN statement. The END statement, consisting solely of the keyword of the same name, is used to terminate a running program. Our previous programs have ended simply by running out of statements (i.e., running past the last statement in the program). As an alternative, the END statement provides you with a means to stop program execution in the middle of a program.

Figure 2-10
Output of Listing 2-8

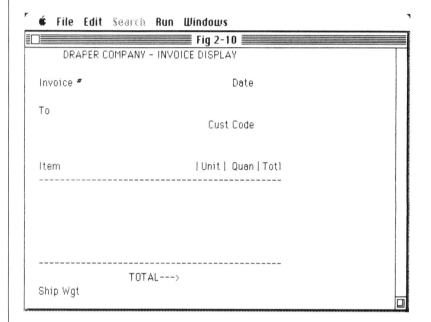

Built-in Numeric Functions

Microsoft BASIC provides a number of built-in numeric functions that support a wide range of mathematical programming. Each built-in function is referenced by its own unique keyword. The format of a function reference is always the same. The function keyword is followed by a left parenthesis, then its argument, and finally a right parenthesis. Such function references may appear anywhere that an expression is legal, and may be combined with other data items via operators to form even more complex expressions. The following is an example of a function reference

```
x = SIN(y)
```

In the above example, the keyword SIN is used to request the trigonometric sine function. The argument, or operand, of the function is the variable *y*, which appears after the function keyword in parenthesis. This statement will calculate the sine of the value in variable *y*, and assign the result to variable *x*.

A complete list of numeric functions available in Microsoft's Macintosh BASIC is shown in Table 2-7. These functions can be divided into two general types. There are the conversion functions, which are used to alter the format of their operands. There are also the mathematical functions, which perform standard math operations such as logarithm, random, and trigonometry. Lets take a closer look at some of them.

Function	Returns
ABS(X)	Absolute (unsigned) value of X.
ATN(X)	Arctangent of X in radians (range of result will be $-Pi/2$ to $+Pi/2$, multiply by $180/Pi$ to convert to degrees).
CDBL(X)	Converts X to double-precision format.
CINT(X)	Converts X to integer format.
COS(X)	Cosine of radian angle X (to convert to radians from degrees, multiply by $Pi/180$).
CSNG(X)	Converts X to single-precision format.
EXP(X)	e^X (Natural base raised to X power).
FIX(X)	Truncates X to an integer.
INT(X)	Largest integer less than or equal to X.
LOG(X)	Natural (base e) logarithm of X.
RND(X)	If $X > 0$ then returns the next random number in the current sequence. If $X = 0$ then returns the same random number as the previous call. If $X < 0$ then restarts the current sequence. All values returned are between 0 and 1.
SGN(X)	Sign of X, returned as -1, 0, or $+1$.
SIN(X)	Sine of radian angle X.
SQR(X)	Square root of X.
TAN(X)	Tangent of radian angle X.

Conversion Functions

The **FIX** function can be used to truncate (remove) the fractional part of a real number, thus converting it into an integer. Figure 2-11 shows how this function can be used in a program to test for exact divisibility by a specific value. In the example shown, the program checks to see if the user's input is exactly divisible by 5. The program works by dividing the number given by 5. The **FIX** function is then used to isolate the integer (whole part) of the result. If this value is equal to the result of the division, then there was no fractional part, so the original number must be evenly divisible by 5. Note that the **FIX** function simply removes any fractional part from its argument.

A similar function, **INT**, also returns the integer part of its argument, but there is a subtle difference. The **INT** function is defined to return *the largest integer which is less than or equal to its* *argument*. The **FIX** and **INT** functions differ only when their arguments are negative. For example

```
FIX(-4.1) = -4
```

but

```
INT(-4.1) = -5
```

A related function is the "convert to integer" function, **CINT**. Unlike **FIX**, which operates by simply truncating the fractional part of its argument, the **CINT** function returns the integer value which is nearest to its argument. It is therefore useful when you need to round a fractional number up or down. For example

```
CINT(5.2) = 5
CINT(5.7) = 6
```

The other conversion functions, **CSNG** and **CDBL**, convert their operands to single or double precision format, respectively. The result returned by these functions must, of course, be assigned to a variable of the appropriate type.

Figure 2-11
Using FIX to Determine Exact Divisibility

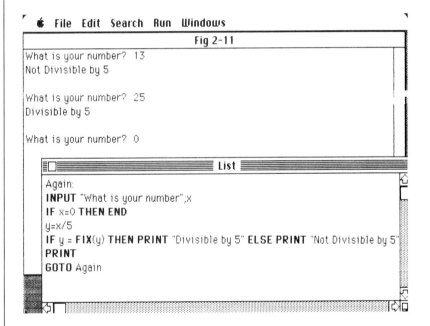

Logarithmic Functions

The logarithmic function **LOG**, and its inverse, **EXP**, both operate using the natural base, e. These functions are used in many equations and formulas that describe our physical universe. For example, the electric voltage on a capacitor, C, that is being charged through a resistor, R, can be described by the formula

$$V = V_0 (1 - e^{-t/RC})$$

This formula can be evaluated using the BASIC expression

```
V = V0 * (1 - EXP(-T/(R*C)))
```

Many applications require the use of the common logarithm, that is, the log to base 10. The common logarithm function can be derived from the natural logarithm function provided in BASIC through use of the formula

$$LOG_{10}(X) = LOG_e(X) / LOG_e(10)$$

Trigonometric Functions

Microsoft BASIC supports the three basic trigonometric functions: sine, cosine, and tangent. The argument of these functions must be provided in radians. The radian is a measure of angular rotation that is designed so that pi radians equal 180 degrees. To convert an angle measured in radians to degrees, multiply the radian value by 180/pi. To convert an angle measured in degrees to radians, multiply the degree angle by pi/180. The value pi is, of course, the ratio of a circle's circumference to its diameter. Pi is approximately equal to 3.14159. My first demo program (Listing 2-1) used both the sine and cosine functions to determine the coordinates of points along the edge of a circle. By allowing the function's arguments to range from 0 to 360 degrees (2 pi radians), complete circles were drawn.

Another demo program is shown in Listing 2-9. This program also varies the argument of the sine function throughout the range 0 to 360 degrees. In this case, however, the result is being used to plot a picture of the sine wave itself on the Output window (see Figure 2-12). This program, like the one in Listing 2-1, uses the **PSET** function. This is a graphics function, and will be described fully in Chapter 5.

Listing 2-9
Plot of a Sine Wave

```
pi = 3.14159
x=1
FOR angle = 0 TO 2*pi STEP .04
y=SIN(angle)
y=75-75*y
PSET(x,y)
x=x +1
NEXT
```

The Random Function

One of the more interesting functions provided by BASIC is the random function, **RND**. This function is used to produce a random (i.e., uncorrelated) sequence of numbers. The use of random number sequences in computer programming is quite common; they are often used to generate data for simulations and mathematical approximation algorithms. Random numbers are also useful for producing special effects, such as those used in video games. Without a random element, the special effect of a ship exploding, or the attack of a wave of aliens, would always appear the same. Eventually, the effect or attack wave would become predictable to the viewer and would lose its appeal.

To obtain a sequence of random numbers, call the **RND** function repeatedly with any argument value greater than 0. To restart the same sequence of random numbers, call **RND** with an argument less than 0. If the **RND** argument is 0, then **RND** will return the same value as was returned on the previous call. To produce different sequences of random numbers, the RANDOMIZE statement must be used. This statement sets the starting seed for BASIC's random number generator. It has the form

RANDOMIZE expression

where expression can evaluate to any integer value. Of course, the random sequence will always be the same for the same RANDOMIZE value. Thus, if you put the statement

RANDOMIZE 258

at the beginning of your program that uses random numbers, then every time the program is run the same sequence of random numbers will be used. To produce a more truly random sequence, one that will be different every time you run the program, use the statement

RANDOMIZE TIMER

This statement invokes the BASIC built-in function TIMER, which requires no argument. The TIMER function returns an integer value that is linked to the system's internal time-of-day clock. The value is thus incremented once every second. Since it is unlikely that your program will be run at the exact same moment each time it is used, this technique effectively provides for a unique random number sequence on each program run.

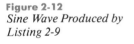
Figure 2-12
Sine Wave Produced by Listing 2-9

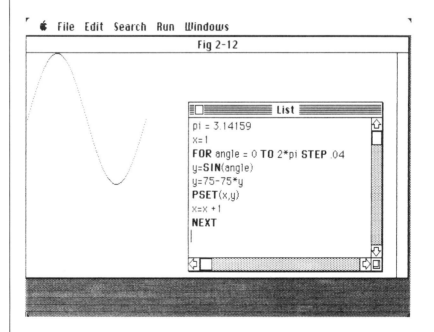

The random numbers returned by the **RND** function will always be real numbers lying in the range 0 – 1. Since most applications will require that the random numbers lie in some other range, it is necessary to perform a conversion on the value returned by **RND.**

Many applications will also work best with integer random numbers. The conversion formula that I will present will only return integer values.

To perform the conversion, you must first decide what range of values you want the random numbers to lie within. Select a lower limit for the desired range and call it L. Then select an upper limit and call it U. The formula to return an integer random number in the range from L to U is

$$X\% = CINT(L + (RND(1) * (U - L)))$$

Listing 2-10 shows how this technique can be used to simulate the rolling of a pair of dice. In this case, we want random numbers in the range from 1 to 6, representing the six different values that can appear on a die roll. A sample run of the program appears in Figure 2-13.

```
RANDOMIZE TIMER
Again:
die1=CINT(1+(RND(1)*5))
die2=CINT(1+(RND(1)*5))
total=die1+die2
PRINT "Rolling dice....";die1;" - ";die2;" (";total;")"
LINE INPUT "Press Return to roll again";a$
GOTO Again
```

```
▤□▤▤▤▤▤▤▤▤▤▤▤▤ Fig 2-13 ▤▤▤▤▤
Rolling dice..... 3 - 6 ( 9 )
Press Return to roll again
Rolling dice..... 4 - 3 ( 7 )
Press Return to roll again
Rolling dice..... 3 - 1 ( 4 )
Press Return to roll again
Rolling dice..... 2 - 5 ( 7 )
Press Return to roll again
Rolling dice..... 6 - 6 ( 12 )
Press Return to roll again
Rolling dice..... 4 - 5 ( 9 )
Press Return to roll again
Rolling dice..... 6 - 1 ( 7 )
Press Return to roll again|
```

Built-in String Functions

BASIC contains a wide variety of built-in functions that deal with character string data. These functions provide a great deal of power for processing and manipulating character strings. In addition, there are a number of functions that facilitate converting data between the numeric and string types.

The built-in string functions are listed in Table 2-8. Note that some of these functions return string data, while others return numeric data. To indicate that a function returns string data, a **$** is appended to the function's keyword (i.e., **STR$**). Some of the functions require more than one argument, and some arguments are strings, while others are numeric. Two of the functions, **MID$** and **INSTR**, can accept either two or three arguments. All in all, many features are available here. Let us take a look at how they can be used.

Table 2-8
Built-in String Functions

Keyword/ Example	Type of Data Returned by Function	Returns
LEN(A$)	NUMERIC	Current length of string A$.
LEFT$(A$,N)	STRING	Leftmost N characters of A$.
RIGHT$(A$,N)	STRING	Rightmost N characters of A$.
MID$(A$,N,M)	STRING	M characters from string A$, starting with the Nth character.
INSTR(A$,B$)	NUMERIC	Searches for string B$ within string A$. Returns starting position of match, or 0 if not found.
STRING$(N,"–")	STRING	String of N dash characters.
UCASE$(A$)	STRING	Converts all lowercase letters to uppercase.
ASC(A$)	NUMERIC	ASCII value for first character in A$.
CHR$(N)	STRING	Character corresponding to ASCII code value N.
VAL(A$)	NUMERIC	Numeric value represented by the contents of string A$.
STR$(N)	STRING	Character string representing the numeric value N.
INKEY$	STRING	Character corresponding to key currently being pressed on the keyboard. Null string if no key is depressed.

Extracting Parts of Strings

I will begin by looking at those functions that allow you to access selected portions of strings. These are the **LEFT$**, **RIGHT$**, and **MID$** functions. The **LEFT$** and **RIGHT$** functions are used to divide a string into two parts at a selected character position, and then isolate either the left or right side. For example, consider a program that has to process the serial numbers on a certain make of automobile. Each serial number is ten characters long. The first three characters of the serial number indicate the car model. The last seven characters are unique for each car as they are assigned sequentially when the cars are manufactured. Assuming the serial number is in variable *SERIAL$*, the following two statements will isolate the model code and sequential number and place them into variables *MODEL$* and *SEQNTL$*, respectively

```
MODEL$ = LEFT$(SERIAL$,3)
SEQNTL$= RIGHT$(SERIAL$,7)
```

If *SERIAL$* contained the string "CPE0003048", then variable *MODEL$* would be set to "CPE" and variable *SEQNTL$* would be set to "0003048".

The **MID$** function is even more powerful than **LEFT$** and **RIGHT$** because it allows you to isolate any desired part of a character string. The string to be acted upon is specified as the first argument of **MID$**. The second argument is a numeric value that specifies the starting position of the part to be isolated. The third argument specifies how many characters to extract from the string. If the third argument is omitted, then all characters in the string, from the starting position onward, will be extracted. Therefore

```
MID$("MICROCOMPUTER",6,4)
```

will extract the sixth through tenth characters of "MICROCOMPUTER," and thus return "COMP" whereas

```
MID$("MICROCOMPUTER",6)
```

will extract all characters from the sixth position onward, and thus return "COMPUTER."

Suppose the automotive serial number described above is modified so that a year of manufacture code (two digits) is placed between the model code and the sequential number. Thus the serial number "SUN840000101" would identify the hundred and first model SUN, made in 1984. The year of manufacture code could then be extracted by using the following statement

```
YEAR$ = MID$(SERIAL$,4,2)
```

Note that the previously shown **LEFT$** and **RIGHT$** function calls would not have to be changed!

The MID$ Statement
The MID$ keyword can also be used to isolate a portion of a string variable to be the target of an assignment statement. Such a statement, in which the MID$ reference appears to the left of the equals sign, is called a MID$ statement. Here is an example of a MID$ statement

```
MID$(a$,5,2) = "**"
```

If variable *a$* contained the value "Computer", then after the statement above was executed *a$* would contain the value "Comp**er". Note that this technique cannot be used to concatenate additional characters onto the end of of existing strings (use the concatenation string operator (+) for that). The MID$

statement can only be used to modify a part of a string that already exists.

If, once again, variable *a$* contained "Computer", then the statement

```
MID$(a$,15,5) = "Happy"
```

would cause an error, because there are no fifteenth through twentieth character positions in string *a$* to be modified.

String Functions that Yield Numeric Results

So far, the character string functions that I have discussed have acted on character strings to produce other character strings. We will now look at some functions that act on character strings to produce numeric results. These functions can be extremely useful when analyzing the contents of strings. The **LEN** function returns the current length of its string argument. It will always return an integer value between 0 and +32767. A return of 0 means that the argument of **LEN** was a null string (i.e. one that contains no characters). For example

```
a$ = "Welcome home!"
x% = LEN(a$)
```

would result in a value of 13 for $x\%$.

The **LEN** function is very useful because many programs contain string variables whose length changes dynamically as the program runs. For example, suppose you have a requirement to change the last (rightmost) character in a string to an asterisk. The string will be stored in variable *a$*, but you may not know its length at the time you write the program. You can still accomplish your objective, as follows

```
MID$(a$,LEN(a$),1) = "*"
```

A more powerful string analysis function is the **INSTR** function. This function is used to search for a particular character or sequence of characters within a given string. The character(s) to search for is specified as a character string itself and is called the search string. The string to be searched is specified as the first argument of **INSTR**. The search string is specified as the second argument. If the search string is not found within the first argument, then the **INSTR** function will return a value of 0. Otherwise, it will return a numeric value corresponding to the starting position of the search string within the first argument. Only a complete match with the search string will be reported. Thus

```
INSTR("STAN","AND")
```

will return 0, whereas

```
INSTR("STANDARD","AND")
```

will return 3.

Suppose you are writing a personnel file database program. You will want to store each person's name with the last name first, for ease of access and lookup. However, to make things more comfortable for the user, you might want to allow the input of the person's name in the conventional first name-last name order. By using the string functions discussed above, you will be able to easily process the user's input and convert it from first-name-first to last-name-first order. The program to perform this kind of processing is shown in Listing 2-11, and a sample run is shown in Figure 2-14. How would you modify this program so that it can accept a title preceding the input name (i.e., Mr., Dr., etc.)?

Listing 2-11
Name Reversing
Program

```
Again:
INPUT "Enter your name, please";n$
x%=INSTR(n$," ")
IF x%=0 THEN PRINT "Invalid name!":END
n$=MID$(n$,x%+1) + ", " + LEFT$(n$,x%-1)
PRINT "Reversed name = ";n$
PRINT
GOTO Again
```

Figure 2-14
Run of the Name
Reversing Program

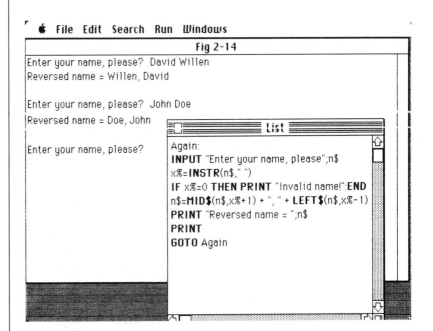

Conversion Functions

The next group of string functions allow you to convert string data to numeric, and vice versa. There are four functions in this category. They are **ASC**, **CHR$**, **VAL**, and **STR$**. The **ASC** and **CHR$** functions are used to convert a single character to the numeric value of its ASCII code, and vice versa. If, for example, you look up the character "C" in Table 2-5, you will find it has an ASCII code value of 67. Thus, the function

```
ASC("C")
```

would return the value 67; and the function

```
CHR$(67)
```

would return the string "C."

The **CHR$** function is often used to generate control characters to be sent to an output device. For example, the ASCII control code form feed is represented by code value 12. This control code will cause most printers to eject paper until the top of the next page is reached. It will work with the Macintosh Imagewriter as well. To send this command to the printer, you can use the statement

```
LPRINT CHR$(12)
```

Another useful example, mentioned earlier in this chapter, is

```
PRINT CHR$(7)
```

This statement sends the ASCII control code bell to the display, which causes the Macintosh to emit an audible beep.

The **VAL** and **STR$** functions are used to convert character strings representing numeric values into the corresponding numeric values, and vice versa. For example, if variable *NUMBER$* contained the string "108" then the function

```
VAL(NUMBER$)
```

would return the numeric value 108. Note that the string argument of **VAL** can contain any valid BASIC representation of a numeric quantity. Thus, strings such as "–98.7" and "4.29E6" will be properly converted to their numeric equivalents.

The **STR$** function performs the opposite of the **VAL** function. It accepts numeric type data as an argument and produces a character string containing an equivalent representation. For example, if variable *TOTAL* contained the value 598, then the function

```
STR$(TOTAL)
```

would return the string " 598". Notice the blank character at the beginning of the returned string. This character position is reserved for a minus sign character in the event that the value being converted is negative. In applications where this blank would be troublesome, it can be easily removed, using the following technique

```
a$ = STR$(x)
IF x > = 0 THEN a$ = RIGHT$(a$,LEN(a$)-1)
```

A program that demonstrates how **STR$** and **VAL** can be used is shown in Listing 2-12. This program asks the user to enter a numeric value. The value is then converted to a string representation. A FOR-NEXT loop then steps through each character in the string, **VAL** converts the characters to their numeric values, and the sum of all of the digits in the number is accumulated. A sample run of the program is shown in Figure 2-15.

Another interesting program is shown in Listing 2-13. This program can be used to encrypt secret messages so that they can be

Listing 2-12
Digit Summing Program

```
PRINT "Digit Summing Program"
PRINT
Again:
INPUT "Enter your number, please ";n%
IF n%<=0 THEN END
a$=STR$(n%)
a$=RIGHT$(a$,LEN(a$)-1) 'remove leading blank
digit.total%=0 'initialize digit total
FOR position%=1 TO LEN(a$)
digit.total%=digit.total% + VAL(MID$(a$,position%,1))
NEXT
PRINT "The sum of the digits is ";digit.total%
PRINT
GOTO Again
```

Figure 2-15
*Run of the Digit
Summing Program*

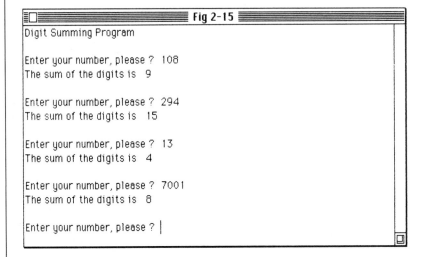

```
Digit Summing Program

Enter your number, please ?  108
The sum of the digits is   9

Enter your number, please ?  294
The sum of the digits is   15

Enter your number, please ?  13
The sum of the digits is   4

Enter your number, please ?  7001
The sum of the digits is   8

Enter your number, please ? |
```

transmitted safely. The program works by converting each character in the message into its ASCII code value, then increasing that code value by 3, and converting back to character format. Thus, for example, the character "A" would become "C" and the character "B" would become "D", etc. A sample run of the program, which contains both the encryption and decryption routines, is shown in Figure 2-16.

The INKEY$ Function
As I mentioned earlier, the **INKEY$** function provides the ability to do sophisticated keyboard input. The **INKEY$** function, which takes no arguments, should only be used in a simple assignment statement reference, such as

```
a$ = INKEY$
```

When this statement is executed, *a$* will be set to the character represented by the key currently being held down at the keyboard. The keystroke will not be automatically echoed to the output window. Because **INKEY$** does not wait for a keystroke, it is usually placed within a program loop so that the program will wait until a key is pressed

```
' This program will encode a character string message so
' that is it unreadable. The program contains both the
' encrypt and decrypt routines.
' The encryption technique accepts only printable ASCII
' characters, i.e. those with codes in the range 32-127.
' They are encrypted by increasing the code value by 3.
' If during encryption a value exceeds 127 it is wrapped to
' values starting with 32.
PRINT "Secret Code Program"
PRINT
Again:
LINE INPUT "Enter message to be encrypted: ";a$
FOR position%=1 TO LEN(a$)
x=ASC(MID$(a$,position%,1))
x=x+3
IF x>127 THEN x=32 + (x MOD 128)
MID$(a$,position%,1)=CHR$(x)
NEXT
PRINT "The encrypted message is: ";a$
' Now decrypt the message:
FOR position%=1 TO LEN(a$)
x=ASC(MID$(a$,position%,1))
x=x-3
IF x<32 THEN x=128 - (32 - x)
MID$(a$,position%,1)=CHR$(x)
NEXT
PRINT "The decrypted message is: ";a$
PRINT
GOTO Again
```

Figure 2-16
*Run of the Message
Encryption Program*

```
┌─────────────────────── Fig 2-16 ───────────────────────┐
│ Secret Code Program                                     │
│                                                         │
│ Enter message to be encrypted: Meet you in the park at midnite! │
│ The encrypted message is: Phhw#|rx#lq#wkh#sdun#dw#plgqlwh$ │
│ The decrypted message is: Meet you in the park at midnite! │
│                                                         │
│ Enter message to be encrypted: The password for tonite is 109FISH │
│ The encrypted message is: Wkh#sdvvzrug#iru#wrqlwh#lv#43<ILVK │
│ The decrypted message is: The password for tonite is 109FISH │
│                                                         │
│ Enter message to be encrypted: The captain will attack at dawn! │
│ The encrypted message is: Wkh#fdswdlq#zloo#dwwdfn#dw#gdzq$ │
│ The decrypted message is: The captain will attack at dawn! │
│                                                         │
│ Enter message to be encrypted: │                        │
└─────────────────────────────────────────────────────────┘
```

```
Again: a$ = INKEY$
IF a$ = " " THEN GOTO Again
```

One common application of **INKEY$** is in obtaining user input
and acting on it immediately. For example, suppose you have a
program that is presenting the user with a menu of choices and
waiting for a selection, as in Figure 2-17. If you use INPUT or
LINE INPUT to obtain the user's reply, he will have to type the
reply and then press the Return key before the program can act
upon it. By using **INKEY$**, the program can obtain and act upon
the user's reply as soon as he presses the appropriate key. This can
help in producing a fast and smooth running program. This
technique is shown in Listing 2-14.

Figure 2-17
*Run of the Menu
Selection Program*

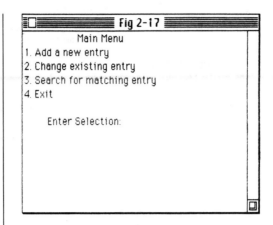

```
▤▦▦▦▦▦ Fig 2-17 ▦▦▦▦
              Main Menu
1. Add a new entry
2. Change existing entry
3. Search for matching entry
4. Exit


    Enter Selection:
```

Listing 2-14
Using INKEY$

```
PRINT TAB(10); "Main Menu"
PRINT "1. Add a new entry"
PRINT "2. Change existing entry"
PRINT "3. Search for matching entry"
PRINT "4. Exit"
PRINT
PRINT TAB(5); "Enter Selection:"
Get.Reply:
a$=INKEY$
IF a$ = "" THEN GOTO Get.Reply
IF a$="1" THEN GOTO Add
IF a$="2" THEN GOTO Change
IF a$="3" THEN GOTO Search
IF a$="4" THEN GOTO quit
GOTO Get.Reply
```

Another application of **INKEY$** involves obtaining keyboard input without echoing it to the display. An example is shown in Listing 2-15. This is a program fragment that you can add to the beginning of your own programs to "password protect" them. When you run this section of the program, it will wait for you to type in your secret password. The password is not echoed to the screen as you type, so no one else can see it. If the password is not entered correctly, the rest of your program will not run. Note how the program detects the < Return > key as ASC(13). How would you modify the program so that it automatically accepted the password as soon as the last correct character was entered?

Listing 2-15
Password Protection

```
PRINT "Enter the password, please"
Try.Again:
pw$="" 'Initialize the password accumulation string
Again:
a$=INKEY$
IF a$="" THEN GOTO Again
IF ASC(a$)=13 THEN GOTO Pw.Entered 'User pressed "Return" key
pw$=pw$ + a$ 'Accumulate the characters entered by the user
GOTO Again
Pw.Entered:
' "Return" key pressed: check for valid password :
IF UCASE$(pw$) <> "SWORDFISH" THEN PRINT "Incorrect password, try again" : GOTO Try.Again
' Program can now proceed here.......
```

Summary

This chapter has covered the various elements that make up Microsoft BASIC programs. The sample programs have been short and simple. In the next chapter, I will discuss facilities for structuring programs. These are vital when building larger programs that actually do meaningful work. At that point, you will be able to start to make use of some of those features that make the Macintosh unique, such as windows, icons, pull-down menus, and the mouse.

Chapter 3

Advanced Programming Structures

As programs become large and complex, it is important to impose some structure upon them. Good structure is vital to insure that programs remain readable, maintainable, and error-free throughout their development cycle. Exactly what is and is not good structure has been debated extensively by computer scientists ever since the concept of program structure was developed, over ten years ago.

Program Structure

As I see it, good program structure in BASIC means several things. Statement labels should be kept to a minimum. While "spaghetti code" (i.e., using lots of GOTO statements to jump to labels all over the program) is certainly undesirable, the GOTO statement is a valid and useful tool and may be used, albeit with moderation.

The program should be clearly understandable, no matter how large, and must be accompanied by thorough documentation. Through use of subroutines and subprograms, needless repetition of code should be avoided.

Each major function of the program should be written as a separate module, so that it can be as independent as possible. Global variables can, however, be used to link modules together. Let us look at how these goals can be achieved.

The WHILE-WEND Loop

The *WHILE-WEND* loop is an advanced BASIC feature that in many applications can eliminate the need for two program labels, an IF-THEN statement and a GOTO statement. In so doing, the WHILE-WEND loop makes the program easier to read and understand. A WHILE-WEND loop begins with a WHILE statement which looks like

```
WHILE expression
```

The expression following the keyword WHILE should evaluate to a logical value, and usually represents a test for a specific condition. One or more statements then follow the WHILE statement; these make up the body of the loop. The end of the loop is denoted by a WEND statement, which consists solely of the keyword WEND.

When the loop is entered, the expression in the WHILE statement is evaluated. If the expression is true, the statements in the body of the loop are executed. If the expression is false, all of the statements in the body of the loop are skipped, and execution continues with the statement following the WEND statement. So far, it seems simple, but now comes the good part. If the expression is true and the loop body is executed, when the WEND statement is reached BASIC returns to the WHILE statement and evaluates the expression again. The entire process then repeats. Thus, the statements in the loop body execute repeatedly, until the WHILE expression is false. Figure 3-1 shows the basic structure of a WHILE-WEND loop, and compares it to the equivalent structure using program labels, IF-THEN, and GOTO statements. By comparing the two structures, you can easily see the advantage to using WHILE-WEND.

As a simple example, consider Listing 3-1. Here the program of

Figure 3-1
*The WHILE-WEND
Loop*

```
                                      Loop.Start:
    WHILE expression                  IF expression THEN GOTO Loop.End

    ...                               ...
    ... (body)                        ... (body)

    ...                               ...
    WEND                              GOTO Loop.Start
                                      Loop.End:
```

Listing 3-1
A WHILE-WEND Loop

```
x=1
WHILE x < 11
PRINT "Hello, x=";x
x=x+1
WEND
```

Listing 2-4 has been rewritten to use a WHILE-WEND loop. In this case, the WHILE-WEND loop replaces the label Again, and the IF-THEN statement of Listing 2-4. The program's clarity and readability are improved.

As a more complicated example, I have redesigned the password protection program of Listing 2-15 to also make use of WHILE-WEND loops. The new program is shown in Listing 3-2. The original program had three labels, three corresponding IF-THEN-GOTO statements, and another GOTO statement. In Listing 3-2, two of the test conditions have been placed into WHILE statements. Note that the two WHILE-WEND loops thus formed are nested, one within the other. When several WHILE-WEND loops are nested in this fashion, each WEND statement is matched to the nearest unmatched WHILE statement. Run the two programs and compare them. Note the slight difference in the way they operate.

As you can now see, the WHILE-WEND loop is an excellent tool for simplifying and clarifying program logic. There are some cases, however, where the logic of the WHILE-WEND loop is difficult to apply. If you encounter such difficulty, I advise simply using the alternate technique (program labels and IF-THEN-GOTO). It is

Listing 3-2
WHILE-WEND Loops

```
pw$="" 'Initialize the password accumulation string
WHILE UCASE$(pw$) <> "SWORDFISH"
PRINT "Enter the password, please"
pw$="" 'Initialize the password accumulation string
Accumulate.Chars:                                                '***
a$=""
WHILE a$ = ""
a$=INKEY$
WEND
IF ASC(a$)=13 THEN GOTO Check.Pw                                 '***
pw$=pw$ + a$ 'Accumulate the characters entered by the user
GOTO Accumulate.Chars                                            '***
Check.Pw:                                                        '***
WEND
' Program can now proceed here.......
```

not worth wrestling with the logic of WHILE-WEND, trying to force it to meet your requirements when it cannot do so. To get an idea of how this kind of problem can arise, consider the four statements in Listing 3-2 which have been marked with the comment '***.' Try to replace these with a WHILE-WEND loop.

Subroutines

Microsoft BASIC for the Macintosh provides two facilities for modularizing a program into independent sections. These are the *subroutine* and the *subprogram*. In this section, I will cover the subroutine; subprograms will be covered later in this chapter.

The fundamental purpose of a subroutine is to reduce or eliminate the needless repetition of statements in a program. When writing many programs, you will often find the need to place the same set of statements at several places in the program. For example, a program with many different menu levels might use the statements

```
a$ = ""
WHILE a$ = ""
a$ = INKEY$
WEND
```

in each place where the program must wait for the user to make a menu selection. (I am not talking about pull-down menus here, they are covered in a later chapter). To avoid repeating the same statements over and over again, they are placed into a subroutine. Then, whenever the statements are needed, a subroutine call is made. The subroutine call consists of a GOSUB statement, which looks like this

```
GOSUB label
```

This statement causes the program execution to branch to the specified program label. The label identifies the start of the subroutine, and should be followed by the statements that make up the body of the subroutine. The end of the subroutine is denoted by a *RETURN* statement, consisting solely of the RETURN keyword. When the RETURN statement is reached it causes the program to resume execution at the point after the subroutine call itself. In this way, the subroutine can be called from many different places within the program. After execution of the statements within the subroutine, execution of the main program will *always* resume at the proper place. Figure 3-2 illustrates the subroutine concept.

Another advantage of using subroutines is they allow you to modularize a program; that is, break the program down into separate sections, each of which performs a different function. To illustrate this, I have rewritten the secret code program of Listing 2-13 to utilize subroutines. The rewritten program is shown in Listing 3-3.

The program now consists of three parts. The main program appears at the beginning of the listing and defines all the input and output that the program will perform. It is supplemented by the two subroutines Encrypt and Decrypt. These routines perform the actual data processing in the program. Note that the purpose of the program is much clearer in this version than in the version of Listing 2-13.

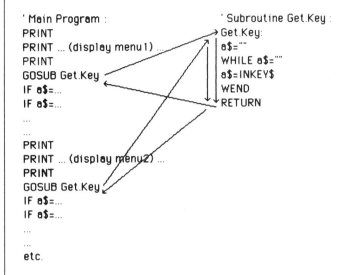

```
' Main Program :                        ' Subroutine Get.Key :
PRINT                                   Get.Key:
PRINT ... (display menu1) ...           a$=""
PRINT                                   WHILE a$=""
GOSUB Get.Key                           a$=INKEY$
IF a$=...                               WEND
IF a$=...                               RETURN
...

...
PRINT
PRINT ... (display menu2) ...
PRINT
GOSUB Get.Key
IF a$=...
IF a$=...
...

...
etc.
```

```
' This program will encode a character string message so
' that is it unreadable.  The program contains both the
' encrypt and decrypt routines.
' Main Program:
PRINT "Secret Code Program"
PRINT
LINE INPUT "Enter message to be encrypted: ";a$
GOSUB Encrypt
PRINT "The encrypted message is: ";a$
GOSUB Decrypt
PRINT "The decrypted message is: ";a$
END
' Subroutine Encrypt.
' Gosub Encrypt with a$ = string to be encrypted
' The encryption technique accepts only printable ASCII
' characters, i.e. those with codes in the range 32-127.
' They are encrypted by increasing the code value by 3.
' If during encryption a value exceeds 127 it is wrapped to
' values starting with 32.
Encrypt:
FOR position%=1 TO LEN(a$)
x=ASC(MID$(a$,position%,1))
x=x+3
IF x>127 THEN x=32 + (x MOD 128)
MID$(a$,position%,1)=CHR$(x)
NEXT
RETURN
'
' Subroutine Decrypt.
' Gosub Decrypt with a$ = string to be decrypted
Decrypt:
FOR position%=1 TO LEN(a$)
x=ASC(MID$(a$,position%,1))
x=x-3
IF x<32 THEN x=128 - (32 - x)
MID$(a$,position%,1)=CHR$(x)
NEXT
RETURN
```

By reading through the main program only, you can discern what the program is all about, and what functions are performed by the subroutines. All this is possible without actually reading the subroutines and getting involved in their detail. The subroutines themselves can also be studied in this fashion, as independent, smaller programs. Once the purpose and operation of a subroutine is understood, its inner details can be forgotten; whenever that function is needed, a reference to the subroutine (i.e. GOSUB xyz) is simply inserted into the main program. This is one of the greatest advantages to the modular approach to programming, and it is why subroutines are so important in BASIC programming.

Nesting Subroutines

Subroutines in BASIC may be nested. That is, one subroutine may call another, which may call another, and so on. Each subroutine RETURN will return to the previous level, so an orderly return to the main program can be orchestrated. Figure 3-3 illustrates the concept of nested subroutines.

There is no actual limit to how deeply subroutines may be nested. The practical limit depends upon how much memory is available at the time the program is run.

Subroutine Placement

The statements that make up the body of subroutines are indistinguishable from those in the main program. (This will not be true of subprograms, discussed later in this chapter.) For this reason, it is important to place subroutines where they will not interfere with the operation of the main program. As a general rule, all subroutines in a program are placed at the end of the program, after the entire main program has been coded. Unless the main program ends with a GOTO statement (as in Listing 2-11), the subroutines should be preceded with an END statement. This will insure that the program flow does not "fall into" the subroutine area. Subroutines are meant to be invoked explicitly by GOSUB statements, and should not be executed in any other fashion.

Figure 3-3
Nested Subroutines

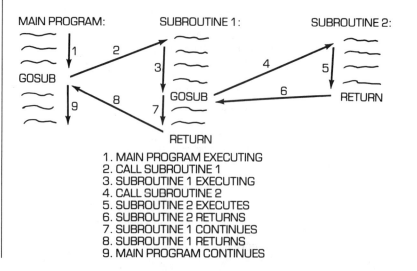

1. MAIN PROGRAM EXECUTING
2. CALL SUBROUTINE 1
3. SUBROUTINE 1 EXECUTING
4. CALL SUBROUTINE 2
5. SUBROUTINE 2 EXECUTES
6. SUBROUTINE 2 RETURNS
7. SUBROUTINE 1 CONTINUES
8. SUBROUTINE 1 RETURNS
9. MAIN PROGRAM CONTINUES

Subroutines and Program Variables

Any variables used in the main program may be referenced in subroutines and will represent the same values. If the subroutine changes the contents of variables, those changes will remain in effect when the subroutine returns to the main program. BASIC subroutines are thus said to share their variables with the main program. Another way of putting it is to say that BASIC variables are *global* to both the main program and its subroutines.

This fact was used in the program of Listing 3-3. In that program, the string being encrypted/decrypted was passed to the appropriate subroutine in variable *a$*. The subroutines altered that variable and returned the new string in the same variable. It is very important to realize, however, that all of the other variables used by the subroutines were also altered from the point of view of the main program. In that case, this was unimportant, because none of the other variables were used by the main program. But, this can cause problems in other programs. Consider, for example, the program shown in Listing 3-4. This program uses the same Encrypt subroutine. Here it is used to encrypt an entire array of character string messages. Study the program carefully. Note that the Encrypt subroutine is called from within a FOR-NEXT loop. This loop accesses each of the elements of array *message$,* and passes each in turn to the Encrypt routine for encryption.

The program will not work, however. This is because the FOR-NEXT loop uses variable *x* as its loop control variable, and this same variable is used for another purpose within subroutine Encrypt. When the first call is made to the subroutine, the value in variable *x* will be altered. Then, when the subroutine returns, the loop control variable *x* will no longer be correct and the program will stop with an error. Try running the program to see this happen.

To correct the error, you can simply use a different variable name for either the loop control variable, or in the subroutine. This kind of program error is very common when using subroutines, so you should look out for it. One way to avoid it is to use subprograms, which solve the problem in an interesting manner. I shall explain how to use subprograms later in this chapter.

User-Defined Functions

Just as subroutines help to reduce needless repetition in program statements, user-defined functions help to reduce needless repetition in expressions. In so doing, they also help to reduce the size and apparent complexity of programs. Many programs have to rely on the same expressions and formulas over and over again. For example, the program of Listing 2-10 uses the same formula to obtain a random number for *die1* and *die2*. By defining a function to represent this formula, you can avoid having to write it over and over again. Whenever you need it, you simply invoke your function instead.

Invoking a user-defined function is much like calling a subroutine. Input parameters are passed to the function as arguments. The output parameter is the value returned by the function. User-defined functions look just like, and can be used in the same fashion as, the built-in BASIC functions.

Listing 3-4
*Program with a
Subroutine Error*

```
' This program uses the Encrypt routine to protect an
' array of character string messages.
' Main Program:
DIM message$(10)  'An array of messages to be encrypted
' Read in the messages:
FOR x=1 TO 10
READ message$(x)
NEXT
' Now encrypt the messages:
FOR x=1 TO 10
a$=message$(x)
GOSUB encrypt
message$(x)=a$
NEXT
' All messages now encrypted
END
' Subroutine Encrypt.
' Gosub Encrypt with a$ = string to be encrypted
' The encryption technique accepts only printable ASCII
' characters, i.e. those with codes in the range 32-127.
' They are encrypted by increasing the code value by 3.
' If during encryption a value exceeds 127 it is wrapped to
' values starting with 32.
Encrypt:
FOR position%=1 TO LEN(a$)
x=ASC(MID$(a$,position%,1))
x=x+3
IF x>127 THEN x=32 + (x MOD 128)
MID$(a$,position%,1)=CHR$(x)
NEXT
RETURN
DATA "Message to : Control"
DATA "From : Agent 009"
DATA "Have infiltrated enemy base"
DATA "using supplied cover"
DATA "Aerial attack is planned for dawn"
DATA "Bomber strength is 27"
DATA "Impossible to reach Gustav"
DATA "Believe his cover was blown"
DATA "Next message at 0200"
DATA "Agent 009 Clear."
```

The DEF-FN Statement

You define your own functions by using the *DEF-FN* statement. Each user-defined function is given a function name. This name, like the keyword names of built-in functions, is subsequently used whenever the function is to be invoked. The function name is made up of the two characters, FN followed by any valid variable name.

The same technique used to define the type of a variable is used to define the type of the function. In other words, if the function name ends with the $ characters (e.g., FNSLICE$), it is a character string function, and will be expected to return a character string value. If no suffix is used on a function name (e.g. FNPROBT), then the function will be expected to return a numeric result. Here is an example of a DEF FN statement

```
DEF FNCUBE(X) = X^3
```

This statement defines the function FNCUBE. This function will accept one argument, and will return a value equal to the argument value cubed. The variable X that appears in the DEF-FN statement is called a dummy parameter. When the function is invoked, the value of its argument is passed to the function definition. It is then used as the value of the *dummy parameter* while the expression in the definition statement is evaluated. Therefore, if the statements

```
arg = 4
PRINT FNCUBE(arg)
```

were executed, the value of arg, 4, would be passed to the FNCUBE definition and used as the value of X. The expression defining the function

```
X^3
```

would thus be evaluated with $X = 4$. The function would therefore return the value 64 ($4\hat{\ }3$). The dummy parameter X does not represent a program variable, and will not conflict with a real program variable of the same name. It is used only to aid in the definition of the function.

True program variables can also be referenced within function definitions, provided those variable names do not appear in the dummy parameter list following the function name. For example, consider the following two statements

```
PI = 3.14159
DEF FNAREA(R) = PI * (R^2)
```

These statements set up and define a function used to calculate the area of a circle as a function of its radius, R. The dummy parameter in the function is R. The function also references the program variable *pi*, which is set to the value 3.14159 in the execution of the main program.

Nested Function Definitions

A function definition may contain references to other user-defined functions, as well as any of the built-in BASIC functions. For example, consider the following definition

```
DEF FNSTL$(X$) = MID$(X$,LEN(X$)-1,1)
```

This defines a function named FNSTL$ which returns the second to last character of its character string argument. Thus the statement

```
PRINT FNSTL$("APPLE")
```

would print the character "L." Another way to implement this function would be

```
DEF FNSTL$(X$) = LEFT$(RIGHT$(X$,2),1)
```

Verify for yourself that these two functions perform the same operation.

Multiple Argument Functions

By specifying multiple dummy parameters on the DEF-FN statement, you can define functions that accept more than one input argument. As an example of this feature, let me define a function to implement the general purpose random number formula introduced in the last chapter. The definition would look like this

```
DEF FNRAND(L,U) = CINT(L + RND(1) * (U - L))
```

This function accepts the two input arguments *L* and *U*, which represent the lower and upper limits of the random number to be generated. The function will return an integer random number in that range. In Listing 3-5, the dice rolling program of Listing 2-10 has been rewritten to utilize this function. Note how the use of the user-defined function helps to modularize and increase the readability of the program.

```
' Generates a pair of random numbers
' in the range 1 - 6.
DEF FNrand(l,u)=CINT(1+RND(1)*(u-1))
RANDOMIZE TIMER
Again:
die1=FNrand(1,6)
die2=FNrand(1,6)
total=die1+die2
PRINT "Rolling dice.....";die1;" - ";die2;" (";total;")"
LINE INPUT "Press Return to roll again";a$
GOTO Again
```

The FNRAND function has another advantage over the "hard-coded" formula used in Listing 2-10. FNRAND is general purpose; it can be used to generate random numbers in any range, not just 1 to 6. This makes it ideal for any job where random numbers may be needed. For example, many popular fantasy role playing games require that players roll various kinds of dice. Besides the conventional 6-sided die, these games use 8-sided, 4-sided, 10-sided and other strange dice. Sometimes the player must roll several dice of one type; if only a handful of these dice are available, many rolls must be made before the game can proceed. The fantasy game dice rolling program of Listing 3-6 can help speed up game play in these cases. It uses the general purpose random number function shown above, and allows the user to specify the number of die rolls to make, and the number of sides per die.

In later chapters, I show you how to make the program even more fun to use by adding the unique Macintosh interface tools (i.e., mouse, pull-down menus) to the program. A sample run of the program in its present form appears in Figure 3-4.

Subprograms

Microsoft added the *subprogram* to their BASIC for the Macintosh to serve as an enhanced subroutine mechanism. The subroutine, discussed earlier in this chapter, is a common feature in most

Listing 3-6
*Fantasy Game Dice
Rolling Program*

```
' Simulates the rolling of any number of dice,
' with any number of sides per die.
DEF FNrand(l,u)=CINT(l+RND(1)*(u-1))
RANDOMIZE TIMER
Again:
INPUT "How many dice to be rolled";number%
INPUT "How many sides per die";sides%
PRINT
PRINT"Rolling...";
total%=0
FOR x%=1 TO number%
die%=FNrand(1,sides%)
total%=total%+die%
PRINT "   ";die%;
NEXT
PRINT
PRINT "Total = ";total%
PRINT
GOTO Again
```

Figure 3-4
*Run of the FRP Dice
Rolling Program*

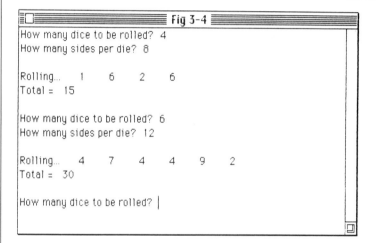

```
▤☐▤▤▤▤▤▤▤▤▤▤▤▤ Fig 3-4 ▤▤▤▤
How many dice to be rolled?  4
How many sides per die?  8

Rolling...    1     6     2     6
Total =  15

How many dice to be rolled?  6
How many sides per die?  12

Rolling...    4     7     4     4     9     2
Total =  30

How many dice to be rolled?  |
```

dialects of BASIC, the subprogram is not. Subprograms address many of the shortcomings of subroutines, and are, in general, a more powerful facility. As a result of this, they can be somewhat more difficult to use.

There are three major differences between subroutines and subprograms. First, subprograms are accessed by the *CALL* statement, whereas subroutines are accessed by the GOSUB statement. Second, unlike subroutines, subprograms do not share all their variables with the main program. This is really the most significant difference between the two forms, and one that shall be of utmost concern when writing subprograms. Finally, subprograms cannot be accidentally executed; it is impossible to "fall through" into subprogram code.

Defining a Subprogram
All subprograms begin with, and are defined by the *SUB* statement. This statement has the following format

```
SUB name (parameters) STATIC
```

The name that follows the keyword SUB will be the name of the subprogram. The rules for subprogram names are the same as for program labels (maximum of 40 characters). The parameters are optional, but if present must be enclosed in parenthesis, as shown. The keyword *STATIC* must always be present in the SUB statement. You will see why in a moment.

The SUB statement is followed by one or more program statements; these make up the body of the subprogram. The end of the subprogram is denoted by the *END SUB* statement, which looks like this

```
END SUB
```

The entire subprogram (Figure 3-5) can be placed anywhere in a program. It will not be executed until it is explicitly called. This means that you could insert a subroutine between any other two lines of your program, although this is certainly not recommended, as it would make the program much harder to read.

As with subroutines, it is best to group all subprograms together at the end of the listing, following the main program. It is not possible to nest subprogram definitions.

Figure 3-5
Defining a Subprogram

```
SUB name (parameters) STATIC
...

...
... (body of subprogram)
...

...
END SUB
```

Invoking a Subprogram

You invoke the execution of a subprogram through use of the CALL statement. This statement has the form

```
CALL name (parameters)
```

This statement specifies the name of the subprogram to be called. The parameters, enclosed in parentheses, are once again optional. Their use will be explained in a moment. When the CALL statement is executed, the program branches to the beginning of the subprogram and executes the statements there. When the end of the subprogram is reached, control is returned to the main program at the point of the CALL statement. Thus, the subprogram behaves identically to the subroutine, in terms of flow of control as shown in Figure 3-6.

Subprograms and Variables

So far, the operation of the subprogram seems not much different from that of the subroutine. The significant difference has to do with the way variables are treated during subprogram calls. Unlike a subroutine, any variables declared or used within a subprogram are considered *local* to that subprogram. This means that they are not known to the main program, outside of the subprogram. If the same variable name is used in a subprogram and in its main program, they are not the same variable. This is illustrated in Figure 3-7. Study this figure carefully, as this is an important concept.

Figure 3-6
Invoking a Subprogram

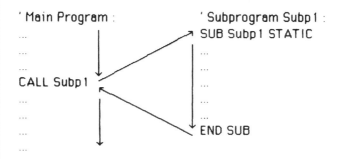

Figure 3-7
Local Variables in Subprograms

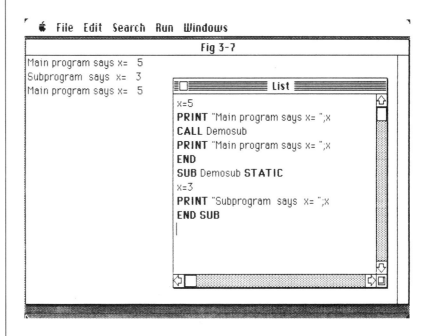

Whatever values are left in the local variables by a subprogram will still be present if and when the subprogram is called again. These local variables are therefore said to be *static*. It is for this reason that Microsoft requires that you specify the STATIC keyword on all SUB statements. This will serve as a reminder for you that any variables declared in the subprogram will be local to the subprogram, and will remain unchanged between invocations of the subprogram.

While this locality of variables within subprograms would seem to be a wonderful new feature (recall the problem with Listing 3-4), it also presents a new problem. How does one transfer information between a main program and its subprograms? This is certainly going to be necessary if the subprogram is to be meaningfully integrated into the main program. To be sure, there are two techniques that can be used to allow communications between the main program and its subprograms. They are *shared variables* and *formal parameters*.

Shared Variables

The easiest way to exchange data between a main program and a subprogram is to make one or more variables shared. A shared variable is declared as such within the subprogram through use of the *SHARED* statement. It looks like this

```
SHARED variable-name, variable name,
. . .
```

The statement lists the names of one or more variables that are to be shared with variables of the same name in the main program. It is only necessary to place the statement in the subprogram; it is not needed in the main program. Variables that are declared as shared in this fashion are not local to the subprogram, and are not static with respect to multiple subprogram calls.

Passing data back and forth between a subprogram and its main program is easy with shared variables. As an example, I have rewritten the program in Listing 3-4; the new program appears in Listing 3-7.

In Listing 3-7, I have converted the Encrypt subroutine into a subprogram with the same name. Within the subprogram, the variable *a$* is shared with the main program. All of the other subprogram variables are local to the subprogram. The main program can now pass the message to be encrypted to the subprogram in variable *a$*. The subprogram performs the encryption and passes the result back to the main program in the same variable.

Because no other communication between the main and subprograms is necessary, all other variables used in the subprogram can be local to it. In particular, this means the variable *x* used in Encrypt is a different variable from the variable *x* used in the main program. There is no conflict, and this program will work. (If you run this program, note that it does not produce any output in its current form.) For comparison, try running the program of Listing 3-4. This program will fail with an error, study it carefully and be sure you understand how this error arises as a result of the conflicting uses of variable *x* in the main program and subroutine.

You may place as many SHARED statements as you like into a subprogram. Because it is not an executable statement but rather a declarative one, the SHARED statement may be placed anywhere within the subprogram without any change in its effect. In spite of this, you should place all SHARED statements at the beginning of the subprogram, immediately after the SUB statement, to aid in program readability.

If you are declaring an array variable as shared, then you must indicate to the subprogram that the variable is indeed an array. This is done by following the variable name with a set of parentheses in the SHARED statement. For example, assuming *DELTAS* is an array in the main program that is to be accessed in a subprogram

```
SHARED DELTAS()
```

```
' This program uses the Encrypt routine to protect an
' array of character string messages.
' Main Program:
DIM message$(10) 'An array of messages to be encrypted
' Read in the messages:
FOR x=1 TO 10
READ message$(x)
NEXT
' Now encrypt the messages:
FOR x=1 TO 10
a$=message$(x)
CALL Encrypt
message$(x)=a$
NEXT
' All messages now encrypted
END
' Subprogram Encrypt.
' Call Encrypt with a$ = string to be encrypted
' The encryption technique accepts only printable ASCII
' characters, i.e. those with codes in the range 32-127.
' They are encrypted by increasing the code value by 3.
' If during encryption a value exceeds 127 it is wrapped to
' values starting with 32.
SUB Encrypt STATIC
SHARED a$
FOR position%=1 TO LEN(a$)
x=ASC(MID$(a$,position%,1))
x=x+3
IF x>127 THEN x=32 + (x MOD 128)
MID$(a$,position%,1)=CHR$(x)
NEXT
END SUB
DATA "Message to : Control"
DATA "From : Agent 009"
DATA "Have infiltrated enemy base"
DATA "using supplied cover"
DATA "Aerial attack is planned for dawn"
DATA "Bomber strength is 27"
DATA "Impossible to reach Gustav"
DATA "Believe his cover was blown"
DATA "Next message at 0200"
DATA "Agent 009 Clear."
```

Formal Parameters

A somewhat more complicated technique for transferring data between a main program and its subprograms is the use of *formal parameters*. Formal parameters provide a means whereby specific data values can be explicitly passed to a subprogram at the time of its invocation. The data items being passed to the subprogram from the main program are called *arguments*. The concept is very similar to the arguments that can be passed to user-defined functions. Within the subprogram, these arguments are referenced via a predefined set of variable names, which are called the formal parameters of the subprogram (or just parameters, for short). The arguments to be passed to the subprogram are specified, in parentheses, following the subprogram name in the CALL statement. These arguments will be assigned to a set of variable names specified, also in parentheses, after the subprogram name and before the keyword STATIC.

An example of how this mechanism works is shown in Listing 3-8. The subprogram in this example, made deliberately simple for illustrative purposes, checks to see whether one value is evenly divisible by another. It uses a technique introduced in the last chapter. The subprogram is named Dcheck. It has three formal parameters; they are named *Dividend%*, *Divisor%*, and *Iquotient%*. These formal parameters represent variables that can be referenced anywhere in the subprogram.

Listing 3-8
Subprogram with
Formal Parameters

```
' Main Program:
x%=28
CALL Dcheck(x%,6,result%)
IF result%=0 THEN PRINT x%;" is not divisible by 6"
IF result%<>0 THEN PRINT "6 goes into ";x%;" -- ";result%;" times."
'
CALL Dcheck(27,3,result%)
IF result%=0 THEN PRINT "27 is not divisible by 3"
IF result%<>0 THEN PRINT "3 goes into 27 -- ";result%;" times."
END
'
' Subprogram DCHECK:
' Call Dcheck(x%,y%,result%)
' Dcheck checks to see if x% is evenly divisible by y%. If not, then
' result% is returned as 0. Otherwise result% is returned as the
' number of times that y% goes into x%.
SUB Dcheck(Dividend%,Divisor%,Iquotient%) STATIC
x=Dividend%/Divisor%
IF x=FIX(x) THEN Iquotient%=x : EXIT SUB
Iquotient%=0
END SUB
```

When the subprogram is called, three arguments are passed to it. Viewing Listing 3-8, you can see that in the first call, these arguments are the variable $x\%$, the constant 6, and the variable *result%*. When the subprogram begins execution, the three (local) variables *Dividend%*, *Divisor%*, and *Iquotient%* will be passed the values of variable $x\%$, 6, and variable *result%*, respectively. In this fashion, information from the main program is passed to the subprogram. So far so good, but how does the subprogram pass information back to the main program?

Information can be passed to formal parameters within a subprogram in two different ways. These are known as *pass by name* and *pass by value*. Both of these ways have been used in the current example. When the argument of the subprogram call is simply a variable name, then the information is said to be passed by name. This is the case for the first and third arguments of our example, $x\%$ and *result*%.

When arguments are passed by name, BASIC sets up a temporary correspondence between the argument variable name and the formal parameter variable name. Thus, any change in the subprogram to the variable name *Dividend*% will be reflected identically in variable $x\%$ when control is returned to the main program. Variables *result*% and *Iquotient*% are similarly linked. It is through this pass by name technique that information from within a subprogram can be passed back to the main program.

When the argument of a subprogram call is anything other than a variable name (i.e., a constant or an expression), then the information is said to be passed by value. In this case, BASIC evaluates the expression or constant and assigns the resulting value to the appropriate formal parameter variable name when the subprogram begins execution. The subprogram may subsequently alter the variable in question, but such changes *will not* be reflected in any manner in the main program.

The second argument in our example call (6) is passed by value. In the second call statement of Listing 3-8, the first and second arguments are passed by value, while the third argument is passed by name.

Formal parameters provide a well-structured technique for communicating data between a main program and its subprograms. It is easy to see what information is being passed to the subprogram because such information is listed explicitly in the subprogram call. General purpose subprograms can be written; their function can then depend upon the actual values passed when they are called. Information being returned to the main program can be clearly identified by the pass by name technique.

Sometimes you may find the need to pass information contained in a variable to a subprogram, but you do not wish to perform the pass by name. You can easily trick BASIC into passing the information by value instead, simply by specifying the (variable) argument as an expression. The easiest way to do this is to enclose the variable in an extra set of parentheses. For example

```
CALL Sample(x,y,(z))
```

In the above example, variables x and y will be passed by name, while the contents of variable z will be passed by value. The subprogram may cause the contents of variable x and y to change, but it will be unable to alter the contents of variable z.

If arrays are to be passed to subprograms via the formal parameter method, then a special nomenclature must be used in the SUB statement. Each formal parameter that represents an array must be followed by the number of array dimensions in parenthesis. For example

```
SUB Sample (x,y(1),z(2)) STATIC
```

This statement defines a subprogram named Sample that will accept three arguments: a scalar, x, a one-dimensional array, y, and a two-dimensional array, *z*. It might be called from a main program containing statements like

```
DIM alpha(100),beta(10,10)
CALL Sample (tryit,alpha,beta)
```

The actual size of an array can be determined from within the subprogram by using the special built-in functions **LBOUND** and **HBOUND**. These functions return the lowest and highest available subscript values for an array dimension. For a one-dimensional array, the argument of **LBOUND** and **HBOUND** is simply the array name. For a multidimensional array, **LBOUND** and **HBOUND** expect two arguments. The first is the array name, and the second is the array dimension in question. For the example above, the following would be true

```
LBOUND(alpha) = 0
HBOUND(alpha) = 100
LBOUND(beta,1) = 0
HBOUND(beta,1) = 10
LBOUND(beta,2) = 0
HBOUND(beta,2) = 10
```

In practice, **HBOUND** is much more important than **LBOUND**. The only possible values that can be returned from **LBOUND** are 0 or 1, depending upon the setting of the OPTION BASE statement, if used.

The EXIT SUB Statement

The EXIT SUB statement is used to exit from a subprogram prior to reaching the defined end of the subprogram. When this statement is executed, the subprogram ends and control is returned to the point in the main program from which the subprogram was called. The values of any formal parameters that were passed by name are sent back to the appropriate variables in the main program. An example of the use of the EXIT SUB statement can be found in Listing 3-8.

The StartDay Subprogram

The StartDay subprogram is the first step towards what will become a complete and useful Macintosh application (the Personal Calendar). This subprogram is used to determine the starting day of the week for a given month and year. It is contained in Listing 3-9, along with a temporary main program that can be run to demonstrate its operation.

Throughout the personal calendar program, any day of the week will be represented by a code number from 1 to 7, where 1 represents Sunday, 2 represents Monday, and so on. The main program dimensions and then initializes the character string array *DayNames$*, which contains the names of the days of the week according to this correspondence. In a similar fashion, the array *MonthNames$* contains the names of the months of the year. Finally, the array *MonthDays%* contains the number of days in each month. It is indexed by a value from 1 to 12, representing the months of January through December. The second entry in this array (February) must be handled in a special manner due to leap years. This will be managed by the StartDay subprogram.

Listing 3-9
The StartDay
Subprogram

```
' First phase in development of the calendar program.
' Initialize array data:
DIM MonthDays%(12)
FOR x%=1 TO 12
READ MonthDays%(x%)
NEXT
DATA 31,28,31,30,31,30,31,31,30,31,30,31
DIM DayNames$(7)
FOR x%=1 TO 7
READ DayNames$(x%)
NEXT
DATA Sunday,Monday,Tuesday,Wednesday,Thursday,Friday,Saturday
DIM MonthNames$(12)
FOR x%=1 TO 12
READ MonthNames$(x%)
NEXT
DATA January, February,March,April,May,June,July,August,September
DATA October,November,December
' Temporary main program to demo the subprogram:
again:
INPUT "Enter month, year",month%,year%
CALL StartDay(month%,year%,day%,days%)
PRINT MonthNames$(month%);" 19";
PRINT USING "##";year%;
PRINT " starts on a ";DayNames$(day%);"   and has ";days%;" days in it"
PRINT
GOTO again
' Subprogram StartDay
' Finds the starting day of the week for a given month and year.
' Call StartDay(Month%,Year%,Day%,Days%)
' with Month% = 1(Jan), 2(Feb), ...., 12(Dec)
' and Year% = 85, 86, ..., 99 (valid for 1985 thru 1999)
' Returns with Day% = 1 (Sun), 2 (Mon), 3 (Tue), ..., 7 (Sat)
' and with Days% = number of days in that month.
SUB StartDay (m%,y%,d%,ds%) STATIC
SHARED MonthDays%()
d%=3 'Jan 85 starts with Tuesday
m1%=1 'start at Jan
y1%=85 'start at 1985
StartDayLoop2:
IF (y1%-84) MOD 4 = 0 THEN MonthDays%(2)=29 ELSE MonthDays%(2)=28 'Leap Years
StartDayLoop1:
IF m1%=m% AND y1%=y% THEN GOTO FoundStartDay
d%=d%+MonthDays%(m1%)
IF m1%<12 THEN  m1%=m1%+1 : GOTO StartDayLoop1
m1%=1
y1%=y1%+1
GOTO StartDayLoop2
FoundStartDay:
d%=d% MOD 7
IF d%=0 THEN d%=7
ds%=MonthDays%(m1%)
END SUB
```

The StartDay subprogram is called with four arguments, all integers. The first two arguments represent input data to the subprogram, whereas the last two represent output from the subprogram passed back to the main program. The subprogram

79 *Advanced Programming Structures*

accepts as input a month code (1 - 12) and a year code (85 - 99). The year code must be in the range 85 through 99, and represents the years 1985 through 1999, the only range in which the subprogram's logic will work. The subprogram returns the day of the week that the specified month starts with (as a code number from 1 - 7). It also returns the number of days in the month. The subprogram shares the array variable *MonthDays%* with the main program, and automatically makes adjustment to the second element of this array when in a leap year.

The logic of the subprogram is very simple. The date January 1, 1985 is "hard coded" into the routine as a Tuesday (code value 3). The routine starts with this value, and adds the number of days in each subsequent month, counting up until the specified month and year are reached. The final day count, modulo 7, represents the day of the week for the month in question. Leap years are detected by subtracting the year code by 84 (1984 was a leap year), taking the modulo 4, and checking for a remainder (i.e. every fourth year after 1984 will be a leap year).

Leap years cause an automatic change in the second element of array *MonthDays%* (February); this change is reflected in the main program.

Eventually, this routine is used to help create the image of a monthly calendar on the Macintosh display. For the moment, however, the main program demonstrates the operation of the subprogram by simply allowing the user to request a specific month and year. The program then displays the starting day for that month, and the number of days in the month. A sample run is shown in Figure 3-8.

Figure 3-8
Testing the StartDay
Subprogram

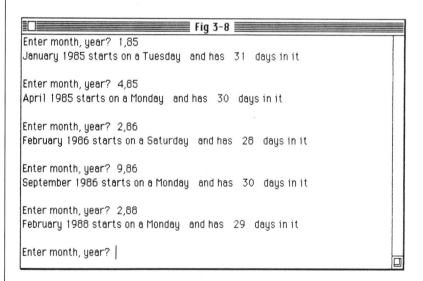

Program Chaining

Microsoft BASIC provides the ability to *chain* from one program to another independently written and filed program. There are two reasons for wanting to do this. The most important reason is that many BASIC programs require more memory than is available in a typical microcomputer configuration. Memory limitations can be overcome by splitting a large program into smaller parts, each of which can run separately. The other reason for breaking a program into smaller parts is to improve the program's structure and readability.

This so called modular approach to programming allows one to attack a programming task that might otherwise be too complex to handle effectively and without errors. The large problem is broken down into smaller ones, which are more manageable. Using this approach, it is even possible to have several people working on one program. Each person works on his (her) own module. A single program coordinator manages the integration of each independently written module into a single, cohesive program.

The subroutine and subprogram mechanisms discussed earlier in this chapter can be used to modularize a program in this manner. In this section, I will introduce yet another mechanism, the chained program. The chained program actually consists of several separate program files which transfer control to each other. This is accomplished through use of the *CHAIN* statement.

The CHAIN statement, when executed, instructs BASIC to load in a new program file and start executing it. Some or all of the current program's variables may be passed to the new program. To pass all of the current program's variables, use the form

```
CHAIN filename,,ALL
```

In the statement above, filename is the name of the Macintosh file containing the new BASIC program to be loaded. The filename should be enclosed in double quotes. The keyword ALL specifies that *all* of the current program's variables should be retained in memory; they will thus be available to the new program file when it begins execution. Any data files that were opened by the current program will remain open (data files are discussed in the next chapter).

The COMMON Statement

If it is not necessary to pass all of the current program's variable to the chained program, then the keyword ALL should be omitted from the CHAIN statement. In this case, a separate *COMMON* statement is used to specify which variables are to remain in memory when the new program is loaded. The COMMON statement begins with the keyword COMMON, and then contains one or more variable names. For example

```
COMMON Days, types, x, y$
```

The above statement specifies that variables *Days*, *types*, *x*, and *y$* be retained and passed to the new program when a CHAIN statement is executed. As with the SHARED statement, if an array variable is specified, the variable name should be followed by a set of parentheses

```
COMMON alpha()
```

The COMMON statement can appear anywhere in a program, although it is best to place it at the beginning of the listing, for better program readability.

The MERGE Option

An alternate form of the CHAIN statement can be used to merge a program file with the current program. In this case, the current program is not lost. The specified program file is simply added to the current program in memory. The same statement can specify that a portion of the current program be deleted at the same time. This feature allows you to create overlays. An overlay structure is useful when the main program and all of its support subroutines (or subprograms) cannot fit in memory. In this case, you can use the CHAIN statement with the *MERGE* option to load in one subroutine at a time, as they are needed. When each subroutine is loaded, the previously loaded subroutine is deleted. In this fashion, a large program can be executed without being totally memory resident. The CHAIN statement with the MERGE option looks like this

```
CHAIN MERGE "filename",,ALL,DELETE
label1-label2
```

The filename specifies the name of the Macintosh file containing the new program segment to be loaded. This file must have been saved in the Text format. The statement also specifies a range of statements to be deleted from the current program. The range is defined by specifying a starting program label, label1, and an ending program label, label2. All statements between the two labels specified will be deleted from the current program in memory before the new program segment is loaded.

Interrupt Driven Structures

An *interrupt* is an event that takes place independently of the currently executing program. One example of such an event might be the clicking of the mouse button. Another might be the Macintosh internal time of day clock reaching a certain preset time. By setting up an interrupt driven structure, your program can be ready for such events. You can then take whatever action is necessary when the event in question actually takes place.

On the Macintosh, there are a total of five different events that you can detect and take special action on. These event types are summarized in Table 3-1. Events related to the mouse, pull-down menus, and dialog boxes are discussed in greater detail in the appropriate chapters later in this book. I will cover the basic techniques involved in setting up for and handling interrupts right now. For the purposes of illustration, I will use the remaining two interrupt types, timer and break.

As shown in Table 3-1, each event type is identified by a unique event name. They are *TIMER, BREAK, MENU, MOUSE,* and *DIALOG.* There are four BASIC statements used to set up and control interrupt structures. In each statement, the specific event

Table 3-1
Interrupt Events

Event Name	Occurs when
TIMER(N)	Every N seconds.
BREAK	User presses Command-. or pulls down the Run menu and selects Stop.
MENU	Custom pull-down menu item selected (see Chapter 9).
MOUSE	Mouse button is clicked (see Chapter 6).
DIALOG	Dialog box button is selected, or entry made into an edit field within a dialog box (see Chapter 8).

type being controlled is specified through use of one of the five names just mentioned. The statements are

```
ON eventname GOSUB label
eventname ON
eventname OFF
eventname STOP
```

The first of these statements is used to set up what is known as an interrupt service subroutine. The label specified on this statement should be the name of a subroutine that will receive control whenever the event specified takes place. It will be the job of this subroutine to handle the event in whatever manner is necessary.

The three remaining statements shown above are used to enable or disable the detection of the specified event. The

```
eventname OFF
```

statement will disable detection of the event indicated. This is the default state for all five event types. After executing an

```
ON eventname GOSUB label
```

statement, you must also execute an

```
eventname ON
```

statement to enable interrupts of that same event type. Once these two steps have been taken, every time the event specified occurs, the normal flow of the program will be interrupted and control will be transferred to the named subroutine. The subroutine should handle the event in the appropriate manner and then execute a RETURN statement. The RETURN statement will cause the normal flow of the program to be resumed at its point of interruption.

If at any point you no longer wish to be interrupted by additional event occurrences, you must execute the

```
eventname OFF
```

statement. In some cases, a portion of a program may require execution without interruption, but you may still want to know if an interrupt event took place while that portion of the program was executing. In this case, precede the sensitive portion of the program with an eventname STOP

statement. This will prevent activation of the interrupt service subroutine, but it will remember if the interrupt event does occur. When the sensitive portion of the program is completed, you can then execute an

eventname ON

statement. If the event did indeed occur during the previous interval, the interrupt service subroutine will be activated immediately. The interrupt control statements are summarized in Table 3-2.

Table 3-2
Interrupt Control Statements

Statement	Action
ON eventname GOSUB label	Sets up the interrupt service subroutine starting at the label specified. The routine will be used to service events of the type specified.
eventname ON	Enables interrupts of the type specified to occur.
eventname OFF	Disables interrupts of the type specified from occurring.
eventname STOP	Temporarily prevents interrupts of the type specified from being serviced. Any interrupts that do occur will be remembered, however, and will be serviced once the 'eventname ON' statement is issued.

BREAK Event Examples

The BREAK event is signalled whenever the user tries to stop program execution, either by pulling down the Run menu and selecting Stop, or by holding down the command key and pressing the period key $<.>$. By setting up an interrupt service subroutine to handle this event, you can prevent the user from halting your program. A simple example of how to do this can be found in Listing 3-10.

The first two statements in Listing 3-10 set up for and enable the BREAK event. The program then enters a loop that prints the values of *x*, *x squared*, and *x cubed* for values of *x* starting at one

Listing 3-10
An Unbreakable Program

```
' WARNING: you must reset or turn off your Macintosh to regain
' control after starting this program !!!
ON BREAK GOSUB Break.Int
BREAK ON
x=1
Again:
PRINT x,x*x,x*x*x
x=x+1
GOTO Again
' Interrupt Service Subroutine for event = BREAK :
Break.Int:
PRINT "You can't stop me now..... hahahaha!!"
RETURN
```

and increasing continually. Since the loop has no programmed stopping point, you would normally halt the program by selecting Stop from the Run menu, or by holding down the command key and pressing the period key. In this program, however, either of these actions will cause the Break.Int subroutine to be entered. This routine prints out the message

You can't stop me now. . . . .hahahaha!!

and then executes a RETURN statement. This causes the program to be resumed at exactly the point where it was originally interrupted. Thus, the program is unbreakable. Figure 3-9 shows a sample run of this program. In this figure, you can see where I attempted to stop the program at two points. If you try running this program, be aware that it cannot be halted, so to regain normal control of your Macintosh you must either turn it off and then on again, or press the <reset> button.

Figure 3-9
*Running the
Unbreakable Program*

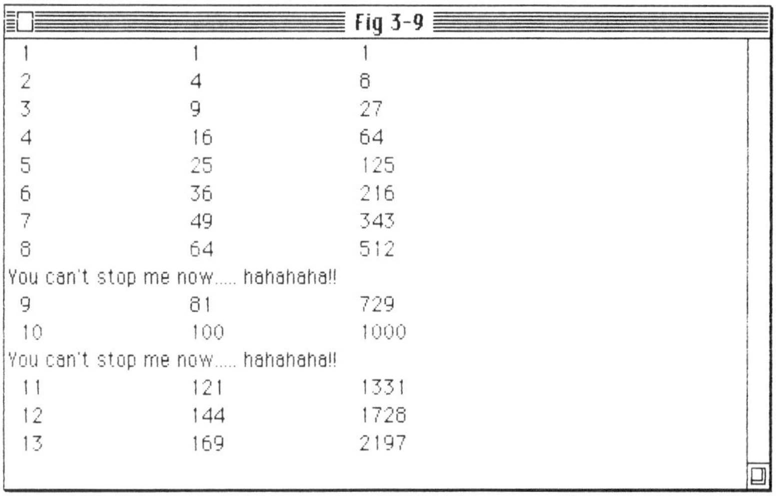

```
╔═════════════════════ Fig 3-9 ═════════════════════╗
 1              1              1
 2              4              8
 3              9              27
 4              16             64
 5              25             125
 6              36             216
 7              49             343
 8              64             512
You can't stop me now..... hahahaha!!
 9              81             729
 10             100            1000
You can't stop me now..... hahahaha!!
 11             121            1331
 12             144            1728
 13             169            2197
```

The reset button is that funny piece of plastic that Apple provides with the computer. It is installed on the left side of the machine, near the back panel, and actually provides two buttons. (To install, simply snap it into the second ventilation slot from the bottom, see Figure 3-10.) The button closer to the front of the machine will be the reset button. It is very useful since it allows you to regain control of the Macintosh without having to turn the machine off.

A BREAK interrupt routine such as this one might be used to protect a sensitive portion of a program from being accidentally halted. For example, a database program might employ this interrupt handler to prevent being halted while it is updating its disk file(s). Once the update part of the program is complete, a

BREAK OFF

statement could be used to allow the program to be halted, if necessary. Figure 3-11 shows how this approach would look.

Figure 3-10
The Reset Button

Figure 3-11
*Protecting a Program
Segment from BREAK*

```
' First, set up interrupt service subroutine :
ON BREAK GOSUB Break.Int
'
' ... Main Program (breakable here) ...
'
BREAK ON
'
' ... Unbreakable portion ...
'
BREAK OFF
'
' ... Program continues (breakable here) ...
'
END
' Interrupt Service Subroutine for event = BREAK :
Break.Int:
RETURN
```

Listing 3-11 illustrates another technique involving **BREAK**
protection. In this case, when the user attempts to halt the program
he is prompted for a password. Without the proper password reply,
the program continues to run. Figure 3-12 shows what happened
when I ran this program. I attempted to halt the program and it
asked for the password; I replied "xyz." The program simply
proceeded on its merry way, producing the same (by now quite
boring) listing. I attempted to halt the program again, this time I
provided the proper password, "archimedes." The program halted,
and the listing window reappeared, as usual.

The *UCASE$* function is used in the interrupt service subroutine
to allow the user to enter the password in either uppercase or
lowercase.

The TIMER Event

The TIMER event is a periodic (constantly repeating) interrupt
keyed to the Macintosh internal time-of-day clock. This clock is
accessible to BASIC programs in fundamental units of one second
each (recall the TIMER function described in the last chapter).
When you set up an interrupt service subroutine for the TIMER
event, you must specify the rate (in whole units of seconds) at which
you want it to occur. The following syntax is used

ON TIMER (n) GOSUB label

In the above statement, a value of 10 for *n* would cause timer events to occur once every ten seconds. Assuming an ON TIMER statement is in effect, this will cause the running BASIC program to be interrupted six times a minute. The value of *n* can range from 1 to 86400, although you will typically want to use values towards the low end of that range (86400 seconds = 24 hours).

Listing 3-11
Password Protection

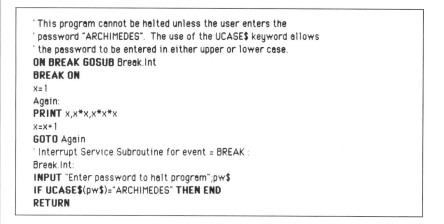

```
' This program cannot be halted unless the user enters the
' password "ARCHIMEDES". The use of the UCASE$ keyword allows
' the password to be entered in either upper or lower case.
ON BREAK GOSUB Break.Int
BREAK ON
x=1
Again:
PRINT x,x*x,x*x*x
x=x+1
GOTO Again
' Interrupt Service Subroutine for event = BREAK :
Break.Int:
INPUT "Enter password to halt program";pw$
IF UCASE$(pw$)="ARCHIMEDES" THEN END
RETURN
```

Figure 3-12
Running the Password Protected Program

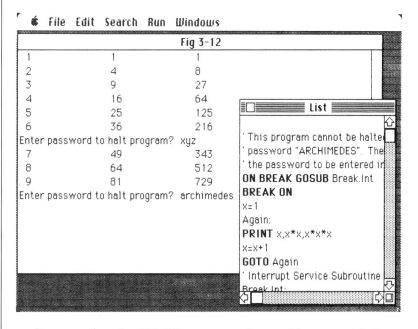

One way that the TIMER event can be used is to provide for a programmed "time-out" on a user input function. Listing 3-12 shows how this is accomplished. Try running this program. It will ask for you to enter your name, and wait for a reply. If you type in your name and press the <Return> key, the program proceeds. If, however, you do not do this within 30 seconds, the program aborts the input wait and informs you that it is going to proceed without your reply.

Listing 3-12
The TIMER Event

```
' Set up for timer interrupts every 30 seconds:
ON TIMER(30) GOSUB Timer.Int
'
LOCATE 5,1
PRINT "You have thirty seconds to reply."
LOCATE 2,1
PRINT "Please enter your name : ";
GOSUB GetReply
IF reply$="" THEN GOTO TimedOut
PRINT "Thank you, proceeding ....."
'
' ... program continues with user reply ...
'
END
TimedOut:
PRINT "Too late,.i'm going ahead without you! "
'
' ... program continues without user reply ...
'
END
' Interrupt service subroutine for event = TIMER :
Timer.Int:
TIMER OFF
RETURN GetReplyTimedOut
' End of Timer.Int Subroutine.
'
' Subroutine GetReply :
' GOSUB GetReply to wait for a user's response.  The user's response must
' be entered within 30 seconds or a programmed "time-out" occurs.
' The user's response is returned in variable reply$.  If the time-out
' occurs, then reply$ is returned as the null string.
GetReply:
TIMER ON  'enable TIMER interrupt
reply$=""  'initialize return value
GetChar:        'Wait for a character using INKEY$ :
a$=INKEY$
WHILE a$=""
a$=INKEY$
WEND
PRINT a$;  'echo users entries on screen, including the "return" keystroke
IF a$=CHR$(13) THEN TIMER OFF : RETURN
reply$=reply$+a$
GOTO GetChar
' Normal program flow is forced to here if a timer interrupt occurs :
GetReplyTimedOut:
reply$=""  ' return a null string to the main program to indicate time-out
PRINT
RETURN
' End of GetReply Subroutine.
```

The main program uses the ON TIMER statement to set up for timer interrupts once every 30 seconds. The interrupts are not yet enabled. The main program then displays the prompt for the input. It then calls subroutine GetReply to actually wait for the input. Subroutine GetReply uses the INKEY$ function to obtain the user's reply, one keystroke at a time. This technique was first illustrated in Chapter 2. As each key is pressed, the character is echoed to the Output window, and the data is accumulated in string *reply$*. When the <Return> key is pressed (CHR$(13)), the subroutine returns to its caller.

The subroutine enables timer interrupts with a ON TIMER statement when it is called. The first timer interrupt will occur 30 seconds later. If the user enters the reply and presses the < Return > key before that time is up, no interrupt occurs, because the subroutine disables the interrupt before returning (TIMER OFF statement). If, however, the time out does takes place (i.e., the user does not reply within 30 seconds), then the subroutine is interrupted and control is transferred to the timer event service subroutine, named Timer.Int. This routine performs an explicit TIMER OFF statement. Normally, interrupts of a particular type are disabled as soon as the interrupt service subroutine for that type is entered. This prevents the subroutine from being interrupted by another occurrence of the same event!

When the interrupt service subroutine RETURNs, however, that event type is re-enabled to allow subsequent interrupts of the same type. In our case, this will not happen, because with the TIMER OFF statement I explicitly requested that the event remain disabled.

The subroutine then executes a RETURN statement with a destination label. Normally, a RETURN statement appears with the keyword RETURN alone, specifying a return to the point of call (or, in the case of an interrupt service subroutine, to the point of interruption). By specifying a label, however, you can force the subroutine to return to a different point. In this case, the subroutine returns to label GetReplyTimedOut, within the subroutine GetReply. This allows the GetReply subroutine to return to the main program, with the *reply$* string set to null to indicate that a time out occurred.

In this example, I have used the TIMER event as a "one-shot" — that is, to produce only a single, timed interrupt. This was achieved by disabling further timer interrupts as soon as the first one was received. If this is not done, however, the TIMER event will occur repeatedly. The interrupt will therefore take place at regular intervals, and can be used to monitor the progress of a program from section to section.

To do this, a "tag" variable is set up to indicate what part of the program is being executed. The timer interrupt service subroutine checks the value of the tag at regular intervals. Since it can detect when the tag changes, it can tell when the program passes from one phase to another. The routine can thus be used to track the total length of time spent in any single program phase. This information can then be used to abort the program if it spends too much time in a particular phase.

This technique, illustrated in Listing 3-13, may be helpful when developing programs that use iterative algorithms to solve problems. Sometimes these algorithms can repeat almost indefinitely without getting any closer to a solution; in these cases it is nice to be able to abort the program in a clean manner. The FOR-NEXT loop that appears in Listing 3-13 is only present so the program can be run as an effective demonstration of this concept.

The loop takes about fifteen seconds to complete, and since the timer interrupt monitors the program's progress once every five seconds, you see the program enter each phase when it is run. Note also that the loop is written on one line by using colons as statement separators. Although I do not normally condone this practice as it can lead to very unreadable programs, in this case it actually makes it easier to see the structure and point of this program. To observe the program's built-in time out, change the upper limit on one of the FOR-NEXT loops from 2000 to 10000 and run the program again.

Another way that the periodic timer interrupt can be used is to produce a ticking clock on the display. I will illustrate how this can be done in a later chapter, when multiple output windows are introduced.

Listing 3-13
Program Tracking with TIMER

```
' Set up the timer interrupt service subroutine :
ON TIMER(5) GOSUB Timer.Int
TIMER ON
tag$="PHASE 1"

'  ... lengthy section 1 ...
FOR x=1 TO 2000:y=LOG(x):NEXT
'
tag$="PHASE 2"

'  ... lengthy section 2 ...
FOR x=1 TO 2000:y=LOG(x):NEXT
'
tag$="PHASE 3"

'  ... lengthy section 3 ...
FOR x=1 TO 2000:y=LOG(x):NEXT
'
END
' The timer interrupt service routine, used to monitor
' what part of the program is currently being executed :
Timer.Int.
IF tag$<>previous$ THEN GOTO New.Phase
' Continue counting ticks in current phase :
Ticks=Ticks + 1
IF Ticks = 12 THEN PRINT "Time limit exceeded, aborting program" : END
RETURN
' A new phase has been entered :
New.Phase:
previous$=tag$
Ticks=0   ' Initialize count of number of timer ticks for this phase
PRINT "Program is now in ";tag$
RETURN
```

Intercepting Program Errors

There are, of course, many possible errors that can occur while executing a BASIC program. Normally, when an error is encountered, execution of the program is halted and a dialog box is presented to the user. The dialog box describes the error condition that has occurred, and has an "OK" button to be clicked when its contents have been read. After clicking this button, the listing window is made active and the program statement that caused the error is highlighted. These actions are very useful to us while we are developing a program. However, once a program is completed and put into production use, it is not pleasant to have it interrupted in this way due to an unexpected error. For this reason, Microsoft

BASIC provides us with a technique whereby we can detect and handle error conditions on our own.

In many ways, the error condition is similar to the other interrupt events that were described in the preceding section. The occurrence of an error is an event that can arise at any time during program execution, and that causes the program flow to be diverted to a special handling routine. Setting up to handle the error event is not unlike setting up to handle any other interrupt event, although there are some syntactic differences in the statements used to do so.

To prepare to receive control when an error occurs, you use the ON ERROR statement, which has the following form

ON ERROR GOTO label

Once this statement has been executed, any program errors that arise will cause the program flow to be diverted to the specified label. Although the keyword GOTO is used instead of GOSUB, the point at which the interruption occurred is remembered. In a moment, you will see how you can return to this point in the program, if desired.

Suppose you have set up to handle errors, as shown above, but at some later point in the program you want to resume the normal, system method of handling errors. This can be accomplished by executing the statement

ON ERROR GOTO 0

Once this statement is executed, your own error handling routine is disabled, and any subsequent errors will be handled by the system in its usual fashion.

Assuming you have set up your own error handling routine and an error does occur, what happens next? Program execution will be diverted to the label you specified in the ON ERROR statement. Starting at this label, you should place your routine to handle the error conditions. To help you write this routine, BASIC provides a built-in function, called ERR, that returns the code number of the error condition that occurred. The code number ranges in value from 1 to 74. Table 3-3 lists the error codes and their descriptions. The function ERR requires no arguments, but should only be used within an error handling routine.

Table 3-3
Error Codes

Error Code	Meaning
1	NEXT without FOR
2	Syntax error
3	RETURN without GOSUB
4	Out of DATA
5	Illegal function call
6	Overflow (a calculation resulted in a number too large to express)
7	Insufficient main memory to continue
8	An undefined label was referenced
9	Subscript out of range
10	Attempt to re-DIMension an array that was already

Table 3-3—cont.

	DIMensioned
11	Attempted to divide by zero, or raise zero to a negative power
12	You entered a statement into the Command window that can only be used from within a program (i.e. it must be entered in the Listing window)
13	Type mismatch (attempting to mix string and numeric data)
14	Insufficient main memory to continue (heap exhausted)
15	String exceeds 32767 characters in length
16	String formula too complex (break it down into smaller expressions)
17	Cannot continue after halting due to error, or because the program listing has been changed since it was halted
18	Attempted to invoke a user-defined function that has not been defined
19	No RESUME statement was found in an error handling routine
20	A RESUME statement was encountered, but not within an error handling routine
21	Undefined error code
22	Missing operand
23	The reply to an INPUT statement is too long
26	FOR without NEXT
29	WHILE without WEND
30	WEND without WHILE
35	Attempted to CALL a subprogram that is not defined
36	Attempted to CALL a subprogram that has already been called and has not yet been ENDed or EXITed
37	The number of arguments in a CALL statement does not match the number of arguments in the SUB statement defining the subprogram
38	An array specified in a SHARED statement has not yet been DIMensioned
50	A FIELD statement specifies more bytes in total than the declared record length of the file
51	Internal Disk i/o error
52	Attempted to access a file number that is not OPEN
53	File not found
54	Illegal file mode specified on OPEN statement, or attempted to use random i/o techniques on a file opened for sequential i/o
55	Attempted to OPEN a file that is already OPEN
57	Device i/o error
58	Attempted to rename a file to a name that is already in use on the disk
61	Insufficient free space on disk
62	Attempted to read past the end of a file
63	Attempted to access a random file record number that is too large, or is zero
64	Illegal file name specified
67	Too many OPEN files
68	Device unavailable
70	Attempted to write to a write-protected disk
74	Attempted to reference a disk name that is not currently in a disk drive

Another built-in function provided for error handling is called
ERL. This function returns the line number of the statement in
which the error occurred. It is not very useful, however, since
Microsoft BASIC does not require line numbers, and ERL cannot

return statement labels. I do not recommend adding line numbers to your program just so that you can detect where an error occurred from within an error handling routine. It simply isn't worth it.

Within your error handling routine, you can choose to handle the error in any way you like. You might use the ERR function to determine exactly what kind of error occurred, and then take different actions for different errors. You can, of course, halt the program with an END statement. Alternatively, you can continue execution of the program. If you choose to continue execution, you have three choices. The program can be continued at the exact point where the error occurred (this is called error retry, and your error handler must have arranged for the statement to not cause the same error again). The program can be continued at the statement following the statement that caused the error (useful when it is not possible to fix the problem that caused the error to occur, but perhaps the program can continue anyway). Finally, the program can be continued at a totally different point, in cases when the normal flow of the program cannot be resumed due to the error situation. Each of these actions is achieved through use of the *RESUME* statement, which signals the end of the error handling routine, and a return to normal program flow. The RESUME statement can be written in three different ways

```
RESUME
RESUME NEXT
RESUME label
```

The first form shown above is used to effect a return to the statement that caused the error condition to arise (error retry). The second form, RESUME NEXT, is used to return to the statement following the statement that caused the error. The third form allows a return to any specified label in the main program.

A simple example of an error handling routine is depicted in Figure 3-13. In the run shown, the error condition raised is division by zero. The RESUME NEXT statement in the error handling routine allows the main program to continue, bypassing the bad data.

A more sophisticated error handling routine is shown in Listing 3-14. This program inputs two parameters, x and y, and then evaluates the formula square root of x divided by y. In the evaluation of this formula, there are two error conditions that can arise. One is a negative value for x (cannot take the square root of a negative number), the other is a value of zero for y (cannot divide by zero). The error handling routine checks specifically for error code 5, which would occur if the program attempted to find the square root of a negative number. If this error occurs, the routine negates the value of x, prints a message indicating that the result will be imaginary, and allows the program to resume at its point of interruption. This will cause the statement that prints out the result to be executed again, but this time the value of x will be positive so that the statement will not result in an error.

Figure 3-13
A Simple Error Handling Routine

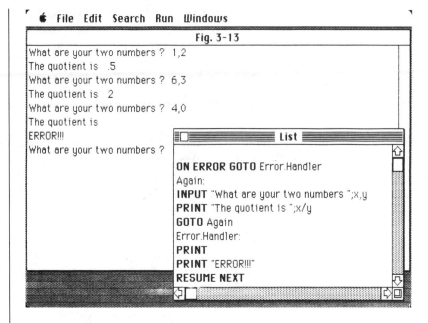

```
 File  Edit  Search  Run  Windows

                    Fig. 3-13
What are your two numbers ?  1,2
The quotient is   .5
What are your two numbers ?  6,3
The quotient is   2
What are your two numbers ?  4,0
The quotient is
ERROR!!!
What are your two numbers ?          List

                              ON ERROR GOTO Error.Handler
                              Again:
                              INPUT "What are your two numbers ";x,y
                              PRINT "The quotient is ";x/y
                              GOTO Again
                              Error.Handler:
                              PRINT
                              PRINT "ERROR!!!"
                              RESUME NEXT
```

Listing 3-14
An Error Handling Routine

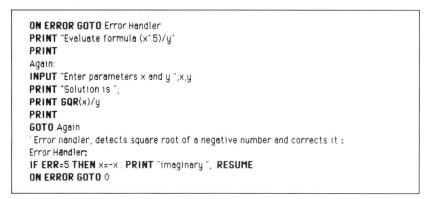

```
ON ERROR GOTO Error.Handler
PRINT "Evaluate formula (x^.5)/y"
PRINT
Again:
INPUT "Enter parameters x and y ";x,y
PRINT "Solution is ";
PRINT SQR(x)/y
PRINT
GOTO Again
' Error handler, detects square root of a negative number and corrects it :
Error.Handler:
IF ERR=5 THEN x=-x : PRINT "imaginary "; :RESUME
ON ERROR GOTO 0
```

Figure 3-14
Run of Listing 3-14

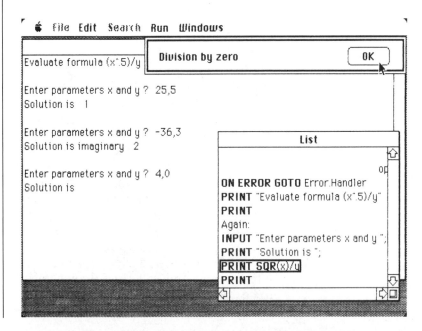

```
 File  Edit  Search  Run  Windows

Evaluate formula (x^.5)/y      Division by zero          OK


Enter parameters x and y ?  25,5
Solution is   1


Enter parameters x and y ?  -36,3
Solution is imaginary   2
                                              List
Enter parameters x and y ?  4,0
Solution is                    ON ERROR GOTO Error.Handler
                               PRINT "Evaluate formula (x^.5)/y"
                               PRINT
                               Again:
                               INPUT "Enter parameters x and y ";
                               PRINT "Solution is ";
                               PRINT SQR(x)/y
                               PRINT
```

Note that, for any other error code, the error handling routine executes the statement

ON ERROR GOTO 0

This results in BASIC's normal error response for any error code other than 5 (Illegal Function Call). A sample run of this program can be seen in Figure 3-14. In this run, I supplied three sets of parameters to be evaluated. The first set produced no error conditions, and the formula was evaluated without incident. On the second set, I supplied a negative value for x; this caused the error handler to be invoked. The error handler indicated that the result would be an imaginary number, corrected x, and allowed the program to continue. On the final set of data, I supplied a value of zero for y. This caused the division by zero error condition. Since this condition is not specifically addressed by the error handler, the usual BASIC error dialog box appeared, and the program was halted.

Chapter 4

BASIC Files

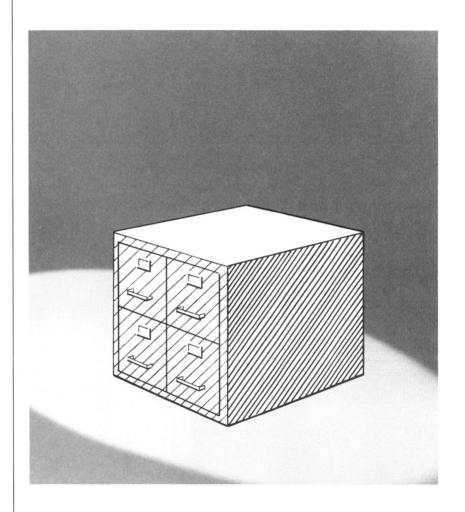

When information is stored in BASIC variables, that information is actually kept in the main memory of the Macintosh. Storing information in main memory allows rapid access and great flexibility of manipulation, attributes that are essential when dealing with most program data. There are some drawbacks to storing information in this manner, however. The primary drawback is a result of the volatility of main memory. When you turn the computer off, the information in memory is lost. Furthermore, if you want to transfer some data in main memory to another computer, there is no easy way to do so.

It is for these reasons that BASIC provides an alternative information storage medium — disk files. In this chapter, I cover techniques for creating and accessing data on disk files. I also explain the general concept of input/output as implemented in Microsoft BASIC. Using these techniques, you will be able to access the Macintosh *clipboard* as if it were a file. As you will see, this can be tremendously useful (if you have used the clipboard with either MacPaint or MacWrite, you already know how valuable a tool it is). This chapter also covers the Macintosh implementation of file types, and how to manipulate them.

Types of File Access

There are two different methods for reading and writing disk file data. These methods are known as *sequential* input/output (i/o) and *random* i/o. Sequential i/o is easy to understand, because it is similar to the i/o techniques used to output to the display and input from the keyboard. Random i/o, although more complex to understand and use, has the advantage of being faster and more flexible. In addition, files containing numeric data that are created using random i/o will take up less disk space than equivalent files created using sequential i/o. Table 4-1 summarizes the differences between these two file i/o techniques.

Table 4-1
Types of File I/O

	Sequential	Random
Complexity	Similar to keyboard/display i/o.	Operation is more complex.
Order of Access	Information must be accessed in the order in which it was written.	Information may be accessed in any order.
Access Time	Moderate access time.	Rapid access.
Media Efficiency	Moderate use of storage media.	Efficient use of storage media.

Files that are created using sequential i/o techniques are called *sequential files*, whereas files created using random i/o techniques are called *random files*. In either case, files are made up of *records*. Each record represents a single entry of information in the file, much like the relationship of a single statement to an entire program (in fact, when storing programs as text files, each program statement is considered a record).

Files are always accessed one record at a time. When a sequential file is created, the records are written to the file one after another, in order. They may subsequently be retrieved from the file, but only in the same order in which they were written. See Figure 4-1.

Figure 4-1
Sequential File Access

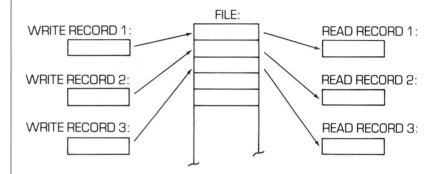

Records stored in random files may be accessed (read or written) in any order, simply by specifying the desired record number. See Figure 4-2. This is the fundamental difference between sequential and random files and i/o techniques.

Figure 4-2
Random File Access

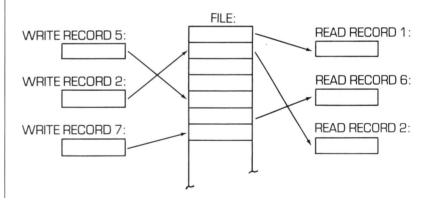

File Access Protocol

Regardless of whether you are using sequential or random files, there is a specific *protccol*, or order of operations, that must be adhered to when accessing files. This protocol is outlined in Figure 4-3.

Before a file can be accessed, it must be *opened*. This is accomplished through use of the *OPEN* statement, described in a moment. Once a file is opened, you can read records from the file into program variables, or write records to the file from program variables. When the file access is completed, the file must always be *closed*. This is accomplished through use of the *CLOSE* statement, also described shortly. Failure to close a file after use can lead to unpredictable results.

Figure 4-3
*Sequential File Access
Protocol*

STEP	BASIC Statement(s) Used
1. Open File.	OPEN

2. Access data in file.
   [Read Record[s],
   Write Record[s]]
	INPUT#
	PRINT#

3. Close File.	CLOSE

When a file is opened, you assign a *file number* to it. Subsequent statements that access the file will refer to it by its file number. This permits keeping track of multiple files within a single program. File numbers are usually assigned starting with 1 and increasing by 1 as necessary. Most programs will not require access to more than a couple of files.

Sequential Files

You are now ready to create a sequential file. The first step, of course, will be to open the file. To do this, you use the OPEN statement. The syntax of the OPEN statement for sequential files is

```
OPEN mode,filenumber,filename
```

In the statement above, the mode is a one-character string equal to either "O," "I," or "A." The mode defines the type of access that will be used in subsequent file accesses. A mode of "O" specifies that the file is being opened for output, that is, the file will be written to. A mode of "I" specifies that the file is being opened for input (the file is going to be read). A mode of "A" stands for append. If a file that already exists is opened for output, its contents will be overwritten by any new data sent to the file. The append mode allows a preexisting file to be opened so that data can be added to its current contents.

The second parameter on the OPEN statement specifies the file number to associate with the file on subsequent references. The third parameter is a character string that specifies the file name. For example, the statement

```
OPEN "O",1,"TESTDATA"
```

will open (or create, as necessary) a file named TESTDATA and assign it a file number of 1. Subsequent statements in the program will be able to write records to the file.

Writing Sequential Files

Writing data to a sequential file is just as easy as writing data to the Output window. Instead of using a PRINT statement, a *PRINT#* statement is used. The PRINT# statement specifies the file number to be accessed. The remainder of the PRINT# statement looks exactly like the PRINT statement. The difference is that the data specified is written to the file instead of to the display screen. The file number to be accessed follows the PRINT# keyword, and is then followed by a comma. For example, the statement

```
PRINT#1,"VALUE OF x=";x
```

would write the characters "VALUE OF x = ", followed by the value in variable *x*, to file number 1. Remember that the file must be opened before this statement can be executed!

When all of the desired data has been written to the file, it must be closed. The CLOSE statement specifies the number of the file to close. For example, the statement

```
CLOSE 1
```

would close file number 1. Listing 4-1 shows a simple program that contains all of these steps. This file will create a disk file named "FRIENDS" that contains a list of names. After executing this program, return to the Macintosh finder, and verify for yourself that the file was indeed created.

Listing 4-1
Creating a Sequential Disk File

```
' This example will create a disk file named "FRIENDS"
' and fill it with a list of names. You can verify that
' the file was indeed created by returning to the
' finder after running this program.
' Step One : Open the file :
OPEN "O",1,"FRIENDS"
' Step Two : Write the data records to the file :
Again:
READ a$
IF a$="END" THEN GOTO Step3          '***
PRINT#1,a$                           '***
GOTO Again
' Step Three : All data written, close the file :
Step3:
CLOSE 1
END
DATA "Peter","David","Fred","Allen"
DATA "Susan","Ted","Alice","END"
```

Reading Sequential Files

Once a sequential file has been created, you can open it using the "I" (input) mode and read its contents into your program's variables. Reading data from a sequential file is similar to reading data from the user at the keyboard. Instead of using the INPUT statement, however, the INPUT# statement is used. When the INPUT# statement is executed, it does not display a "?" and wait for the user to type in data. Instead, it reads the next data item from the file specified. For example, the statement

```
INPUT#1,x,y
```

will read the next two data values in file number 1 into variables *x* and *y*. Remember that the file must be opened before it can be read! The sample program shown in Listing 4-2 will open and read the data in file FRIENDS, displaying the information on the Output window. Assuming you have run the previous program (Listing 4-1), which created the file, you can now run this program and see the information retrieved. Figure 4-4 shows what happens when the program of Listing 4-2 is run.

```
' This example will read the disk file named "FRIENDS"
' that was created by program listing 4-1, and display
' the data contained therein in the output window.
' Step One : Open the file :
OPEN "I",1,"FRIENDS"
' Step Two : Read the data records from the file :
PRINT "Contents of file FRIENDS : "
PRINT
Again:
INPUT#1,a$
PRINT a$
GOTO Again
```

Figure 4-4
*Reading a Sequential
File*

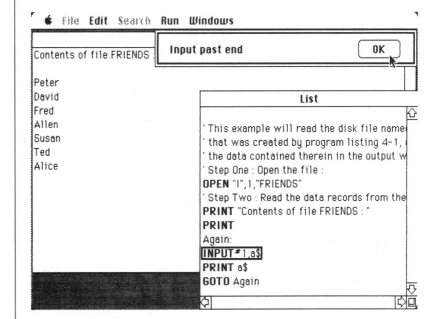

Detecting End of File

Note that, although the program works (the data is successfully
retrieved), it ends with an "Input past End" error. This occurs
because the program, running in an infinite loop, eventually reads
all of the records that had been placed in the file by the previous
program. When it tries to read past the *end of file* (that is, read
more data than is there), the error is given.

One way to avoid this problem would be to write a special marker
at the end of the file so that the retrieval program would know when
all of the data has been read. This can be easily accomplished by
exchanging the order of the two statements marked "***" in Listing
4-1. This would cause that program to write the data item "END" to
the file before closing the file.

The program of Listing 4-2 could then be modified to check for
this special marker record, and terminate in a more orderly fashion.
The modification would simply require the addition of a statement
as follows

```
IF a$="END" THEN CLOSE 1 : END
```

Can you determine where this statement should be inserted in Listing 4-2? While this is an often used and quite effective technique, you should realize that an alternative approach should be available. "After all," you ask, "if BASIC could know that the end of the file has been reached (which it must, since it was able to give us the error message), then I should be able to find this out as well, without having to resort to adding a special 'marker' record."

Indeed, BASIC does provide a method to determine when you have read all of the data in a file. It is the **EOF** function. The **EOF** function has a single argument that represents the number of the file in question. It returns a logical value of false (numeric 0) if there is more data in the file, and a logical value of true (numeric -1) if the file's contents have been completely read. In Listing 4-3, I have modified the read file example program to make use of the **EOF** function.

Listing 4-3
Reading a Sequential Disk File with EOF Detection

```
' This example will read the disk file named "FRIENDS"
' that was created by program listing 4-1, and display
  the data contained therein in the output window.
' Through use of the EOF function, the end of the file
' will be detected and no error will occur.
' Step One : Open the file :
OPEN "I",1,"FRIENDS"
' Step Two : Read the data records from the file :
PRINT "Contents of file FRIENDS : "
PRINT
WHILE NOT EOF(1)
INPUT #1,a$
PRINT a$
WEND
' Step Three: Close the file when done :
CLOSE 1
END
```

The INPUT$, LOC, and LOF Functions

An alternate technique for reading data from sequential files is possible through use of the **INPUT$** function. This technique assumes that you are only interested in accessing the file as a stream of characters, one character at a time. After opening the file for input, the function is used on the right side of an assignment statement, in the following fashion

```
x$ = INPUT$(length,#filenumber)
```

This function will read the number of characters specified (length) from the file specified and return it as a string variable (x$ above). For example, the statement

```
filedata$ = INPUT$(10,#3)
```

will read the next ten characters from the file opened as number 3 and place them in variable *filedata$*. Example programs using **INPUT$** appear later in this chapter.

To aid in using the **INPUT$** function, BASIC provides two additional functions, **LOC** and **LOF**. Both take a single argument that indicates the file number being referenced. The **LOF** function returns the total length of the file in bytes. The file must previously have been opened before this function can be used. For example

```
OPEN "I",1,"INQUIRE"
x=LOF(1)
```

The statements above might be used to determine the size of the file named INQUIRE (result returned in variable *x*).

The **LOC** function returns the current position in the file and is useful when you want to find out how far into a file you may have already read. It returns a number that represents the number of bytes read from the file so far, divided by the file's buffer size. This size defaults to 128, but can be specified on the OPEN statement as follows

```
OPEN mode,filenumber,filename,
buffersize
```

The buffer size is the number of bytes set aside by BASIC for actual i/o to the disk. A larger buffer size will promote faster disk i/o operations, but will leave less memory available to your program (the buffer size cannot exceed 32767 bytes). Unfortunately, if the buffer size is not the same as the length of your data records, the **LOC** function by itself is not too useful. Since sequential file records are often of variable length, the **LOC** function is really best employed when using random files (discussed later in this chapter).

For sequential files, you can multiply the value of the **LOC** function by the file buffer size (128 if not explicitly specified), and then compare that value to the value returned by **LOF**. This will give you a rough idea of what percentage of the file has been read so far. In Listing 4-4, I have modified the simple file reading program of Listing 4-3 to employ this technique. The program now displays the percentage of the file left to be read after each record is read and displayed. A sample run is shown in Figure 4-5.

Note that, because the demonstration file FRIENDS is so small, a buffer size of 1 is used in Listing 4-4. This buffer size is too small to provide adequate throughput with any reasonably sized file. I used it here for demonstration purposes only. For any file larger than 1K bytes, the default buffer size of 128 can be used. In this case, the percentage remaining formula must be altered appropriately, as follows

```
100-CINT(100*(LOC(1)*128/filesize))
```

File Structure

The organization of information within a file is critical to the use of that file. As the designer of programs that will create and use files, it is your responsibility to define the organization or structure of those files. In the preceding example, the file structure was quite simple — a list of character strings representing people's names. When I changed the file organization by embedding my own end of file marker in the file, that represented a change in file structure, and required a corresponding set of changes in the processing programs. Most programs will require even more complex file structures. Both character and numeric data are often mixed in files.

Listing 4-4
Using LOC and LOF

```
' This example will read the disk file named "FRIENDS"
' that was created by program listing 4-1, and display
' the data contained therein in the output window.
' The LOC function is used to keep track of how far in the file we have
' read so far.  This value is related to the LOF function value to provide
' a percentage.
' Step One : Open the file :
' NOTE: a buffer size of 1 is used here because the total file size is too
' small to be able to get an accurate percentage calculation with the
' default buffer size of 128.
OPEN "I",1,"FRIENDS",1
filesize=LOF(1)
' Step Two : Read the data records from the file :
PRINT "Contents of file FRIENDS : "
PRINT
WHILE NOT EOF(1)
INPUT#1,a$
PRINT a$;
PRINT TAB(20);"Percentage of file remaining = ";100-CINT(100*(LOC(1)/filesize))
WEND
' Step Three: Close the file when done :
CLOSE 1
END
```

Figure 4-5
Monitoring File Size Remaining

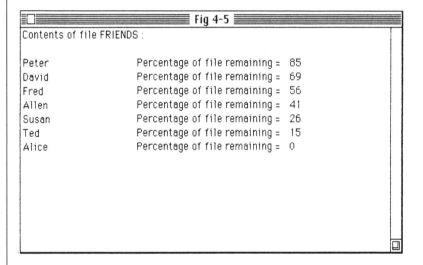

```
Fig 4-5
Contents of file FRIENDS :

Peter           Percentage of file remaining =  85
David           Percentage of file remaining =  69
Fred            Percentage of file remaining =  56
Allen           Percentage of file remaining =  41
Susan           Percentage of file remaining =  26
Ted             Percentage of file remaining =  15
Alice           Percentage of file remaining =  0
```

When this is done, care must be taken to insure that character data is read into character string variables, and numeric data into numeric variables. For example, a file created using a statement such as

```
PRINT#1, a$,x
```

will contain records that consist of a character string followed by a numeric value. This file should be read using a similar statement

```
INPUT#1, a$,x
```

To avoid possible problems, once the layout of a file has been determined, it is best to use the same types of statements to read and write the file.

Even when a great deal of care is taken, problems can arise. For example, consider the following statement

```
PRINT#1, "Hello There"
```

If you attempt to retrieve the information written above by using the following statement

```
INPUT#1, a$
```

you may be surprised to discover that *a$* will be returned as "Hello." The statement

```
INPUT#1, a$,b$
```

would return *a$* as "Hello" and *b$* as "There." This is because BASIC considers the blank character as a terminator when reading data items from a file. Other terminator characters that BASIC is sensitive to include the comma, the semicolon, and the "carriage return" character (CHR$(13)). The latter is written to the file after each PRINT# statement and thus delimits the individual records of the file. By surrounding a string of characters with the double-quote character (CHR$(34)), you allow BASIC to read the string into a single variable, even though the string may contain embedded terminator characters. Thus the statement

```
PRINT#1, CHR$(34)+"Hello There"
+CHR$(34)
```

would create a file record that could subsequently be retrieved into a single character string variable.

Because the above statement is so unwieldy, an alternative technique is provided. It is the *WRITE#* statement. The WRITE# statement works exactly like the PRINT# statement, except it automatically encloses string data items in a set of doublequotes. In addition, if multiple variables are specified on a single WRITE# statement, they are written with a single comma separator between them. This format insures that the data written can be easily retrieved. For example, the statements

```
x=5
a$="Hi Again!"
WRITE#1,a$,x
```

would produce a single file record that looked like this

```
"Hi Again!",5
```

In contrast, the statement

```
PRINT#1,a$,x
```

would produce a single file record that looked like this

```
Hi Again!       5
```

Device Independent I/O

You should now be quite aware of the similarity between the way BASIC accesses sequential files and the way it accesses the standard computer input/output devices of screen and keyboard. Other than where the data actually goes, there is, in fact, no functional difference between sequential file output and output to the Macintosh display screen. There is also no functional difference between sequential file input and input from the Macintosh keyboard. To turn this striking similarity to our advantage, Microsoft BASIC implements a concept called *device independent i/o*.

Device independent i/o means that you can use a common set of statements to perform i/o operations without knowing in advance what i/o device those operations will be directed to. This is accomplished by using the sequential file i/o statements PRINT#, INPUT#, and WRITE# to program the desired i/o operations. Then, through use of the appropriate filename in the OPEN statement, you can assign a variety of devices to the file number referenced in those statements.

An ordinary filename will, of course, represent a disk file, but Microsoft also provides a set of special predefined filenames that represent the standard i/o devices of display, keyboard, printer, etc. These special names are shown in Table 4-2.

The first few names in Table 4-2 represent those common computer devices that you are, no doubt, by now familiar with. These are followed by some special devices of greater interest. The Macintosh clipboard, for example, is accessible to your programs through this mechanism. The Macintosh's built-in asynchronous communications port is also accessible in this manner. Don't get too excited, now. I will cover the more mundane devices first!

The Screen Device

Opening a file to device name *SCRN:* for output provides a channel to the current Output window. Data sent to that file number will appear on the display screen just as if an ordinary PRINT statement was used. "So what's the advantage?," you ask. Well, suppose you really want to send some data to a disk file. While developing and testing your program, you could use the name SCRN: instead of the real disk file name desired. In this fashion, you will be able to see the data that the program would be sending to the disk. When the program is working and the data looks correct, you simply change the filename from SCRN: to a real disk file name. This scenario illustrates the advantages and flexibility that device independent i/o can offer.

The Keyboard Device

Opening a file to device name *KYBD:* for input provides a channel to the Macintosh keyboard. A **LOC** function for that file number will return 1 if there is a keystroke waiting to be read, 0 otherwise. The **LOF** function on the keyboard device will always return 0.

Table 4-2
*Predefined Filenames
for Device Independent
I/O*

Filename	Device	Comments
SCRN:	Display screen	Should only be opened for output. Any data sent to this device will be directed to the current output window.
KYBD:	Keyboard	Should only be opened for input.
LPT1:	Imagewriter printer	Should only be opened for output. Standard print quality. Graphics are supported.
LPT1:PROMPT	Imagewriter printer	Should only be opened for output. User can select print quality via dialog box. Graphics are supported.
LPT1:DIRECT	Any printer	Should only be opened for output. Data is output as ASCII text. Graphics not supported, but many printers other than the Imagewriter can be used.
CLIP:	Macintosh clipboard	Can be opened for input or output. Used to transfer text data in tabular format between BASIC and other applications.
CLIP:TEXT	Macintosh clipboard	Can be opened for input or output. Used to transfer text in any format between BASIC and other applications.
CLIP:PICTURE	Macintosh clipboard	Can be opened for input or output. Used to transfer graphics images between BASIC and other applications. See Chapter 7 for more information.
COM1:parms	Asynchronous serial communications port	Should be opened for both input and output at the same time via a different format of the OPEN statement (see text). The 'parms' specify the serial communications parameters to be used. Their format is:

COM1: baud-rate, parity, word-length, stop-bits.
See Table 4-3 for more information about 'parms.'

The Printer Device

Opening a file to device name *LPT1:* for output provides a channel to the Macintosh Imagewriter printer. As you now know, it is generally true that performing a PRINT#x where file *x* is opened to SCRN: is the same as performing a PRINT; and performing an

INPUT#x (where file *x* is opened to KYBD:) is the same as performing an INPUT. So you would naturally assume that performing a PRINT#x where file x is opened to LPT1: is the same as performing a LPRINT. While this is true, there are some advantages to using the device independent i/o approach.

When the printer is accessed through device LPT1:, you have additional control over the way the data will be sent to the printer. This control is exercised by appending a modifier word to the device name. The device name with modifier appears as either filename LPT1:DIRECT or LPT1:PROMPT. The DIRECT modifier instructs BASIC to send the printer data as a stream of ASCII bytes. This results in the fastest print speed, and also allows you to interface with printers other than the Imagewriter. Unfortunately, this mode does not support Macintosh graphics. The PROMPT modifier causes two dialog boxes to appear when the data is about to be sent to the printer. These dialog boxes allow the user to adjust the quality of the printout, as well as such parameters as paper size and style. They are illustrated in Fig. 4-6. Note that specifying LPT1: without a modifier is the same as LPT1:PROMPT with *Standard Quality* printout selected. Either of these modes will support Macintosh graphics and should be used with the Imagewriter.

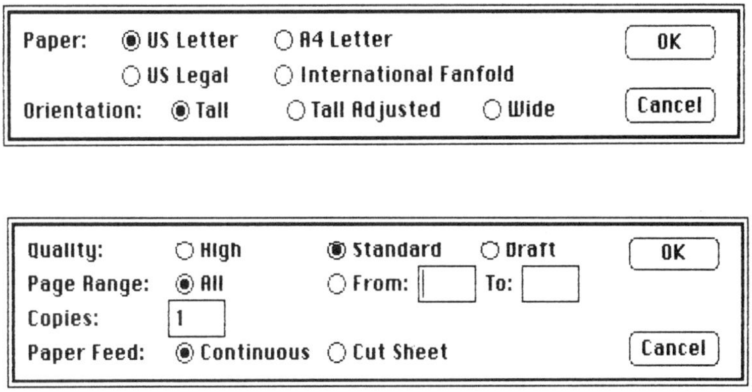

Figure 4-6
*LPT1:PROMPT Dialog
Boxes*

Accessing the Clipboard

By opening a file to device name CLIP:, you can obtain access to the Macintosh clipboard. This gives you the powerful ability to exchange information between your own BASIC program and most other Macintosh applications. This is possible because most Macintosh applications support the clipboard. Depending upon the application, the type and format of data used in the clipboard may vary. For example, MacPaint will read and write graphics images to the clipboard, while MacWrite will read and write text. The type and format of data will be an important consideration when writing programs to access the clipboard.

To define the type of data being accessed, there are two modifiers that can be appended to the CLIP: device name. These modifiers are *TEXT* and *PICTURE*. Opening a file to device CLIP:TEXT will allow access to unformatted text information in the clipboard. Opening a file to device CLIP:PICTURE will allow access to graphics data in the clipboard. More information on the graphics format will be presented in Chapter 7. Finally, opening a file to device CLIP: (no modifier) will allow access to text information in a tabular format. The tabular format is useful when preparing reports using a wordprocessor such as MacWrite, and can also be used to interface with spreadsheet programs such as MultiPlan.

Tabular Clipboard Data

As an example of how the clipboard access feature can be used, suppose you are the manager of an ice cream parlor. You are preparing a report for the owner that will highlight sales for a six month period. Using MacWrite, you prepare the report and enter the sales figures. See Figure 4-7A.

Figure 4-7A
*The Sales Report
Document in MacWrite*

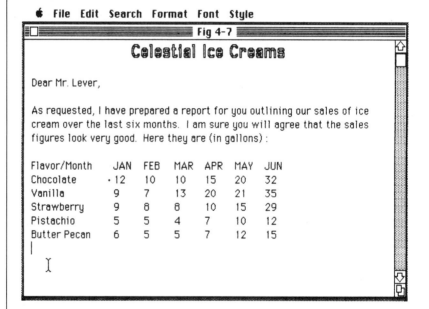

What you would now like to do is show the totals for each month, and for the entire six month period. To accomplish this, you select the sales data from the document and use Copy from the Edit menu to copy it to the clipboard. Then, you run a BASIC program that opens the clipboard for input, read the data into an array, perform the necessary calculations, and write the results back out to the clipboard.

Going back to MacWrite and the original document, you then use Paste from the Edit menu to copy the new data on the clipboard into the document. (Of course, for this simple example it would be much easier to perform the calculations by hand and enter them directly into the MacWrite document. The technique is a useful one however, because a real application might have a great deal more data, as well as more complex calculations to perform.)

To perform this operation, use the tabular data format in the clipboard. This format assumes that each line of text in the clipboard contains several data items, and that these items are separated by tab characters (CHR$(9)). Figure 4-7B shows how I set up the MacWrite tabs prior to entering the sales data in the document. In Figure 4-7C, I have selected the information that I want to send to my BASIC program and am about to copy it to the clipboard.

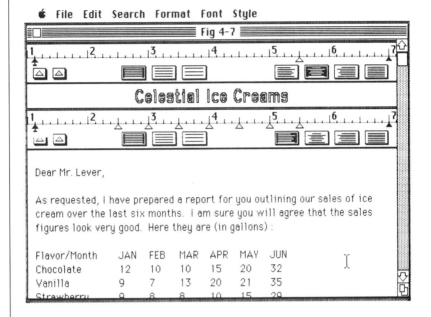

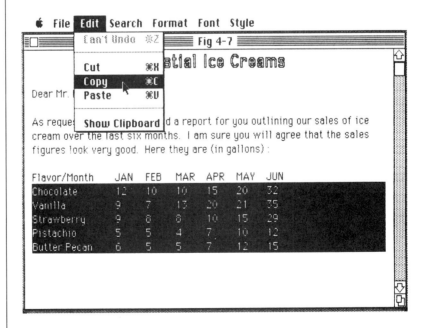

Listing 4-5 shows a BASIC program that reads the data from the clipboard, calculates the totals for each month, as well as a grand total, and writes these results back to the clipboard. This program should be run next. The BASIC application is then exited, MacWrite is entered once again, and the document is opened.

```
' This program will read the ice cream sales data from
' the clipboard, calculate sales totals, and write those
' results back to the clipboard for inclusion in the original
' document. See text for more information.
DIM sales(5,6)
' Step One: Read sales data from clipboard :
OPEN "I",1,"CLIP:"
FOR flavor=1 TO 5
INPUT #1,flavor$
PRINT "Reading data for flavor = ";flavor$
FOR month=1 TO 6
INPUT #1,sales(flavor,month)
NEXT
NEXT
CLOSE 1
PRINT "All data read"
' Step Two: Calculate new data from sales data :
DIM totals(7)
totals(7)=0 'initialize grand total
FOR month=1 TO 6
totals(month)=0 'initialize month sub-total
FOR flavor=1 TO 5
totals(month)=totals(month)+sales(flavor,month)
NEXT
totals(7)=totals(7)+totals(month) 'accumulate grand total
NEXT
' Step Three: Write totals data to clipboard :
OPEN "O",1,"CLIP:"
WRITE #1,"Total",totals(1),totals(2),totals(3),totals(4),totals(5),totals(6)
WRITE #1,"Grand Total",totals(7)
CLOSE 1
END
```

Figure 4-7D shows the document just before I pasted in the new contents of the clipboard. The insertion point is at the end of the document, just below the words "Butter Pecan." Figure 4-7E shows the document after the data has been pasted into place. Notice that the character strings "Total" and "Grand Total" written by the BASIC program have been enclosed in doublequotes. This was due to use of the WRITE# statement. These doublequotes can be removed manually. Figure 4-8 shows the contents of the clipboard before and after the program of Listing 4-5 is executed.

When using the clipboard in this fashion, you must be very careful not to destroy the clipboard contents between steps. This is all too easy for an inexperienced Macintosh user to do. You should always keep in mind that any Cut or Copy operation in the Edit menu of any application (including the Finder itself) will overwrite the existing contents of the clipboard. In other words, when using the clipboard to transfer data between two different applications, be sure that you do not perform any Cut or Copy operations between the time that you exit from the first application and the time that you enter the second application.

Figure 4-7D
*Copy Totals Data from
Clipboard into
MacWrite Document*

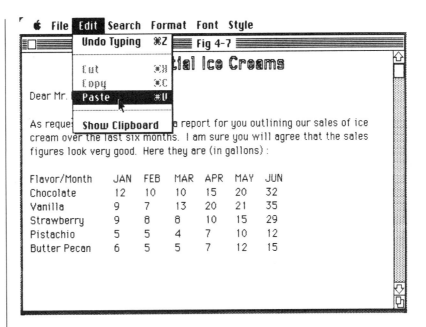

Figure 4-7E
*The Document with
Totals Data from BASIC*

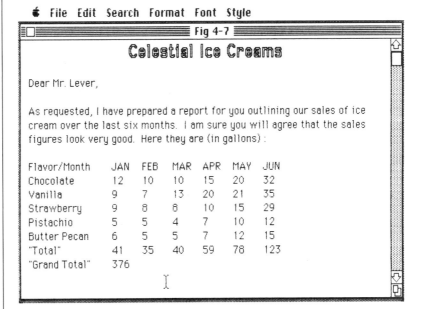

Text Clipboard Data

The preceding example illustrated the tabular format of clipboard data. This format causes tab characters to be used as separators when a WRITE# statement is used to write multiple data items to the clipboard. I used this to great advantage in the example by presetting the MacWrite tab positions to produce an attractive and orderly document. As an alternative to this format, the clipboard text format can be used.

The *CLIP:TEXT* device name provides access to the clipboard in this format. In this format, the data on the clipboard is assumed to be a simple stream of characters. Multiple lines are delimited in the usual fashion by a single carriage return character (CHR$(13)) at the end of each line. From within BASIC, data can be read from the clipboard in this format using either the INPUT# or INPUT$ statements. Data can be written to the clipboard using either PRINT# or WRITE# statements.

Figure 4-8
The Clipboard before and after running Listing 4-5

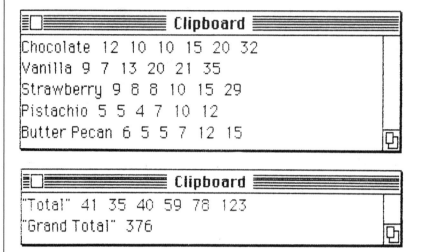

The data itself can be cut from or pasted into any application that supports plain text data (e.g., MacWrite, MacPaint). As an example, the program of Listing 4-6 is presented.

This program uses the sine and random functions to produce a series of text lines that portray an interesting mathematical shape. By running this program, this set of text lines is sent to the clipboard. You can then exit from BASIC and start the MacPaint application. Select the Monaco font type, in a size of 9 point. Then select Paste from the Edit menu. The image will be brought in from the clipboard to your MacPaint document. Figure 4-9 shows what it will look like.

Note that the entire image produced by the BASIC program does not fit into the MacPaint document. As an exercise, you could modify the BASIC program so that it writes the text image in sections. You could then paste each section into the MacPaint document separately. In this fashion, the entire image, representing two double sine wave cycles, could be accumulated into a single MacPaint document.

Accessing the Communications Port

Opening a file to device name COM1: allows access to the Macintosh asynchronous serial communications port. This port can, in turn, be connected to another computer to allow data exchange between the two machines. Alternatively, the port can be connected to a modem so that a much larger, remotely located computer system can be contacted. Such a system, called a *host* computer, can provide many useful and interesting services to users of personal computers. Some of the more popular dial-up systems

Listing 4-6
Creating Text Data for the Clipboard

```
' This program generates an interesting pattern using
' all text characters and writes this pattern to the clipboard.
' From the clipboard, the data can be pasted into a MacPaint document.
' See text for more information.
DEF FNrand(l,u)=CINT(1+RND(1)*(u-l))
RANDOMIZE TIMER
pi=3.14159
OPEN "O",1,"CLIP:TEXT"
FOR angle=0 TO 4*pi+.3 STEP .3
x=6+CINT(6*SIN(angle)) 'numerical value ranging sinusoidally from 0 to 12
IF x=0 THEN x=1
image$=""
FOR i=1 TO 25-x
image$=image$+MID$(".,: ",FNrand(1,5),1)
NEXT
image$=image$+STRING$(2*x,"*")
FOR i=1 TO 25-x
image$=image$+MID$(".,: ",FNrand(1,6),1)
NEXT
PRINT#1, image$
NEXT
CLOSE 1
END
```

Figure 4-9
Text from BASIC Pasted into a MacPaint Document

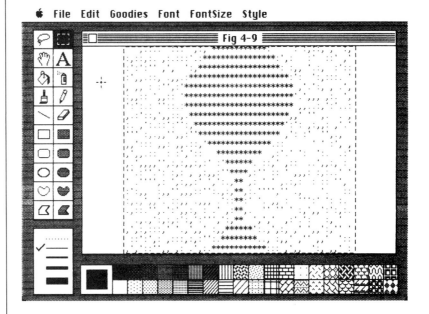

of this type are American People/Link, CompuServe, Dow Jones, and The Source.

Serial Communications Parameters

Whenever asynchronous serial communications are used, the two communicating devices must agree on a set of communications parameters. In all, there are four different parameters that must be specified. They are *baud rate*, *parity*, *word length*, and *stop bits*.

Table 4-3
*Serial Communications
Parameters*

Parameter	Meaning	Possible Values
Baud-rate	Speed at which data is transferred.	110, 150, 300, 600, 1200, 1800, 2400, 3600, 4800, 7200, 9600, 19200, 57600.
Parity	Type of error detection to use, or none.	E (even), O (odd), N (none)
Word Length	Size (in bits) of each unit of data that is transferred.	5, 6, 7, 8.
Stop Bits	Minimum wait time between transfer of successive units of data.	1, 2.

Table 4-3 outlines these parameters and indicates what values may be selected for each.

Perhaps the most important parameter is the baud rate, which determines the speed at which data will be transferred between the two communicating devices. The higher the baud rate the faster the transmission of data. The rate of data transmission in characters per second is equal to roughly one tenth the baud rate.

When communicating with a remote device over the telephone lines, the baud rate that you can use depends upon the *modem* you have available. The modem interfaces the electrical output of the Macintosh serial port with the telephone line itself. Most modems can operate at either 300 or 1200 baud.

For a direct wire connection between your Macintosh and another device, you can use up to 9600 baud without difficulty. Such a direct wire connection should be no longer than 50 feet. Figure 4-10 shows how to wire a connector to the serial port for either modem or direct connection.

When the COM1: device is opened, a set of modifiers must be appended to the device name to specify the four communications parameters. The format of the device name is as follows

```
COM1:baud-rate,parity,word-length,
stop-bits
```

Remember, you must select these parameters to match those of the device or system that you intend to communicate with. If the device is another computer that is connected locally, you can probably pick a set of parameters yourself, and program them into both machines. On the other hand, if you are dialing up a remote service, you must conform to the set of parameters defined by that service. Most 300 baud dial up services can communicate using one stop bit and either an eight bit word and no parity, or a seven bit word and even parity.

Opening the Serial Port

Because the COM1: device allows both input and output operations, a different syntax for the OPEN statement is required.

Figure 4-10
Connecting to the Serial Communications Port

Macintosh
Serial Port
5 4 3 2 1
9 8 7 6

Conventional "DB-25"
Serial Connector
13   3 2 1
25   14

Pin numbering is shown from the wiring side of these connectors.   Not all pins are used.

Wiring Macintosh to modem :

Macintosh	Modem (DB-25)
1 – Ground	1 – Ground
3 – Ground	2 – Receive
5 – Transmit	3 – Transmit
7 – Handshake	4 – Request to Send
9 – Receive	5 – Clear to Send
(Note: arrows show	6 – Data Set Ready
direction of data	7 – Ground
flow)	20 – Data Terminal Ready

Wiring Macintosh directly to another Macintosh :

Macintosh 1	Macintosh 2
1 – Ground	1 – Ground
2 – +5 volts	2 – +5 volts
3 – Ground	3 – Ground
5 – Transmit	5 – Transmit
7 – Handshake	7 – Handshake
9 – Receive	9 – Receive

Wiring Macintosh directly to other computer or terminal :

Macintosh	Computer/Terminal (DB-25)
1 – Ground	1 – Ground
2 – +5 volts	2 – Receive
3 – Ground	3 – Transmit
5 – Transmit	4 – Request to Send
7 – Handshake	5 – Clear to Send
9 – Receive	6 – Data Set Ready
	7 – Ground
	20 – Data Terminal Ready

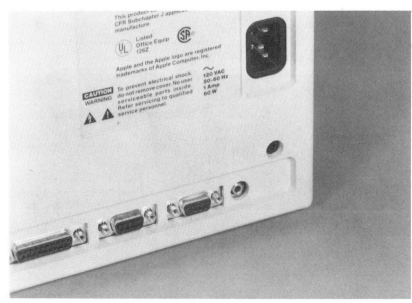

This syntax is as follows

```
OPEN device-name AS file-number
LEN=buffer-size
```

Notice that no "mode" is specified in this statement. Thus, the device can be read from and written to. The file number functions in the same way as always, and the buffer size defines how much space BASIC will set aside to buffer (hold) incoming serial data. This is very important, especially at higher baud rates, because the data may be coming in to the Macintosh faster than our program can read it. In this case, a large buffer area is necessary to hold this incoming data until the program can deal with it.

A Simple Terminal Program

To illustrate how the COM1: device can be used, the program of Listing 4-7 is presented. This program allows the Macintosh to act as a simple data communications terminal. In this capacity, the Macintosh displays in the Output window every character it receives from the serial port. Any characters typed on the keyboard are in turn sent out over the serial port.

Listing 4-7
Simple Terminal Communications Program

```
' This program can be used to communicate with most 300 baud
' dial up services. Line feed characters received from the host
' computer are automatically suppressed. The program provides
' an "underline" cursor on the terminal screen at all times.
' The screen will support up to eighty columns of text on a line.
CALL TEXTFONT(4)
CALL TEXTSIZE(9)
PRINT "SIMPLE TERMINAL PROGRAM"
PRINT
PRINT "1. 300 Baud, 8 Bits, No Parity, 1 Stop Bit"
PRINT "2. 300 Baud, 7 Bits, Even Parity, 1 Stop Bit"
PRINT
Retry:
LINE INPUT "Select parameter choice (1 or 2) ==> ";r$
IF r$="1" THEN p$="300,N,8,1" ELSE IF r$="2" THEN p$="300,E,7,1" ELSE GOTO Retry
PRINT
PRINT "Terminal Ready :"
PRINT
OPEN "COM1:"+p$ AS 1 LEN=5000
PRINT CHR$(95);
Again:
WHILE LOC(1)>0
a$=INPUT$(1,#1)
a$=CHR$(ASC(a$) AND 127)
IF a$<>CHR$(10) THEN PRINT CHR$(8);a$;CHR$(95);
WEND
a$=INKEY$
IF a$="" THEN GOTO Again
PRINT #1,a$;
GOTO Again
```

Note that characters typed on the keyboard will not appear on the display unless the device attached to the serial port explicitly echoes them. Most host computers perform this echoing operation most of the time, so you can see what you are typing and sending to them.

If you do not have a dial up service and/or modem available, you can test this program in another way. Simply use a piece of wire or electrical test clip to short together pins 5 and 9 of the serial port connector. This connects the serial port output to the serial port input. Such a connection is called a loopback test, because it loops the output signal right back into the input. If you do this and then run the program in Listing 4-7, you should be able to see any characters you type appear on the display. This verifies that the program, and the Macintosh serial port, are working properly.

How the Terminal Program Works

The first two statements in the program are CALL statements to special built-in subprograms. These subprograms will be explained in greater detail in Chapter 7. I am using them here to force all text sent to the Output window to appear in the Monaco font and with a text size of 9 points.

This is necessary for two reasons. First, it allows up to eighty columns of text to fit across the Macintosh screen. Second, the Monaco font is not a proportional font, meaning that all characters in this font take up the same amount of space. This allows a backspace character to be sent to the output window to erase any previously displayed text on the current line. I will make use of this characteristic in putting up the terminal screen cursor.

The program begins by presenting a menu allowing the user to select from the two most often used parameter sets. After this selection, the COM1: device is opened with the desired parameters. Note that I use a buffer size of 5000 characters, which is more than adequate for a program of this type running at 300 baud. This insures that no incoming data will be lost. The terminal screen cursor character will be the underscore symbol, displayable as CHR$(95).

A WHILE-WEND loop is executed as long as there are characters waiting in the serial port input buffer. The number of characters currently in the buffer is always available via the **LOC** function call.

The characters are read using the **INPUT$** function. The next statement insures that all data received will be interpreted as seven bit ASCII codes. This statement effectively masks off the eighth bit of each received data byte. This avoids any difficulty that might arise if the host computer is sending data as seven bits with parity, and the Macintosh receives it as eight bits with no parity. In such a case, the parity bit will often make the received data look like non-ASCII characters.

The next statement actually displays the received data. The IF-THEN statement filters out any line feed characters (CHR$(10)) that are received. Since many terminal devices require both a carriage return and a line feed to move the cursor to the next line, most hosts send both of these characters.

In the case of the Macintosh, however, simply displaying the carriage return character will cause the cursor position to drop down to the beginning of the next line. It is therefore necessary to filter the line feed characters to avoid double spacing on the terminal screen.

Note that before each received character is displayed, the backspace character (CHR$(8)) is displayed. This causes the terminal cursor character to be erased, and the received data to be displayed in its place. This data is then followed by a new CHR$(95), which displays the cursor in its new position.

When there is no data waiting in the input buffer, the program checks the keyboard through use of the **INKEY$** function. Any characters typed on the keyboard are sent out the serial port via a PRINT# statement. This completes all the functional requirements of a simple terminal program.

The Check Writing Program—Version 1

My next sample program, Listing 4-8, makes use of all of the concepts discussed so far. It is a check writing program—one that you can use to prepare and keep track of your own personal checks. If you find that each month you write out a series of checks, always to the same payees (e.g. electric bill, phone bill, credit card bills, etc.), then you will appreciate the value of this program. You will need to have custom check forms preprinted, with your name, your bank's name, and your checking account number.

Listing 4-8
The Check Writing
Program — Version 1

```
' This program will help you to maintain your personal check-book.
' The program allows you to add entries that represent deposits.
' You can also add entries that represent payments (checks).
' In this case, the subroutine Check.Print will be used to actually
' fill out the fields in a check on the Imagewriter printer.
' Continuous forms checks can be ordered from many sources with
' your name, your bank name and your account number pre-printed.
' You will probably have to modify the print field locations in
' subroutine Check.Print to match the specific format of the checks
' that you order.
' The check register is maintained on disk in a file named CHECKS.
' The program maintains a constantly updated balance and can produce
' a printed copy of the register at any time.
' The program allows you to set up a list of predefined accounts to which
' you often write checks. This saves time when actually using the program
' to write checks to the same payees each month. Define your payees in
' the data statements indicated below:
' You may have up to 10 predefined payee accounts:
DIM Account$(10),Accountno$(10)
Predefined=0
GetPredefined:
READ a$ 'get a predefined account name
IF a$="END" THEN GOTO EndPredefData
Predefined=Predefined+1
Account$(Predefined)=a$
READ Accountno$(Predefined)
GOTO GetPredefined
EndPredefData:
' Predefined data has been setup, variable Predefined = # of Predefined accounts
' Place your predefined account names here, two strings per account:
' The first string will be the payee name for the check, the second will be
' placed on the comment line of the check and usually set to your account
' number with that payee. Sample data follows:
DATA "ABC Telephone Company","555-1212"
DATA "HTD Power and Light","123-456789-01"
DATA "XYZ Heating Oil Co.","001-58726724"
DATA "SUPERCARD Credit Company","5123-456-7890"
DATA "Book of the Hour Club","0012233445566"
' --------end of predefined accounts data.
DATA "END"
```

Listing 4-8—cont.

```
DIM Numbers$(19), Numbers10$(9)
FOR i=1 TO 19
READ Numbers$(i)
NEXT
FOR i=2 TO 9
READ Numbers10$(i)
NEXT
DATA ONE,TWO,THREE,FOUR,FIVE,SIX,SEVEN,EIGHT,NINE,TEN,ELEVEN
DATA TWELVE,THIRTEEN,FOURTEEN,FIFTEEN,SIXTEEN,SEVENTEEN
DATA EIGHTEEN,NINETEEN,TWENTY,THIRTY,FOURTY,FIFTY,SIXTY
DATA SEVENTY,EIGHTY,NINETY
BalanceKnown=0 'set flag to show current balance not known yet
FileOpen=0 'set flag to show CHECKS file not open
Today$=DATE$   'Get date and reformat it to mm/dd/yy format.
Today$=LEFT$(Today$,6)+RIGHT$(Today$,2)  'remove '19' from year
MID$(Today$,3,1)="/"
MID$(Today$,6,1)="/"
' Main Menu :
Main:
CLS
LOCATE 1,10
PRINT "CHECK WRITING PROGRAM"
LOCATE 3,1
PRINT "1. Display Register and Current Balance"
PRINT "2. Print Register"
PRINT "3. Write Checks"
PRINT "4. Add Deposits"
PRINT "5. Initialize New Register"
PRINT "6. End Program"
LOCATE 10,10
PRINT "Select Choice : "
TryAgain:
GOSUB WaitKey
a%=VAL(a$)
IF a%<1 OR a%>6 THEN GOTO TryAgain
ON a% GOTO Rdisp,Rprint,Cwrite,Deposit,Rinit,Finish
'
' Display Register Function:
Rdisp:
CLS
LOCATE 1,10
PRINT "DISPLAY REGISTER"
OPEN "O",2,"SCRN:"
MergeDispPrint: 'both disp and print functions are the same from this point on
GOSUB GetStartDate
GOSUB ScanFile
IF Cdate$="" THEN PRINT "No records found for that start date" :CLOSE 2: GOTO Restart
' display the register info:
DispAgain:
PRINT #2, STRING$(70,"-")
PRINT #2, TAB(35),"Balance",TAB(45);
PRINT #2, USING "$$#### ##",Bal
PRINT #2, MID$(Cdate$,3,2)+"/"+MID$(Cdate$,5,2)+"/"+MID$(Cdate$,1,2),"    ";
IF Camt>0 THEN PRINT #2, "** DEPOSIT ** ";
PRINT #2, Cdesc$
IF Camt<0 THEN PRINT #2, TAB(10);"Check # ";Cno%;
PRINT #2, TAB(45);
IF Camt>0 THEN PRINT #2, USING "$$####.##",Camt ELSE PRINT #2, USING "$$#### ##";-Camt
' get next record :
IF EOF(1) THEN GOTO DispEnd
INPUT #1,Cdate$,Cdesc$,Cno%,Camt,Bal
GOTO DispAgain
'
' End of file reached on display/print function :
DispEnd:
CLOSE 1
PRINT #2, STRING$(70,"-")
PRINT #2, TAB(29);"Closing Balance";TAB(45);
```

Listing 4-8—cont.

```
PRINT#2, USING "$$**** **";Bal+Camt
Balance=Bal+Camt
BalanceKnown=1 'set flag to show that the current balance is known
CLOSE 2

' Come to here to wait before returning to main menu :
Restart:
PRINT
PRINT "Press any key to continue"
GOSUB WaitKey
GOTO Main

' Print Register Function :
Rprint:
CLS
LOCATE 1,10
PRINT "PRINT REGISTER"
OPEN "O",2,"LPT1:"
GOTO MergeDispPrint 'both Disp and Print functions are the same
                                     from this point on.

' Check Write Function :
Cwrite:
CLS
LOCATE 1,10
PRINT "CHECK WRITING"
IF BalanceKnown = 0 THEN GOSUB GetBalance
LOCATE 3,1
PRINT "Today is ";Today$
LOCATE 3,20
PRINT "Your current balance is ";
PRINT USING"$$**** **",Balance
LOCATE 5,1
FOR i=1 TO Predefined   'show all predefined account codes :
PRINT USING "**";i;
PRINT ". ";Account$(i)
NEXT
PRINT "99. All other accounts"
PRINT
GetacRetry:
PRINT TAB(10);"Select account number ==> ";
INPUT ac
IF ac<1 OR (ac>Predefined AND ac<>99) THEN GOTO GetacRetry
IF ac<>99 THEN GOTO UsePredefined
' Get account name and number from user:
PRINT "Enter name of payee ==> ";
LINE INPUT payee$
PRINT "Enter additional text to go on check, if any ==> ";
LINE INPUT payee2$
GOTO GetDesc
UsePredefined:   ' use a predefined account name and number for check payee:
payee$=Account$(ac)
payee2$=Accountno$(ac)
PRINT "Check will be made out to ";payee$
PRINT "Additional text on check will read : ";payee2$
GetDesc:   ' get any additional info to be stored with this check entry:
PRINT "Enter additional text to go in register, if any ==> ";
LINE INPUT desc$
PRINT
PRINT "Enter Check Amount ==> ";
INPUT Ckamt
IF Ckamt<=Balance THEN GOTO AmtOK
PRINT "That will cause an overdraft, proceed anyway? (Y/N) ==> ";
GOSUB GetYN
IF yn$="N" THEN GOTO NextCheck
PRINT yn$
AmtOK:
```

Listing 4-8—cont.

```
CLS
LOCATE 1,10
PRINT "PLEASE CONFIRM"
LOCATE 3,1
PRINT Today$," Check #";
PRINT USING "###";Cno%+1;
PRINT " to ";payee$;"  ";
PRINT USING "$$#### ##";CKamt
PRINT TAB(20);payee2$;"  ";
PRINT TAB(20);desc$
PRINT
PRINT "Proceed to write this check? (Y/N) ===> ";
GOSUB GetYN
IF yn$="N" THEN PRINT : PRINT "CHECK ABORTED" : GOTO NextCheck
PRINT yn$
Cno%=Cno%+1
Camt=-CKamt  ' show amount as negative to indicate check and not deposit
GOSUB TextAmount  'convert CKamt to TextCKamt$
'
' print the check on the Imagewriter printer. the following LPRINT
' statements must be modified to conform to the specific check forms
' that you use.
LPRINT TAB(60);"No. ";  'column location for check number, upper right corner
LPRINT USING "###"; Cno%
LPRINT TAB(60);   'column location for date, beneath check number
LPRINT Today$
LPRINT
LPRINT                  'number of blank lines before payee line is reached
LPRINT TAB(5);payee$  'column location for payee
LPRINT TAB(5);           'column location for text of amount of check
LPRINT TextCKamt$        'print out amount of check in text
LPRINT TAB(60);         'column location for check amount in numeric form
LPRINT USING "$$#### ##";-Camt
LPRINT
LPRINT                  'number of blank lines before comment line is reached
LPRINT TAB(5);payee2$   'column location for comment on check
LPRINT
LPRINT
LPRINT                  'number of blank lines to top of next check form
'---------end of check printing statements that need custom modification.
'
' Now add entry to the CHECKS file for this check:
IF FileOpen=0 THEN OPEN "A",1,"CHECKS" : FileOpen=1
GOSUB SetCdate
Cdesc$=payee$+"/"+desc$
' Cno% is already set
' Camt is already set
Bal=Balance 'balance prior to this check
Balance=Balance+Camt  'keep program's balance current
WRITE#1,Cdate$,Cdesc$,Cno%,Camt,Bal 'write register record to file

NextCheck:
PRINT
PRINT "Do you want to write another check? (Y/N) "
GOSUB GetYN
IF yn$="Y" THEN GOTO Cwrite
CLOSE 1 'close CHECKS file
FileOpen=0 ' show that file not open
GOTO Main
'--------------End of Check Write Function.

' Deposit Function :
Deposit:
CLS
LOCATE 1,10
PRINT "MAKE DEPOSITS      ";Today$
LOCATE 3,1
LINE INPUT "Enter Deposit description ==> ";desc$
INPUT "Enter amount of deposit ==> ";DPamt
```

Listing 4-8—cont.

```
PRINT
PRINT Today$;" DEPOSIT from ";desc$;" ";
PRINT USING "$$####.##";DPamt
PRINT
PRINT "Proceed to register this deposit ? (Y/N) ";
GOSUB GetYN
IF yn$="N" THEN PRINT : PRINT "DEPOSIT ABORTED" : GOTO NextDeposit
IF BalanceKnown=0 THEN GOSUB GetBalance
' Now add entry to the CHECKS file for this deposit:
IF FileOpen=0 THEN OPEN "A",1,"CHECKS" : FileOpen=1
GOSUB SetCdate
Cdesc$=desc$
' Cno% is already set - it remains same as last check number for deposit entries
Camt=DPamt
Bal=Balance 'balance prior to this check
Balance=Balance+Camt  'keep program's balance current
WRITE#1,Cdate$,Cdesc$,Cno%,Camt,Bal 'write register record to file

NextDeposit:
PRINT
PRINT "Do you want to make another deposit? (Y/N) "
GOSUB GetYN
IF yn$="Y" THEN GOTO Deposit
CLOSE 1 'close CHECKS file
FileOpen=0 ' show that file not open
GOTO Main
'---------------End of Deposit Function.

' Initialize CHECKS file function :
Rinit:
CLS
LOCATE 1,10
PRINT "INITIALIZE CHECK REGISTER"
LOCATE 3,1
PRINT "WARNING! - This function will destroy any previous register contents!"
PRINT "Be sure to rename the CHECKS file and obtain a printout of the current"
PRINT "register before proceeding  !!!"
PRINT
INPUT "Enter a starting balance for the new register ==> ";Camt
INPUT "Enter a starting check number ==> ";Cno%
PRINT
PRINT Today$;" Opening Balance = ";
PRINT USING "$$####.##";Camt;
PRINT "   Next Check Number will be ";Cno%
PRINT
PRINT "Proceed to initialize new register ? (Y/N) ";
GOSUB GetYN
IF yn$="N" THEN PRINT : PRINT "INIT ABORTED" : GOTO InitFinish
GOSUB SetCdate
Cdesc$="OPENING BALANCE"
Cno%=Cno%-1 'adjust so next check written will be correct number
' Camt is already set up
Bal=0
Balance=Camt
BalanceKnown=1
OPEN "O",1,"CHECKS"
WRITE#1,Cdate$,Cdesc$,Cno%,Camt,Bal 'write register record to file
CLOSE 1
PRINT
PRINT "INIT COMPLETED."
InitFinish:
PRINT
PRINT
PRINT "Press any key for menu."
a$=INKEY$
WHILE a$=""
a$=INKEY$
WEND
GOTO Main
```

Listing 4-8—cont.

```
'-------------------End of INIT Function.
'
' End of Program:
Finish:
END
'
' Subroutine to wait for the user to press any key.
' The keystroke is returned in a$
WaitKey:
a$=INKEY$
WHILE a$=""
a$=INKEY$
WEND
RETURN
'
' Subroutine to obtain starting date for display or print functions:
' Returns value in format yymmdd in variable d$
GetStartDate:
LOCATE 3,1
GSDretry:
LINE INPUT "Enter start date as mm/dd/yy ==> ",d$
' Verify valid input:
IF LEN(d$)<>8 THEN GOTO GSDerr
IF MID$(d$,3,1)<>"/" OR MID$(d$,6,1)<>"/" THEN GOTO GSDerr
d$=MID$(d$,7,2)+MID$(d$,1,2)+MID$(d$,4,2)
RETURN
GSDerr:
PRINT "Invalid input, try again please"
GOTO GSDretry
'
' Subroutine to open the CHECKS file and scan until the date in d$
' is reached, returning with the first file record at or beyond that
' date in variables Cdate$,Cdesc$,Cno%,Camt,Bal and the file left opened
' to that position.  If the date could not be found, then the file is closed
' and Cdate$ is returned as null.
ScanFile:
OPEN "I",1,"CHECKS"
ScanAgain:
IF EOF(1) THEN CLOSE 1 : Cdate$="" : RETURN
INPUT#1,Cdate$,Cdesc$,Cno%,Camt,Bal
IF Cdate$<d$ THEN GOTO ScanAgain
RETURN
'
' Subroutine to read the CHECKS file completely for the purposes of
' obtaining a current balance. The file is closed when the
' operation is complete, and the current balance is returned
' in variable Balance.  In addition, the variable BalanceKnown is set
' to 1 to indicate that the current balance is now available.
GetBalance:
OPEN "I",1,"CHECKS"
WHILE NOT EOF(1)
INPUT#1,Cdate$,Cdesc$,Cno%,Camt,Bal
WEND
CLOSE 1
Balance=Bal+Camt
BalanceKnown=1
RETURN
'
' Subroutine to wait until the user presses either the Y or N keys,
' in response to a yes or no question.  Will not return until one of these
' keys is pressed.  The keystroke character is returned in yn$.
GetYN:
yn$=INKEY$
WHILE UCASE$(yn$)<>"Y" AND UCASE$(yn$)<>"N"
yn$=INKEY$
WEND
yn$=UCASE$(yn$)
RETURN
'
```

Listing 4-8—cont.

```
' Subroutine to convert Today$, in the format mm/dd/yy into
' Cdate$, in the format yymmdd :
SetCdate:
Cdate$=RIGHT$(Today$,2)+LEFT$(Today$,2)+MID$(Today$,4,2)
RETURN

' Subroutine to convert a numeric dollar amount to a textual description
' as used on a bank check. The amount is input in variable CKamt and the
' result is returned in string variable TextCKamt$.
TextAmount:
TextCKamt$=""
IF CKamt>.99 THEN GOTO NotNoDollars
TextCKamt$="NO DOLLARS AND "+STR$(CKamt*100)+" CENTS"
RETURN
NotNoDollars:
IF CKamt<1000 THEN GOTO NoThousands
amt=FIX(CKamt/1000)
CKamt=Ckamt-amt*1000
GOSUB Textamt
TextCKamt$=Textamt$+" THOUSAND "
NoThousands:
IF CKamt<100 THEN GOTO NoHundreds
amt=FIX(CKamt/100)
CKamt=CKamt-amt*100
GOSUB Textamt
TextCKamt$=TextCKamt$+Textamt$+" HUNDRED "
NoHundreds:
amt=FIX(CKamt) 'remove any cents
CKamt=Ckamt-amt 'isolate just the cents
GOSUB Textamt
TextCKamt$=TextCKamt$+Textamt$+" DOLLARS "
IF CKamt=0 THEN TextCKamt$=TextCKamt$+"AND NO CENTS" : RETURN
TextCKamt$=TextCKamt$+" AND "+STR$(CINT(Ckamt*100))+" CENTS"
RETURN

' Subroutine to convert a value from 0-99 in variable amt into a textual
' description of that amount in variable Textamt$
Textamt:
IF amt=0 THEN Textamt$="" : RETURN
IF amt<20 THEN Textamt$=Numbers$(amt) : RETURN
amt10=FIX(amt/10) 'get tens digit of number
amt=amt-amt10*10
Textamt$=Numbers10$(amt10) 'tens digit in text
IF amt=0 THEN RETURN
Textamt$=Textamt$+" "+Numbers$(amt) 'append ones digit in text
RETURN
```

There are many business supply houses that will now do this for you, in quantities as low as 500 checks. The checks come complete with sequence numbers, as continuous forms with detachable tractor-feed edges. They are ideal for use with an Imagewriter printer. You can customize the check writing program to include a predefined list of the accounts you pay most often. Then, when the bills arive each month, all you have to do is run the program on your Macintosh.

You select the account to pay from your predefined list and enter the amount. The rest is automatic! The check will be made out to the correct party, showing your account number, and the date and amount. Your record ("checkbook register") is stored as a sequential disk file named CHECKS, from which you can make a printout. All you then have to do is detach the checks as they come out of the Imagewriter, sign them, and place them in the proper envelopes and mail them. I find that this approach can save a lot of time when doing the monthly bills; and it makes an otherwise unpleasant task more fun as well!

The program presented at this time is fairly large, as it must handle all of the functions described above. In its present form, however, it does not do justice to the Macintosh. This is because it does not make extensive use of those unique Macintosh features such as the mouse, windows, and pull-down menus. In fact, this version of the program relies on old fashioned screen menus and prompts to provide a user interface.

I have done this on purpose; at this point I want to focus on the internals of the program and not the user interface. I will explain in detail how the program maintains the checkbook register as a sequential data file, and how it manipulates the data that it has to work with.

In later chapters of this book, as you learn how to implement user interfaces, I will keep bringing this program back. We will then modify the user interface parts of the program so that, by the end of the book, it will be a true Macintosh style implementation. In this final form, I am sure it will be a program you will enjoy using.

How to Use the Program

Before I explain how the program works, I will describe how it is intended to be used. Figure 4-11 shows the "main menu" of the program. The five major functions provided by the program are *Display Register*, *Current Balance*, *Print Register*, *Write Checks*, *Add Deposits*, and *Initialize New Register* (this will eventually be a pull-down menu). As you know, the program maintains your checkbook register as a disk file named CHECKS.

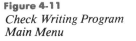

Figure 4-11
Check Writing Program Main Menu

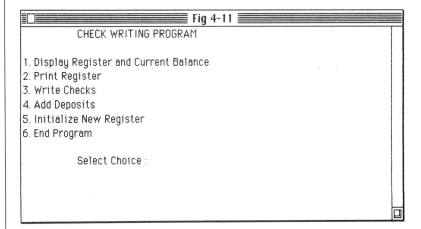

When you first start using the program, you must select the Initialize New Register function to initialize this disk file. This function will prompt you to supply a starting checking account balance, as well as a starting check number for the next check to be written. This data will then be used to create and place the first record in the CHECKS file, as shown in Figure 4-12. Subsequently, you may use any of the other four program functions, as needed. You may make deposits to the account, write checks against it, or display or print the account register.

Figure 4-12
*Initialize New Register
Function*

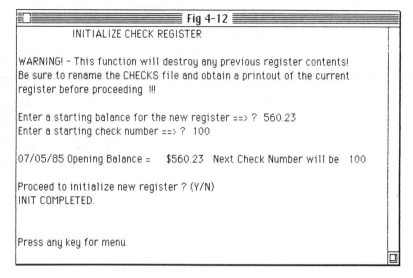

Figure 4-12
*Initialize New Register
Function*

To make a deposit to the account, select the Add Deposits function and supply a deposit description and amount, as shown in Figure 4-13. Notice that the program automatically stamps the deposit with the current date.

Figure 4-13
Add Deposits Function

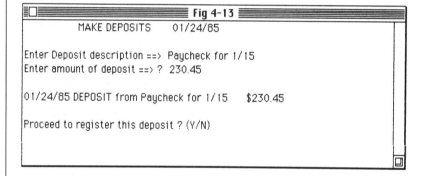

Figure 4-13
Add Deposits Function

To write out a check, select the Write Checks function. You will be provided with a list of predefined payees, as shown in Figure 4-14. Notice that the program also supplies the date and your current checking account balance. You can either select a predefined payee, or enter the payee manually.

In Figure 4-14, I have selected one of the predefined payee accounts. The program shows the name of the account and my account number with that payee, both of which will appear on the check itself. The program then prompts for the check amount, and any additional text you will want to put in the checkbook register for this entry.

Once this information is supplied, the program displays a screen showing what the check and checkbook register entry will look like, and asks for confirmation. This is shown in Figure 4-15. Figure 4-16 shows the check as it was printed by the Imagewriter on plain paper. When you actually receive your continuous forms checks, you can modify that portion of the program that prints the check so that all of the print fields line up properly.

Figure 4-14
Check Writing Function

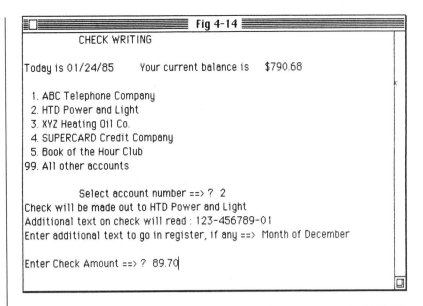

Figure 4-15
*Check Writing
Confirmation*

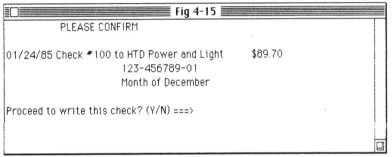

Notice that the program converts the numeric value of the check amount into an English language textual description. The program gives you the option of writing additional checks, or returning to the main menu.

The program's Display Register and Print Register functions are identical, except for the target device to which the output is directed. Either function allows you to select a starting date from which the checkbook register entries will be selected. All entries from that date on will be displayed (or printed) by these functions.

In Figure 4-17, I have used this function to obtain a complete display of my checkbook register for this ongoing example. Note that the first register entry (titled "OPENING BALANCE") was placed in the register by the Initialize function.

The CHECKS File Structure

The heart of this program is the structure of the CHECKS file, in which the checkbook register entries are maintained. Each record in this file is created using the following statement

```
WRITE#1, Cdate$, Cdesc$, Cno%, Camt, Bal
```

The five variables specified above represent the total amount of information necessary in each file record to make the check writing program work. Each check and each deposit made using the program will appear as a single file record. A description of each variable and its purpose can be found in Table 4-4.

Figure 4-16
The Check as Printed by the Imagewriter

```
┌                                                      No. 100 ┐
                                                      01/24/85

  HTD Power and Light
  EIGHTY NINE DOLLARS   AND   70 CENTS
                                                       $89.70

  123-456789-01
└                                                             ┘
```

Figure 4-17
Checkbook Register Display

```
≣□≣════════════════ Fig 4-17 ≣════════════════
 Enter start date as mm/dd/yy ==>  01/01/85
 -----------------------------------------------
                              Balance      $0.00
 07/05/85    ** DEPOSIT ** OPENING BALANCE
                                          $560.23
 -----------------------------------------------
                              Balance    $560.23
 01/24/85    ** DEPOSIT ** Paycheck for 1/15
                                          $230.45
 -----------------------------------------------
                              Balance    $790.68
 01/24/85    HTD Power and Light/Month of December
             Check *  100                 $89.70
 -----------------------------------------------
                         Closing Balance  $700.98

 Press any key to continue
                                                    ▣
```

Notice that the date is stored in the file in the format yymmdd (year, month, day). This format is used because two dates in this format can be compared simply as character strings to determine if one date is greater than the other. This is possible because the most significant information (year) appears to the left of the string while the least significant information (day) appears to the right. Using this format will prove to be quite helpful when implementing the search for start date component of the Display and Print Register functions.

The description field, *Cdesc$*, is a variable length character string used to provide a description of deposit, or additional description text for checks. The *Cno%* field holds the check number for entries that represent checks. For entries that represent deposits, this field contains the check number of the last check entry.

When a new check is to be written, the program can simply read the file to the last record to obtain the last check number used. It then adds one to that value to obtain the next check number to use. When the Initialize function is used to create the file, it asks the user for a starting check number. One less than the value supplied by the user will appear in the *Cno%* field of the initialization record written to the file.

Table 4-4
Variables in Each
CHECK File Record

Variable	Type	Holds
Cdate$	String of length 6	Date of transaction described by this record in format yymmdd.
Cdesc$	String of variable length	Description of this transaction.
Cno%	Integer	Check number for check transactions. Last check number used for all other transactions.
Camt	Single-precision	Amount of this transaction. If negative, then this record represents a check, otherwise it represents a deposit.
Bal	Single-precision	Account balance prior to the transaction described by this record.

The *Camt* field holds the dollar amount of the transaction represented by the record. It is this field that determines whether or not the record represents a deposit or a check. If the field is positive, then the record represents a deposit, otherwise it represents a check.

The final field, *Bal*, represents the checking account balance prior to the transaction represented by the record. The program can obtain the current account balance at any time by simply reading to the last file record, and adding the *Bal* field and the *Camt* fields together. The *Bal* field in the initialization record will be set to zero, and the *Camt* field for that record will be set to the opening balance provided by the user.

How the Program Works

The program relies heavily on subroutines to provide a readable, structured form. The main program implements each of the functions available in the main menu, obtaining help from the appropriate subroutines when necessary. A complete list of subroutines used in the program is shown in Table 4-5.

You may find some of these subroutines useful in your own programs. The subroutines can be grouped into three basic types. WaitKey, GetYN, and GetStartDate obtain information from the user, format it appropriately, and return that information to the caller. ScanFile and GetBalance both open the CHECKS file for input and read information for return to their callers.

In some cases the file is left open and positioned to a particular record to be read; in other cases the file is closed before a return. The main program must take this into account, since all files must be closed when their processing is completed.

Finally, the subroutines SetCdate, TextAmount, and Textamt perform computational functions, accepting data in input variables, and returning results in output variables. Since subroutines, and not subprograms, are used, all variables are shared and known to the main program and all of the subroutines.

Subroutine Name	Input Variables	Output Variables	Function
WaitKey		a$	Waits for a key to be pressed, returns it in a$
GetStartDate		d$	Prompts for and obtains start date from user. User enters date in mm/dd/yy format, but d$ is returned as yymmdd.
ScanFile	d$	Cdate$, Cdesc$, Cno%, Camt, Bal	Opens CHECKS file and reads until a record dated d$ or later is found. Returns variables for that entry and leaves file open. If no entries in file for date, then close file and return Cdate$ as null string.
GetBalance		Cdate$, Cdesc$, Cno%, Camt, Bal, Balance, BalanceKnown	Reads CHECKS file to end to obtain the current account balance.
GetYN		yn$	Waits until the user presses either the Y or the N key. Returns key pressed in yn$ as upper case even if lower case 'y' or 'n' was pressed.
SetCdate	Today$	Cdate$	Converts date in input variable from mm/dd/yy format to yymmdd format in output variable.
TextAmount	CKamt	TextCKamt$	Converts numeric dollar amount in input variable to textual description of that amount in output variable.
Textamt	amt	Textamt$	Converts value from 0 to 99 in input variable into textual description of that value in output variable.

The main program begins by defining a pair of array variables to hold the predefined payee accounts. The variable *Predefined* will hold the total number of such accounts available, and will be used later when the check writing function provides a menu of the predefined accounts.

A loop (starting with the label GetPredefined) is then used to read the predefined account information from a set of DATA statements. The end of this information is signalled by an account name of END, which must be present in the DATA statements that follow. The loop will automatically set variable *Predefined* for later use.

The program, as provided, contains the names and account numbers of five fictitious accounts. Be sure to replace these with your own real accounts before using the program. The DATA statements appear immediately after the GetPredefined loop.

The next step in the main program is to define and initialize a set of string arrays named *Numbers$* and *Numbers10$*. These arrays are initialized from DATA statements by a set of simple FOR-NEXT loops. The information they hold is used by the TextAmount and Textamt subroutines to convert a numeric quantity into an English language textual description of the quantity. For example, the number 123 is converted into "ONE HUNDRED TWENTY THREE."

If you decide to use these subroutines in your own programs, be sure to also copy the initialization and DATA statements for the arrays.

Next, a set of *flag* variables are initialized. Flag variables can contain various different values to indicate different conditions during program execution. In this case, the flag variable *BalanceKnown* is set to 0 when the current account balance is not yet known; it is set to 1 once the current account balance is known.

The flag variable *FileOpen* is set to 0 when the CHECKS file is not open, it is set to 1 once the file is opened; this variable is only used during the check writing and deposit functions.

As the final initialization step, the built-in function **DATE$** is used to obtain the current date. It is returned in the format mm-dd-yyyy; the program immediately converts this to the more familiar format of mm/dd/yy and stores it in variable *Today$*. Later, the program will also use the format yymmdd for the date.

The main menu of the program is displayed using PRINT statements, and a user selection is obtained from the keyboard via subroutine WaitKey. Later in the book, I will replace this part of the program with a custom pull-down menu, making the program feel much more "at home" on the Macintosh.

An ON-GOTO statement is used to transfer control to the appropriate part of the main program based upon the user's menu selection. The ON-GOTO statement has the general format

```
ON variable GOTO label1, label2, label3,
   . . .
```

Control is transferred to label1 if the variable specified contains a value of 1, to label2 for a value of 2, and so on.

Each of the five program functions begins with the statement CLS, which clears the current Output window. LOCATE and PRINT statements are then used to present a secondary menu appropriate to the function. At this point, each function requests and obtains input from the user. In later chapters, I will replace these sets of PRINT and INPUT statements with custom dialog boxes.

Both the custom pull-down menus and the custom dialog boxes allow the user to control the program with the mouse, and thus help to provide the program with a Macintosh-style user interface.

Since the Display and Print Register functions are identical except for the target of their output, I put Microsoft's device independent i/o to good advantage here. The two functions will share most of their code, beginning at statement label MergeDispPrint. Prior to that point, each function opens file number 2 for output. The Display function opens it to the SCRN: device, while the Print function opens it to the LPT1: device.

The bulk of the common code, which formats and outputs the checkbook register data, uses file number 2 for the target of the output. This allows you to avoid having to rewrite the same set of statements for the two functions.

The check write function obtains the current account balance and date, and displays these for the user along with a list of the predefined payee accounts. The user may select either a predefined account, or fill in his own. The multitude of PRINT and INPUT statements here can also be replaced with a pull-down menu and/or dialog box. In any case, the program also requests a check amount, then clears the screen and redisplays all of the pertinent check information for confirmation. Note that the program also checks for account overdrafts, though it allows the user to proceed with an overdraft if desired.

In this version of the program, if the user makes a mistake, he must cancel the operation at the confirmation checkpoint and reenter all pertinent data. With a dialog box interface, this will not be necessary. The dialog box is clearly a better user interface.

When the user confirms that he wants to write the check, the TextAmount subroutine is used to convert the check amount to a text description. A series of LPRINT statements are then employed to send the pertinent information to the Imagewriter. You will have to customize these statements so that the proper information appears in the proper places for the actual checks that you receive from the business forms supplier.

Once the check is printed, the program writes a record to the CHECKS file. The variable *FileOpen* is used to keep track of whether or not the CHECKS file is already open, since the program allows multiple checks to be written from within this function. When the function is finally exited, the file is closed. Note the use of the append mode when the file is opened for this function.

The Deposit function allows the user to specify an amount and description for deposits to the account. Once again, PRINT and INPUT statements are used where a dialog box will be substituted later. This function must call subroutine GetBalance before writing the deposit record to the CHECKS file. This allows the program to propagate the values for balance and check number from the last record in the file to the record to be added. Once again, append mode is used.

The Initialize function obtains a starting account balance and check number. This data is placed in a record written to the CHECK file using the output mode and not the append mode. Since output mode is used, the file, if it was already present, is reset to zero records. The initialization record is thus the first record in the file. Since the program always adds one to the check number found in the last file record when writing a new check, the user supplied check number is decremented by one before it is placed in the initialization record.

If you use the program for a long time, eventually the CHECKS file may become so large as to impact the speed of the program. When this happens, you can simply rename it so as to save it as an archive of old checking account data. Then use the initialize function to create a new CHECKS file, carrying over the balance and next check number by manually supplying that information to the initialize function.

Random Files

As I mentioned at the beginning of this chapter, there are two kinds of disk files, sequential and random. Having spent a good amount of time on sequential files, it is now time to look at random files. As I have already noted, you have considerably greater control over file access with random files than you do with sequential files. The cost, of course, is the additional and complicated programming that must be used to implement the extra control.

In what cases, then, would random files be useful? Random files are best employed when a large database of information must be maintained; one that may be too large to fit entirely in memory; and one in which you need to have immediate access to any specific database entry.

Consider, for example, a bank that maintains its customer's accounts in a computer database. Each entry in the database must contain the customer's name, address, and current account balance. An example of such an entry is shown in Figure 4-18. Each database entry must also be keyed to a specific account number, since that is the manner in which the database will be accessed. When a customer comes into the bank to make a deposit or withdrawal, he gives his account number to the teller, who enters it into the computer. The computer must be able to use the account number to immediately access the customer's entry in the database.

If you specified that each customer's account number corresponds to the record number of his database entry, then you could use a random file to implement the bank's program. Using random i/o techniques, you can directly access a specific customer account, as long as you know the account number (record number). I will now develop the file structure and program necessary to do this.

Figure 4-18
A Database of Bank Account Records

Account #	Customer Name	Address	Balance
Record 1	JOHN DOE	112 AMERICA ST.	$1115.70
Record 2	...	...	...
Record 3	...	...	...
...	...	...	...

File Structure:

```
Account #       = Record #
Customer Name = 40 characters
Address         = 80 characters
Balance         = Single-precision value [4 bytes]
```

Total Record Length = 40 + 80 + 4 = 124 Bytes.

CUSTOMER NAME:	ADDRESS:	BALANCE
40	80	4

Defining Ramdom Files

When working with random files, you must have a clear definition of the format (data structure) of the file's records. This format must be explicitly stated in the program before you can access the file. Refer to Figure 4-18. The record is organized into fields, each of which is assigned a fixed length in bytes. Fields containing character string information require one byte per character, whereas fields containing numeric data require 2, 4, or 8 bytes, depending upon the numeric data type. Numeric data types are shown in Table 4-6.

Table 4-6
Bytes Required for Numeric Fields (Random Files)

Numeric Data Type	Bytes Required	To Place Data in File, Use: (change to string)	To Retrieve Data From File, Use: change to numeric
Integer	2	MKI$	CVI
Single-Precision	4	MKS$	CVS
Double-Precision	8	MKD$	CVD

Once the fields are organized, and their respective lengths determined, you calculate the total record length. This length must be specified in the OPEN statement for the random file. The statement looks like this

```
OPEN "R",file number,filename,total
record length
```

For the example shown in Figure 4-18, the OPEN statement might be written as

```
OPEN "R",1,"ACCOUNTS",124
```

The "R" stands for random file. The file number is 1 and the filename is ACCOUNTS. The new parameter, 124, defines the length in bytes of each record in the file. This parameter should always be specified when using random files.

After the file is opened, its record layout must be defined to BASIC. This is accomplished by using the *FIELD* statement, which defines the length and position of each field in the record. The FIELD statement also assigns a specific BASIC variable name to be used when accessing the contents of each record field.

To continue the example, the FIELD statement might look like this

```
FIELD 1, 40 AS Custname$, 80 AS Address$, 4
AS Bal$
```

The number 1 appearing after the FIELD keyword is the file number. This is followed by a list of field definitions. The length of each field is specified, as is the variable name through which the contents of that field will be accessed. Note that only character string variables may be used to access fields in random access file records.

For numeric fields, special functions are employed to convert the numeric data to/from character string format (a list of the special functions are given in Table 4-6). The procedure for doing so will be described in a moment.

Accessing Random File Data

Once the file has been OPENed and FIELDed, you can read and write records to/from it. The BASIC statements GET and PUT are used to accomplish this. In either case, the number of the record to be accessed must be specified. Thus, for example, the statement

```
GET 1,7
```

will read the seventh record from (open) random file number 1.

The statement

```
PUT 1,23
```

will write the 23rd record to the file. When a record is read, the contents of each of its fields are placed into the corresponding variable names defined in the FIELD statement for that file number. Conversely, when a record is written, its contents are taken from the contents of these variables. When you are finished accessing the file, you must, of course, close it in the usual fashion. The complete file access protocol for random files is outlined in Figure 4-19.

The LSET and RSET Statements

When preparing to write a random file record, you cannot use the standard BASIC assignment statement to place data into the FIELD variables. Special assignment statements, using the keywords *LSET* and *RSET*, must be used.

Figure 4-19
*Random File Access
Protocol*

STEP	BASIC Statement(s) Used
1. Open File.	OPEN
2. Define Record Fields	FIELD
3. Access data in file. [Read Record(s), Write Record(s)]	GET LSET, RSET, PUT
4. Close File.	CLOSE

The LSET statement is used to place data into a FIELD variable, aligned to the left side of the field. The RSET statement aligns data to the right side of the field. For example, if you wanted to set the customer's name field to "JOHN DOE," you could use the statement

```
LSET Custname$ = "JOHN DOE"
```

This would cause the 40-character-long customer name field to be set to equal to the eight characters "JOHN DOE" followed by 32 blanks.

Alternatively, the statement

```
RSET Custname$ = "JOHN DOE"
```

would cause the 40-character-long customer name field to be set equal to 32 blanks followed by the eight characters "JOHN DOE".

In a similar fashion, you might set the address field using the statement

```
LSET Address$ = "112 AMERICA ST."
```

Setting the last field, which contains a numeric value, is slightly more difficult. The field variable, *Bal$*, is a character string, but you want to place a numeric value in it. To do so, you must use the special conversion function *MKS$*.

The keyword stands for "make single precision character string." This function converts a single precision number into a four character long string so that it can be stored in a random file. In the current example, you would use it as follows

```
LSET Bal$ = MKS$(1115.70)
```

The alternative special conversion functions MKI$ and MKD$ would be used to convert integer and double-precision values, respectively. MKI$ returns a two-character-long string and MKD$ returns an eight-character-long string.

What happens when you wish to read the file? Well, fields containing character string data are easy; you simply access the FIELD variable as if it were any other variable. Thus, for example, the statements

```
GET 1,6
PRINT Custname$
```

would result in a display of the customer name field for the sixth record in the file. To access numeric data fields, you must use the other set of special conversion functions listed in Table 4-6. These functions are CVI, CVS, and CVD. The keywords stand for convert to integer, convert to single precision, convert to double precision. An example of their use

```
Get 1,6
x = CVS(Bal$)
```

The above statements will obtain the balance for account number 6 and place it in single precision variable *x*.

When using random files, you must be very careful to never use a FIELDed variable name as the target of an assignment or INPUT statement. To do so would break the relationship between that variable name and the random file records. Be sure to use the LSET or RSET keywords whenever placing such variable names to the left of an equals sign.

The Appointment Calendar Program — Version 1
As a way of illustrating the use of random file i/o, I will now introduce the first version of the appointment calendar program. The main purpose of this program is to allow your Macintosh to help you maintain a personal appointment calendar. In its final form (several chapters hence), this program will display a graphic image of a selected calendar month, and allow you to use the mouse to select a particular date as shown in Figure 7-57 (Chapter 7). For each date in the year, you will be able to specify a list of appointments.

In the version shown here, the program's user interfaces do not make it very practical to use, but you will be able to see the details of how the program builds and maintains the appointment data itself. This central component of the total program is what I will focus on now. Once it is in place and fully understood, the program's user interface can be enhanced (in subsequent chapters).

The Linked List Structure
The heart of the appointment calendar program is the CALENDAR file itself, which maintains all of your personal appointment data. The CALENDAR file is a random file. It is created by running the special initialization program shown in Listing 4-9, after which the appointment calendar program itself can be run (Listing 4-10).

The way the file is structured, each file record can store a single appointment. The first 366 records correspond to each individual day in a single year period (365 days for most years, 366 days for leap years). Using these records, it will be possible to set a different appointment for each day of the year.

A problem arises, however, when you want to set more than one appointment for the same day. In general, every day of the year may not have appointments scheduled; some days may have quite a few appointments, while other days may have none. For these reasons, it is not feasible to set aside a fixed number of records for each day of the year. Instead, a special data structure called a *linked list* is employed. Using this structure, it will be possible to allocate as many or as few records as are needed to any particular day of the year.

```
' This program creates and initializes the CALENDAR file.
' It must be run before any version of the Appointment
' Calendar Program can be run.
' Records numbered 1 through 366 represent their corresponding
' julian dates for a one year period (including the possibility of
' leap years). Each record has two fields: Appoint$ and Link$.
' Records numbered 1 - 366 are initialized so that Appoint$ = "@"
' which indicates no appointments. Also, Link$ is initialized to 0.
' Record 367 is a special record as its Link$ field points to the
' start of the free record chain. It is initialized to 368. Any new
' free records that are needed will be allocated from record number
' 368 onward.
' See text for more information.
OPEN "R",1,"CALENDAR",42
FIELD 1, 40 AS Appoint$, 2 AS Link$
LSET Appoint$ = "@"
LSET Link$ = MKI$(0)
FOR Record.number% = 1 TO 366
PUT 1,Record.number%
NEXT
LSET Link$ = MKI$(368) 'Initialize start of the free record chain
PUT 1,367 'Write the special record containing the start of free chain ptr
CLOSE 1
PRINT "CALENDAR FILE INITIALIZED."
END
```

```
' This version of the program does not have the Macintosh style
' user interfaces installed yet, but it does illustrate the use of a
' random access file and the concept of a linked list to implement
' the appointment database. See the text for more information.
Today$=DATE$   'Get date and reformat it to mm/dd/yy format:
Today$=LEFT$(Today$,6)+RIGHT$(Today$,2) 'remove '19' from year
MID$(Today$,3,1)="/"
MID$(Today$,6,1)="/"
Tmonth%=VAL(LEFT$(Today$,2))
Tday%=VAL(MID$(Today$,4,2))
Tyear%=VAL(RIGHT$(Today$,2))
' Initialize array data:
DIM MonthDays%(12)
FOR x%=1 TO 12
READ MonthDays%(x%)
NEXT
DATA 31,28,31,30,31,30,31,31,30,31,30,31

' Determine the starting day of the week for the current year, save
' it in variable NewYearsDay% :
CALL StartDay(1,Tyear%,NewYearsDay%,Days%)
' Set up month of February for the current year :
IF (Tyear%-84) MOD 4 = 0 THEN MonthDays%(2)=29 ELSE MonthDays%(2)=28 'Leap Years
CALL DayofWeek(Tmonth%,Tday%,Tdayw%,Tjday%)

DIM DayNames$(7)
FOR x%=1 TO 7
READ DayNames$(x%)
NEXT
DATA Sunday,Monday,Tuesday,Wednesday,Thursday,Friday,Saturday
DIM MonthNames$(12)
FOR x%=1 TO 12
READ MonthNames$(x%)
NEXT
DATA January, February,March,April,May,June,July,August,September
DATA October,November,December
```

Listing 4-10—cont.

```
' Set up a complete textual description of the current date :
Tdate$=DayNames$(Tdayw%)+" "+MonthNames$(Tmonth%)+" "+STR$(Tday%)
Tdate$=Tdate$+", 19"+RIGHT$(Today$,2)+"    (Day #"+STR$(Tjday%)+")"
' Prepare for access to random file CALENDAR :
OPEN "R",1,"CALENDAR",42
FIELD 1, 40 AS Appoint$, 2 AS Link$
HighestRecord%=LOF(1)/42    'current highest record number in the file
Main.Menu:
CLS
LOCATE 1,10
PRINT "Appointment Calendar Program - Version 1"
LOCATE 3,5
PRINT "Today is ",Tdate$
LOCATE 5,1
PRINT "1. Check/Delete Appointments"
PRINT "2. Enter Appointments"
PRINT "3. Exit Program"
LOCATE 9,5
PRINT "Select Choice ==> "
TryAgain:
GOSUB WaitKey
a%=VAL(a$)
IF a%<1 OR a%>3 THEN GOTO TryAgain
ON a% GOTO CheckA,EnterA,Finish

' Check Appointments function :
CheckA:
CLS
PRINT "This function will let you check to see if you have"
PRINT "any appointments. In this version, you must supply"
PRINT "the date that you wish to check. Any appointment may"
PRINT "be deleted from the calendar using this function."
PRINT
GOSUB GetDate  'get date from user via keyboard
' determine day of week and julian day # for selected date :
CALL DayofWeek(Month%,Day%,Dayw%,Jday%)
' display the selected date nicely :
PRINT
PRINT DayNames$(Dayw%)+" "+MonthNames$(Month%)+" "+STR$(Day%)
' search CALENDAR file for appointments for selected date :
' ( the initial record number to read is the julian date, Jday% )
GET 1,Jday%
Link%=CVI(Link$)
IF LEFT$(Appoint$,1)="@" AND Link%=0 THEN PRINT "No appointments for this date !": GOTO NextCheck
' display each appointment in the chain :
Apno=1 'number each appointment starting with 1
Apno.fix=0  'handles case where appoint#1 was deleted but appoint#2 exists
FollowChain:
IF LEFT$(Appoint$,1)<>"@" THEN PRINT Apno;". ",Appoint$ : Apno=Apno+1 ELSE Apno.fix=1
IF Link%=0 THEN GOTO EndofChain
GET 1,Link%
Link%=CVI(Link$)
GOTO FollowChain
EndofChain:
PRINT "---- End of Appointments for selected date ----"
PRINT
PRINT "Do you wish to delete any of these appointments ? (Y/N) "
GOSUB GetYN
IF yn$="N" THEN GOTO NextCheck
RetryApno:
INPUT "Enter appointment number to delete ==> ",Dapno
IF Dapno<1 OR Dapno>=Apno THEN PRINT "Invalid choice" : GOTO RetryApno
Dapno=Dapno+Apno.fix 'handles case where appoint#1 was deleted but appoint#2 exists
' Delete the selected appointment entry from the calendar :
IF Dapno>1 THEN GOTO DeChain 'all entries except the 1st must be returned to the free chain
GET 1,Jday%
LSET Appoint$="@"
PUT 1,Jday%
```

Listing 4-10—cont.

```
GOTO DeletedIt
DeChain:    ' find the entry to be deleted and break it out of the chain :
GET 1,Jday%           'start at the head of the chain
Link%=Jday%
Apno=1               'keep track of the position number (appointment #)
WHILE Apno+1 <> Dapno
Link%=CVI(Link$)
GET 1,Link%          'chain forward and keep looking for it
Apno=Apno+1
WEND
' Now Link% = the record preceding the record to be deleted :
PreLink%=Link%
Link%=CVI(Link$)
GET 1,Link%          'get the record to be deleted
DelLink%=Link%       'the record # to be returned to the free chain
Link%=CVI(Link$)     'Link% = the next entry after the one to be deleted
GET 1,PreLink%       'get the preceding record
LSET Link$=MKI$(Link%)  'connect it to the entry following the deleted one
PUT 1,PreLink%       'this effectively disconnects the deleted entry from the
'                              current appointment chain.
' Now put the deleted entry on the free record chain:
GET 1,367            'get pointer to start of free chain
NextFreeLink%=CVI(Link$)
LSET Link$=MKI$(DelLink%)   'make the deleted entry the first on the free chain
PUT 1,367
GET 1,DelLink%        'get the deleted entry
LSET Link$=MKI$(NextFreeLink%)  'attach the rest of the free chain to it
PUT 1,DelLink%
' Deletion process complete.
DeletedIt:
PRINT "That appointment has been deleted."
NextCheck:
PRINT "Do you wish to check another date ? (Y/N) "
GOSUB GetYN
IF yn$="Y" THEN GOTO CheckA
GOTO Main.Menu

' Enter Appointments Function :
EnterA:
CLS
PRINT "This function will let you add appointments to any date in"
PRINT "the current year.  In this version, you must manually specify"
PRINT "the date desired."
PRINT
GOSUB GetDate
CALL DayofWeek(Month%,Day%,Dayw%,Jday%)
' display the selected date nicely :
PRINT
PRINT DayNames$(Dayw%)+" "+MonthNames$(Month%)+" "+STR$(Day%)
PRINT
LINE INPUT "Enter the description of the appointment ==> ";Apdesc$
' search CALENDAR file for appointments for selected date :
' ( the initial record number to read is the julian date, Jday% )
GET 1,Jday%
Link%=CVI(Link$)
PrevLink%=Jday%
IF LEFT$(Appoint$,1)="@" AND Link%=0 THEN LSET Appoint$=Apdesc$ : PUT 1,Jday% : GOTO Appoin
tmentMade
WHILE Link%<>0
GET 1,Link%
PrevLink%=Link%
Link%=CVI(Link$)
WEND
' found end of chain, allocate and insert a new record at PrevLink%
GET 1,367    'get start of free record chain
NextFreeLink%=CVI(Link$)
IF NextFreeLink%>HighestRecord% THEN LSET Link$=MKI$(NextFreeLink%+1) : HighestRecord%=High
estRecord%+1 : GOTO AllocateNextFree
GET 1,NextFreeLink%    'get the link to the next free record available
```

Listing 4-10—cont.

```
AllocateNextFree:
PUT 1,367   'setup the new start of the free chain
GET 1,PrevLink%   'get previously last record for appointment date chain
LSET Link$=MKI$(NextFreeLink%)   'attach the new record to the end of the chain
PUT 1,PrevLink%
LSET Appoint$=Apdesc$   'set up the new appointment record
LSET Link$=MKI$(0)   'end of chain indicator for appointment date chain
PUT 1,NextFreeLink%   'write the new appointment record
' the appointment has been added.
AppointmentMade:
PRINT "Do you wish to enter another appointment ? (Y/N) "
GOSUB GetYN
IF yn$="Y" THEN GOTO EnterA
GOTO Main.Menu

' End of Program :
Finish:
CLOSE 1
END
'

' Subroutine to wait for the user to press any key.
' The keystroke is returned in a$
WaitKey:
a$=INKEY$
WHILE a$=""
a$=INKEY$
WEND
RETURN
'

' Subroutine to obtain the date from the user.
' Returns value in format mm/dd in variable d$, also returns
' month in Month% and day in Day%
GetDate:
LINE INPUT "Enter desired date as mm/dd ==> ",d$
' Verify valid input:
IF LEN(d$)<>5 THEN GOTO GDerr
IF MID$(d$,3,1)<>"/" THEN GOTO GDerr
Month%=VAL(LEFT$(d$,2))
IF Month%<1 OR Month%>12 THEN GOTO GDerr
Day%=VAL(RIGHT$(d$,2))
IF Day%<1 OR Day%>MonthDays%(Month%) THEN GOTO GDerr
RETURN
GDerr:
PRINT "Invalid input, try again please"
GOTO GetDate
'

' Subroutine to wait until the user presses either the Y or N keys,
' in response to a yes or no question.  Will not return until one of these
' keys is pressed.  The keystroke character is returned in yn$.
GetYN:
yn$=INKEY$
WHILE UCASE$(yn$)<>"Y" AND UCASE$(yn$)<>"N"
yn$=INKEY$
WEND
yn$=UCASE$(yn$)
RETURN
'

' Subprogram StartDay
' Finds the starting day of the week for a given month and year.
' Call StartDay(Month%,Year%,Day%,Days%)
' with Month% = 1(Jan), 2(Feb), ..., 12(Dec)
' and Year% = 85, 86, ..., 99 (valid for 1985 thru 1999)
' Returns with Day% = 1 (Sun), 2 (Mon), 3 (Tue), ..., 7 (Sat)
' and with Days% = number of days in that month.
SUB StartDay (m%,y%,d%,ds%) STATIC
SHARED MonthDays%()
d%=3 'Jan 85 starts with Tuesday
m1%=1 'start at Jan
```

Listing 4-10—cont.

```
y1%=85 'start at 1985
StartDayLoop2:
IF (y1%-84) MOD 4 = 0 THEN MonthDays%(2)=29 ELSE MonthDays%(2)=28 'Leap Years
StartDayLoop1:
IF m1%=m% AND y1%=y% THEN GOTO FoundStartDay
d%=d%+MonthDays%(m1%)
IF m1%<12 THEN  m1%=m1%+1 : GOTO StartDayLoop1
m1%=1
y1%=y1%+1
GOTO StartDayLoop2
FoundStartDay:
d%=d% MOD 7
IF d%=0 THEN d%=7
ds%=MonthDays%(m1%)
END SUB
'
' Subprogram DayofWeek
' Call DayofWeek(month%,day%,dayw%,jday%)
' Variables month% and day% are inputs to this routine.
' Variables dayw% and jday% are outputs from this routine.
' This routine takes a month (1-12) and a day (1-31) and
' returns a day of the week (1(Sun), 2(Mon), ..., 7(Sat)) and
' a julian day (1-366). The current year (Tyear%) is assumed.
SUB DayofWeek(m%,d%,dw%,jd%) STATIC
SHARED MonthDays%(),NewYearsDay%
dw%=NewYearsDay%
jd%=1
m1%=1
WHILE m1%<m%  'Accumulate days for each full month prior to desired month :
dw%=dw%+MonthDays%(m1%)
jd%=jd%+MonthDays%(m1%)
m1%=m1%+1
WEND
' Now in desired month, find desired day :
dw%=dw%+d%-1
jd%=jd%+d%-1
' Adjust day of week to range 1 - 7 :
dw%=dw% MOD 7
IF dw%=0 THEN dw%=7
END SUB
```

Each entry in a linked list structure contains two elements: the data for the entry, and a special *link field*. The link field is used to connect the current entry to any additional related entries in the structure. Several entries connected together via their link fields form what I shall call a *chain*. This concept is illustrated by Figure 4-20. The last entry of a chain is denoted by placing a special value (usually 0) in the link field.

For the calendar program, each date with multiple appointments will form a chain. Each entry in the chain will represent an

Figure 4-20
A Linked List Structure

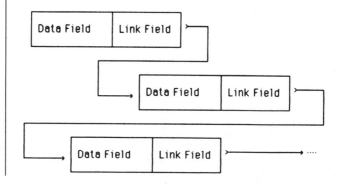

individual appointment for that date. The CALENDAR file will contain one additional chain, called the *free record chain*. This will be a chain of entries that are no longer in use. Entries will be added to this chain when appointments are deleted from the calendar.

When additional appointments are made, the entries used to hold them will be allocated from the free record chain. In this fashion, the amount of disk space needed is kept to a minimum, while the storage requirements of the program are met.

The CALENDAR File

The CALENDAR file is a random access file with 42 byte records. Each record contains a data field (used to hold a single appointment), and a link field (used to implement linked list chains). The record structure is defined by the following FIELD statement

    FIELD 1, 40 AS Appoint$, 2 AS Link$

Variable *Appoint$* holds a string with a maximum length of 40 characters, used to describe the user's appointments. Variable *Link$* holds an integer value (2 bytes) that represents the link information. The file always has a minimum of 367 records. Records numbered 1 through 366 correspond to the days of a single calendar (Julian) year. Record number 366 is only used for leap years.

Records 1 through 366 are initialized so that the Appoint$ field contains the "@" character, and the Link$ field contains zero. This indicates no appointments for each day of the year. When the first appointment for a specific day is made, that appointment is placed in the corresponding day's record (i.e., Jan 10th would appear in record # 10).

Subsequent appointments for the same day will be stored in new file records (starting with record number 368). These additional

Figure 4-21
Calendar File Structure

Record Number	Appoint$	Link$
001 (Jan 1)	@	0
002 (Jan 2)	@	0
003 (Jan 3)	@	0
... ...	...	...
016 (Jan 16)	Dentist, 9 AM	368
017 (Jan 17)	@	0
... ...	...	...
152 (Jun 1)	@	0
153 (Jun 2)	Dad's Birthday !!!	371
... ...	...	...
364 (Dec 30)	@	0
365 (Dec 31)	@	0
366 (leap yr)	@	0
367 (free ptr)	@	373
368	Staff Meeting, 1 PM	369
369	New Employee Interviews	370
370	Racquetball, 7 PM	0
371	Theater Tickets for 2 PM	372
372	Dinner Reservations for 6	0

**************** END OF FILE ****************

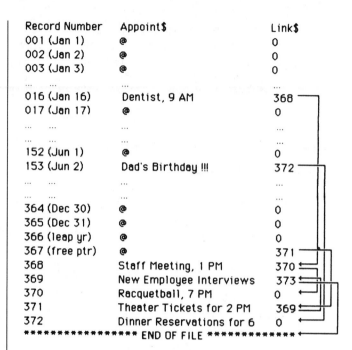

Figure 4-22
Calendar File Structure with Deletions

Record Number	Appoint$	Link$
001 (Jan 1)	@	0
002 (Jan 2)	@	0
003 (Jan 3)	@	0
... ...	...	...
016 (Jan 16)	Dentist, 9 AM	368
017 (Jan 17)	@	0
... ...	...	...
... ...	...	...
152 (Jun 1)	@	0
153 (Jun 2)	Dad's Birthday !!!	372
... ...	...	...
... ...	...	...
364 (Dec 30)	@	0
365 (Dec 31)	@	0
366 (leap yr)	@	0
367 (free ptr)	@	371
368	Staff Meeting, 1 PM	370
369	New Employee Interviews	373
370	Racquetball, 7 PM	0
371	Theater Tickets for 2 PM	369
372	Dinner Reservations for 6	0

**************** END OF FILE *************

entries will be logically connected to the first record via the Link$ field. Record number 367 is a special record. Its *Link$* field holds the starting record number of the free record chain. If this number is greater than the total number of records currently in the file, then the next free record must be allocated by adding a new record to the end of the file.

Eventually, however, as new records are allocated and then deleted, the free record chain will contain existing (unused) records in the file. These records will be reclaimed and reused when additional appointments are added. This overall strategy is illustrated by Figures 4-21 and 4-22.

In Figure 4-21, a set of appointments has been made for the dates January 16th, and June 2nd. Since there is more than one appointment for each of these dates, new records have been allocated at the end of the file (records numbered 368 and higher) to hold the data.

In Figure 4-22, several of the appointments have been deleted. Note how the corresponding records have been added to the free record chain (which starts at record number 367). If new appointments were added at this time, these free records would be used before any new records are added to the file.

How to Use the Program

Once again, let me stress that this version of the program is not meant for serious use. It is only presented in this form so that you can focus on how to handle a random access file and linked list structure. In a later chapter, a much improved version of the same program is presented; that version can be put to real and practical use. With this caveat in mind, let me show you how the current version of the program operates.

If you want to follow through these steps on your own Macintosh, remember that you must run the program of Listing 4-9 once before the program of Listing 4-10 can be run.

Figure 4-23 shows the main menu of the program. The two significant choices are Check/Delete and Enter appointments. The first function is used to interrogate the CALENDAR file for appointments made on a specific date. Any appointments found can then be deleted from the file if so desired. The second function is used to actually place new appointments into the CALENDAR file.

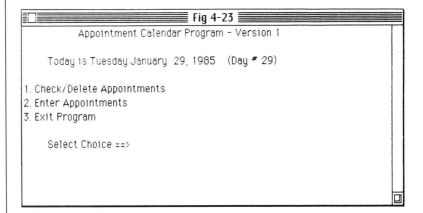

In Figure 4-24, I have selected the Check/Delete function, and supplied a date of January 16th. Note that the program calculates the day of the week for the selected date, and displays this information for the user (in this case, Wednesday). The program indicates that, at the present time, no appointments have been made for that date. The final prompt shown in Figure 4-24 allows you to inquire about another date, or return to the main menu.

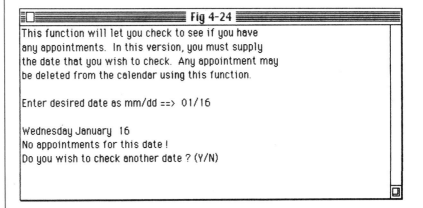

In Figure 4-25, I have selected the Enter Appointments function. Once again, I have supplied the program with the date; it has replied with the day of the week. I then entered an appointment for that date, which the program adds to the CALENDAR file.

The final prompt shown in the figure allows me to either enter another appointment, or return to the main menu. Continuing to use the Enter Appointments function, I supplied all of the appointments shown in Figure 4-21.

Figure 4-25
*The Enter
Appointments Function*

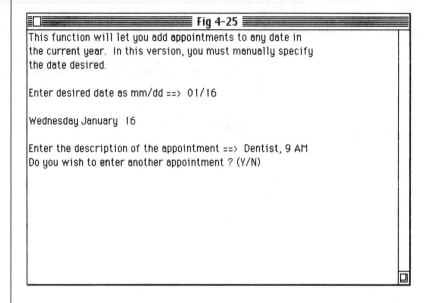

Going back to the Check/Delete function, I requested those dates for which I just added appointments—the results are shown in Figures 4-26 and 4-27. Note that the program numbers all appointments and displays them in the order in which they were entered. In addition, the program gives you the option at this point to delete any appointment displayed. Appointments to be deleted are specified by the numbers supplied by the program.

In Figure 4-27, I have deleted appointment number 2 ("Theater Tickets...") from the June 2nd list. If I were to proceed in the same fashion and delete the appointments numbered 2 and 3 in Figure 4-26, the CALENDAR file would then be structured as shown in Figure 4-22. As you can see, the program fulfills all of the requirements of a simple automated appointment calendar, although the user interface is not very friendly at this point.

How the Program Works
The program is divided into several parts: a main program, several subroutines, and two subprograms. The main program implements the main menu and its subfunctions, which rely on the subroutines and subprograms for support. The subroutines WaitKey, GetDate and GetYN are either identical or very similar to those used in the checkbook program, so they do not require additional explanation.

Subprogram StartDay was developed in an earlier chapter; its purpose is to calculate the starting day of the week (e.g. Sunday, Monday, Tuesday, etc.) for a given month and year. This routine will work for any month-year combination between January 1985 and December 1999. It is used in this program to determine the starting day of the week for the current year.

Figure 4-26
Appointments Made for 01/16

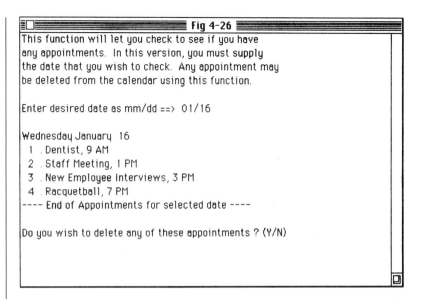

Figure 4-26
Appointments Made for 01/16

Figure 4-27
Appointments Made for 06/02, with Deletion Request

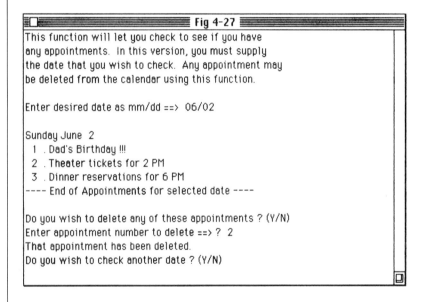

Figure 4-27
Appointments Made for 06/02, with Deletion Request

Since the CALENDAR file only holds data for a single year, StartDay need only be called once. The value for the first day of the current year is thereafter maintained in variable *NewYearsDay%*, as a number in the range 1 to 7 (where 1 corresponds to Sunday, 2 to Monday, etc.). Subprogram DayofWeek uses this information to calculate the day of the week for any date in the current year.

DayofWeek also calculates and returns the Julian day for the requested date. The Julian day is a number that begins with 1 for January 1st and increases by 1 for each day thereafter. Thus December 31st is Julian day 365, except in a leap year, when it is Julian day 366. The Julian day corresponds to the starting record number in the CALENDAR file for any given date within the year.

The main program begins by obtaining the current date from the built-in function DATE$. The *MonthDays%* array is then initialized from DATA statements to show the number of days in each month of the year. This array is shared by the two date manipulation subprograms. Subprogram StartDay is then used to obtain a value for *New YearsDay%*, and then subprogram DayofWeek is used to determine the current day of the week.

Arrays DayNames$ and MonthNames$ are initialized from DATA statements; they contain the text for the days of the week and months of the year, respectively. Using this information, the program can now create a complete textual description of the current date, which is placed in variable *Tdate$*. The initialization is completed by opening and fielding the random access CALENDAR file.

Note how the **LOF** function is used to calculate the current highest record number in the file (LOF value divided by record size). Most linked list chains in the CALENDAR file are terminated by a link value of zero. However, the free record chain is terminated by a link value that exceeds the highest record number in the file. This is used to indicate when a new record should be allocated.

The program's main menu is implemented using PRINT statements, the WaitKey subroutine, and an ON-GOTO statement. In later chapters, you will see how they can be replaced by a custom pull-down menu. The Check/Delete function begins at label CheckA. Subroutine GetDate is used to obtain the date to be checked from the user.

In a later implementation, the program will display a graphics image of an entire calendar month, and allow the operator to use the mouse to select a particular day.

The DayofWeek subprogram is used to determine the day of the week for the selected date, and this information is supplied to the user. The Julian day (variable *Jday%*) returned by the subprogram is used as a starting file record number, and the CALENDAR file is accessed.

If the appointment field for the record contains the special indicator "@" and the link field is zero, then there are no appointments scheduled for the date in question. If the appointment field does not contain "@," it is displayed, and the link field is used to determine if additional appointments are scheduled for this day. When the value of the link field is nonzero, it is used as a record number, and that record is read from the CALENDAR file. The process is repeated until a link value of zero is encountered. In this fashion, each appointment in the linked list chain for this day is found and displayed.

Note that the program numbers each appointment found and keeps track of the total number of appointments as variable *Apno*. The appointment number is simply a reference value which allows the user to define a specific appointment to be deleted. A special case exists if the user has deleted the first appointment in a multiappointment chain. In this case, the primary file record (record number = Julian day) for the day in question will contain the "@" symbol in the *Appoint$* field, but it will also contain a nonzero link field. This situation is indicated by setting the variable *Apno.fix* to 1 (it is normally 0).

This is important, because the delete function uses the appointment reference number to determine how far to chain through the linked list before reaching the record to be deleted. In the special case where the primary appointment record has already been deleted, this chaining operation would be off by one. Variable *Apno.fix* corrects for this situation.

Once all of the appointments for the selected date have been displayed, the user is given the option to delete any listed appointment. In the present version, the appointment to delete is selected by manually entering the appropriate reference number. Eventually, such a selection will be made via the mouse.

For now, the appointment number to delete is input to variable *Dapno*. Variable *Apno.fix* is added to *Dapno* to handle the special case described above. If the appointment number to be deleted is 1, then the process is simple. The primary record for the date is read, its Appoint$ field is set to "@," and then the record is written back to the file. Note that the record's link field is not altered. This insures that any additional appointments in the chain are not affected.

If, however, the appointment number to delete is greater than 1, the process is quite complex. The appointment record in question must be removed from the appointment chain, and the chain must then be reconnected so that any preceding appointments are still linked to any following appointments.

A WHILE-WEND loop is used to chain through the appointment records until the record preceding the record to be deleted is reached. The link field of this record is then changed to contain the value in the link field of the deleted record. This effectively breaks the delete record out of the chain, while leaving the chain intact.

Now, the deleted record must be added to the free record chain. Doing this allows the record to be reused by a subsequent Enter Appointment function, and conserves space in the CALENDAR file. The deleted record is thus placed at the very beginning of the free record chain, by placing its record number in the link field of special record number 367. The previous value in the link field of record 367 is placed into the link field of the deleted record, thus insuring that the complete free record chain is intact.

The Enter Appointments function also relies on subroutine GetDate to obtain a date from the user. It then prompts the user for a text description of the appointment to be added for that date. The DayofWeek subprogram converts the date into a Julian day, and this value is used to obtain the primary file record for that day.

If this record is unused, then the appointment is simply inserted into the record, and the function is complete. Otherwise, a WHILE-WEND loop is used to chain through each record in the existing appointment chain until a link field of zero is found. This is the point at which the new appointment will be appended to the chain. This will be done by allocating a new record, and placing its record number into the link field of the current last record in the chain. The new record's link field will be set to zero to indicate that it is now the end of the chain.

The new record is allocated from the free record chain, which is interrogated by reading special record number 367. The first record in this chain is taken off the chain and used as the new appointment record. If, however, the record number indicated as the next free record is greater than the current total number of records in the file, then there are no (previously allocated and deleted) free records available for use, so a new record is allocated at the end of the file. The free record chain pointer (link field of record number 367) and the variable *HighestRecord%* are updated accordingly in this case.

This completes my discussion of how the appointment calendar program works. As I have already mentioned, the guts of this program will be reused later when the user interface is extended to a Macintosh style. Study the program listing and accompanying figures carefully, and be sure you understand how the program works in its current form. This is important, because the program becomes much more complex when reincarnated in later chapters.

File Types

Each Macintosh disk file has an attribute called its *file type*. The file type identifies how the file was created and how it can be used. If you are an experienced Macintosh user, you are probably aware that MacPaint will only open MacPaint documents, MacWrite will only open MacWrite documents, and so on. In fact, Microsoft BASIC will only open Microsoft BASIC documents. In general, each Macintosh application defines a file type that it will work with.

Most applications have an Open function in the File pull-down menu that will display all files of the appropriate type available on the current disk. Since Microsoft BASIC gives you the ability to create and access disk files, it also gives you some control over the file type attribute of those files.

The file type attribute is a four character string. All files created by your BASIC programs will have a default file type of TEXT. You can set the file type attribute of any file from within BASIC by using the *NAME* statement. The primary purpose of this statement is actually to rename the file, but the ability to set the file's type is provided at the same time. The format of the NAME statement is as follows

`NAME oldfilename AS newfilename, filetype`

For example, the statement

`NAME "CHECKS" AS "CHECKS1984", "OLDC"`

would change the name of disk file "CHECKS" to "CHECKS1984" and simultaneously change its file type to "OLDC." You can make up your own file types in order to classify different files created by different programs.

Through use of the **FILE$** function, which is described in the following section, you can limit access by a program to only those files that are of a specific type.

The file type TEXT is of special interest, because it usually represents a general file structure that is used by many applications.

When you save a BASIC program with the Text option (see Chapter 1), the file type TEXT is used. In addition, many word processing programs allow you to save documents as "text" or "ASCII-only"; these formats represent the TEXT file type.

Most of these applications define a TEXT file as a very simple structure. The file is a sequential one, in which each record represents a line (or perhaps a paragraph) of text. The length of each record in the file is not constant. Each record is terminated by a single carriage return character (CHR$(13)). This simple structure makes it easy to write a BASIC program and to list the contents of the file. Such a program will be introduced in the following section.

The FILES$ Dialog Boxes

Earlier I mentioned the File Open function as it appears in many familiar Macintosh application programs. While establishing the Macintosh user interface, one of Apple's basic ground rules was to provide the user with a consistent way of doing things across many different applications. A fine example of this is the file open dialog box shown in Figure 4-28.

Figure 4-28
File Open Dialog Box, Type 1

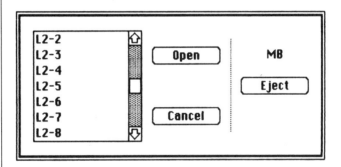

I am sure that you are by now familiar with using this dialog box, as almost every Mac program makes use of it in one way or another. Fortunately for us, Microsoft felt that we should be able to use this dialog box in our programs as well. They therefore provided the special Macintosh function FILES$.

The **FILES$** function is a built-in character string function (that is, it returns a character string result when referenced). When the **FILES$** function is referenced in a program, it causes a file open dialog box to be presented to the user. The program does not proceed until the user enters the data requested by the dialog box, or clicks the dialog box cancel button with the mouse.

The character string returned by the function describes the actions taken by the user on the dialog box. A **FILES$** function reference should look like one of the following

```
stringvariable$ = FILES$(0,prompt
string)
```

```
stringvariable$ = FILES$(1,file type
string)
```

The two different formats allow two different kinds of file open dialog boxes to be used. When the first argument of **FILES$** is 0, the dialog box displays a message to the user and allows him to manually enter a file name. Save, Cancel, and Eject buttons are provided. The message displayed in the dialog box is specified as the second argument of the function reference. For example, the statement

```
x$ = FILES$(0,"Tell me what file to use
please")
```

will cause the dialog box shown in Figure 4-29 to be presented to the user.

Figure 4-29
*File Open Dialog Box,
Type 0*

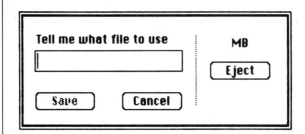

Note that the dialog box only has room for the first 24 characters of the prompt string. The Save button is dimmed until some text is entered from the keyboard. After entering text, pressing the <Return> key will have the same effect as clicking the Save button. The dialog box also displays the name of the current disk (in this case, "MB").

An Eject button allows the user to eject the current disk and replace it with a different disk. If you have more than one disk drive attached to the Mac, the dialog box will appear as shown in Figure 4-30. In this case, one additional button, labelled "Drive," will be present. This button allows you to select either disk drive for the filename that you specify. If only one of the drives actually has a disk inserted, then the Drive button will be dimmed and unusable.

The program does not proceed until the user exits from the dialog box either by supplying a file name or clicking the Cancel button. The file name supplied is returned as a character string value to the caller of the **FILES$** function. This character string will contain the disk name followed by a colon and then the file name (e.g., "MB:TestFile").

In this format, with the disk name preceding the file name, the entire string can be used in an OPEN statement. In multiple disk systems, you can automatically reference files on more than one disk in this fashion. I do not recommend using the disk name feature in a one drive system, however. This results in numerous requests to swap disks, which rapidly becomes frustrating for the user. If the dialog box is exited via the Cancel button, the **FILES$** function returns a null string.

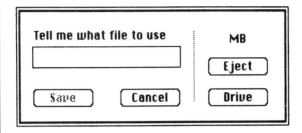

Figure 4-30
File Open Dialog Box, Type 0, with Two Disk Drives in System

When the first argument of **FILES$** is 1, the other style of file open dialog box is displayed. This style of dialog box is shown in Figure 4-28. In this case, the dialog box presents the user with a list of files and allows him to select the particular file desired. A prompt string is not displayed. Instead of a prompt string, we can pass a file type string to the **FILES$** function.

The file type string specifies one or more types of files. Only files that match the file type(s) specified are displayed in the dialog box. If the file type string is not supplied, then all files on the disk are displayed. Each file type must be specified as a four-character string; multiple types are simply concatenated as needed. Thus, for example, the statement

```
x$ = FILES$(1,"OLDCNEWCTEXT")
```

provides a list of all files of types "OLDC," "NEWC," or "TEXT" on the current disk. As with the other dialog box, an Eject button allows the user to swap disks. The file name selected is returned by the function, preceded by the disk name. If the Cancel button is clicked, the function returns a null string. A Drive button appears if more than one disk drive is available in the system.

In Listing 4-11, the **FILES$** function is used to create a general purpose text file read program. The program begins by presenting

Listing 4-11
General Purpose Text File Read Program

```
' Illustrates use of the FILES$ function to create a file
' open dialog box.
f$=FILES$(1,"TEXT")
IF f$="" THEN END
OPEN "I",1,f$
PRINT "File ";f$;" contains ";LOF(1);" bytes."
PRINT "Contents of file :"
PRINT
i=0
WHILE NOT EOF(1)
a$=INPUT$(1,#1)
PRINT a$;
IF a$=CHR$(13) THEN i=i+1
WEND
CLOSE 1
PRINT "***** End of File, total records = ";i
END
```

the user with a dialog box displaying all files of type TEXT on the current disk. The user selects one of these and clicks the Open button. The program opens the file, and displays the file name and its size in bytes (obtained from the LOF function).

The program then displays each line of text in the file. The file is read one character at a time by use of the INPUT$ function, and the characters so received are simply output to the display. Individual file records are delimited by the carriage return character; this fact is used to keep a count of the number of records (text lines) as the file is read. When the end of the file is reached, the total number of records in the file is displayed.

Chapter 5

BASIC Graphics

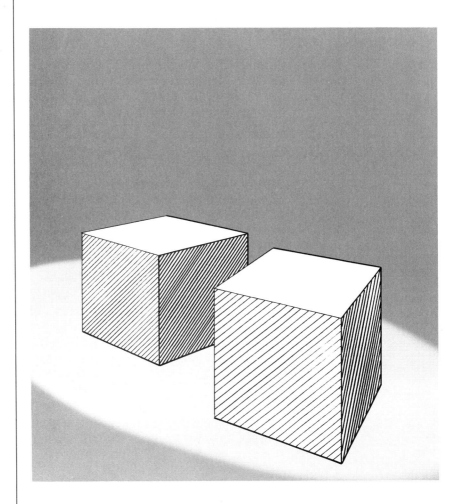

Straight out of the box, the Macintosh computer truly excels in graphics capabilities that are easily accessible to the user. Creating graphics from within a BASIC program requires considerably more time and planning, however, than simply drawing a picture with MacPaint. In spite of this, you will find that the effort is well spent. The power of custom-made software combined with the Mac's graphics can produce some truly remarkable results.

Microsoft BASIC for the Macintosh includes two general classes of statements for creating graphics images. The first class is a set of Microsoft BASIC graphics statements, most of which are available in other implementations of Microsoft BASIC for other computers (such as the IBM PC). This class includes such statements as LINE, CIRCLE, and PSET. If you have worked with Microsoft BASIC graphics before, these will be familiar to you.

The second class of graphics statements are, at least for now, unique to the Macintosh. Most of these correspond very closely to a set of routines called the Macintosh *Toolbox*, which is resident in the ROM of the machine. In this chapter, I cover the first class of graphics statements. The second class will be covered later, in Chapter 7.

Pixels and Graphics Coordinates

The Macintosh screen uses a technology called raster scan display. All displays using this technology can be represented as a simple matrix of individual dots, or picture elements. Since talking about "dots" doesn't sound very impressive, the term pixel (short for picture element) is usually used.

With the current Macintosh screen, you can address each individual pixel and set it to either black or white. From within a BASIC program, you can access pixels only within an Output window.

Individual pixels within an Output window are addressed using a very simple coordinate system. Each pixel location is defined by a pair of coordinates. There is an x-coordinate (horizontal coordinate) and a y-coordinate (vertical coordinate).

In Microsoft BASIC graphics statements, the two coordinates are separated by a comma and enclosed in parentheses. The x-coordinate always appears first. Thus, the coordinate expression

```
(5,9)
```

would refer to the pixel at horizontal coordinate 5 and vertical coordinate 9. Coordinate (0,0) is always the upper left corner of the Output window being accessed. This scheme is illustrated by Figure 5-1.

The simplest graphics statement is the *PSET* statement, which allows you to set a specific pixel in the Output window to either black or white. Its format is as follows

```
PSET (x-coord, y-coord), color
```

The statement specifies the pixel location as a coordinate pair, and the color as a value of either 30 or 33. The value 30 represents white, and the value 33 represents black. If color is not specified, black is used.

An almost identical statement is the *PRESET* statement. The PRESET statement has the same format and function, except if the color is not specified, white is used. Normally, the color parameter is not specified, and PSET is used to set pixels (to black) while PRESET is used to reset pixels (to white).

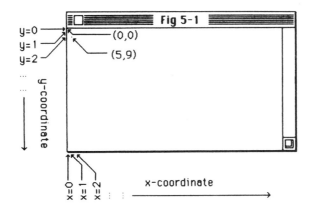

Either statement can be used with the color parameter in cases where it is necessary to reference a particular pixel and set its color to a value that is determined dynamically (that is, at the time the program runs).

Listing 5-1 shows how the PSET statement can be used to produce a plot of the **LOG** function. Note the way this program scales the y-coordinate. This is necessary for two reasons. First, the value returned by the **LOG** function has a range that is too small to show the detail of the curve on the screen. This is handled by multiplying it by 25.

Listing 5-1
Using the PSET
Statement

```
' Note the scaling of the y-coordinate.
CLS
LOCATE 1,10
PRINT "THE LOG FUNCTION"
FOR x=1 TO 400
y=LOG(x)
y=150-(y*25)
PSET (x,y)
NEXT
```

Second, the y-coordinate on the screen increases in value as you go down the screen. Since the graphs that we are used to viewing normally have the y-coordinate increasing as we look up towards the top of the graph, an additional adjustment must be made. This is accomplished by simply subtracting the y-coordinate value from 150, which is the largest value it will reach for the programmed x-coordinate range. This results in the conventional graph shown in Figure 5-2.

Figure 5-2
Plotting the LOG Function

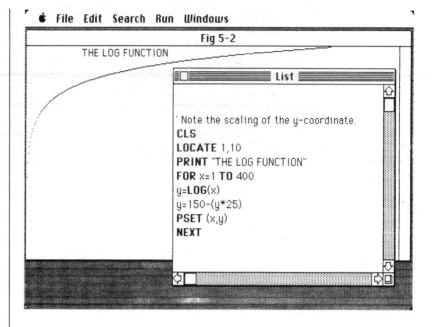

Figure 5-2
Plotting the LOG Function

While a program is running, BASIC keeps track of the last graphics coordinate referenced at any time. Instead of specifying a pixel location by *absolute* coordinates, as I have done above, you can specify it relative to the previously referenced pixel location. To do this, you use *relative* coordinates.

Relative coordinates are used by simply prefacing the coordinate expression with the keyword STEP. For example, the statement

```
PSET STEP (3,1)
```

would set the location three pixels to the right and one pixel below the last referenced location. That location would then become the last referenced location for any subsequent relative coordinate. Negative values may be used in relative coordinates. A negative x value means that many pixels to the left of the previous location; a negative y value means that many pixels above the previous location.

Prior to using a relative coordinate reference, at least one absolute coordinate reference must be made. Figure 5-3 shows an example of how relative coordinates can be used.

The Point Function

The **POINT** function can be used to interrogate the current state of any pixel in the Output window. The **POINT** function requires two arguments that represent a pair of absolute pixel coordinates. It returns the numeric value 30 if the specified location currently contains a white pixel, or the value 33 for a black pixel. For example, the statement

```
color = POINT(10,20)
```

will set variable color to the current color of the pixel at horizontal coordinate 10, vertical coordinate 20. If a pixel location that lies outside the current Output window is referenced, the POINT function will return a value of –1. You could therefore use the function to determine the size of the current Output window. This is not necessary, however, since Microsoft provides a special WINDOW function for that purpose (described in Chapter 8).

Figure 5-3
Relative Coordinate Example

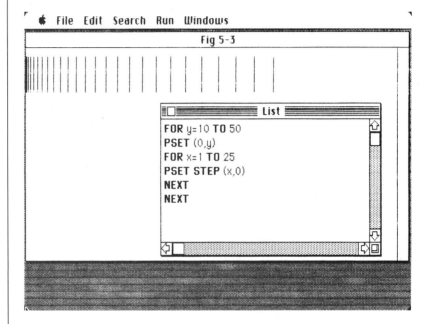

The "animated pixel" program in Listing 5-2 utilizes the graphics functions introduced so far to produce an amusing display. By allowing a set of FOR-NEXT loops to cycle through a sequence of adjacent pixel coordinates, lines can be easily drawn. In this fashion, a box is drawn on the Output window. The random function is then employed to draw a set of "walls" within the box. The walls are of varying length and are placed at random locations within the box. Finally, a random point within the box is selected and the "animated pixel" is displayed.

The pixel is moved about on the screen in a direction which is also determined randomly. To produce the animation effect, the new location of the pixel is calculated, then a PRESET statement erases the pixel from its old location and a PSET statement places it at the new location.

The **POINT** function is used to detect when the pixel is about to collide with a wall. When this occurs, the *BEEP* statement is used to produce an audible beep, and a new random direction is choosen for the pixel.

The Line Statement
In the preceding example, I placed the PSET statement in a loop to produce a line of pixels across the display. This is not necessary,

however, as BASIC provides a *LINE* statement. The LINE statement can be used to rapidly produce lines, boxes, and filled boxes. The simplest form of the LINE statement is as follows

```
LINE (x1,y1)-(x2,y2)
```

This statement specifies two pixel coordinates; a line is drawn between these two locations on the screen. By default, the line is drawn in black. You can specify a color value, as follows

```
LINE (x1,y1)-(x2,y2),color
```

```
' This program causes a single pixel to move in a random manner
' around the screen.  Initially the pixel is placed in the middle
' of a box.  The pixel is not allowed to escape the box.
' Several walls are placed inside the box, the pixel bounces off
' these walls when it encounters them.  The program produces an
' audible "beep" whenever the pixel bounces.
DEF FNrand(l,u)=CINT(l+RND(1)*(u-l))
RANDOMIZE TIMER
' draw the enclosing box :
FOR x=5 TO 400
PSET (x,5)
PSET (x,250)
NEXT
FOR y=5 TO 250
PSET (5,y)
PSET (400,y)
NEXT
' draw a bunch of randomly located and sized walls :
FOR walls = 1 TO 20
x=FNrand(50,350)
y=FNrand(50,200)
d=FNrand(1,4)
IF d=1 THEN dx=1 : dy=0
IF d=2 THEN dx=-1 : dy=0
IF d=3 THEN dx=0 : dy=1
IF d=4 THEN dx=0 : dy=-1
size=FNrand(15,40)
PSET (x,y)
FOR draw=1 TO size
x=x+dx
y=y+dy
PSET (x,y)
NEXT
NEXT
' all walls have been set up.
TryAgain:       'pick a random starting point for the roving pixel :
x=FNrand(20,300)
y=FNrand(20,200)
IF POINT(x,y)=33 THEN GOTO TryAgain 'dont start the pixel inside a wall !
PSET (x,y)
NewDirection:   'select a random (diagonal) direction for the pixel to move in :
d=FNrand(1,4)
IF d=1 THEN dx=1 : dy=1
IF d=2 THEN dx=1 : dy=-1
IF d=3 THEN dx=-1 : dy=1
IF d=4 THEN dx=-1 : dy=-1
Again:       'move the pixel in the selected direction until it hits a wall
newx=x+dx
newy=y+dy
PRESET (x,y)
IF POINT (newx,newy) = 33 THEN BEEP : GOTO NewDirection
x=newx
y=newy
PSET (x,y)
GOTO Again
```

As before, a color value of 30 represents white, and a color value of 33 represents black. Figure 5-4 illustrates the effect of this form of LINE statement.

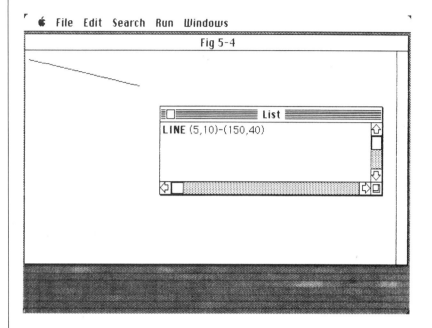

Relative Coordinates

Either coordinate in the LINE statement may be specified as a relative coordinate, simply by prefacing it with the keyword STEP. A relative first coordinate is always relative to the last graphics pixel location referenced. A relative second coordinate will always be relative to the first coordinate in the same LINE statement. Thus, for example, the statement

```
LINE (5,5)-STEP(95,65)
```

will draw a line from coordinates (5,5) to (100,70).

The Box and Box Filled Options

The LINE statement can also be used to produce outlined and solid boxes on the display. This is accomplished by appending an additional parameter to the LINE statement. This parameter is specified as either "B" for an outlined box, or "BF" for a filled (solid) box.

The two pixel locations specified in the LINE statement represent the diagonal corners of the box when these options are used. Examples are shown in Figure 5-5. Note the double comma between the second coodinate and the B/BF specification. The double comma indicates that the color parameter is not specified, thus the default color of black is used. If desired, a color specification can be placed in the statement; in this case, boxes of either black or white can be produced.

Figure 5-5
*The Box and Box Filled
Options*

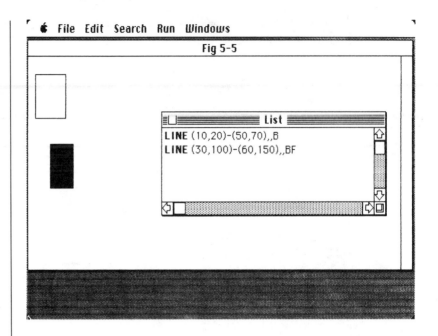

Sample Programs

In Listing 5-3, LINE statements with and without the box option
are combined with a little trigonometry to produce a three-
dimensional image of a cube. The user enters the size of the cube as
a single dimension in pixels (d). The program then draws the cube,
using the specified dimension for each edge.

Listing 5-3
*Producing a Three-
Dimensional Image*

```
' This program produces the image of a cube on the
' Macintosh display.  The length (in pixels) of each
' cube dimension is supplied by the user when the
' program starts.
Retry:
INPUT "Enter cube dimension in pixels ";d
IF d<10 OR d>100 THEN PRINT "Invalid dimension" : GOTO Retry
' Draw back face of cube :
LINE (20,20)-STEP(d,d),,B
' Calculate offset to front face of cube, 3rd dimension must = d :
offset=d*COS(3.14159/4)*COS(3.14159/4)
' Draw front face of cube :
LINE (20+offset,20+offset)-STEP(d,d),,B
' Now connect front face to back face :
LINE (20,20)-(20+offset,20+offset)
LINE (20,20+d)-(20+offset,20+d+offset)
LINE (20+d,20)-(20+d+offset,20+offset)
LINE (20+d,20+d)-(20+d+offset,20+d+offset)
END
```

First, the back face of the cube is drawn, using a simple LINE
statement with the box option. The offset from the corner of the
back face to the corner of the front face is calculated as the cosine
of 45 degrees (pi/4) times the user specified dimension. This value
is multiplied once again by the cosine of 45 degrees to take into

account the fact that each screen pixel is a perfect square (thus the diagonal dimension of a single pixel is 1/cos 45 times its height or width). This calculation assures that the connecting lines drawn from the back face to the front face will be appear to be "d" pixels long. Using this offset, the front face is drawn, again with the box option. Finally, four LINE statements are used to connect the back face corners to the front face. A sample run is shown in Figure 5-6.

In Listing 5-4, LINE statements are combined with random numbers to produce a constantly changing display image. The LINE statement is used to produce a filled box, with the coordinates of the box choosen at random. For each box, a random number from 1 to 6 is selected. If the number is 1 or 2, the box is drawn in white, otherwise it is drawn in black. This results in twice as many black boxes as white boxes, on the average. Run the program on your own Macintosh to see the effect produced.

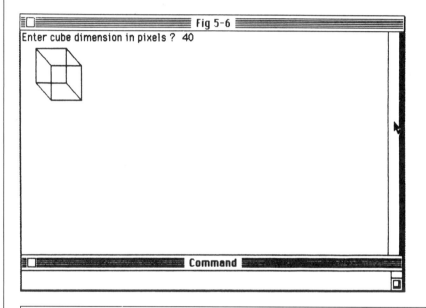

```
DEF FNrand(l,u)=CINT(1+RND(1)*(u-1))
RANDOMIZE TIMER
Again:
x1=FNrand(1,400)
y1=FNrand(1,250)
x2=FNrand(1,400)
y2=FNrand(1,250)
color=FNrand(1,6)
IF color <3 THEN color=30 ELSE color=33
LINE (x1,y1)-(x2,y2),color,BF
GOTO Again
```

Listing 5-5 employs a sequence of closely spaced LINE statements to produce beautiful moire patterns on your Macintosh screen. The program works by selecting at random a point somewhere near the center of the screen. Lines are then drawn from this point to the outer edge of the screen. When the image is complete, the program uses the built-in function **TIMER** to produce a five second pause, then goes on to produce a different pattern. Figure 5-7 shows an example of one of the patterns produced by this program.

Listing 5-5
Producing Moire Patterns

```
DEF FNrand(1,u)=CINT(1+RND(1)*(u-1))
RANDOMIZE TIMER
Again:
CLS
x1=FNrand(100,200)
y1=FNrand(75,150)
FOR x2=0 TO 400 STEP 2
LINE (x1,y1)-(x2,0)
NEXT
FOR y2=0 TO 250 STEP 2
LINE (x1,y1)-(400,y2)
NEXT
FOR x2=400 TO 0 STEP -2
LINE (x1,y1)-(x2,250)
NEXT
FOR y2=250 TO 0 STEP -2
LINE (x1,y1)-(0,y2)
NEXT
' now wait about five seconds before doing another
t=TIMER
Delay:
IF TIMER<t+5 THEN GOTO Delay
GOTO Again
```

Figure 5-7
Moire Pattern

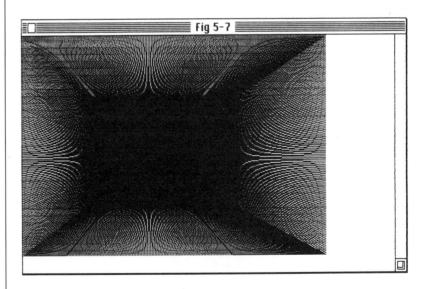
Fig 5-7

The Circle Statement

The *CIRCLE* statement can be used to draw circles, ellipses, arcs, or pie pieces (i.e., segments of a circle). The simplest form of the CIRCLE statement is as follows

```
CIRCLE (x,y),radius
```

In this statement, the coordinates (x,y) specify the center of the circle, and the radius specifies the circle's radius, in pixels. The coordinates can be specified as relative to the last referenced graphics location by using the STEP option. In any event, after the CIRCLE statement has been executed, the last referenced graphics location is taken to be the center of the circle. A simple example of the CIRCLE statement is shown in Figure 5-8.

Figure 5-8
A Simple CIRCLE Statement

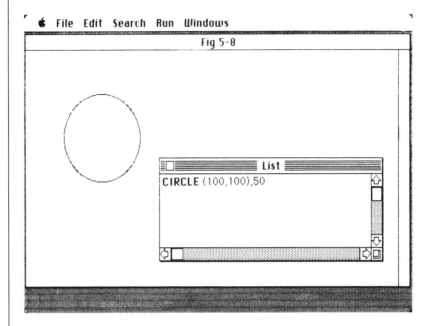

Once again, the default color for the CIRCLE statement is black. It can be specified, however, as follows

```
CIRCLE (x,y),radius,color
```

As usual, a color value of 30 represents white, and a color value of 33 represents black.

Drawing Arcs

By specifying a start and end angle, it is possible to draw only a portion of a circle, the result being an arc. The start and stop angles are specified in radians on the CIRCLE statement as follows

```
CIRCLE (x,y),radius,color,start,stop
```

The start and stop values use the conventional mathematical coordinate system where zero degrees is due east, 90 degrees due north, 180 degrees west, and so on. This coordinate system is shown in Figure 5-9. Thus, for example, the statement

```
CIRCLE (x,y),radius,,0,pi/2
```

would draw a quarter circle arc (assuming variable pi was set to 3.14159). An example is shown in Figure 5-10. Note the use of two commas to skip the specification of the color parameter. This causes the default color of black to be used.

In Listing 5-6, a sequence of CIRCLE statements is used to produce the image of a nautilus shell. This is accomplished by continually increasing the circle radius while simultaneously increasing the size of the arc drawn. The result is shown in Figure 5-11.

Figure 5-9
*Coordinate System for
Start and Stop Angles*

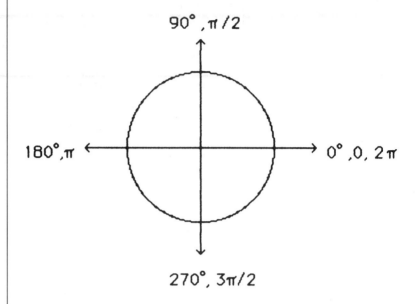

Figure 5-10
*Using CIRCLE to
Produce an Arc*

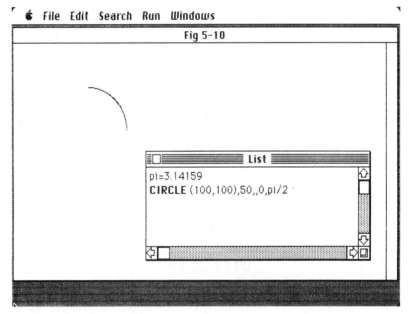

Listing 5-6
*Producing a Nautilus
Shell Image*

```
' The radius of the circle is continually increased as the
' size of the arc increases.
Pi=3.14159
Radius=10
FOR Angle=1 TO 360 STEP 5
StopAngle=Angle*Pi/180
CIRCLE (100,100),Radius,,0,StopAngle
Radius=Radius+1
NEXT
```

Figure 5-11
A Nautilus Shell

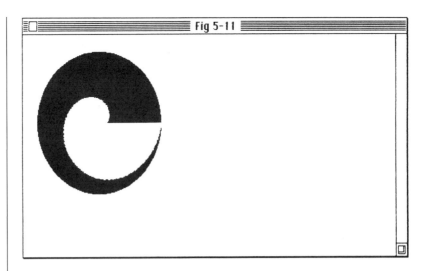

Drawing Pie Pieces

By preceding the start and stop angles in a CIRCLE statement with
a minus sign, you request that BASIC draw connecting lines from
the ends of the arc to the circle's center. The result is a pie piece. An
example is shown in Figure 5-12.

Figure 5-12
A Simple Pie Piece

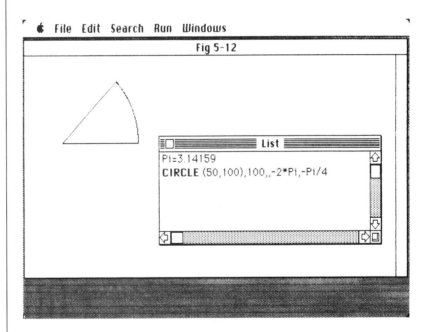

Note that the start angle was specified as 2pi instead of as zero.
This is because BASIC cannot detect that the value zero is negated.
In all other respects, an angle of 2pi is equivalent to an angle of
zero.

When you negate angles in a CIRCLE statement for the purpose
of creating pie pieces, the angle values are still interpreted as if they
were positive. The fact that they are negative is only used to indicate
that the connecting lines to the center should be drawn. It is

important to understand this concept, because in standard mathematics an angle such as −pi/2 is interpreted as reverse (i.e. clockwise) rotation, and represents a true angle of +3pi/2. This is not the case here.

One good use for the pie piece option of the CIRCLE statement is the creation of pie charts. A program to do this is shown in Listing 5-7. This is only the first version of this program, as I will be enhancing it later in the book.

Listing 5-7
The Pie Chart Program
— Version 1

```
' This program allows the user to enter up to six values that
' represent percentages. The total of all values entered must
' equal 100 percent. The program then produces a pie chart using
' the CIRCLE statement with negative start and end angles.
' In a subsequent version, labels will be added to the various
' circle pieces. See text for further information.
'
DIM pc(6)          ' Array pc holds each pie piece percentage
Pi=3.14159
' Obtain user input :
Retry:
INPUT "How many items in the pie chart ";Items
IF Items<2 OR Items>6 THEN PRINT "Invalid number of Items" : GOTO Retry
FOR i=1 TO Items
PRINT "Enter percentage for item ";i;
INPUT pc(i)
NEXT
' Check for valid input data :
Total=0
FOR i=1 TO Items
Total=Total+pc(i)
NEXT
IF Total<>100 THEN PRINT "Invalid input, total does not equal 100%" : GOTO Retry
' Produce pie chart :
CLS
StartAngle=0
FOR i=1 TO Items
EndAngle=StartAngle+(2*Pi*pc(i)/100)
IF StartAngle=0 THEN ST=2*Pi ELSE ST=StartAngle    'zero is a special case
CIRCLE (100,110),75,,-ST,-EndAngle                 'draw the pie piece
StartAngle=EndAngle                                'set up for next pie piece
NEXT
LOCATE 15,1
PRINT "Do another ? (Y/N) "
GOSUB GetYN
IF yn$="Y" THEN CLS : GOTO Retry
END
'
' Subroutine to wait until the user presses either the Y or N keys,
' in response to a yes or no question. Will not return until one of these
' keys is pressed. The keystroke character is returned in yn$.
GetYN:
yn$=INKEY$
WHILE UCASE$(yn$)<>"Y" AND UCASE$(yn$)<>"N"
yn$=INKEY$
WEND
yn$=UCASE$(yn$)
RETURN
```

The program accepts user input describing the way the pie chart should appear. The input consists of a list of items; there may be from 2 to 6 items in the list. Each item represents a percentage of the whole. The sum of all items in the list must total 100%. Once this data is supplied, the program uses the CIRCLE statement to produce a circle divided into pie pieces sized to represent the various percentages. Figure 5-13 shows a sample input session with this program and Figure 5-14 shows the pie chart produced as a result.

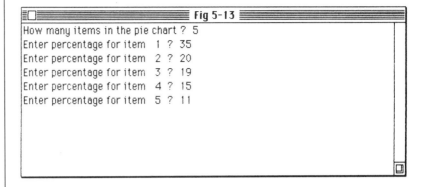

```
How many items in the pie chart ?  5
Enter percentage for item  1  ?  35
Enter percentage for item  2  ?  20
Enter percentage for item  3  ?  19
Enter percentage for item  4  ?  15
Enter percentage for item  5  ?  11
```

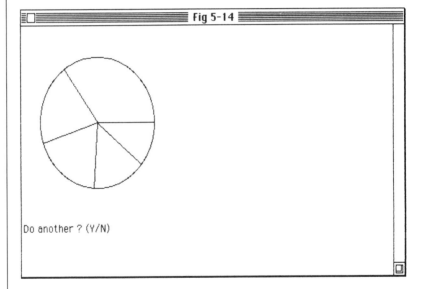

Do another ? (Y/N)

The program begins by requesting the number of items in the user's data; this value goes into variable Items. The percentage for each item is then input into array pc. A FOR-NEXT loop sums the array entries and insures that they total 100%; if not, an error is reported. The program begins producing the pie pieces that will make up the chart. The beginning StartAngle is set to zero, and a FOR-NEXT loop is entered.

For each item in the input data, an EndAngle is calculated as the current StartAngle plus that item's percentage of a whole circle (2pi, or 360 degrees). The pie piece for that item is then drawn using the CIRCLE statement with the start and stop angles negated. Note the special check for a start angle of zero prior to the CIRCLE statement. In this special case, 2pi is substituted to allow the negation sign to have effect. Once the pie piece is drawn, its

EndAngle becomes the new StartAngle. In this fashion, the complete chart is produced.

The program uses the by now familiar subroutine GetYN to allow the user to produce another chart or quit. Later in the book, I show you how to add labels to each of the pie pieces. This makes the program more valuable.

Changing the Aspect Ratio

There is one more parameter that can be added to the CIRCLE statement. It is called the aspect ratio, and it appears after the end angle parameter. If the color, start angle, and/or end angle parameters are not used, then the appropriate number of commas must precede the aspect ratio parameter,

```
CIRCLE (x,y),radius,,,,aspect
```

When not specified, the aspect ratio defaults to one. This produces the perfectly symmetrical circle that I have shown in the previous examples. The aspect ratio represents the ratio of the horizontal dimension of the circle to its vertical dimension. Thus, an aspect ratio less than one will produce an ellipse that is elongated at the sides and compressed at the top and bottom, as shown in Figure 5-15.

An aspect ratio greater than one will produce an ellipse that is elongated at the top and bottom and compressed at the sides, as shown in Figure 5-16.

Figure 5-15
Ellipse Produced Using Aspect Ratio Less Than One

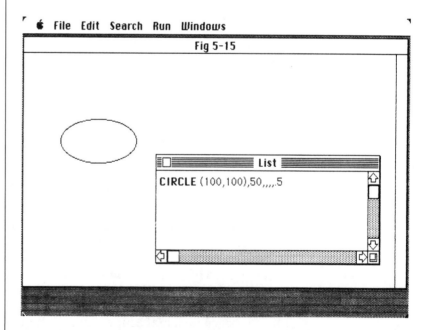

Animating Graphics Images

Microsoft BASIC provides a set of special statements that enable you to animate graphics images on the Macintosh screen. The statements that allow you to do this are called the graphics GET and PUT statements. Although these statements begin with the same GET and PUT keywords as random file i/o statements (see Chapter 4), they have a completely different function.

BASIC automatically distinguishes between random file and graphics GET and PUT statements by the syntax of the operands that follow the keywords. It is important that you, as a BASIC programmer, also be able to distinguish between these two types of statements.

Figure 5-16
Ellipse Produced Using Aspect Ratio Greater Than One

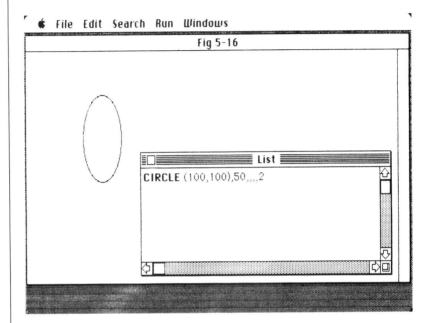

The graphics GET statement allows you to capture a graphics image from the screen and store it as a set of data values in an array variable. Conversely, the graphics PUT statement allows you to take such data stored in an array and place it on the screen for display. Both GET and PUT statements allow you to specify exactly what portion of the current Output window is to be acted upon.

By executing multiple PUT statements at different locations, you can rapidly reproduce an image in several places on the screen. If you execute a sequence of PUT statements, changing the location slightly for each subsequent PUT, and erasing the previous image at the same time, you can create the effect of an image moving across the screen. Sample programs illustrating these techniques follow.

The Graphics GET Statement

The graphics *GET* statement specifies a rectangular area in the current Output window. The contents of this area will be captured and saved by the execution of the statement. The rectangular area is specified by a pair of graphics coordinates, as follows

```
(x1,y1)-(x2,y2)
```

The coordinate (x1,y1) specifies the upper left corner of the rectangle, and the coordinate (x2,y2) specifies the lower right corner. The graphics data present within the rectangle is stored in an array variable that must also be specified on the GET statement. For best results, I recommend using only integer array variables for this purpose.

The array must be dimensioned to contain enough elements to store all of the graphics data in the rectangle. The size of the array therefore depends upon the size of the rectangle, and is given by the formula shown in Listing 5-8. This formula yields the number of elements of an integer array needed to store the graphics data contained in a rectangle of a specific size.

```
' The array size depends upon the size of the rectangular area to
' be captured.  ONLY INTEGER ARRAYS SHOULD BE USED ! ! !
' For a statement such as :
'              GET (x1,y1)-(x2,y2),Image%
' The array Image% should be dimensioned to contain
'              (4+(((y2-y1)+1)*2*INT(((x2-x1)+16)/16)))/2
' elements.  Don't forget that subscript 0 will be the first element
' of the array to be used, thus the value in the DIM statement can be
' one less than the value returned by the formula.

DEF FNasiz(x1,x2,y1,y2)=(4+(((y2-y1)+1)*2*INT(((x2-x1)+16)/16)))/2
PRINT "Graphics GET array size calculation"
PRINT
INPUT "Enter upper left coordinate (x1,y1) ";x1,y1
INPUT "Enter lower right coordinate (x2,y2) ";x2,y2
PRINT "To capture an image of that size, you need an"
PRINT "integer array with ";FNasiz(x1,x2,y1,y2);" elements."
END
```

Note that the GET statement fills the array starting with subscript 0, so the number specified in the DIM statement can be one less than the number given by the formula. For example, suppose you want to capture graphics data within the area defined by the coordinates

```
(5,5)-(35,35)
```

Plugging these values into the formula (or just running Listing 5-8), you find that you need 64 elements. You can thus define your array as follows

```
DIM Image%(63)
```

The complete GET statement would look like this

```
GET (5,5)-(35,35),Image%
```

The statement specifies the coordinates of the rectangular area, as well as the name of the array to be used. Compare the syntax of this statement to the random file i/o GET statement described in Chapter 4.

The Graphics PUT Statement

Once an image has been captured with the GET statement, it can be redisplayed anywhere on the current Output window by using the *PUT* statement. The PUT statement specifies a single coordinate that represents where the upper left corner of the rectangular image should be placed. The array containing the image is, of couse, also specified. The syntax is as follows

```
PUT (x,y),arrayname
```

In Figure 5-17, the basic operation of graphics GET and PUT is demonstrated. The array *Image%* is dimensioned, and then a CIRCLE statement is used to produce the image of a circle centered at (20,20) and with a radius of 10. The rectangle defined by the coordinates

```
(5,5)-(35,35)
```

completely encloses the image of the circle. A GET statement is used to capture the image in array *Image%*. The image is then redisplayed with a PUT statement. The PUT statement specifies that the image in *Image%* be displayed so that its upper left corner is aligned to coordinate (30,30). This results in the second circle (lower and to the right of the first) shown in the figure.

Creating Multiple Images

The program in Listing 5-9 shows one way that the GET and PUT statements can be used. This program draws the image of a smiling face, and then captures it using the GET statement. The screen is then cleared using the CLS statement. A graphics PUT statement within a pair of nested FOR-NEXT loops is then employed to produce many copies of the smiling face image at evenly spaced intervals. The result is a screen that rapidly fills with smiling faces as shown in Figure 5-18.

The image of the face used in this program is produced by a combination of CIRCLE, LINE, and PSET statements. The first CIRCLE statement is the same as was used in Figure 5-17, and produces the outline of the face. A pair of LINE statements then produces the eyes, and then a LINE and a PSET statement produce the nose.

Finally, a CIRCLE statement draws an arc to represent the mouth. The CIRCLE statement uses the same center as the first CIRCLE statement, but a smaller radius. The statement specifies start and stop angles of 220 and 340 degrees, respectively. This results in an arc that is well positioned and sized for the mouth of the face. The entire image fits within the same rectangle that was used in the simple demo of Figure 5-17.

Changing the Dimensions of an Image

The PUT statement allows you to change the dimensions of the image being displayed. To do this, you specify a pair of coordinates instead of a single coordinate on the PUT statement. This pair of coordinates defines a rectangular area in which the image should be displayed. The horizontal and/or vertical dimensions of this rectangle can be different from those of the rectangle used to GET the image.

The PUT statement will automatically scale the image specified to fit into the area specified. This feature can thus be used to grow, shrink, or stretch an image. In Figure 5-19, the same smiling face image is drawn and captured using the GET statement, then redrawn using this new form of the PUT statement. In this example, both the horizontal and vertical dimensions are increased uniformly. The result is a well proportioned, but larger, image of the smiling face.

Figure 5-17
Basic Operation of Graphics GET and PUT

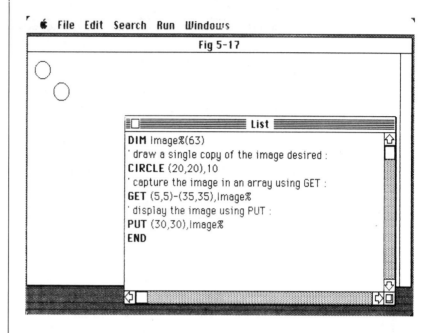

Listing 5-9
Demo of Graphics GET and PUT

```
' This program uses the graphics GET and PUT statements
' to produce multiple copies of a predefined image.
' The image in this example is that of a smiling face and is
' created using the CIRCLE, LINE and PSET statements.
pi=3.14159
DIM Image%(63)
' draw a single copy of the image desired :
CIRCLE (20,20),10              'the face outline
LINE (14,16)-(16,16)          'left eye
LINE (24,16)-(26,16)          'right eye
LINE (20,18)-(20,21)          'nose
PSET (19,21)                  'nose
CIRCLE (20,20),6,,220*pi/180,340*pi/180   'mouth
' capture the image in an array using GET :
GET (5,5)-(35,35),Image%
' now clear the screen and make multiple copies of the image :
CLS
FOR y=10 TO 210 STEP 40
FOR x=20 TO 400 STEP 40
PUT (x,y),Image%
NEXT
NEXT
END
```

By increasing one dimension to a greater extent than the other, "stretched" images can be created. Examples are shown in Figures

5-20 and 5-21. The base image in each case is the same, original smiling face.

Figure 5-18
Duplicating Images with GET and PUT

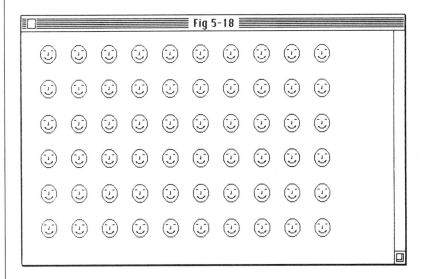

Figure 5-19
Growing an Image with GET and PUT

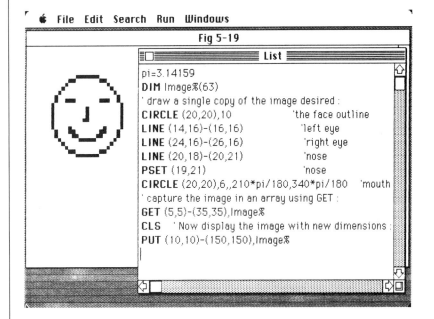

Image Transfer Modes

Up to this point, I have allowed the graphics PUT statement to use its default image transfer mode. In general, however, there are five different image transfer modes that can be used with the PUT statement. The modes determine the way in which the image is placed on the screen. This controls how the image will affect, or will be affected by, any previous graphics data already present in the relevant area of the screen.

Different modes can be used to produce different kinds of special effects, and an understanding of the modes is vital to the production of animation effects. To be able to understand the modes, however, you must first understand how the graphics data is represented within the Macintosh.

Figure 5-20
Stretching the Image Horizontally

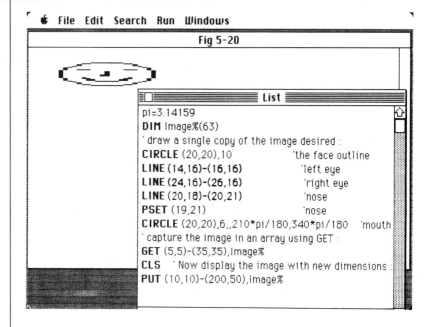

Figure 5-21
Stretching the Image Vertically

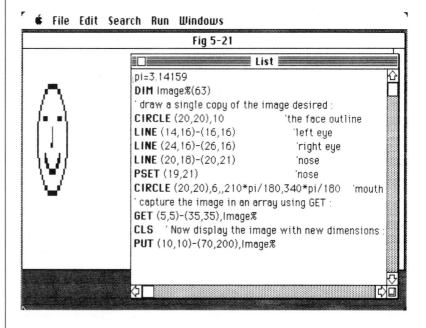

Each graphics pixel on the Macintosh screen is represented by a single bit in the Macintosh memory. As you should already know, a bit is the smallest unit of information storage within a computer, and can take on either the value 0 or the value 1. The Macintosh display hardware is set up so that bits containing zeros represent white pixels, while bits containing ones represent black pixels.

When you GET a graphics image off the screen, you simply store a matrix of bits that, via ones and zeros, represent the black and white pixels of the image. This concept is illustrated by Figure 5-22. The figure shows the image of a diagonal line, and its representation as a matrix of one and zero bits.

Figure 5-22
*Graphics Pixel
Representation*

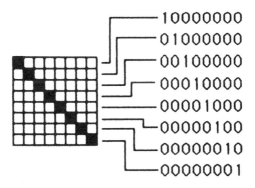

10000000
01000000
00100000
00010000
00001000
00000100
00000010
00000001

0 bits = White pixels
1 bits = Black pixels

When you use the PUT statement to place a graphics image on the screen, the image transfer mode determines how the bits of the image will be combined with the existing bits in the screen memory.

The five image transfer modes are called *XOR*, *AND*, *OR*, *PSET*, and *PRESET*. The default mode (used if no mode is specified on the PUT statement) is XOR. This mode causes the bits of the image to be logically XORed with the bits already present on the screen. When two bits are XORed together, the result is zero if both bits are the same, and one if they are different.

If the image consists of black pixels against a white background, and the screen area in question contains all white pixels, such a PUT operation will result in the display of the black pixel information representing the image. You already know this, of course, from the results of our previous experiments.

The XOR mode has some other properties, however, that are not as readily apparent. If, for example, the screen area contains all black pixels before the PUT operation, the image (defined by black pixels) will appear as white against the black background. This is illustrated by Figure 5-23.

In this example, the smiling face image is used once again. A LINE statement with the box filled option is used to blacken the background area prior to redisplaying the image with a PUT statement. The XOR image transfer mode is used. This mode can be summarized as only those pixels of the image that are black are significant, and they will appear on the screen as either black or white, depending upon the state of the screen prior to the operation.

Table 5-1 defines the effect produced by each of the five image transfer modes. Compare the previous example with that shown in

Figure 5-24, where the PSET mode is used. The PSET mode ignores the previous contents of the screen pixels, and simply stuffs the image defined in the array onto the appropriate area of the screen. Thus, both black and white pixels of the image will be significant when using the PSET image transfer mode. Note also the syntax for specifying an image transfer mode on the PUT statement

```
PUT (x,y),arrayname,mode
```

Although the precise action taken in all situations by each mode is well defined in Table 5-1, it is not immediately obvious how to best employ each mode.

Figure 5-23
*Using XOR Mode
Against a Black
Background*

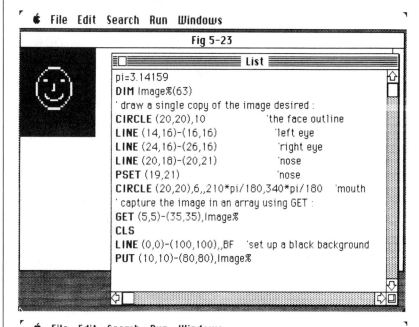

Figure 5-24
*Using PSET Mode
Against a Black
Background*

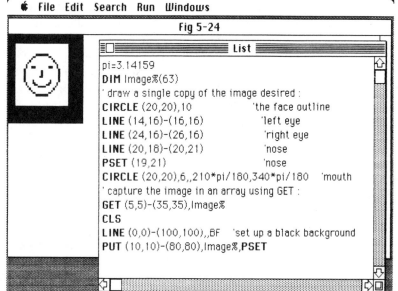

Table 5-1
Image Transfer Modes

Mode	Effect
XOR	Displays an image (defined as black pixels against a white background) in black if the affected area was previously white, or in white if the affected area was previously black. Only black pixels in the image have an effect on the screen. This is the default mode, and is also useful for creating animation effects. See text for more information.

Image pixel	*Previous pixel on screen*	*Resulting pixel on screen*
White	Either	Unchanged
Black	White	Black
Black	Black	White

Mode	Effect
AND	Forces the screen to white wherever the image pixels are white. Only white pixels in the image have an effect on the screen. Can be used to display images (defined as white against a black background) in white if the affected area was previously black. Cannot be used to set screen pixels to black.

Image pixel	*Previous pixel on screen*	*Resulting pixel on screen*
White	Doesn't matter	White
Black	Either	Unchanged

Mode	Effect
OR	Forces the screen to black wherever the image pixels are black. Only black pixels in the image have an effect on the screen. Can be used to display images (defined as black against a white background) in black if the affected area was previously white. Cannot be used to set screen pixels to white.

Image pixel	*Previous pixel on screen*	*Resulting pixel on screen*
White	Either	Unchanged
Black	Doesn't matter	Black

Mode	Effect
PSET	Forces an exact copy of the image (both black and white pixels) onto the affected screen area. The previous appearance of the affected area of the screen is of no consequence when this mode is used.

Image pixel	*Previous pixel on screen*	*Resulting pixel on screen*
White	Doesn't matter	White
Black	Doesn't matter	Black

Mode	Effect
PRESET	Forces an inverted copy of the image (black pixels appear as white, and white pixels appear as black) onto the affected screen area. The previous appearance of the affected area of the screen is of no consequence when this mode is used.

Image pixel	*Previous pixel on screen*	*Resulting pixel on screen*
White	Doesn't matter	Black
Black	Doesn't matter	White

So far, you have seen that the XOR mode can be used when you want to insure that an image is seen, regardless of any background already present on the screen. The image in this case is only defined by the black pixels in the array, as the white pixels will not affect the screen. In addition, the image will appear as black on white or white on black, depending upon preexisting conditions.

A good example of how this mode is used is the I-beam cursor present in an active List window under BASIC. The cursor appears as black against a white background, but when you move it against the text in the List window, it automatically inverts to white.

The XOR mode has one other important characteristic. If you PUT an image using the XOR mode and then PUT it again at the same location, the image will disappear. This feature will prove vital in creating animation effects, as you will soon see.

The PSET mode is best employed to force an image onto the screen, regardless of what was on the screen previously. When using PSET, both white and black pixels within the image array are significant, and any graphics data previously on the screen will always be lost.

An alternative to the PSET mode is the PRESET mode. The PRESET mode has the same effect as the PSET mode, except white and black pixels defined in the image array are inverted before being stuffed onto the screen. Thus, all black areas will appear as white, and vice versa.

The OR mode causes the bits of the image array to be logically ORed with those already present on the screen. This causes the black pixels of the image to appear as black on the screen. If the area of the screen was already black, however, the pixels may not be noticeable. Only black pixels in the image are significant when using OR mode, and only areas of the screen that were previously white will be affected. This mode is best used when it is desired to overlay one image on another.

The AND mode causes the bits of the image array to be logically ANDed with those already present on the screen. Only the white pixels of the image array will be significant in this case. The screen will be forced to white in those areas where the image array pixels are white.

Of course, this may not be noticeable unless that area of the screen was previously black. Areas of the screen that were previously white will not be affected by the AND mode. This mode can be used to erase selected black images, or to display white images against a (preexisting) black background.

Creating Animation

Animated graphics can be created by using either the XOR or the PSET modes. The choice of which mode to use depends upon the type of background that the image will be moving against. If the image is to move against a plain white background, then the PSET mode can be used, and the technique is very simple. The image is defined and captured with a GET statement so that it is surrounded by a border of white pixels.

The border must be at least as wide as the maximum number of pixels that the image will move in a single step. In this fashion, the border itself will take care of erasing the old copy of the image. The program in Listing 5-10 uses this technique to move the smiling face image back and forth across the Output window.

Listing 5-10
Animation Using the PSET Mode

```
' This program will move the smiling face image back
' and forth across the display window five times, with
' ever increasing speed.
' This technique is appropriate for moving images against
' a white background. The image must be captured with
' an adequately sized white border. See text for more information.
pi=3.14159
DIM Image%(63)
' draw a single copy of the image desired :
CIRCLE (20,20),10              'the face outline
LINE (14,16)-(16,16)           'left eye
LINE (24,16)-(26,16)           'right eye
LINE (20,18)-(20,21)           'nose
PSET (19,21)                   'nose
CIRCLE (20,20),6,,210*pi/180,340*pi/180   'mouth
' capture the image in an array using GET :
GET (5,5)-(35,35),Image%
CLS
' Now begin the animation process :
FOR speed=1 TO 5                         '********
FOR x=10 TO 400 STEP speed
PUT (x,10)-(x+60,70),Image%,PSET
NEXT
FOR x=400 TO 10 STEP -speed
PUT (x,10)-(x+60,70),Image%,PSET
NEXT
NEXT
```

The program begins by drawing the base image of the face and capturing it in the usual fashion. The screen is cleared. The image is then redisplayed, using the grow option to make it appear larger. A pair of FOR-NEXT loops cycle the starting location of the image across the Output window, from left to right, and then back again. An outer loop controls the rate at which the image starting location is changed, and thus controls the perceived speed with which the image moves. As the speed increases, the movement becomes more choppy and less attractive to view.

If the speed is increased too far, the border width of the image will be exceeded, and the image will leave a "trail" behind it as it moves. This can be seen by changing the FOR statement marked with asterisks in Listing 5-10 so that it reads

FOR speed = 10 to 25

The technique just illustrated cannot be used if the image is to move against a background that is other than all white. (Actually, you could use PRESET mode and an all black background—try it as an exercise.)

In many applications, you will want to display your image against a detailed background drawing, and then move the image without disturbing that background. This can be accomplished using a different animation technique and the XOR image transfer mode.

The image is drawn at its starting location using the XOR mode. Then, just before it is to be moved, the image is erased by drawing it once again at the same location with the XOR mode. This causes the image to disappear and restores the background that it was drawn on. The next location for the moving image is then calculated, and the process is repeated. An example is provided in Listing 5-11. Try running this program now.

The program of Listing 5-11 displays an amplified image of the smiling face, and causes it to move back and forth across the Output window.

Prior to producing the animation, the program fills the Output window with a cross-hatch pattern made up of two sets of intersecting diagonal lines. If you are running the program now, you will note that the face image moves against this background without disturbing it in any way.

This is only possible when using the XOR mode animation technique. Because this technique tends to cause the animated image to flicker as it moves across the screen, the timing of the various animation steps is very critical. You must provide an adequate delay between the time that the image is displayed and the time that it is erased. In addition, you must try to minimize the time required between the moment when the image is erased and the moment when it is redisplayed at its next location.

In the example program, I wanted to use an amplified copy of the smiling face image. The amplification feature of the PUT statement, however, takes a bit of time to be processed. Since this would cause an undesirable amount of flicker, I perform the amplification once prior to the start of the animation process. The amplified image is then recaptured using a graphics GET statement. The screen is then cleared, and the background image is drawn.

The background image is produced by a pair of LINE statements within a single FOR-NEXT loop. The animation process itself begins by drawing the image using the XOR mode. Since the image was recaptured in its larger size, no additional processing time is needed at this point to amplify it. A delay subroutine is then used to wait a moment before erasing the image. The amount of time delay needed here will depend upon the specific image being animated, and how fast and far it is moving. It must be adjusted in each case by experimentation.

After the time delay, the image is erased by simply drawing it again, at the same location, with the XOR mode. This causes the background to reappear where the image was just seen. The next location for the image is then determined (in this case by the action of the FOR-NEXT loop), and the process is repeated. By using a pair of FOR-NEXT loops, the image is made to move in both directions across the screen. The program remains in this "infinite" loop forever; it must be halted manually.

Listing 5-11
Animation Using the
XOR Mode

```
' This program will move the smiling face image back
' and forth across the display window without altering
' the background image in that window.
' This technique is appropriate for moving images against
' a non-uniform background. The image must be defined as
' black on white. See text for more information.
pi=3.14159
DIM Image%(487)
' draw a single copy of the image desired :
CIRCLE (20,20),10              'the face outline
LINE (14,16)-(16,16)           'left eye
LINE (24,16)-(26,16)           'right eye
LINE (20,18)-(20,21)           'nose
PSET (19,21)                   'nose
CIRCLE (20,20),6,,210*pi/180,340*pi/180   'mouth
' capture the image in an array using GET :
GET (5,5)-(35,35),Image%
CLS
' redisplay the image in a larger size :
PUT (10,10)-(90,90),Image%
' recapture the image in the larger size :
GET (10,10)-(90,90),Image%
CLS
' Set up the background image, a cross-hatch pattern :
FOR x=2 TO 450 STEP 10
LINE (x,100)-(x+50,0)
LINE (x+50,100)-(x,0)
NEXT
' Now begin the animation process :
Again:
FOR x=10 TO 400 STEP 2
PUT (x,10)-(x+80,90),Image%
GOSUB Delay
PUT (x,10)-(x+80,90),Image%
NEXT
FOR x%=400 TO 10 STEP -2
PUT (x%,10)-(x%+80,90),Image%
GOSUB Delay
PUT (x%,10)-(x%+80,90),Image%
NEXT
GOTO Again
' Subroutine Delay : provides a small time delay between the time
' the animated image is displayed and the time that it is erased.
' This delay time helps to reduce flickering of the animated image.
' The delay time will need to be adjusted for best results in each
' application of this technique.
Delay:
FOR d=1 TO 200
NEXT
RETURN
```

Summary

In this chapter, you have learned how to create a variety of graphics images with your Macintosh. As you are no doubt aware, the Macintosh screen, with its pixel structure, can represent text in a wide range of different fonts, or type styles. These and other graphics capabilities of the Macintosh have yet to be explored.

Before proceeding in that direction, however, it is time to discuss the Macintosh mouse. In the following chapter, I will show you how you can make use of the mouse in your own programs. Armed with this new ability, you will be able to make even greater use of graphics and the Macintosh user interface.

Chapter 6

The Mouse

No, look, you see what happened was that we used to do experiments on them.

—Arthur Dent

The Macintosh is the first successful microcomputer to employ a mouse as a pointing and input device. Through the use of clever software such as MacPaint, Apple has produced an environment in which a great deal of productive work can be performed without ever taking one's hand off the mouse.

After using the Mac for a while, control of the computer via the mouse becomes almost second nature. Once this transition is made, it becomes hard to conceive of making a menu selection, initiating a function, or moving data around without the mouse.

Microsoft realized that persons writing their own software for the Macintosh would also want to be able to take advantage of this unique input device. Their BASIC language therefore provides a number of functions and statements that deal with the mouse.

In addition, Microsoft BASIC permits the programmer to define custom pull-down menus, dialog boxes, and windows. Since these entities are implicitly controlled by mouse action, a great deal of mouse control is possible from within BASIC programs.

In this chapter, I show you how to detect the mouse position, mouse movement, and mouse button clicks from within your own BASIC programs. I also cover the mouse program interrupt, and the Toolbox (ROM) calls that control the appearance of the mouse cursor. These features can be used to spice up many BASIC programs that would otherwise be quite ordinary in operation.

In later chapters, you will see how to create custom pull-down menus and dialog boxes and thus provide the user of your programs with even greater mouse control.

The MOUSE Function

The *MOUSE* function is used to determine the mouse position and button status. The function is designed to detect the types of mouse activity that are standard to the Macintosh user interface. These types of activities should be familiar to you. They include such actions as positioning the mouse to a particular item on the screen and clicking the mouse button; positioning the mouse to a particular location, clicking and holding the button, and then moving the mouse to another position before releasing the button (the so-called "drag"); and positioning the mouse to a particular item and double-clicking. Each of these types of activities can be detected through a series of calls to the MOUSE function.

The MOUSE function always requires a single argument; it must be a number in the range 0 to 6. The argument of the function determines what kind of mouse information is to be returned by the function. Table 6-1 summarizes the seven different items of mouse information that can thus be obtained from the MOUSE function.

It is important to realize that a specific protocol must be used when obtaining information via this function. Of course, all of the items shown in Table 6-1 need not be used by your program. However, those that are used must be referenced in a specific order.

Table 6-1
The MOUSE Function

Function	Returns
MOUSE(0)	Mouse button status as follows: 0 = Button is not depressed and has not been depressed since the last call to MOUSE(0). 1 = Button was single-clicked since the last call to MOUSE(0). 2 = Button was double-clicked since the last call to MOUSE(0). 3 = Button was triple-clicked since the last call to MOUSE(0). –1 = Button has been single-clicked and is still held down. –2 = Button has been double-clicked and is still being held down. –3 = Button has been triple-clicked and is still held down.
MOUSE(1)	X-coordinate of mouse pointer at time of last call to MOUSE(0). This is the current mouse horizontal coordinate.
MOUSE(2)	Y-coordinate of mouse pointer at time of last call to MOUSE(0). This is the current mouse vertical coordinate.
MOUSE(3)	X-coordinate of mouse pointer at the time of the most recent button click since the last call to MOUSE(0). This is the horizontal coordinate of the starting position of a drag action.
MOUSE(4)	Y-coordinate of mouse pointer at the time of the most recent button click since the last call to MOUSE(0). This is the vertical coordinate of the starting position of a drag action.
MOUSE(5)	X-coordinate of mouse pointer at the last time that the button was released since the last call to MOUSE(0). If the button was still down at the time of the last call to MOUSE(0), then the x-coordinate of the pointer at that time. This is the horizontal coordinate of the ending position of a drag action.
MOUSE(6)	Y-coordinate of mouse pointer at the last time that the button was released since the last call to MOUSE(0). If the button was still down at the time of the last call to MOUSE(0), then the y-coordinate of the pointer at that time. This is the vertical coordinate of the ending position of a drag action.

Mouse Button Status

When your program is ready to interrogate the current state of the mouse, it must begin by calling the MOUSE function with an argument of 0. The operating system in the ROM of the Macintosh automatically remembers any mouse activity that has taken place and returns the most recent mouse button action when MOUSE(0) is called.

If no button clicks have taken place since the previous call to MOUSE(0), then the function will return a value of 0. Otherwise, the function returns a value of 1, 2, or 3 to indicate that a single-click, double-click, or triple-click of the mouse button has been made. If such an action has occurred, and the button is still being held down (i.e., a "drag" is still in progress), then the value returned will be negative (–1, –2, or –3).

At the same moment that the MOUSE(0) function returns its value, it freezes the values associated with MOUSE function calls 1 through 6. Thus, the protocol for interrogating a user's mouse action is as follows. First, obtain the value for MOUSE(0). If it is zero, no mouse activity has occurred; your program can wait if necessary. If MOUSE(0) returns a nonzero value, a mouse selection has been made; if the value is negative, the selection is still in progress. At this point, you can call any of the other mouse functions to determine the mouse coordinates pertinent to the action. I will show you how to deal with the mouse coordinates in a moment.

Figure 6-1 contains a simple example that is concerned only with the mouse button, and not the mouse location. The figure actually shows two techniques for pausing a program until the user requests that it proceed.

Figure 6-1
Detecting Mouse Button Clicks

```
' The old way (using the keyboard) :
'
PRINT "Press any key to continue."
'
WaitKey:
a$=INKEY$
IF a$="" THEN GOTO WaitKey
'
PRINT "Thank you.....proceeding....."
'

' The new way (using the mouse button) :
'
PRINT "Click the mouse button to continue."
'
WaitMouse:
IF MOUSE(0) <> 1 THEN GOTO WaitMouse
'
PRINT "Thank you.....proceeding....."
'
'
END
```

The first technique, which you have seen before, prompts the user to press any key to continue the program. The **INKEY$** function is used to effect the desired action.

The second technique prompts the user to click the mouse button to proceed with the program. In this case, the MOUSE(0) function is used to wait until the proper mouse activity occurs.

The Current Mouse Position

For some applications, you may want to determine the current position of the mouse pointer, without concern for whether or not the mouse button has been clicked. The current mouse position can be obtained from function calls MOUSE(1) and MOUSE(2), but you must still call on MOUSE(0) first.

Since you will not be concerned with the state of the mouse button, you can ignore the value returned by MOUSE(0). The call is made to freeze the current values for MOUSE(1) and MOUSE(2). These values represent the horizontal and vertical position of the mouse pointer at the moment that the MOUSE(0) call occurs.

The horizontal and vertical values correspond to the pixel coordinates explained in the previous chapter. The resolution of the mouse pointer is one pixel width in both the horizontal and vertical dimensions. The coordinate system is identical to that used to address graphics points within the current Output window. The mouse position will therefore always be returned relative to the upper left corner of the current Output window (coordinate position (0,0)).

If the mouse pointer is moved above the top of the Output window, or to the left of the left edge of the Output window, then the corresponding coordinate value will become negative.

The program shown in Listing 6-1 demonstrates this concept. When run, it displays in the Output window the current horizontal and vertical coordinate values of the mouse pointer. The values are continually updated, so you can watch them change as you move the mouse pointer about on the screen.

Listing 6-1
Demo of Current Mouse Coordinates

```
' This program displays the current mouse coordinates in
' the output window. These values are continually updated
' so that you can watch them change as you move the mouse
' pointer about on the sceen.
CLS
LOCATE 3,5
PRINT "Horizontal Value" TAB(30) "Vertical Value"
Again:
t=MOUSE(0)        'freeze the current mouse coordinate values
x=MOUSE(1)        ' get mouse horizontal coordinate value
y=MOUSE(2)        ' get mouse vertical coordinate value
LOCATE 4,5
PRINT x TAB(30) y
GOTO Again
```

When you run this program, be sure you try moving the mouse pointer outside of the Output window to see what effect this has. Also, try moving the pointer until you get both coordinates to equal zero. You should then be pointing to the upper left corner of the Output window.

Listing 6-2 contains the first version of a basic drawing program. This program allows you to use the mouse pointer as a "graphics pen" to draw freehand pictures in the Output window. Instructions explaining how to use the program will appear when it is run.

Listing 6-2
BASIC Drawing
Program

```
' This program illustrates how to obtain and use current mouse coordinates.
' It permits the mouse to be used as a "graphics pen" in the creation of
' free hand drawings.
CLS
PRINT "BASIC Drawing Program - Version 1"
PRINT "Click and drag to draw with the mouse"
PRINT "Double Click to clear the screen"
PRINT "Triple Click to end the program"
Again:
b=MOUSE(0)  'get button status AND freeze the current mouse coord values
x=MOUSE(1)       ' get mouse horizontal coordinate value
y=MOUSE(2)       ' get mouse vertical coordinate value
IF b=2 THEN CLS : GOTO Again        ' a double click clears the screen
' "drag" action allows drawing with a "pen" the size of a 4 pixel square :
IF b=-1 THEN PSET (x,y) : PSET(x+1,y) : PSET(x,y+1) : PSET(x+1,y+1)
IF b=3 THEN END                     'a triple click ends the program
GOTO Again
```

The program works by obtaining values for the MOUSE
functions 0, 1, and 2 in quick succession. The first MOUSE call
obtains the status of the mouse button and freezes the current
mouse coordinates, which are then returned by the subsequent two
calls.

The program then proceeds to take different actions depending
upon the button status, held in variable b. If b is 2 then the mouse
button was double-clicked; this causes the output window to be
cleared. If b is 3 then the mouse button was triple-clicked; this
causes the program to end. For all other cases except $b = -1$, no
action is taken. This allows you to move the mouse pointer around
on the screen without drawing, as long as you do not press the
mouse button.

To draw, you must press and hold the mouse button while moving
the mouse. This action is reflected by a value in b of -1 (single-
click, button still down). In this case, the mouse coordinates
(returned via MOUSE(1) and MOUSE(2)) are used to plot graphics
pixels on the screen. The version I have presented uses a "graphics
pen" that is two pixels wide and two pixels high, so a total of four
PSET statements are used.

Determining Drag Coordinates
The four remaining MOUSE function calls (MOUSE(3) through
MOUSE(6)) are used to determine the coordinates of mouse drag
actions. As you already know, a mouse drag action consists of
clicking the mouse button (one or more times), holding the button
down, and moving the mouse to another position before releasing
the button. When such an action takes place, the program
processing it will be concerned with two pairs of coordinates. These
are the starting coordinates, which represent the mouse position
when the drag action began (i.e., when the mouse button was first
clicked), and the ending coordinates, which represent the mouse
position when the drag action was completed (i.e., when the mouse

button is finally released).

Functions MOUSE(3) and MOUSE(4) return respectively the horizontal and vertical starting coordinates, while functions MOUSE(5) and MOUSE(6) return the horizontal and vertical ending coordinates. As always, the MOUSE(0) function must be called prior to using any of these functions. In addition, a nonzero value must be obtained from MOUSE(0) for any of these other values to be meaningful.

If MOUSE(0) returns a value of 1, 2, or 3, then a single-click, double-click, or triple-click action took place, and MOUSE(3) through MOUSE(6) contain the starting and ending mouse positions for that action (if the user just clicked the mouse and did not drag it, then MOUSE(3) will equal MOUSE(5) and MOUSE(4) will equal MOUSE(6)).

If MOUSE(0) returns a negative value, then the mouse button is still being held down, so the drag action may still be taking place. In this case, the values of MOUSE(5) and MOUSE(6) may still be changing; additional calls to MOUSE(0) and MOUSE(5) and MOUSE(6) will be necessary to obtain the final values of the ending coordinates.

The program shown in Listing 6-3 illustrates the use of drag coordinates. It is also a basic type of drawing program. In this case, however, the program produces lines and circles instead of simply dots. When you run this program, you will be given instructions on how to use it.

Listing 6-3
Detecting Mouse Drag Activities

```
' This program shows how you can detect a mouse drag action
' and determine the starting and ending coordinates of the drag.
CLS
PRINT "Click once and drag to draw a line."
PRINT "Click twice and drag to draw a circle."
PRINT "Click three times to end program."
Again:
b=MOUSE(0)
startx=MOUSE(3)
starty=MOUSE(4)
endx=MOUSE(5)
endy=MOUSE(6)
IF b=1 THEN LINE (startx,starty)-(endx,endy)
IF b=2 THEN CIRCLE (startx,starty),SQR(((endx-startx)^2)+((endy-starty)^2))
IF b=3 THEN END
GOTO Again
```

To draw a line, position the mouse pointer to the starting point for the line, click and hold the mouse button, and drag to the ending point for the line. Release the button, and the line will appear. To draw a circle, position the mouse pointer to the desired center of the circle, double-click and hold the mouse button, and drag out to the desired size (radius) of the circle. Release the button, and the circle will appear. Triple-click the mouse button to terminate the program.

The program works by calling MOUSE(0) to obtain the button status, then calling MOUSE(3) through MOUSE(6) to obtain the starting and ending positions of the drag action (if any). These coordinates are returned to variables (*startx,starty*) and (*endx,endy*). The button status, in variable *b*, is then interrogated. If *b* is 1, then a single-click drag took place; a LINE statement is used to draw the line between the appropriate coordinates.

If *b* is 2 then a double-click drag took place; a CIRCLE statement is used to draw the circle desired. The center of the circle is at (*startx,starty*). I then employ a basic formula from geometry to calculate the radius of the circle as a function of the circle's center coordinates and a single coordinate given on the circle itself (the ending point of the drag). Finally, if *b* is 3 then a triple-click took place and the program is ended.

Mouse Interrupts

Use BASIC's program interrupt facility (see Chapter 3) to enable interrupts on mouse button activities. To do this, you must set up a subroutine to handle the mouse interrupts. If the subroutine were named MouseInt, the following statement would be used

```
ON MOUSE GOSUB MouseInt
```

To actually enable the interrupt to take place, you would then execute the statement

```
MOUSE ON
```

Once these statements were executed, any mouse button activity (i.e., any time that MOUSE(0) would return a nonzero value) would interrupt the normal flow of execution of the program, and activate the MouseInt subroutine. The RETURN from the subroutine would then resume execution of the main program at its point of interruption.

A Simple Arcade Game

A sample program that illustrates the use of mouse interrupts is presented in Listing 6-4. This is a simple example of an arcade style game utilizing animated Macintosh graphics and the mouse as a player input device. Before executing this program, resize the Output window so that it occupies the maximum amount of space possible on the Macintosh screen. Later, in Chapter 8, I will show you how you can make the program set the window size automatically.

When you execute this program, the image of a ship appears near the top of the screen. This ship moves back and forth across the top of the screen. The XOR animation technique, described in the previous chapter, is used. This ship is the player's target. The player shoots missiles at the ship by positioning the mouse and clicking the mouse button. Player missiles move vertically up from their launch position towards the top of the screen, and then disappear. At any time, the player may have up to four missiles on the screen.

```
' NOTE: The output window should be resized to maximum size before
' starting this program !!!!!!
' In this game, a ship moves back and forth across the top of the screen.
' The player uses the mouse to launch missiles at the ship.  Up to four
' missiles may be on the screen at any time.  Player scores for each
' missile that hits the ship.  The score value is greater for missiles
' launched at a greater distance from the ship.
' Position mouse to launch location and click to launch a missile.
' Double click the mouse to end the game.
' Score is displayed near bottom left of screen.
' See text for more information.
' Array to keep track of up to four missiles at once :
DIM Missiles%(4,5)
FOR i%=1 TO 4          'initially no missiles
FOR j%=1 TO 5
missiles(i%,j%)=0
NEXT
NEXT
' Note : Missiles%(i,1) is current x position of missile
' Note : Missiles%(i,2) is current y position of missile
' Note : Missiles%(i,3) is next x position of missile
' Note : Missiles%(i,4) is next y position of missile
' Note : Missiles%(i,5) is scoring value of missile, if it hits the ship

' Arrays to hold graphics images of ship and missiles :
DIM RShipImage%(23)
DIM LShipImage%(23)
DIM MissileImage%(23)
' Define the images :
CLS
' image of ship moving to right :
LINE (10,10)-(30,15)
LINE (10,20)-(30,15)
LINE (10,10)-(10,20)
GET (10,10)-(30,20),RShipImage%
CLS
' image of ship moving to left :
LINE (10,15)-(30,10)
LINE (10,15)-(30,20)
LINE (30,10)-(30,20)
GET (10,10)-(30,20),LShipImage%
CLS
' image of missile (moves upwards only) :
LINE (10,30)-(15,10)
LINE (20,30)-(15,10)
LINE (10,30)-(20,30)
GET (10,10)-(20,30),MissileImage%
CLS
'
ON MOUSE GOSUB Mouseint      ' set up mouse interrupt handling subroutine
MOUSE ON                     'enable mouse interrupts
'
Score%=0                              'start with zero score points
ShipLoc%=10                           'starting ship location (x-dim)
ShipDirc%=0                           'ship starts moving to the right
Again:
' display ship at new location :
IF ShipDirc%=0 THEN PUT (ShipLoc%,10),RShipImage% ELSE PUT (ShipLoc%,10),LShipImage%
' display any missiles at their new locations :
FOR i%=1 TO 4
IF Missiles%(i%,1)<>0 THEN PUT (Missiles%(i%,1),Missiles%(i%,2)),MissileImage%
NEXT
' check all four missiles for potential hits :
Hit%=0
FOR i%=1 TO 4
IF Missiles%(i%,2)<20 AND Missiles%(i%,1)+6>ShipLoc% AND Missiles%(i%,1)<ShipLoc%+16 THEN Hit
%=i%
```

Listing 6-4—cont.

```
NEXT
IF Hit%<>0 THEN GOSUB MissileHit
' calculate next position for the ship :
IF ShipDirc%=0 AND ShipLoc%<450 THEN NewShipDirc%=0 : NewShipLoc%=ShipLoc%+4
IF ShipDirc%=0 AND ShipLoc%>=450 THEN NewShipDirc%=1 : NewShipLoc%=ShipLoc%
IF ShipDirc%=1 AND ShipLoc%>10 THEN NewShipDirc%=1 : NewShipLoc%=ShipLoc%-4
IF ShipDirc%=1 AND ShipLoc%<=10 THEN NewShipDirc%=0 : NewShipLoc%=ShipLoc%
' calculate next position for missiles :
FOR i%=1 TO 4
IF Missiles%(i%,1)=0 THEN GOTO NextMissile
IF Missiles%(i%,2)<10 THEN Missiles%(i%,3)=0 : Missiles%(i%,4)=0 : GOTO NextMissile
Missiles%(i%,3)=Missiles%(i%,1) ' next x-dim set to current x-dim
Missiles%(i%,4)=Missiles%(i%,2)-3 'next y-dim moves missile upwards
NextMissile:
NEXT
' erase ship from old location :
IF ShipDirc%=0 THEN PUT (ShipLoc%,10),RShipImage% ELSE PUT (ShipLoc%,10),LShipImage%
' set up for new ship location :
ShipDirc%=NewShipDirc%
ShipLoc%=NewShipLoc%
' erase missiles from old locations and set up for new missile locations :
FOR i%=1 TO 4
IF Missiles%(i%,1)<>0 THEN PUT (Missiles%(i%,1),Missiles%(i%,2)),MissileImage%
Missiles%(i%,1)=Missiles%(i%,3)
Missiles%(i%,2)=Missiles%(i%,4)
NEXT
' check for any new missiles launched by the user via the mouse :
IF Mx%=0 THEN GOTO Again
' a new missile was launched, see if there is room in the Missiles array for it :
i%=1
TryLaunch:
IF Missiles%(i%,1)=0 THEN Missiles%(i%,1)=Mx% : Missiles%(i%,2)=My% : Missiles%(i%,5)=My%\10 : Mx%=0 : GOTO Again
i%=i%+1
IF i%<5 THEN GOTO TryLaunch
Mx%=0
BEEP ' beep to show that missile could not be launched
GOTO Again
'
' Subroutine to handle a hit of the ship by player's missile :
MissileHit:
BEEP
Score%=Score%+Missiles%(Hit%,5)
' erase the missile that struck the ship immediately :
PUT (Missiles%(Hit%,1),Missiles%(Hit%,2)),MissileImage%
Missiles%(Hit%,1)=0       ' make this missile go away on the next cycle
Missiles%(Hit%,3)=0
LOCATE 15,1
PRINT Score%                'display the new score
RETURN
'
' The Mouse Interrupt handling subroutine :
' A single mouse click launches a new missile if the mouse
' coordinates are in an acceptable range.  The new missile starting
' coordinates are returned to the main game loop in variables Mx% and My%.
' If an attempt is made to launch a missile in an invalid location, this
' routine issues a "beep" and returns Mx% = 0.
MouseInt:
b%=MOUSE(0)
IF b%=2 THEN END          ' a double-click ends the program !
IF b%<>1 AND b%<>-1 THEN RETURN
Mx%=MOUSE(3)
My%=MOUSE(4)
IF My%<75 OR My%>300 THEN BEEP : Mx%=0 : RETURN
IF Mx%<10 OR Mx%>450 THEN BEEP : Mx%=0 : RETURN
RETURN
```

If a missile on its way up intercepts the ship, the player scores points. The point value of each hit depends upon the vertical position of the mouse at the time the scoring missile was fired.

Thus, shots released from near the bottom of the screen (much harder to strike) are worth more than those released when closer to the ship's path of travel.

The player's score is displayed near the bottom left of the screen. In this version, the game terminates when the mouse button is clicked twice (this discourages overzealousness in the launching of missiles). Figure 6-2 shows what the game looks like when it is in progress.

Figure 6-2
*The Arcade Game in
Progress*

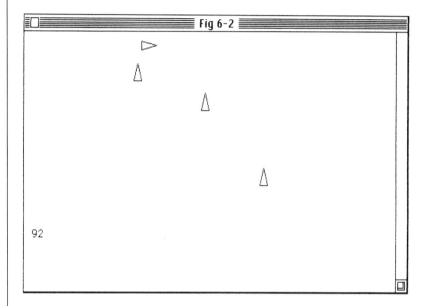

How It Works
The program begins by dimensioning array *Missiles%*. This array holds the necessary information to keep track of four missiles. Each missile is maintained using a different subscript value for the first dimension of the array. For each missile, five data values are needed, and so the second dimension subscript of the array ranges from 1 to 5.

As shown in the comments of the listing, two of these values hold the current coordinates of the missile, two of them hold the missile's next coordinates, and the last value maintains the score value of the missile. If the current x-coordinate value of a missile is zero, then the missile is not currently active (i.e., on the screen).

The program then dimensions arrays *RShipImage%*, *LShipImage%*, and *MissileImage%* to hold the graphics images of the ship and the missile. Two images are used for the ship, one when it is moving from right to left, and the other when it is moving from left to right. Since the missile only moves straight up the screen, it requires only one image. Each image is then defined by a trio of LINE statements, and stored in the arrays using the graphics GET statement.

The mouse interrupt is set up and mouse interrupts are enabled. The variable *Score%* is initialized to zero and the main action of the game commences. The game consists of a large loop starting with the label Again. Each time through the loop, each object that can move on the screen is moved. For each object, the program must maintain two sets of coordinates: one set indicates the object's position before the move (the "current" position), and the other indicates the position the object will occupy after the move (the "new" position). For the four missile objects, this information is maintained in the *Missiles%* array. The target ship's horizontal location is maintained in the variables *ShipLoc%* and *NewShipLoc%*.

Since the ship always maintains the same vertical position, no variable is needed for that dimension. The ship does move in two different directions, however, and so variables *ShipDirc%* and *NewShipDirc%* are used to keep track of this. The direction variables use a value of zero to indicate left to right motion, and a value of one to indicate right to left motion.

The main game loop begins by displaying all currently active objects. The proper ship image is selected based upon the value of *ShipDirc%*. A FOR-NEXT loop cycles through the four possible missiles, displaying any active ones at their appropriate (current) coordinates.

The next step is to check for missile strikes ("hits"). Another loop scans through the missiles, comparing their locations against the ship's location. If a hit is indicated, subroutine MissileHit is called with variable *Hit%* indicating which missile made contact.

Note that the way the loop is coded, only one missile can score at a time. Subroutine MissileHit sounds a "beep" to indicate the strike and then increases the score by the missile's scoring value, which is kept in the *Missiles%* array, and is set when the missile is launched.

Finally, the subroutine erases the missile from the screen and alters its array entries so that it will go away at the end of the current game cycle.

Back in the main loop, the next step is to determine the new location for all objects on the screen. A set of four IF-THEN statements handles the four possible cases for the target ship. Either the ship continues to move to the left or the right, or, when it reaches either end of travel, its direction is reversed.

In the current version, the ship moves at a rate of 4 pixels per game cycle. A FOR-NEXT loop then calculates the next position for each active missile.

The missiles move up at a rate of 3 pixels per game cycle, and they disappear (become inactive) when they reach vertical coordinate 9. Once a new position has been calculated for each object, the objects are erased from their current locations by redrawing at their current locations using the XOR image transfer mode. The "new" locations then become the "current" locations so that when the objects are redrawn at the beginning of the next cycle, they will appear to have moved.

Before the main game loop is closed, however, a check is made to see if any new missiles are to be launched. Missiles are launched by a single mouse click, detected in the MouseInt subroutine. Since the interrupt can occur at any time, the subroutine simply obtains the mouse coordinates for the launch and places them in a pair of dedicated variables, $Mx\%$ and $My\%$.

Normally, these variables are zero. They become nonzero only when a launch request is made. At the end of the game loop, these variables are checked. If they are nonzero, then the *Missiles%* array is searched for an unused (inactive) entry. This entry is then used for the new missile, and the missile's starting coordinates are stored within it.

At this time, the score value of the missile is calculated as one tenth the vertical coordinate of the missile. This value is also stored in the *Missiles%* array, for use if and when the missile scores a hit.

Study the mouse interrupt handling subroutine, MouseInt, carefully. It begins by obtaining the mouse button status via a MOUSE(0) call. A double-click terminates the program. A single-click indicates a missile launch request. Note that the routine accepts a button status of either 1 or −1 for this case. This is necessary because the interrupt subroutine gets control immediately upon detection of any mouse button activity. Thus, depending upon how fast the user releases the mouse button, the button status can come back as either 1 (button released) or −1 (button still down).

Note also that the routine checks to make sure the launch coordinates are in a specific range. In this game, a maximum height limit must be enforced for missile launches, or it would be too easy to score every time.

This game can be enhanced into one that can be played competitively by several people. To do this, you would add a time limit to the main game loop. Each game would therefore progress for a fixed amount of time, at which point it would end. Players would take turns and compete by trying to obtain the highest score in the time allotted. The time remaining in the current game can be displayed on the screen as a continuously decreasing number, near the score. I have left these enhancements as an exercise for the reader.

Controlling the Mouse Cursor

The *mouse cursor* is the image of the mouse pointer. As you know, the Macintosh uses different mouse cursors under different conditions. The two most commonly used cursors are the arrow and the I-beam (see Figure 6-3). Control of the mouse cursor is possible from within a BASIC program. This control is exercised by accessing some of the Macintosh's built-in ROM routines. Collectively, these routines are known as the *Macintosh Toolbox*.

All toolbox routines are accessed from BASIC through use of the CALL statement. The routine names are reserved names and are always known to BASIC; no special defining statements are needed to use them. In this section, I will cover those routines that provide control over the mouse cursor; most of the other routines will be explained in the next chapter.

There are five toolbox routines concerned with the mouse cursor. They are called *INITCURSOR*, *HIDECURSOR*, *OBSCURECURSOR*, *SHOWCURSOR*, and *SETCURSOR*. Only

Figure 6-3
Mouse Cursors

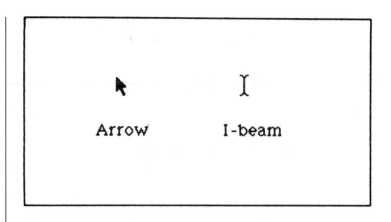

the last of these, SETCURSOR, requires an argument. The routines are summarized in Table 6-2.

Three of the routines are concerned only with whether or not the cursor is visible on the screen. At any time, the cursor can be visible, invisible, or momentarily obscured. A momentarily obscured cursor is invisible until the mouse is moved, at which time it immediately becomes visible again. This state is often used in text editing windows.

For an example, activate the List window of Microsoft BASIC. Move the I-beam mouse cursor around a bit, then click to set the insertion point. Now, watch the mouse cursor very closely and enter some text. Notice that the cursor disappears as soon as you press the first key. This is the momentarily obscured state. The mouse cursor is still there, but it is not visible. If, however, you move the mouse (even the slightest amount), the cursor will immediately become visible again.

Most of these toolbox routines are very easy to use in your own programs. If you wish to make the mouse cursor invisible at some point, simply insert the statement

CALL HIDECURSOR

To counteract this statement and make the cursor appear, the statement

CALL SHOWCURSOR

can be used.

The momentarily obscured state can be entered with the statement

CALL OBSCURECURSOR

The INITCURSOR call makes the cursor visible and also resets its appearance to that of the standard and familiar pointing arrow.

Table 6-2
Mouse Cursor Toolbox Routines

Statement	Action
CALL INITCURSOR	Initializes mouse cursor to the standard system cursor (an arrow) and makes it visible.
CALL HIDECURSOR	Makes mouse cursor invisible.
CALL SHOWCURSOR	Makes mouse cursor visible.
CALL OBSCURECURSOR	Makes mouse cursor momentarily obscured. The cursor will be made invisible immediately, but it will become visible as soon as the mouse itself is moved.
CALL SETCURSOR (VARPTR(Cursor%(0)))	Sets the mouse cursor to the image defined by the contents of Cursor%, and makes it visible. Cursor% is a 34 element integer array containing the following information:
Cursor%(0) Cursor%(1) . . . . Cursor%(15)	Cursor Image (see text)
Cursor%(16) Cursor%(17) . . . . Cursor%(31)	Cursor Mask (see text)
Cursor%(32) Cursor%(33)	Vertical coordinate of hot spot Horizontal coordinate of hot spot

The most interesting routine of all, however, is the SETCURSOR routine. This routine allows you to define your own image for the mouse cursor. The image is passed to the routine, along with other information, in an integer array.

All toolbox routines require that array arguments be passed to them in the form of Macintosh memory addresses, so the VARPTR function must be used (see Chapter 2).

Defining the Cursor Image
A mouse cursor image is defined by 256 pixels, arranged in a 16 pixel wide by 16 pixel high square. The image is defined by 256 bits, or 32 bytes. As we have already seen, white pixels are represented by zero bits, and black pixels are represented by one bits. The 256 bits that represent the cursor image are stored in the first sixteen elements of the integer array passed to the SETCURSOR routine. This organization is illustrated by Figure 6-4. The cursor image in the figure would be that of a thin diagonal line, sloping from upper left to lower right. Additional information is also passed in the array, but I will get to that in a moment.

To be able to use the SETCURSOR routine, you need to set the appropriate bit positions in the appropriate array elements, as shown in Figure 6-4, so as to create the desired cursor image. It is easy to see which array element must be affected for each pixel you want to turn on in the cursor image.

Figure 6-4
Defining the Mouse Cursor Image

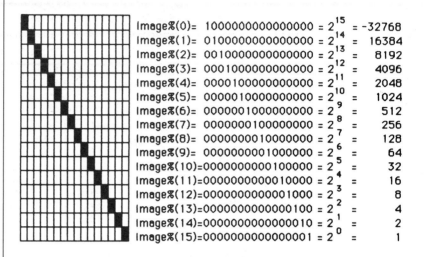

$Image\%(0) = 1000000000000000 = 2^{15} = -32768$
$Image\%(1) = 0100000000000000 = 2^{14} = 16384$
$Image\%(2) = 0010000000000000 = 2^{13} = 8192$
$Image\%(3) = 0001000000000000 = 2^{12} = 4096$
$Image\%(4) = 0000100000000000 = 2^{11} = 2048$
$Image\%(5) = 0000010000000000 = 2^{10} = 1024$
$Image\%(6) = 0000001000000000 = 2^{9} = 512$
$Image\%(7) = 0000000100000000 = 2^{8} = 256$
$Image\%(8) = 0000000010000000 = 2^{7} = 128$
$Image\%(9) = 0000000001000000 = 2^{6} = 64$
$Image\%(10) = 0000000000100000 = 2^{5} = 32$
$Image\%(11) = 0000000000010000 = 2^{4} = 16$
$Image\%(12) = 0000000000001000 = 2^{3} = 8$
$Image\%(13) = 0000000000000100 = 2^{2} = 4$
$Image\%(14) = 0000000000000010 = 2^{1} = 2$
$Image\%(15) = 0000000000000001 = 2^{0} = 1$

The array element (0 – 15) is simply the vertical coordinate of that pixel (coordinates being measured on the 16 × 16 pixel grid, starting with (0,0) for the upper left corner). Each bit position within that array element represents a different numeric value. These numeric values are shown in Figure 6-4.

Each array element holds an integer value, using a storage technique called binary two's complement. Thus the bit positions, going from right to left, each represent a power of 2 ($2^0 = 1$, $2^1 = 2$, $2^2 = 4$, $2^3 = 8$, and so on).

The leftmost bit position is special in that it represents the sign bit, indicating that the integer value is negative. This bit position represents the numeric value –32768. If more than one bit position is to be set in a given element, the values for each bit position are simply added together for that element. Thus, if the two rightmost bits in an element were set, the element value would be $1 + 2$, or 3. The next program I present will automatically calculate the array element values for you, given a specific image.

The Cursor Mask

The SETCURSOR routine requires more than just the mouse cursor image. As shown in Table 6-2, a total of 34 integers (in the form of a 34 element array) are passed to the routine. The first 16 of these define the cursor image itself, in the manner explained above.

The next 16 define another image, but this one is called the cursor mask. The cursor mask determines how the cursor image affects the existing contents of the screen in the area where the mouse pointer is positioned.

To simply display the cursor image as black against whatever is present on the screen, you would define the cursor image as black pixels (one bits) against a white background (zero bits), and set the cursor mask bits identically. Wherever the cursor mask bits are one, the contents of the cursor image are forced onto the screen.

In those positions where both the cursor image and mask bits are zero, the screen image will be unaltered. One way that the cursor mask can be used is to extend the mask by adding a border of additional one bits around the cursor image. This helps to make the (black) cursor visible when it is moved against a black or almost-black area of the screen. The system's standard arrow cursor uses this technique.

Look closely at the arrow cursor as you move it against the grey of the desktop and you will notice the white border surrounding it. This is caused by setting extra bits in the cursor mask. Another way that the cursor mask can be used is to leave some of its bits as zero in positions where the cursor image bits are one. These positions will cause the corresponding screen image pixels to be inverted when the mouse pointer is positioned on the screen. Table 6-3 summarizes the effects that can be produced using different combinations of cursor image and mask bits.

Table 6-3
Cursor Image and Mask Bit Combinations

Cursor Image Bit	Cursor Mask Bit	Effect on screen pixel
0	1	force to white
1	1	force to black
0	0	leave unchanged
1	0	invert (white becomes black, and black becomes white)

The Hot Spot
There are still two more elements in the array passed to SETCURSOR. These two elements are used to define what is called the cursor's *hot spot*. The hot spot is a point that may be defined anywhere on the cursor image. As you already know, the mouse coordinates represent a single pixel position on the screen. The hot spot is used to determine where these coordinates are, relative to where the mouse cursor image has been positioned at any time. For example, the standard arrow cursor would have its hot spot defined at the tip of the arrowhead itself.

The hot spot is defined as a pair of coordinates, but it does not represent a pixel position within the mouse image. The hot spot represents an imaginary point that lies at the boundary between adjacent pixels. Hot spot coordinates are illustrated in Figure 6-5; each dimension can range in value from 0 to 16. The upper left corner of the image would be at (0,0) and the lower right corner would be at (16,16).

The Mouse Cursor Development Workshop
Listing 6-5 contains a useful program I call the Mouse Cursor Development Workshop. This program lets you use the Macintosh

tools to build your own custom mouse cursors. Using the program, you define a cursor image, cursor mask, and hot spot. The program allows you to make these definitions easily, by moving the standard mouse pointer against a grid such as that shown in Figure 6-4.

Figure 6-5
Defining the Mouse Cursor Hot Spot

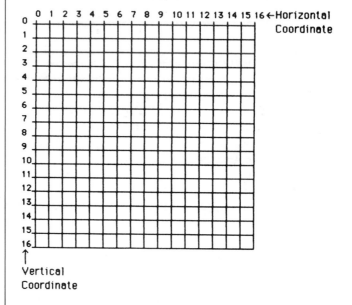

Listing 6-5
The Mouse Cursor Development Workshop

```
' This program allows you to design and test your own mouse
' cursor images. You define the cursor in three steps.
' First, you define the image of the cursor itself.
' Second, you define the cursor mask.
' Finally, you specify the cursor's hot spot.
' When you have completely defined the cursor, it will be presented to you
' on the screen, and you can test the hot spot by clicking the mouse
' button to turn on pixels at the hot spot.
' When you are satisfied with the cursor you have designed, this program
' can be instructed to save the cursor definition as a set of DATA
' statements to the Macintosh Clipboard. From there, the definition
' can be included for use in other programs. See text for more information.
DIM Image%(15)          'holds the image you define on the screen
DIM Cursor%(33)         'holds the complete mouse cursor definition
DIM SaveImage%(848)     'holds screen image for quick redrawing
StartAgain:
CLS
LOCATE 15,1
PRINT "Define mouse cursor image, triple-click when done"
' init image data to all zero, all white pixels :
FOR i=0 TO 15
Image%(i)=0
NEXT

GOSUB DefineImage       'let the user define the 16 x 16 pixel image
FOR i=0 TO 15           'place the image the user defined into Cursor% :
Cursor%(i)=Image%(i)
NEXT
GET (0,0)-(100,120),SaveImage%  'get a snapshot of the screen for quick redisplay
CLS
LOCATE 15,1
PRINT "Define mouse cursor mask, triple-click when done"
PUT (0,0)-(100,120),SaveImage%    'redisplay the mouse cursor image
PUT (100,0)-(200,120),SaveImage%  'redisplay the mouse cursor image
GOSUB DefineImage       'let the user define the 16 x 16 pixel mask
FOR i=0 TO 15                'place the mask the user defined into Cursor% :
Cursor%(i+16)=Image%(i)
NEXT
```

```
CLS
LOCATE 15,1
PRINT "Define hot spot, triple-click when ready"
PUT (100,0)-(200,120),SaveImage%   'redisplay the mouse cursor image
GOSUB DrawGrid          'draw a fresh 16 x 16 grid for the user to select on
' Prepare to get hot spot from user, set up default hot spot at (0,0) :
Hotx=0
Hoty=0
GetHot:
LOCATE 13,1
PRINT "Hot spot at ";Hotx,Hoty;
GetHotClick:                        'wait for user to make a mouse selection
GOSUB MouseWait
IF b=3 THEN GOTO GotHot         ' a triple-click enters the hot spot data
IF x<10 OR x>90 OR y<10 OR y>90 THEN GOTO GetHotClick
x=x-10                          'adjust coordinates to zero base
y=y-10
' The selection must be exactly on a set of grid lines :
IF x MOD 5 <> 0 OR y MOD 5 <> 0 THEN GOTO GetHot
Hotx=x\5                        'convert screen coords to grid coords
Hoty=y\5
GOTO GetHot   'stay in this section until the user enters the data via triple-click

' The user entered the hot spot data :
GotHot:
Cursor%(32)=Hoty         'place user's hot spot definition into Cursor%
Cursor%(33)=Hotx

' Cursor% array now complete.
CLS
PRINT "New cursor defined and now active for testing"
PRINT "Press S to save cursor definition to the clipboard"
PRINT "Press C to change definition"

' make the defined cursor active for a demo :
CALL SETCURSOR(VARPTR(Cursor%(0)))

' let the user play with the new cursor, also check for keyboard commands
' as defined above :
DemoCursor:
a$=INKEY$
IF a$="S" OR a$="s" THEN GOTO SaveFile
IF a$="C" OR a$="c" THEN CALL INITCURSOR : GOTO StartAgain
' check for mouse button clicks so the hot spot can be checked :
b=MOUSE(0)
IF b<>1 AND b<>-1 THEN GOTO DemoCursor
x=MOUSE(3)
y=MOUSE(4)
IF x<0 OR y<0 THEN GOTO DemoCursor
PSET (x,y)              'show where the hot spot is at button click
GOTO DemoCursor

' Save the cursor definition on the clipboard.
' The cursor definition is saved as a set of five DATA statements.
SaveFile:
OPEN "O",1,"CLIP:TEXT"
i=0
FOR j=1 TO 4
PRINT#1,"DATA ",
FOR k=1 TO 7
PRINT#1, Cursor%(i),",",
i=i+1
NEXT
PRINT#1, Cursor%(i)
i=i+1
NEXT
PRINT #1,"DATA ",Cursor%(i),",",Cursor%(i+1)
CLOSE 1

CLS
PRINT "Image data saved on clipboard"
END
' Subroutine to allow the user to define a graphics image on a
' 16 pixel by 16 pixel grid, and return the graphics data in array Image%
```

Listing 6-5—cont.

```
' This subroutine returns when the user triple-clicks the mouse.
DefineImage:
GOSUB DrawGrid              'displays the 16 x 16 grid at (10,10) on the screen
GetLoc:
GOSUB MouseWait            'wait for and get a mouse selection
IF b=3 THEN RETURN         'mouse was triple-clicked
' mouse must be clicked within the 16 x 16 grid.
IF x<10 OR x>90 OR y<10 OR y>90 THEN GOTO GetLoc
' convert screen coord to 16 x 16 grid coord :
x=(x-10)\5           'adjust x to range 0-15
y=(y-10)\5           'adjust y to range 0-15
' convert x coord into a single bit position value in integer variable x% :
IF x=0 THEN x%=-32768! ELSE x%=2^(15-x)
' invert that bit position in the appropriate entry of the Image% array :
Image%(y)=Image%(y) XOR x%
' determine whether the bit just altered is now zero or one :
Pixel=Image%(y) AND x%
' and set the screen display of that pixel accordingly :
IF Pixel=0 THEN GOSUB ResetPixel ELSE GOSUB SetPixel
GOTO GetLoc          'stay here until the user triple-clicks

' Subroutine to reset a pixel position on the 16 x 16 grid.
' The pixel is reset both on the grid and in the smaller, real image
' interpretation below.
ResetPixel:
PRESET (x+10,y+100)   'reset the pixel in the smaller, real image interpretation
' convert grid coords to screen coords :
x=x*5+11
y=y*5+11
LINE (x,y)-(x+3,y+3),30,BF       'reset the pixel on the grid
RETURN

' Subroutine to set a pixel position on the 16 x 16 grid.
' The pixel is set both on the grid and in the smaller, real image
' interpretation below.
SetPixel:
PSET (x+10,y+100)     'set the pixel in the smaller, real image interpretation
' convert grid coords to screen coords :
x=x*5+11
y=y*5+11
LINE (x,y)-(x+3,y+3),33,BF         'set the pixel on the grid
RETURN

' Subroutine to display the 16 x 16 grid :
' The grid is composed of a set of horizontal and vertical lines that are
' spaced five pixels apart. The grid is origined at screen coord (10,10).
' Each "cell" (pixel position) in the grid will actually occupy a 2 x 2 pixel
' area on the screen.
DrawGrid:
FOR i=10 TO 90 STEP 5
LINE (i,10)-(i,90)
LINE (10,i)-(90,i)
NEXT
RETURN

' Subroutine to wait until the user takes a mouse action.
' This subroutine will only return on a single or triple-click.
' It returns b = value of MOUSE(0) = button status
'              x= value of MOUSE(3) = x coord at time of click
'              y= value of MOUSE(4) = y coord at time of click
MouseWait:
b=MOUSE(0)
IF b=3 THEN RETURN
IF b<>1 THEN GOTO MouseWait
x=MOUSE(3)
y=MOUSE(4)
RETURN
```

As you define the image, a "life-sized" copy of it is also displayed. Based upon your input, the program calculates the appropriate values for the SETCURSOR array. You can test the cursor you build by making it active, and you can see where you placed the hot spot by clicking to alter screen pixels.

Finally, the program can be instructed to generate a set of DATA statements containing the SETCURSOR array values. The program will automatically write these statements to the clipboard, from which they can be easily included in your own programs. It is a very useful program indeed!

When you run this program, it begins by displaying a copy of the 16 × 16 pixel grid shown in Figure 6-4. The program prompts you to define the cursor image. You do so by moving the mouse pointer to each pixel position on the grid and clicking. You can click once to turn the pixel on (black); clicking again will turn the pixel off (back to white).

As you build the image in this fashion, a "life-size" copy of it appears below the grid. This gives you the opportunity to see what your cursor looks like as you define it. Figure 6-6 shows this phase of the program; I am creating a mouse cursor image that looks like a fat arrow pointing directly to the left. When you are satisfied with the image, triple-click the mouse button. Your image will be moved to the right on the screen.

Figure 6-6
Defining the Cursor Image with the Workshop

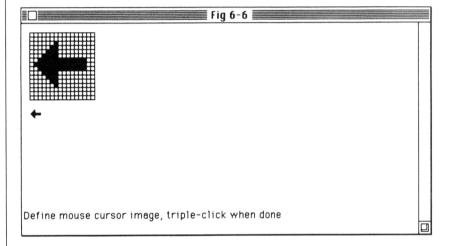

A new grid then appears on the left, and it contains a duplicate of the image you just defined. The prompt now instructs you to define the cursor mask. If you simply triple-click the mouse button now, the program provides a "default" mask that is identical to your image. This allows your image to appear in black against any screen background, although it may be hard to discern if moved against a black background.

To alleviate this problem, you can manually add a border of additional black pixels to the cursor mask at this point. Figure 6-7 shows that I have done this with my sample custom cursor. You can also experiment with screen inverting cursors by resetting some of the image pixels in the mask at this point. In any event, you must triple-click the mouse button when you are satisfied with the mask image.

Figure 6-7

*Defining the Cursor
Mask with the
Workshop*

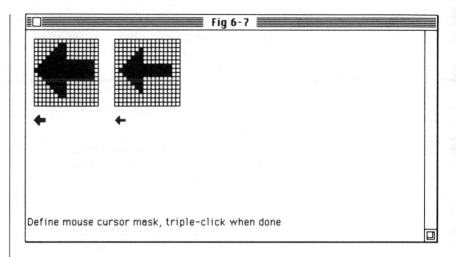

The program will then display a fresh grid and prompt you to define your hot spot. The default hot spot coordinates are (0,0) and are displayed near the prompt at the bottom of the screen. To select a different hot spot, very carefully position the mouse pointer to any point where a set of grid lines intersect and click the mouse button. Since valid selection points exist only at specific locations on the screen, you may find it difficult at first to make this selection. Watch the screen display, as it will change when you make a successful selection and will indicate the new hot spot coordinates. In Figure 6-8, I am selecting the hot spot for my cursor, at coordinates (1,7).

Figure 6-8

*Defining the Hot Spot
with the Workshop*

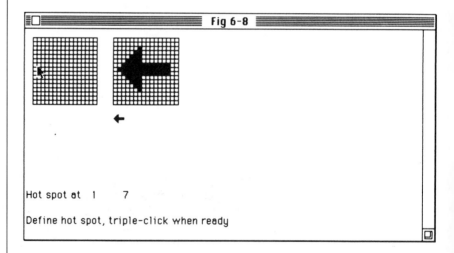

When you are satisfied with the hot spot, triple-click the mouse button. This will activate your cursor and present you with the cursor test screen. The cursor test screen allows you to move your cursor around on the screen to see what it will look like against various screen backgrounds. While this screen is active, you can test the location of the hot spot by simply clicking the mouse button. Each mouse click will set the pixel at the current mouse coordinates. Figure 6-9 shows the test screen with my custom cursor.

There are two ways to exit from the test screen. You can press the <C> key to change the cursor definition. This effectively restarts the program. Alternatively, you can press the <S> key to save your current definition as a set of DATA statements on the clipboard. Figure 6-10 shows the data produced for my example. Selecting this option also causes the program to terminate.

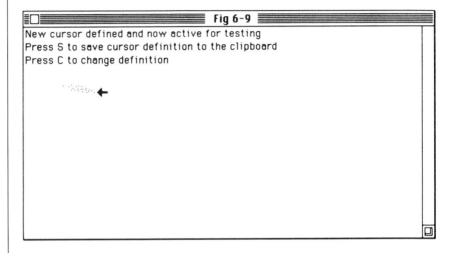

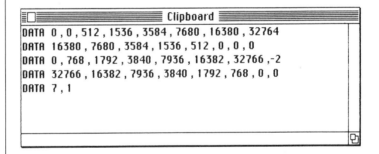

Using this program, you can now design your own custom cursors. When you are satisfied with the cursor you have created, use the Save option to save the pertinent data on the clipboard. From the clipboard, you can copy this data into your own programs. This is done by simply loading in the program desired, selecting an appropriate insertion point, and using the Paste command to insert the contents of the clipboard. Be sure that you do not destroy the clipboard contents between the time that you save the cursor data and the time that you perform the Paste. This can, unfortunately, be easily done by accident when using the Cut or Copy functions of the edit menu.

Once you have the data in your own program, it is an easy matter to use it. Define an integer array with 34 elements, READ the data into the array with a simple FOR-NEXT loop, and then reference the array in a SETCURSOR call. Listing 6-6 shows what this arrangement will look like.

Listing 6-6
*Sample Cursor Data
with Demo*

```
' This program contains the data statements used to create the sample
' mouse cursors shown in the text. When run, this program demos each
' cursor in turn. The program will end with an out-of-data error message.
DIM Cursor%(33)
CLS
PRINT "Press any key to see next cursor example."
PRINT "Click mouse to see location of hot spot."
Again:
FOR i=0 TO 33              'get next set of cursor data from DATA statements :
READ Cursor%(i)
NEXT
CALL SETCURSOR(VARPTR(Cursor%(0)))   'define new cursor
WaitKey:
a$=INKEY$
IF a$<>"" THEN CALL INITCURSOR : GOTO Again 'any key goes on to next sample
b=MOUSE(0)
IF b<>1 AND b<>-1 THEN GOTO WaitKey   'only detect single mouse clicks
x=MOUSE(3)                           'get mouse coords at time of click
y=MOUSE(4)
IF x<0 OR y<0 THEN GOTO WaitKey
PSET (x,y)                  'show location of hot spot via a pixel
GOTO WaitKey
'
' The sample cursor data follows:
' .
' Left-pointing arrow cursor :
DATA 0 , 0 , 512 , 1536 , 3584 , 7680 , 16380 , 32764
DATA 16380 , 7680 , 3584 , 1536 , 512 , 0 , 0 , 0
DATA 0 , 768 , 1792 , 3840 , 7936 , 16382 , 32766 ,-2
DATA 32766 , 16382 , 7936 , 3840 , 1792 , 768 , 0 , 0
DATA 7 , 1
' Diagonal Cross-hairs, flickers when moved against standard
' Macintosh grey desktop pattern :
DATA -32766 , 16388 , 8200 , 4112 , 2080 , 1088 , 896 , 640
DATA 896 , 1088 , 2080 , 4112 , 8200 , 16388 ,-32766 , 0
DATA -16378 ,-8178 , 28700 , 14392 , 7280 , 4064 , 1984 , 1984
DATA 1984 , 4064 , 7280 , 14392 , 28700 ,-8178 ,-16378 , 0
DATA 7 , 7
' Diamond shaped cross-hair with hot spot at center :
DATA 0 , 256 , 896 , 1344 , 2336 , 4368 , 8456 , 32508
DATA 8456 , 4368 , 2336 , 1344 , 896 , 256 , 0 , 0
DATA 256 , 896 , 1984 , 4064 , 8176 , 16376 , 32764 ,-2
DATA 32764 , 16376 , 8176 , 4064 , 1984 , 896 , 256 , 0
DATA 7 , 7
' Solid caret with hot spot at top :
DATA 0 , 0 , 0 , 0 , 0 , 0 , 0 , 128
DATA 448 , 992 , 2032 , 4088 , 8188 , 16382 , 0 , 0
DATA 0 , 0 , 0 , 0 , 0 , 0 , 128 , 448
DATA 992 , 2032 , 4088 , 8188 , 16382 , 32767 , 32767 , 0
DATA 7 , 8
' A mouse cursor that looks like a mouse !
' The hot spot is at the tip of the mouse's tail :
DATA 0 , 0 , 0 , 0 , 496 , 520 , 1028 ,-30670
DATA 18482 , 12290 , 2050 , 4094 , 0 , 0 , 0 , 0
DATA 0 , 0 , 0 , 0 , 496 , 520 , 1028 ,-30670
DATA 18482 , 12290 , 2050 , 4094 , 0 , 0 , 0 , 0
DATA 7 , 0
' Similar to the standard Mac arrow, but pointing up and to the right
' instead of up and to the left :
DATA 0 , 2 , 6 , 14 , 30 , 62 , 126 , 254
DATA 510 , 62 , 54 , 98 , 96 , 192 , 192 , 0
DATA 3 , 7 , 15 , 31 , 63 , 127 , 255 , 511
DATA 1023 , 1023 , 127 , 247 , 243 , 480 , 480 , 480
DATA 1 , 15
```

In writing the program shown in Listing 6-6, I used the Mouse Cursor Development Workshop to create six custom cursors. The first one is the left pointing arrow of Figure 6-6. The second appears as a pair of diagonal cross hairs, with the hot spot at the center. This cursor is interesting in that, when moved against the standard desktop "grey" pattern, it flickers. It is shown in Figure 6-11.

The third cursor is a diamond shaped cross hair that obliterates any image it is moved against; it also has the hot spot at the center, and is shown in Figure 6-12. The fourth cursor is a solid "caret" symbol with the hot spot at the top and is shown in Figure 6-13. The fifth cursor looks like a mouse itself! The hot spot is at the tip of the mouse's tail, as seen in Figure 6-14.

Figure 6-11
The Diagonal Cross-hairs Cursor

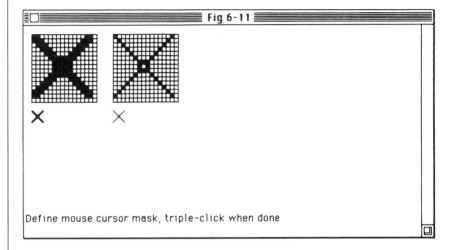

Figure 6-12
The Diamond Cross-hairs Cursor

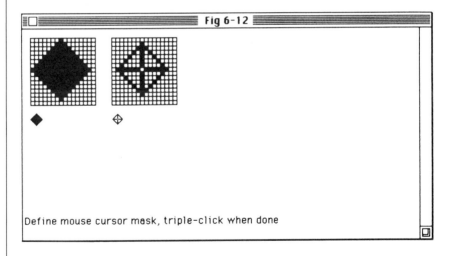

Finally, my last custom cursor is almost identical to the standard arrow cursor, except that it points upward and to the right instead of upward and to the left, as shown in Figure 6-15.

The data for each of these cursors was pasted from the clipboard into the test program, and appears in Listing 6-6. When you run the program you can try out each of them. After trying the last example, the program will end with an "Out-of-Data" error.

Figure 6-13
The Solid Caret Cursor

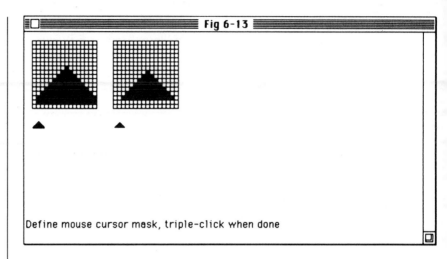

Figure 6-14
*The Mouse Cursor that
Looks Like a Mouse*

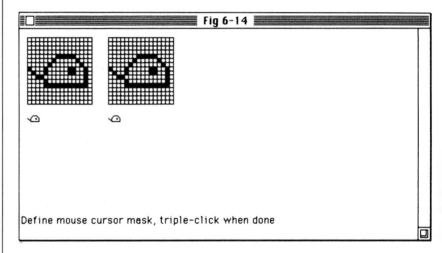

How the Cursor Development Program Works

The cursor development program in Listing 6-5 is in itself an excellent demonstration of the various functions covered in this chapter. It is therefore worth studying in greater detail.

The program begins by defining three integer arrays: array *Image%* has sixteen elements and is used to hold a cursor or mask image, as defined by the user on the development grid; array *Cursor%* has 34 elements and will ultimately hold the complete mouse cursor definition; array *SaveImage%* is much larger, and is used with a set of graphics GET and PUT statements to manipulate sections of the Output window during the program's execution.

A major component of the program is the subroutine named DefineImage. This routine is responsible for presenting the user with the 16 × 16 pixel development grid, detecting mouse clicks within the grid, and converting those clicks into a complete image.

The routine displays the image on the screen and returns it in the contents of array *Image%*. The routine does not return until the user triple-clicks the mouse button. Its first action is to call on another subroutine, named DrawGrid, which simply displays the development grid on the screen.

Figure 6-15
The Left-handed Arrow Cursor

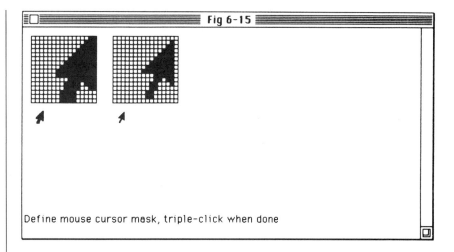

Define mouse cursor mask, triple-click when done

The development grid consists of a set of sixteen horizontal and sixteen vertical lines. Each line is separated from its neighbors by five pixels. This provides a four pixel square area for each cell within the grid. Mouse clicks within these cell areas must be detected and converted into the appropriate coordinates (0–15 in each dimension).

The program relies on another subroutine, MouseWait, for mouse input. This routine waits for either single or triple mouse button clicks, and then returns with the mouse coordinates at the time of the click in variables x and y. Variable b indicates the number of times the mouse was clicked. When the routine returns $b = 3$, subroutine DefineImage knows that the user triple-clicked the mouse and so it returns to its caller.

For single-clicks, the mouse coordinates are inspected. The grid area is eighty pixels wide and high, and its upper left corner starts at screen location (10,10). If the mouse coordinates are not within the grid area, the click is ignored. Otherwise, each coordinate is decreased by ten and then integer-divided by five to convert it into a value in the range 0–15. The x-coordinate is converted into the value representing a single bit position, as per Figure 6-4. The y-coordinate selects the appropriate element of the *Image*% array.

The logical function XOR is used to invert the selected bit position in the array. Thus, each mouse click in a given cell will flip that cell back and forth between the white and black states.

The logical function AND is then used to test the current state of the bit by isolating it within its element. If the result of this operation is zero, then the bit is currently zero; any other value indicates that the bit is currently one. Based upon this outcome, the program knows whether to set or reset the pixel on the screen. This is done by either subroutine SetPixel or ResetPixel. In each case, the pixel must be altered both on the grid and in the smaller "life-size" version of the image.

The "life-size" version appears with its upper left corner at (10,100) and is easy to address. The grid copy of the pixel is a two pixel by two pixel square area whose upper left corner is calculated by multiplying each coordinate by five and then adding eleven. A

LINE statement with the BF (box filled) option is then used to fill in the selected area.

The main program begins by initializing an all zero (all white) image, and then calling subroutine DefineImage. In this step, the user defines his custom cursor image. When the routine returns, the data in *Image%* is copied into the first sixteen elements of *Cursor%*. A graphics GET statement is then employed to save a copy of the grid and "life-size" images of the cursor. Of course, with the data in *Cursor%*, we could always manually reconstruct these images, but this approach is much easier.

The screen is cleared, and the prompt for the cursor mask is displayed. Before calling DefineImage, graphics PUT statements are used to redisplay the image, both in the development grid area, and slightly to the right. The copy on the right serves as a reference for the user in defining the mask.

Once again, the DefineImage subroutine is called to allow the user to turn selected pixels on and off in the development grid. On return, the sixteen elements of *Image%* are copied into elements 16 through 31 of *Cursor%*. The screen is cleared and the default hot spot coordinate (0,0) is set into variables *Hotx* and *Hoty*.

Along with the text prompt, a graphics PUT statement displays a reference copy of the cursor image, as defined by the user in the previous step. Subroutine DrawGrid is called upon once again to display the development grid. Subroutine MouseWait is employed to wait until the user clicks the mouse button. If the mouse is clicked outside of the grid area, the click is ignored. Otherwise, ten is subtracted from each coordinate to base their values at zero (this is necessary because the grid is aligned to screen coordinate (10,10)).

If either coordinate value modulo five is not zero, then the selection was not made at an exact intersection of the grid lines, and so the selection is ignored. If the selection is valid, then a simple integer division by five converts the screen coordinate selected to a grid coordinate in the range 0 - 16. These values are used for *Hotx* and *Hoty*, and are displayed at the bottom of the screen. This section of the program is exited when the user triple-clicks the mouse button. At that time, the values for *Hotx* and *Hoty* are inserted into the last two elements of the *Cursor%* array.

At this time, the *Cursor%* array is complete and ready to be used. The screen is cleared and the test screen prompts are displayed. The SETCURSOR routine is called with the memory address of the first element of the *Cursor%* array (VARPTR(Cursor%(0))). This activates the cursor that was just defined and places it on the screen.

The loop beginning with statement label DemoCursor checks for a keyboard command (either <S> or <C>) via the **INKEY$** function, and also checks for single mouse button clicks. The latter are used to set the corresponding pixels on the screen, thus helping to identify the new cursor's hot spot.

The keyboard command <C> causes the program to restart at statement label StartAgain (note that the INITCURSOR call is used in this case to restore the normal system cursor). The keyboard command <S> causes the program to continue at label SaveFile, where the data for the cursor will be saved.

The save function opens the CLIP:TEXT device for sequential output. File number 1 is used. A set of PRINT#1 statements output the contents of the *Cursor*% array in the form of DATA statements. When all of the data has been output (five DATA statements in all), the file is closed and the program terminates.

Chapter 7

Graphics Revisited

Now it is time to look at the more sophisticated graphics capabilities of Macintosh. Many of these capabilities come from the Macintosh Toolbox, a set of routines that come built into the ROM (read-only memory) of the machine. In the last chapter, you saw how such toolbox routines could be invoked from within a BASIC program. In this chapter, I expand upon these concepts and introduce many more toolbox routines. You will learn how to control text format and appearance as well as text fonts and styles. Other routines allow you to define a graphics "pen" with which you can "draw" lines on the screen.

The familiar shapes that make up much of the Macintosh user interface (rectangles, rounded rectangles, ovals, etc.) can also be quickly created using these routines. Finally, you will see how these graphics commands can be combined with Microsoft BASIC graphic commands (discussed in Chapter 5) under a single unifying structure. In this fashion, a complete graphics image, as defined by a sequence of many and varied graphics commands, can be stored and manipulated as a single entity.

Controlling the Appearance of Text

You may wonder why I have chosen to discuss control of text appearance in a chapter that is supposed to be about graphics. The Macintosh provides you with extremely powerful control over text appearance, and it does this so well because it actually treats all text as a special case of graphics images. This is not immediately apparent, because you create text with PRINT statements, while a whole world of other statement types are used to create graphics images (i.e., LINE, CIRCLE, and PUT).

It is important to realize that each character you print is nothing more than a special, predefined graphics image; all Macintosh characters are formed by appropriate combinations of those black and white pixels that you have learned so much about in the last few chapters.

Character Fonts

A collection of graphics images that makes up a complete character set is called a *font*. There are many different fonts available for use with the Macintosh and at any time you may have a variety of such fonts available for use by your program. Some examples are shown in Figure 7-1.

Figure 7-1
Sample Text Fonts

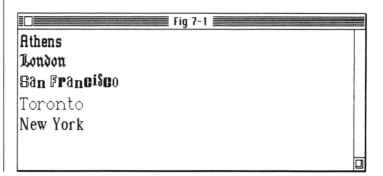

Fonts are provided in different sizes. The size of a font is specified in pixels and represents the vertical size (height) of the characters produced. Font sizes typically vary from 9 (very small characters) to 36 (fairly large characters). Representative font sizes are shown in Figure 7-2.

Figure 7-2
Sample Text Sizes

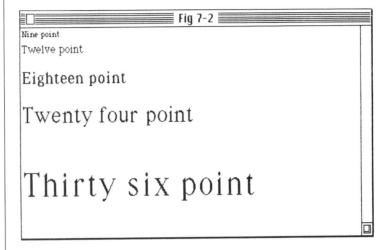

When specifying a font, be sure that the font is available in the character size that you intend to use. If it is not, there can be undesirable side effects (which I will explain shortly).

Fonts are stored as part of the system file on bootable disks. To determine whether a font is available on a particular disk, you must use an Apple utility program called The Font Mover.

The Font Mover lets you copy fonts into and out of the system. Fonts copied out of the system are held in a file named Fonts, which you can use to transfer fonts from one disk to another.

The reason why all of this bother is necessary is because fonts take up a lot of space on disk. If you had all of the fonts that I will demonstrate available on a single disk, little room would be left for your own programs. Most people keep only the fonts that they intend to use in their system, to maximize the available disk space. Unused fonts are kept in the Fonts file on a backup disk. You can therefore see why it is important to insure that a font is available before using it in a program.

Font Size Scaling

If you specify that you wish to use a particular font in a particular size, and the font is not available in that size, the Macintosh will automatically try to scale the characters (in whatever size it does have available) to the size requested. In general this is very undesirable process and you should try to avoid it. The scaling process takes time, and so any program that displays a lot of characters in an unavailable font size will be seriously slowed down.

Another problem is that many fonts do not scale well to certain sizes. Figure 7-3 shows what happened when I tried to display some data in the Monaco-12 font when only the Monaco-9 font was available in the system. As you can see, the scaling process damaged the legibility of the characters.

Figure 7-3
*Font Size Scaling
(Monaco-9 Available,
Monaco-12 Scaled)*

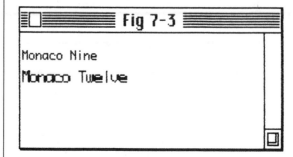

Default Font Designations

There are certain fonts that you can rely on always to be present the system. These fonts are used by the system itself and therefore must always be available. As of this writing, the system uses Chicago-12 for window titles, Geneva-9 and -12 for miscellaneous information displays, and Monaco-9 for small nonproportionally spaced text.

The Monaco font is unique in that it is not a proportional font, and so all characters in Monaco take up the same amount of horizontal space. Geneva-12 is the default font used by Microsoft BASIC. I caution that these designations may be changed by Apple in later releases of the Macintosh Finder.

The TEXTFONT and TEXTSIZE Routines

You can set the font to be used when displaying data through use of the *TEXTFONT* and *TEXTSIZE* toolbox routines. The TEXTFONT routine takes a single input parameter that indicates the desired font, as per Table 7-1. The TEXTSIZE routine takes an input parameter that specifies the size of that font.

Table 7-1
*TEXTFONT Input
Parameter*

0	Chicago
1	Default font used by BASIC (currently Geneva)
2	New York
3	Geneva
4	Monaco
5	Venice
6	London
7	Athens
8	San Francisco
9	Toronto
10	Seattle
11	Cairo

If you call either routine with invalid values, the active font will not be changed. Sample programs demonstrating the use of these routines are shown in Listings 7-1 and 7-2. They produce the outputs shown in Figures 7-1 and 7-2, respectively. You will not be able to reproduce those results, however, unless you have the specified font available on your disk when the programs are run.

```
CALL TEXTSIZE (18)          ' set size to 18 point
LOCATE 1,1  'set starting display position appropriately for 18 point
FOR i=1 TO 5
READ font,nf$
CALL TEXTFONT(font)          ' make the specified font active
PRINT nf$
NEXT
' Sample font codes. For each font sampled, the name of that
' font is displayed :
DATA 7,Athens
DATA 6,London
DATA 8,"San Francisco"
DATA 9,Toronto
DATA 2,"New York"
```

```
' The program displays several different sizes of the
' "New York" font. See text for more information.
CALL TEXTFONT(2)          ' set New York font
FOR i=1 TO 5
READ size,sizename$
CALL TEXTSIZE(size)          ' set specified text size
LOCATE i,1  ' set starting display position for that text size
PRINT sizename$
NEXT
END
' Sample data showing commonly used font sizes. A textual
' description of the size is used as the demonstration data
' for each size.
DATA 9,"Nine point"
DATA 12,"Twelve point"
DATA 18,"Eighteen point"
DATA 24,"Twenty four point"
DATA 36,"Thirty six point"
```

These two demonstration programs are basically very simple and straightforward, although there is an important point that can be learned from them. Notice the LOCATE statement in each program. At first glance, these LOCATE statements would seem superfluous—they do not set the display position to a row-column location other than where it would have been anyway at the moment(s) they are employed.

Why then, are they present? All text displayed within a Macintosh window is displayed starting at a particular location. This location is called the pen position, and it is specified as the coordinates of any pixel within that window (the standard convention assigning coordinate (0,0) to the upper left corner is used).

When you tell BASIC that you want to display text at a specific row and column via the LOCATE statement, it calculates the pen position based upon that row and column, as well as the current text size. It is therefore important to use the LOCATE statement after initially setting a specific text size, so that any PRINT statements that follow will produce text that is properly positioned.

If the pen position is allowed to remain set to a value calculated on the basis of a smaller text size, then some of your displayed text will be lost or will overlap other text. You can see this for yourself by removing the LOCATE statements from the sample programs in Listings 7-1 and 7-2, and then executing the altered programs. The pen position concept will be covered in more detail later in this chapter.

Fancy Text Styles

Because all text characters are actually graphics images, it is easy for Apple to offer basic style enhancement options for all fonts. The style enhancement options allow you to display characters in italics, boldface, and underlined, among others. You can enable any of these options through use of the TEXTFACE routine. This routine accepts a single numeric input parameter that selects the enhancement options desired. Calling the routine with an input parameter of zero turns off all options.

Each option is represented by a different numeric value, as shown in Table 7-2. You can turn on more than one option at the same time by simply adding together two or more of the values shown in the table. Thus, for example, a value of five would represent both the bold and underlined options (bold $= 1$, underlined $= 4$, $1 + 4 = 5$).

Table 7-2
TEXTFACE Input Parameter

0	Turn off all style enhancements
1	Boldface
2	Italic
4	Underlined
32	Compressed
64	Expanded

Exercise restraint when using several options at once, as the composite effect of too many options can often be unattractive to look at. Also, some fonts do not lend themselves well to certain style enhancements. In fact, the italic enhancement only really works well with the Monaco font.

Listing 7-3 contains a sample program that demonstrates the use of style enhancement options and the TEXTFACE routine. Figure 7-4 shows the output produced when this program is run. The Monaco-18 font is used.

Text Display Modes

Recall the image transfer mode option of the graphics PUT statement. That option allowed us to control how the pixels of the image being displayed would affect the pixels in the relevant area of the screen. In a similar fashion, you can instruct the Macintosh to

Listing 7-3
Style Enhancement
Demo

```
CALL TEXTSIZE(18)        ' set 18 point size
LOCATE 1,1               ' set pen position as per point size
CALL TEXTFONT(4)          'set Monaco font
FOR i=1 TO 8
READ style,stylename$
CALL TEXTFACE(style)
PRINT stylename$
NEXT
END
' Each of the single style options, as well as two combinations, are
' sampled by the following data :
DATA 0,Plain
DATA 1,Bold
DATA 2,Italic
DATA 4,Underlined
DATA 32,Condensed
DATA 64,Expanded
DATA 3,"Bold and Italic"
DATA 68,"Underlined and Expanded"
```

Figure 7-4
Text Style Enhancements

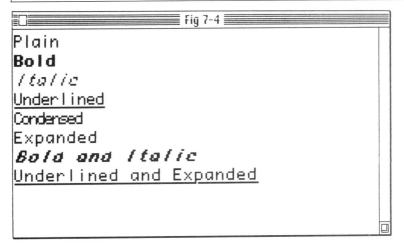

use different text display modes whenever text is displayed. The default text display mode simply causes the character image to replace the previous contents of the screen.

Characters are, of course, defined as black pixels against a white background, and this is how they normally appear on the Macintosh screen. There are three alternative text display modes; they are called OR, XOR, and BIC.

The OR and XOR modes are identical to their counterparts as used in the graphics PUT statement. The OR mode combines the black pixels of the character being displayed with any previously black pixels on the screen. Thus, if the screen background is black, you would not see any text displayed using the OR mode.

The XOR mode causes the black pixels in the character image to invert the corresponding pixel positions on the screen, the white pixel positions in the character image do not alter the previous screen contents. This mode could thus be used to display text automatically in black when the background is white, and in white if the background is black. (The default mode, analogous to the PSET mode of the graphics PUT statement, would display characters as black on white regardless of the preexisting screen background.)

The *BIC* mode stands for *Black Is Changed*. This mode has no counterpart in the mode options of the graphics PUT statement. When this mode is used, all of the black pixels in the character image are displayed on the screen as white. The existing screen pixels are not altered in those positions where the character image pixels are white. This mode can thus be used when you want to display characters in white only; they will be visible if displayed against a black background, but invisible against a white background.

Using a text display mode other than the default is only necessary when you want to display text combined with, or in a manner determined by, the preexisting contents of the screen. The prevailing text display mode is set by a call to the TEXTMODE routine. The numeric input parameter to this routine selects the desired mode, as per Table 7-3.

The sample program of Listing 7-4 demonstrates the action taken by each text display mode. The output produced by this program is shown in Figure 7-5. The program begins by setting up three different background areas on the screen. There is a white area, a black area (produced using a LINE statement with the box filled option), and a grey area composed of a pattern of evenly spaced lines.

The program displays the same message, against each of these backgrounds, using each of the text display modes. Figure 7-5 provides a visually succinct summary of the effect of each of the modes. The default mode (PSET) displays text as black against a white background, regardless of any preexisting material on the screen. The OR mode will produce visible text in black against a

Listing 7-4
Text Display Modes
Demo

```
' This program begins by setting up several different backgrounds
' on the screen, so that the significant differences between each
' mode can be illustrated.
LINE (100,0)-(200,300),,BF        ' set up a black area on the screen
FOR y=0 TO 300 STEP 2             'set up a grey area on the screen
LINE (200,y)-(350,y)
NEXT
LOCATE 4,1                        'set starting position for the demo
FOR i=0 TO 3       'display the same message using each of the four modes :
CALL TEXTMODE(i)
PRINT "Look at all of these wonderful different modes ! ! ! "
NEXT
```

Table 7-3
TEXTMODE Input
Parameter

0	PSET (Text, in black on white, replaces whatever is currently on the screen.)
1	OR (Text in black is superimposed on any other black image already on screen.)
2	XOR (Image of text inverts any previous data on screen. Text will therefore appear in black if screen was previously white. Text will appear in white if screen was previously black.)
3	BIC (Text is displayed in white, but the screen area must have previously been set to black or text will not be visible.)

preexisting white background. Text produced using the OR mode will be invisible against a preexisting black background. The XOR mode will display text in black if the preexisting background is white, and in white if the preexisting background is black.

Finally, the BIC mode will display text in white against a preexisting black background. Text produced using the BIC mode will be invisible against a preexisting white background.

Figure 7-5
Text Display Modes

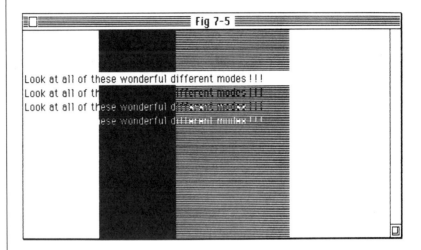

The Pen Position

As mentioned earlier, the graphics images (including text) that are produced by the toolbox routines are drawn with an imaginary "graphics pen." The position of the pen at any time determines where the next image will appear. In this section, I show you the toolbox routines that you can use to manipulate the pen position.

Controlling the pen position allows you to specify where text will appear, right down to a specific pixel location. This is a much finer degree of control than you have when using the LOCATE statement, which only allows you to position text on (character) row column boundaries.

The *GETPEN* routine can be used to determine the current pen position. It returns the pen position in a two element integer array. The array must be predefined and its address must be passed to the GETPEN routine using the **VARPTR** function. The vertical coordinate of the pen position will be returned in the first element of the array, while the horizontal coordinate will be returned in the second element. Figure 7-6 illustrates how the GETPEN routine may be used.

The *MOVETO* routine is used to actually set a new pen position. It accepts two numeric values as input parameters; these specify the horizontal and vertical coordinates for the pen. Thus, for example, the statement

```
CALL MOVETO(10,30)
```

would set the pen position to pixel location (10,30) within the current output window.

Figure 7-6
The GETPEN Routine

```
' The GETPEN routine is used to obtain the current
' pen position as a set of screen coordinates.
' First, dimension an integer array with two elements
' to hold the result returned by GETPEN :
DIM PenLoc%(1)
' Now, call the routine, passing the address of the
' array through use of the VARPTR function :
CALL GETPEN(VARPTR(PenLoc%(0)))
' On return, PenLoc%(0) holds the vertical coordinate
' and PenLoc%(1) holds the horizontal coordinate of the
' pen position :
PRINT "Pen was positioned at x=";PenLoc%(1);"    y=";PenLoc%(0)
END
```

The MOVE routine can also be used to set a new pen position. Unlike MOVETO, however, the coordinates specified in a MOVE routine call are considered relative to the current pen position. Thus, for example, the statement

```
CALL MOVE(5,10)
```

would move the pen five pixels to the right and ten pixels below its current position.

Negative values can be passed to the MOVE routine. A negative *x* value causes the pen location to be moved to the left, while a negative *y* value causes the pen location to be moved up.

Recall the pie chart program in Listing 5-7. At the time I introduced that program, I mentioned that it would be nice to be able to add descriptive labels to each pie piece. Using the pen positioning techniques just described, this can be easily accomplished. Version 2 of the pie chart program is shown in Listing 7-5.

Listing 7-5
*The Pie Chart Program
— Version 2*

```
' In this version, labels are automatically added to each
' circle piece through use of the MOVETO toolbox routine.
DIM pc(6)        ' Array pc holds each pie piece percentage
DIM Plabel$(6)   ' Holds the label for each pie piece
Pi=3.14159
' Obtain user input .
Petry:
INPUT "How many items in the pie chart ",Items
IF Items<2 OR Items>6 THEN PRINT "Invalid number of Items" : GOTO Petry
FOR i=1 TO Items
PRINT "Enter label for item ",i;
INPUT Plabel$(i)
PRINT "Enter percentage for item ",i;
INPUT pc(i)
NEXT
' Check for valid input data :
Total=0
FOR i=1 TO Items
Total=Total+pc(i)
NEXT
IF Total<>100 THEN PRINT "Invalid input, total does not equal 100%" : GOTO Retry
' First, calculate the size of each pie piece, so that the
' centerpoint for that pie piece can be calculated, based upon that
' centerpoint, position the pen and display the pie piece label :
CLS
```

Listing 7-5—cont.

```
StartAngle=0
FOR i=1 TO Items
EndAngle=StartAngle+(2*Pi*pc(i)/100)
MiddleAngle=StartAngle+ ((EndAngle-StartAngle)/2)
x=100 + 40*COS(MiddleAngle)
y=100 - 40*SIN(MiddleAngle)
CALL MOVETO (x,y)
PRINT Plabel$(i);
StartAngle=EndAngle            'set up for next pie piece
NEXT

' Now produce the pie chart itself .
StartAngle=0
FOR i=1 TO Items
EndAngle=StartAngle+(2*Pi*pc(i)/100)
IF StartAngle=0 THEN ST=2*Pi ELSE ST=StartAngle    'zero is a special case
CIRCLE (100,110),75,,-ST,-EndAngle                 'draw the pie piece
StartAngle=EndAngle                                'set up for next pie piece
NEXT
LOCATE 15,1
PRINT "Do another ? (Y/N) "
GOSUB GetYN
IF yn$="Y" THEN CLS : GOTO Retry
END
'
' Subroutine to wait until the user presses either the Y or N keys,
' in response to a yes or no question. Will not return until one of these
' keys is pressed. The keystroke character is returned in yn$.
GetYN:
yn$=INKEY$
WHILE UCASE$(yn$)<>"Y" AND UCASE$(yn$)<>"N"
yn$=INKEY$
WEND
yn$=UCASE$(yn$)
RETURN
```

This version is essentially the same as the previous version, except for the addition of the label feature. A new array has been added to the program. It is called *Plabel$* and it holds the label for each pie piece. Data is input to the elements of this array by the user when he enters the percentage data for each pie piece. The "obtain user input" loop is modified to handle this requirement. The next step, in which the input data is verified, remains unaltered.

In the original program, the next step was to create the pie pieces themselves. In this new version, the pie piece labels are produced first, and then the pie pieces are drawn. It is necessary to do things in this order because the user might enter a long label which, if drawn on top of the pie chart, would obliterate part of the chart.

The label display loop is similar to the pie piece drawing loop. *StartAngle* is initialized to zero. For each item, an *EndAngle* is calculated as that item's percentage of a complete circle (360 degrees). The objective here is to find the proper location on the screen to place the item's label. To this end, an angle that lies exactly between the *StartAngle* and the *EndAngle* is calculated. This angle is called the *MiddleAngle*.

Using simple trigonometry, a point lying near the center of the pie piece is calculated as a function of the *MiddleAngle*, the centerpoint of the pie (100,100), and a radius less than the pie's radius (40). The coordinates of this point are used as the input to the MOVETO routine. This positions the graphics pen to the center of the pie piece being processed. An ordinary PRINT statement is then employed to display that pie piece label at that position.

Once all of the labels have been displayed, the orginal pie chart drawing loop is employed to create the pie chart itself. Figure 7-7 shows some sample input data to this program, and Figure 7-8 shows the pie chart produced as a result.

Figure 7-7
Sample Pie Chart Data

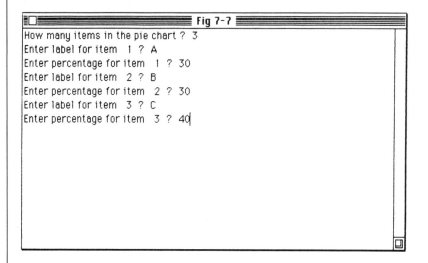

Figure 7-8
Sample Pie Chart with Labels

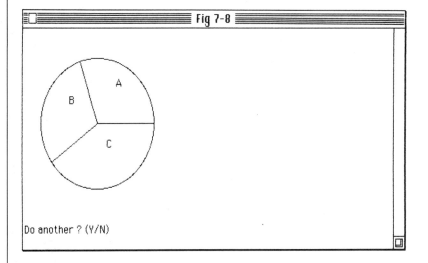

Drawing With the Graphics Pen

There are toolbox routines that let you draw lines with the graphics pen. Combined with the pen positioning routines, these give you the ability to draw lines between any two points on the screen. Of course, the Microsoft BASIC statement **LINE** also gives you this ability, but there are some advantages to using the toolbox routines, so they are worth consideration.

The *LINETO* routine draws a line from the current pen position to the coordinates specified in the routine call. Assuming the graphics pen is positioned to coordinate (10,10), the statement

```
CALL LINETO(100,20)
```

would draw a line from (10,10) to (100,20). The routine leaves the graphics pen positioned to the endpoint of the line just drawn, so in this example the pen would be left at position (100,20).

The LINE routine is similar to the LINETO routine, except that it accepts coordinates that are relative to the current pen position. For example, the statement

```
CALL LINE(100,50)
```

would draw a line from the current pen location to a point 100 pixels to the right and 50 pixels below. At the conclusion of the statement, the pen would be positioned to that new location.

A simple example illustrating how these statements can be used is shown in Figure 7-9. Here, a set of LINE routine calls is used to draw a five pointed star. A set of LINETO routine calls is then used to enclose that star in a box. Note how the MOVETO routine is used to reposition the pen between the two stages of the program.

Figure 7-9
Drawing with the Grapics Pen

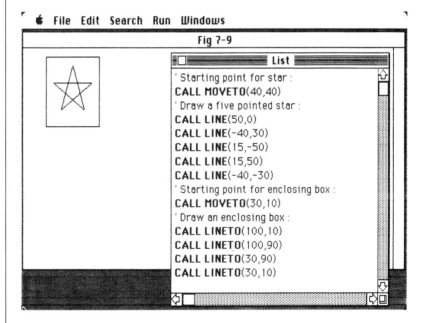

Setting the Pen Size
Thus far, I am sure you can see no advantage to using the line drawing toolbox routines over the standard Microsoft BASIC LINE statement. There is an advantage, however, and it becomes apparent when you discover that you have greater control over the graphics pen. The default pen is comprised of a single black pixel, and so it draws lines that are one pixel thick, as seen in the previous example.

It is possible, through use of yet another toolbox call, to change the dimensions of the pen itself. This allows you to draw thicker and wider lines. The size of the pen is defined by two values: a horizontal size and a vertical size. The size is set by calling the PENSIZE routine. For example, the statement

```
CALL PENSIZE(3,2)
```

would cause the pen to draw lines that are three pixels thick in the horizontal dimension and two pixels thick in the vertical dimension.

To illustrate this concept, I have provided the program in Listing 7-6. This program is identical to the demonstration of Figure 7-9, with the addition of a single CALL PENSIZE statement. The results produced by this program are illustrated in Figure 7-10. Notice that the same image is drawn, but with thicker lines.

Listing 7-6
Drawing with the Graphics Pen

```
' Set the graphics pen size to 3 x 3 :
CALL PENSIZE(3,3)
' Starting point for star :
CALL MOVETO(40,40)
' Draw a five pointed star :
CALL LINE(50,0)
CALL LINE(-40,30)
CALL LINE(15,-50)
CALL LINE(15,50)
CALL LINE(-40,-30)
' Starting point for enclosing box :
CALL MOVETO(30,10)
' Draw an enclosing box :
CALL LINETO(100,10)
CALL LINETO(100,90)
CALL LINETO(30,90)
CALL LINETO(30,10)
```

Figure 7-10
Using a Thicker Grapics Pen

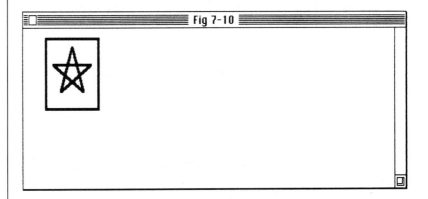

Setting the Pen Pattern
In the previous example, the graphics pen was expanded to a three pixel by three pixel square area, and all of the pixels in the area remained black. Not only is it possible to expand the pen size in this fashion, but a custom pen pattern can be specified as well. This means that the pen does not have to draw only with black pixels, but there can be white pixels within the pen area as well.

The largest allowable pen size is eight pixels high by eight pixels wide. For any pen size greater than a single pixel, you can specify a custom pattern for the pen. This is done through the PENPAT toolbox call.

The PENPAT routine accepts as input an integer array with four elements. The contents of the array define an eight pixel square pattern, in much the same way as the mouse cursor images were defined to the *SETCURSOR* routine. Since each element of an integer array can hold 16 bits, each element represents two consecutive rows of the complete image. This is why only four elements are needed for an image with eight rows and eight columns. This arrangement is illustrated by Figure 7-11.

Figure 7-11
Defining the Pen Pattern

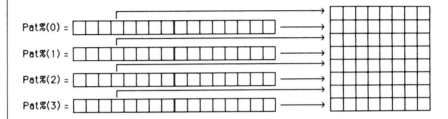

Each element of Pat% is an integer comprised of 16 bits, as shown above. The pen pattern is an eight bit by eight bit array.

Once a pen pattern has been set up in an array (say *Pat%*), it can be made active by calling the PENPAT routine, as follows

```
CALL PENPAT(VARPTR(Pat%(0)))
```

The pen size should also be set at this time. I have provided a Pattern Development Workshop program, similar to the Mouse Cursor Development Workshop program. It is shown in Listing 7-7. This program can be used to design and test your own custom pen patterns. Like the mouse cursor program, it can generate a set of DATA statements for the pattern you create, and store these on the clipboard for inclusion in your own programs.

Listing 7-7
*The Pen Pattern
Development Workshop*

```
' This program allows you to design and test your own pen and background
' patterns. You define the pattern on an 8 pixel by 8 pixel grid.
' When you are satisfied with the pattern you have designed, this program
' can be instructed to save the pattern definition as a DATA
' statement on the Macintosh Clipboard. From there, the definition
' can be included for use in other programs. See text for more information.
DIM Image%(3)          'holds the image you define on the screen
DIM SaveImage%(1000)     'holds screen image for quick redrawing
GridColor=30      'grid color=30=white=no grid line display by default
StartAgain:
CLS
' init image data to all one bits, all black pixels :
FOR i=0 TO 3
Image%(i)=-1
NEXT

' set up the initial screen display :
LINE (100,10)-(130,40),,B   'display the "Toggle Grid Lines" box
LOCATE 2,18
PRINT "Toggle Grid Lines",

' display default, all black image :
```

Listing 7-7—cont.

```
LINE (10,10)-(50,50),,BF          ' the grid copy
LINE (10,60)-(17,67),,BF          'the "life-size" copy
'
GOSUB DrawGrid              'displays the 8 x 8 grid at (10,10) on the screen
'
GET (10,10)-(250,70),SaveImage%  'get a snapshot of the screen for quick redisplay
Again:
CLS
PUT (10,10)-(250,70),SaveImage%  'redisplay development screen
LOCATE 15,1
PRINT "Define pattern, triple-click when done"
GOSUB DefineImage           'let the user define the 8 x 8 pixel image
GET (10,10)-(250,70),SaveImage%  'get a snapshot of the screen for quick redisplay
'
' Demo the pattern for the user :
'
CLS
PRINT "New pattern defined and now on display"
PRINT "Press S to save pattern definition to the clipboard"
PRINT "Press C to change current definition"
PRINT "Press N to create a new definition"
'
' make the defined pattern active for a demo :
CALL PENPAT(VARPTR(Image%(0)))  '
'
' display some graphics images using the new pattern :
'
. x=0
y=100
x2=330
FOR psize=2 TO 8  'draw three lines (diag, horiz, vert) in each pen size :
CALL PENSIZE(psize,psize)
' draw a diagonal line in this pen size :
CALL MOVETO(x,200)
CALL LINETO(x+80,100)
x=x+20
' draw a horizontal line in this pen size :
CALL MOVETO(220,y)
CALL LINETO(300,y)
y=y+20
' draw a vertical line in this pen size :
CALL MOVETO(x2,100)
CALL LINETO(x2,200)
x2=x2+20
NEXT
'
' now fill in a nice sized area of the screen with the pattern :
FOR y=220 TO 280 STEP 8
CALL MOVETO(10,y)
CALL LINETO(80,y)
NEXT
'
' demonstration images now on view,
' check for keyboard commands as defined above :
WaitKey:
a$=INKEY$
IF a$="S" OR a$="s" THEN GOTO SaveFile
IF a$="C" OR a$="c" THEN CALL PENNORMAL: GOTO Again
IF a$="N" OR a$="n" THEN CALL PENNORMAL: GOTO StartAgain
GOTO WaitKey
'
' Save the pattern definition on the clipboard.
' The cursor definition is saved as a single DATA statement.
SaveFile:
OPEN "O",1,"CLIP:TEXT"
PRINT#1,"DATA ",
FOR i=0 TO 2
PRINT#1, Image%(i);",";
NEXT
PRINT#1, Image%(3)
```

Listing 7-7—cont.

```
CLOSE 1
CLS
PRINT "Pattern data saved on clipboard"
END
'
' Subroutine to allow the user to define a graphics image on an
' 8 pixel by 8 pixel grid, and return the graphics data in array Image%
' This subroutine returns when the user triple-clicks the mouse.
' Clicking in the "Toggle Grid Lines" box will turn the display
' of the grid lines on or off.
DefineImage:
GetLoc:
GOSUB MouseWait              'wait for and get a mouse selection
IF b=3 THEN RETURN           'mouse was triple-clicked
' check for mouse click in the "Toggle Grid Lines" box :
IF x>100 AND x<130 AND y>10 AND y<40 THEN GOSUB Toggle
' otherwise, mouse must be clicked within the 8 x 8 grid :
IF x<10 OR x>50 OR y<10 OR y>50 THEN GOTO GetLoc
' convert screen coord to 8 x 8 grid coord :
x=(x-10)\5          'adjust x to range 0-7
y=(y-10)\5          'adjust y to range 0-7
' convert x coord into a single bit position value in integer variable x% :
IF y MOD 2 = 0 THEN IF x=0 THEN x%=-32768! ELSE x%=2^(15-x) ELSE x%=2^(7-x)
' invert that bit position in the appropriate entry of the Image% array :
y2=y\2             'convert y to select the proper element of Image%
Image%(y2)=Image%(y2) XOR x%
' determine whether the bit just altered is now zero or one :
Pixel=Image%(y2) AND x%
' and set the screen display of that pixel accordingly :
IF Pixel=0 THEN GOSUB ResetPixel ELSE GOSUB SetPixel
GOTO GetLoc         'stay here until the user triple-clicks
'
' Subroutine to reset a pixel position on the 8 x 8 grid.
' The pixel is reset both on the grid and in the smaller, real image
' interpretation below.
ResetPixel:
PRESET (x+10,y+60)   'reset the pixel in the smaller, real image interpretation
' convert grid coords to screen coords :
x=x*5+11
y=y*5+11
LINE (x,y)-(x+3,y+3),30,BF       'reset the pixel on the grid
RETURN
'
' Subroutine to set a pixel position on the 8 x 8 grid.
' The pixel is set both on the grid and in the smaller, real image
' interpretation below.
SetPixel:
PSET (x+10,y+60)     'set the pixel in the smaller, real image interpretation
' convert grid coords to screen coords :
x=x*5+11
y=y*5+11
LINE (x,y)-(x+3,y+3),33,BF         'set the pixel on the grid
RETURN
'
' Subroutine to display the 8 x 8 grid :
' The grid is composed of a set of horizontal and vertical lines that are
' spaced five pixels apart.  The grid is origined at screen coord (10,10)
' Each "cell" (pixel position) in the grid will actually occupy a 2 x 2 pixel
' area on the screen.
' Variable GridColor toggles between 30 (white) and 33 (black) to
' determine whether or not the grid is visible.
DrawGrid:
FOR i=10 TO 50 STEP 5
LINE (i,10)-(i,50),GridColor
LINE (10,i)-(50,i),GridColor
NEXT
RETURN
'
' Subroutine Toggle is called when the user clicks in the
' "Toggle Grid Lines" box.  It causes the grid line display to be
```

Listing 7-7—cont.

```
' turned off or on by flipping the value of variable GridColor
' between 30 (white) and 33 (black).
Toggle:
IF GridColor=30 THEN GridColor=33 ELSE GridColor=30
GOSUB DrawGrid
RETURN

' Subroutine to wait until the user takes a mouse action.
' This subroutine will only return on a single or triple-click.
' It returns b = value of MOUSE(0) = button status
'            x= value of MOUSE(3) = x coord at time of click
'            y= value of MOUSE(4) = y coord at time of click
MouseWait:
b=MOUSE(0)
IF b=3 THEN RETURN
IF b<>1 THEN GOTO MouseWait
x=MOUSE(3)
y=MOUSE(4)
RETURN
```

Some sample pen patterns are provided in Listing 7-8; that program also shows how to use the DATA statements generated by the workshop program.

Listing 7-8
Sample Pen Patterns

```
ON ERROR GOTO EndofData     ' to catch the out-of-data error condition
DIM Pat%(3)                 'array to hold the pattern definition
Patno=0                     'keeps count of which pattern is currently on view
CLS
PRINT "Pen Pattern Demo Program"
PRINT "Click and drag to draw lines in current pattern"
PRINT "Triple-click to go on to next pattern"
CALL PENSIZE(4,4)           ' set a 4 pixel by 4 pixel pen size
GetNextPat:
FOR i=0 TO 3                'read in the next pattern definition
READ Pat%(i)
NEXT
Patno=Patno+1               'count up and display the pattern number
LOCATE 4,1
PRINT "Pattern ",Patno
CALL PENPAT(VARPTR(Pat%(0)))   'now make the pattern active
' wait for user input via the mouse :
MouseWait:
b=MOUSE(0)
IF b=3 THEN GOTO GetNextPat         'triple click goes on to next pattern
IF b<>1 THEN GOTO MouseWait         'wait for a single click-drag action
x1=MOUSE(3)                 'drag start coords
y1=MOUSE(4)
x2=MOUSE(5)                 'drag end coords
y2=MOUSE(6)
IF x1=x2 AND y1=y2 THEN GOTO MouseWait     'skip if no drag was done
IF x1<0 OR y1<0 OR x2<0 OR y2<0 THEN GOTO MouseWait
CALL MOVETO(x1,y1)          'position pen to start drag coords
CALL LINETO(x2,y2)          'draw a line to end drag coords
GOTO MouseWait

EndofData:                  'get here when run out of data statements :
CALL PENNORMAL
END

' Sample pattern data follows:
'
' Medium grey :
DATA 21930 , 21930 , 21930 , 21930
' Diagonal stripes :
DATA 26231 , 13243 ,-26147 ,-13074
' Light grey :
DATA 13260 , 13260 , 13260 , 13260
```

Listing 7-8 —cont.

```
' Dark grey :
DATA -86 ,-86 ,-86 ,-86
' Vertical jagged stripes :
DATA -8773 , 30651 ,-8773 , 30651
```

The Pattern Development Workshop Program

Although the Pattern Development Workshop is very similar to the Mouse Cursor Development Workshop, there are some interesting differences. When you run the program of Listing 7-7, you will be presented with an eight pixel by eight pixel grid on which you can define a pattern.

Unlike the mouse cursor grid, this grid starts out with all the pixels black. This is the default pattern, and is a better starting point for custom patterns than an all white pattern. Because the pattern is all black, the grid lines are not shown (see Figure 7-12).

If the grid lines were shown, the development grid area would appear as a solid black square, and it would be impossible to accurately select individual pixels within it. A "life-size" copy of the pen pattern appears below the development grid. If you are developing a pattern that has quite a few white pixels in it, you may want to turn the grid lines on to help identify the individual pixel positions. This can be accomplished by clicking the mouse in the "Toggle Grid Lines" box, just to the right of the development grid.

Figure 7-13 shows the program being used to develop a pattern containing a diagonal white stripe. In Figure 7-14, the same pattern is shown with the grid lines turned on. Once a pattern has been designed, triple click the mouse to display a demonstration of the pattern. The demonstration screen shows the pattern used to draw horizontal, vertical, and diagonal lines in various widths, as well as a solid area filled in with the pattern, as in Figure 7-15.

From the demonstration screen, you can save the pattern data by pressing the <S> key. The data is saved as a single BASIC DATA statement on the Clipboard. Figure 7-16 shows the data produced for the sample pattern of Figures 7-13, 7-14, and 7-15. Alternatively, you can press the <C> key to go back to the development grid and change the pattern, or the <N> key to start developing a new pattern.

I have used the program to generate the required data for some commonly used Macintosh patterns. Figure 7-17 shows a light grey pattern formed by alternating white and black pixels. Figure 7-18

Figure 7-12
Default Pen Pattern

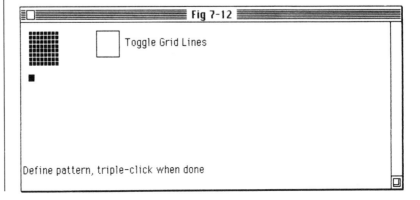

shows this pattern on the demonstration screen. In Figure 7-19, a medium grey pattern is shown; the demonstration screen is seen in Figure 7-20. A dark grey pattern is shown in Figures 7-21 and 7-22. Finally, a pattern containing jagged vertical stripes appears in Figures 7-23 and 7-24.

Figure 7-13
Diagonal Striped Pen Pattern

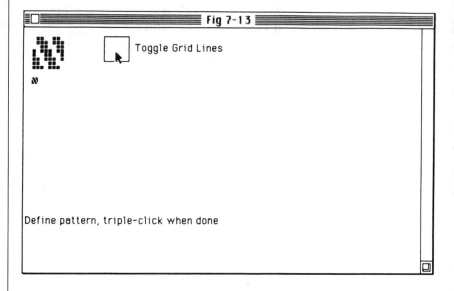

Figure 7-14
Pen Pattern with Grid On

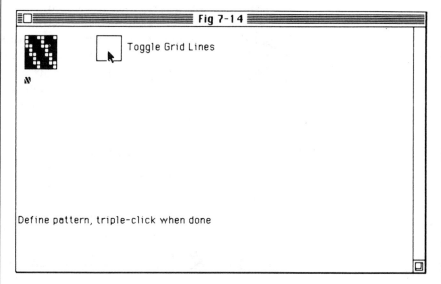

The data for each of these sample patterns appears in Listing 7-8. When that program is run, it defines a four pixel by four pixel pen and allows the user to draw lines with the pen by clicking and dragging the mouse. Each time the mouse is triple-clicked, the program goes on to the next sample pattern.

Most of the programming techniques used in the pattern development program are similar to those used in the mouse cursor development program. One important difference involves the conversion of coordinates on the eight pixel by eight pixel development grid into a bit position in one of the *Pat%* array elements.

Figure 7-15
Testing Diagonal Striped Pen Pattern

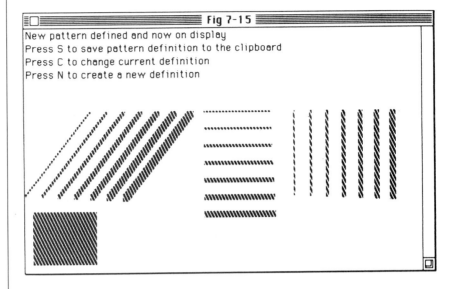

Figure 7-16
Data for Diagonal Striped Pen Pattern

Figure 7-17
Light Grey Pen Pattern

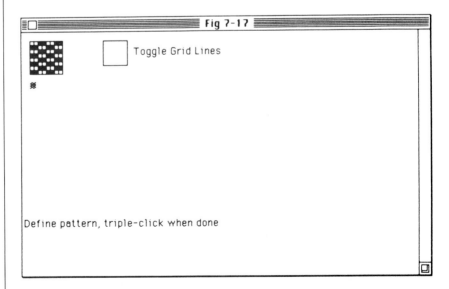

Since the grid is 8 × 8, and not 16 × 16 as it was for the mouse cursor, it is possible to store two lines of pixel information in a single array element (each array element still holds 16 bits). This arrangement was illustrated in Figure 7-11.

Figure 7-18
Testing Light Grey Pen Pattern

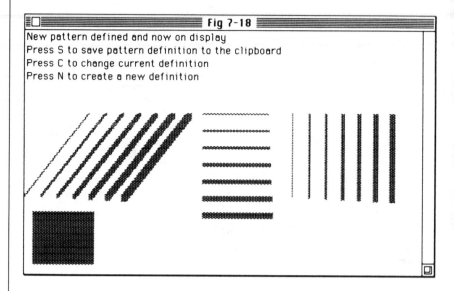

Figure 7-19
Medium Grey Pen Pattern

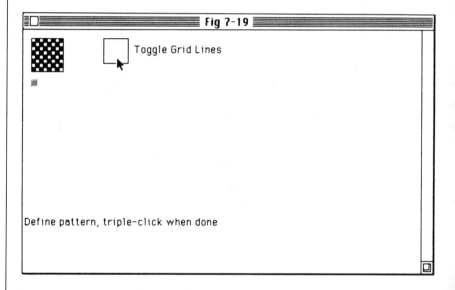

Study the code in Listing 7-7 that handles this structure. The x-coordinates and y-coordinates of the mouse click are converted to development grid coordinates using the same formula that was used for the mouse cursor development grid. This time, however, each coordinate has a range of 0–7, instead of 0–15.

The x-coordinate is converted into a bit position using a formula that depends upon whether the y-coordinate is even or odd. The y-coordinate thus determines whether the upper or lower half of the array element is used.

Variable *y2* is then created by integer dividing the y coordinate by 2. This variable is used to index into the *Pat%* array. In this fashion, y-coordinate values of 0 and 1 both access array element 0, values of 2 and 3 both access array element 1, and so on. Once a bit position and array element have been determined, the rest of the DefineImage code works the same.

Figure 7-20
Testing Medium Grey Pen Pattern

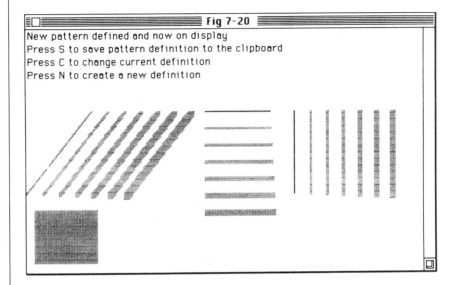

Figure 7-21
Dark Grey Pen Pattern

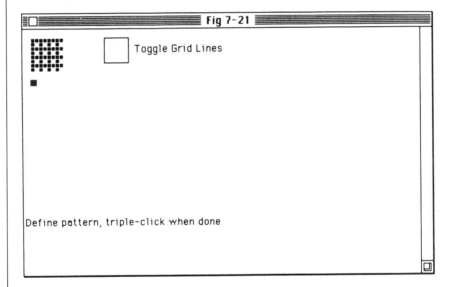

One additional feature of this program is the "Toggle Grid Lines" box. This feature illustrates how an area of the screen can be set aside, and a program can be made sensitive to mouse clicks within that area. The effect is not unlike that of the control buttons within dialog boxes. In this case, I displayed the control box using a LINE statement with the "box" option. Mouse clicks within the x-coordinate range of 100 to 130, and within the y-coordinate range of 10 to 40 lie within this box, and are used to trigger the desired action. Note that a single, albeit compound, IF-THEN statement is all that is needed to detect this condition.

Figure 7-22
*Testing Dark Grey Pen
Pattern*

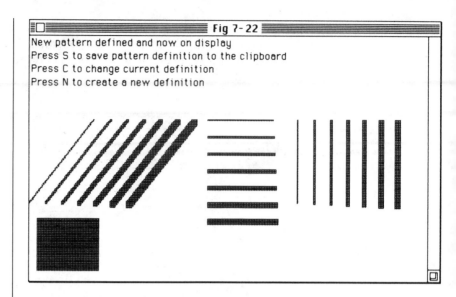

The desired action, that of toggling the development grid lines off and on, is effected by a call to subroutine Toggle. This subroutine alternates the value of variable GridColor between 30 and 33. Subroutine DrawGrid references this variable when it actually draws the grid lines.

Figure 7-23
*Jagged Vertical Striped
Pen Pattern*

Additional Graphics Pen Options

There are additional toolbox calls that you can use to control the way the graphics pen draws images. The most interesting of these is the PENMODE routine. This routine allows you to define the image transfer mode used by the pen when drawing lines using the LINE and LINETO routines. It will also affect the creation of other graphics images that I will cover later in this chapter.

The image transfer mode choices are similar to those available for the TEXTMODE routine. The prevailing mode is set by passing a single numeric parameter to the PENMODE routine, as follows

```
CALL PENMODE(parameter)
```

The parameter values that can be used in this statement are summarized in Table 7-4. The first four entries in this table correspond to the four text display modes shown in Table 7-3 (page 226). The last four entries are the same as the first four, except that they first invert the pattern definition. This allows you to design a pattern and then use both it and its inverse without having to define the inverse pattern separately. The applications of the four basic transfer modes have been explained earlier in this chapter.

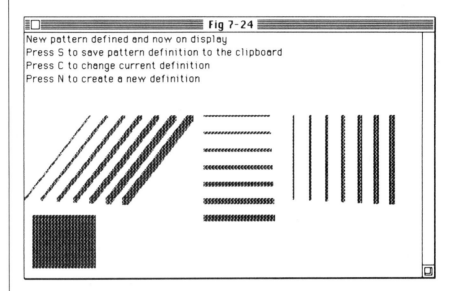

8	PSET (Pen image completely replaces previous contents of screen.)
9	OR (Black pixels of pen image are displayed on screen, previous contents of screen not altered where pen image pixels are white.)
10	XOR (Existing screen pixels are inverted where pen image pixels are black, previous contents of screen not altered where pen image pixels are white.)
11	BIC (Black pixels of pen image are displayed on screen as white, previous contents of screen not altered where pen image pixels are white.)
12	PRESET (Pen image is inverted and then completely replaces previous contents of screen.)
13	NOT OR (Same as OR mode, except pen image is inverted before processing.)
14	NOT XOR (Same as XOR mode, except pen image is inverted before processing.)
15	NOT BIC (Same as XOR mode, except pen image is inverted before processing.)

Three more toolbox calls complete our repertoire of graphics pen control routines. They are *PENNORMAL*, *HIDEPEN*, and *SHOWPEN*. None require any arguments. The PENNORMAL routine simply restores the graphics pen to its default state. This state consist of an all black pattern, a pen size of a single pixel, and a pen transfer mode of PSET. It is used in the programs of Listings 7-7 and 7-8.

The HIDEPEN routine is used to temporarily inhibit the creation of any graphics pen images. Once a call is made to HIDEPEN, any subsequent toolbox calls that draw with the graphics pen will have no visible effect on the screen. The pen is still there, and can be moved about on the screen, but it is "hidden" in that it produces no readable image. To counteract the effect of the HIDEPEN routine, simply call the SHOWPEN routine.

The program shown in Listing 7-9 illustrates the operation of these routines. When executed, the program sets a pen size of four by four pixels, and the XOR pen transfer mode. The default pen pattern (all black) is used. Starting at pixel coordinate (100,100), the program draws lines using the graphics pen. The point to which each line is drawn is chosen randomly.

Since the LINETO routine is used, each line originates where the previous line ended. Because the pen transfer mode has been set to XOR, the lines are drawn in white where they cross each other. A mouse interrupt routine is used to detect when the user clicks the mouse button. This is used to toggle the pen state between "hidden" and "shown."

Execute the program and observe the lines that are drawn. Now click the mouse button. Notice that the image appears to stop changing on the screen. The main loop of the program is still executing but because the mouse click caused the HIDEPEN routine to be called, no further images are produced. Click the mouse once again. This causes the SHOWPEN routine to be called, causing the images to start appearing once again. Note that the line drawing picks up at a new point on the screen, and not at the end of the last line that was visibly drawn before.

Setting a Background Pattern

When you use the CLS ("clear screen") statement, BASIC's Output window is filled in with a background pattern. You would not normally realize this, because the default background pattern is all white. The background pattern can be changed, however, through use of the BACKPAT toolbox routine. The background pattern is defined on an eight pixel by eight pixel grid, exactly like the pen pattern. You can therefore use the Pattern Development Workshop program to create custom patterns for use as screen backgrounds. The BACKPAT routine is called in the same way as the PENPAT routine

```
CALL BACKPAT(VARPTR(Pat%(0)))
```

Once again, *Pat%* is a four element integer array that defines the pattern image. Use the data produced by the pattern development program to initialize the array. Once the BACKPAT call has been made, you should use the CLS statement to actually fill in the Output window with your pattern.

```
' When run, this program starts filling the screen with thick blacks lines
' drawn in various random directions. Each line starts where the previous
' line left off. Because the XOR pen transfer mode is used, the lines are
' clearly visible where they cross one another. By clicking the mouse,
' the user can "hide the pen," thus turning off the display of the lines.
' Clicking the mouse again will turn "show the pen" and turn the display
' of new lines back on.
DEF FNrand(1,u)=CINT(1+RND(1)*(u-1))
PenOn=1                              'keeps track of whether pen is on or off
CALL MOVETO(100,100)                 'set starting point
CALL PENMODE(10)                     'set XOR pen transfer mode
CALL PENSIZE(4,4)                    'set up a thick pen
ON MOUSE GOSUB MouseInt              'detect mouse clicks via an interrupt
MOUSE ON
Again:
x=FNrand(0,500)                  'select a random point for the next line to go to
y=FNrand(0,300)
CALL LINETO(x,y)            'draw the line to that point
FOR delay=1 TO 50          'waste some time to slow things down a bit
NEXT
GOTO Again
' Come to here on whenever the user presses the mouse button :
MouseInt:
b=MOUSE(0)                              'get mouse button status
IF b<>1 AND b<>-1 THEN RETURN       'only concerned with single clicks
IF PenOn=0 THEN PenOn=1 ELSE PenOn=0 'toggle state of pen between on and off
IF PenOn=0 THEN CALL HIDEPEN ELSE CALL SHOWPEN
RETURN
```

```
' Note : This program requires the London font.
DIM Pat%(3)
FOR i=0 TO 3              'initialize the image array
READ Pat%(i)
NEXT
CALL BACKPAT(VARPTR(Pat%(0)))        'set a new background pattern
CLS                      ' fill the output window with the background pattern
CALL TEXTFONT(6)            'set London font
CALL TEXTSIZE(72)             'set text size
CALL TEXTMODE(3)              'set BIC text transfer mode
LOCATE 2,2              'position for centered text
PRINT "Dramatic";
END
' Pattern data generated by pattern development program :
' Diagonal stripes :
DATA 26231 , 13243 ,-26147 ,-13074
```

Listing 7-10 shows how the *BACKPAT* routine can be used. The "diagonal stripe" pattern, developed earlier in this chapter, is.

defined as the background pattern. The program then selects the London font, in a rather large text size of 72. The BIC ("Black is Changed") text transfer mode is also selected at this time. The appearance of text produced in this fashion and against this background is quite dramatic, if not just plain dizzying. It is illustrated by the execution of this program, provided in Figure 7-25.

Drawing Shapes

The next set of toolbox routines that I will discuss all use the graphics pen. They are therefore affected by the pen size, mode, pattern, and whether or not the pen is hidden. These routines allow you to rapidly create images of various shapes. Most of these shapes are rectangles or variations of basic rectangles. For each shape, there are five basic actions that you can perform. These actions are summarized in Table 7-5.

Figure 7-25
Dramatic Text Display

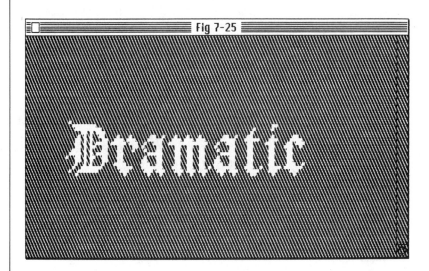

Table 7-5
Basic Drawing Actions for Shapes

FRAME	Draw an outline of the defined shape.
PAINT	Fill in the defined shape with the current pen pattern.
ERASE	Fill in the defined shape with the current background pattern.
INVERT	Invert all screen pixels within the defined shape (white becomes black and black becomes white).
FILL	Fill in the defined shape with the supplied pattern.

The *FRAME* action is used to create an outline of the shape selected, while the *PAINT* action creates a solid image of the shape.

The *ERASE* action replaces the shape with the background pattern. The *INVERT* action reverses all of the existing pixels within the area defined by the shape. This can be very useful, as you will see later in this chapter. Finally, the *FILL* action can be used to fill in the shape with a user-specified pattern.

Rectangles

Let me introduce you to each of these actions by starting with the simplest shape, a rectangle. The name of the toolbox routine used to produce an action on a shape is formed by combining the action verb, from Table 7-5, with the name of the shape. Thus, since rectangles have the shape name RECT, we have the five toolbox routines named *FRAMERECT, PAINTRECT, ERASERECT, INVERTRECT*, and *FILLRECT*. The five different shapes and their names are summarized in Table 7-6.

RECT	Rectangle.
ROUNDRECT	Rectangle with rounded corners.
OVAL	Oval or circle.
ARC	Segment of an oval or circle, or the pie piece created by connecting the endpoints of the segment to the oval center by a pair of straight lines.
POLY	Polygon (Three or more sides, each side can be of arbitrary length, sides can be joined at arbitrary angles.)

For each shape type, there is a different method for defining the shape to the toolbox routine. Rectangles are easily defined by four numeric values representing the upper left and lower right coordinates of the shape. These values are passed in a four element integer array. The placement of coordinate values in the array is shown in Figure 7-26. Figure 7-27 shows how the FRAMERECT routine would be used to draw the image of a rectangle on the screen.

Figure 7-26

Rectangle Shape Definition

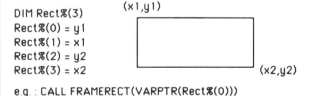

```
DIM Rect%(3)
Rect%(0) = y1
Rect%(1) = x1
Rect%(2) = y2
Rect%(3) = x2

e.g.: CALL FRAMERECT(VARPTR(Rect%(0)))
```

The example in Figure 7-27 does not reveal the true power of these toolbox routines. After all, the image produced by that example could have been generated more easily with the Microsoft BASIC statement LINE (with the "box" option). The real advantage to the toolbox routines comes as a result of the control you have over the graphics pen. For example, by simply adding one statement to the example of Figure 7-27, you can increase the thickness of the lines that make up the rectangle. This would be accomplished by adding a CALL PENSIZE statement. In a similar fashion, you can use an alternate pen pattern and/or pen transfer mode when drawing the rectangle.

Figure 7-27
*The FRAMERECT
Routine*

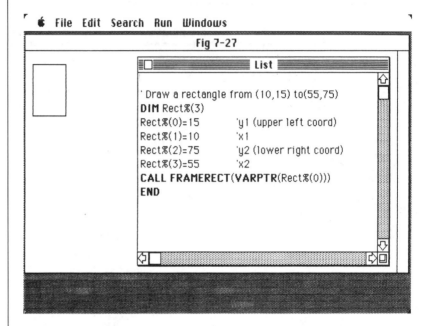

The PAINT action fills in the entire area bounded by the shape with the current pen pattern. You can thus use the PAINTRECT routine to fill arbitrary rectangular areas of the Output window with any pattern desired. Obviously, an all-black or all-white pattern would not be used in these cases, as it is easier to use the LINE statement with the "box filled" and "color" options. If, however, you wanted to fill an area of the Output window with, for example, a grey pattern, the PAINTRECT routine would be the way to go. An example is shown in Figure 7-28.

The ERASE action is very similar to the PAINT action. It also fills the entire area bounded by the shape with a specific pattern. Unlike the PAINT action, which uses the current pen pattern, however, the ERASE action uses the current background pattern. The action will therefore set the area to match the background color as set by the CLS statement. The default background pattern is, of course, all white.

The program of Listing 7-11 contains the sample program of Figure 7-28, with the addition of an ERASERECT call. The results of running this program are shown in Figure 7-29. Note that, for this example, the default background pattern of all white has been used.

The *INVERT* action alters the current screen contents in the entire area bounded by the shape. All black pixels within that area become white, and all white pixels become black. This is a very important action, and is used extensively in the Macintosh user-interface. Whenever you click a button in a dialog box, or select an item in a pull-down menu, the selection is highlighted by this kind of INVERT action. It is therefore quite fortunate that this capability is available to us from within a BASIC program. This allows us to write programs that mimic the standard Macintosh interface.

Figure 7-28
*The PAINTRECT
Routine*

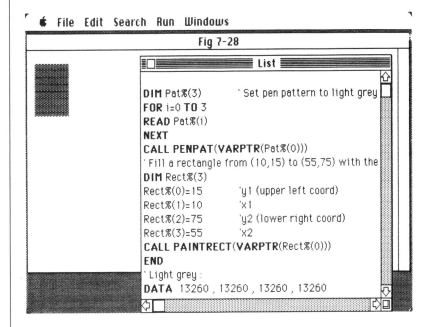

```
 File  Edit  Search  Run  Windows

                         Fig 7-28

                                        List

DIM Pat%(3)          ' Set pen pattern to light grey
FOR i=0 TO 3
READ Pat%(i)
NEXT
CALL PENPAT(VARPTR(Pat%(0)))
' Fill a rectangle from (10,15) to (55,75) with the
DIM Rect%(3)
Rect%(0)=15          'y1 (upper left coord)
Rect%(1)=10          'x1
Rect%(2)=75          'y2 (lower right coord)
Rect%(3)=55          'x2
CALL PAINTRECT(VARPTR(Rect%(0)))
END
' Light grey :
DATA  13260 , 13260 , 13260 , 13260
```

Listing 7-11
*The PAINTRECT and
ERASERECT Routines*

```
DIM Pat%(3)          ' Set pen pattern to light grey :
FOR i=0 TO 3
READ Pat%(i)
NEXT
CALL PENPAT(VARPTR(Pat%(0)))
' Fill a rectangle from (10,15) to (55,75) with the pen pattern :
DIM Rect%(3)
Rect%(0)=15          'y1 (upper left coord)
Rect%(1)=10          'x1
Rect%(2)=75          'y2 (lower right coord)
Rect%(3)=55          'x2
CALL PAINTRECT(VARPTR(Rect%(0)))
' Now erase a smaller rectangle within the filled rectangle :
' This smaller rectangle is defined by the coordinates :
'        (20,30)-(40,50)
Rect%(0)=30          'y1 (upper left coord)
Rect%(1)=20          'x1
Rect%(2)=50          'y2 (lower right coord)
Rect%(3)=40          'x2
CALL ERASERECT(VARPTR(Rect%(0)))
END
' Light grey :
DATA 13260 , 13260 , 13260 , 13260
```

We can display a variety of items on the Output window, and, when the user selects one of these items, the selection can be highlighted by using an INVERT routine. Listing 7-12 illustrates the programming techniques used to accomplish this.

Figure 7-29
Effects of ERASERECT

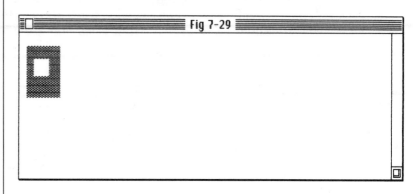

Listing 7-12
The Ice Cream Flavor Selection Program

```
' When run, this program presents the user with a choice of four items
' (they happen to be ice-cream flavors).  Each item is enclosed in a
' rectangular box.  The user selects an item by clicking in the box with
' the mouse.  The selected box is highlighted by inverting its contents.
' When the user releases the mouse button, the selected item is
' un-highlighted and the program ends.
DIM Flavors$(3)                      'holds the names of the four choices
FOR i=0 TO 3
READ Flavors$(i)
NEXT
DATA Chocolate,Vanilla,Strawberry,Banana

CLS
LOCATE 1,3                           'display prompt and the four choices
PRINT "Select desired flavor :"
FOR i=0 TO 3
LOCATE i*2+3,5                       'seperate each choice by a blank line
PRINT Flavors$(i)
NEXT

' The Rect% array will hold the definitions of four rectangles.
' Four elements are required for each rectangle definition.
DIM Rect%(15)
y=30
FOR i=0 TO 12 STEP 4   'initialize the array to hold the four rectangle defs
Rect%(i)=y
Rect%(i+1)=30                 'x coords always the same
Rect%(i+2)=y+25
Rect%(i+3)=120               'x coords always the same
y=y+30
NEXT

FOR i=0 TO 12 STEP 4                     'draw the four rectangles
CALL FRAMERECT(VARPTR(Rect%(i)))
NEXT

MouseWait:          'wait for the user to make a selection with the mouse
b=MOUSE(0)
x=MOUSE(3)
y=MOUSE(4)
IF x<30 OR x>120 THEN GOTO MouseWait 'selection must be in one of the rects
IF b<>-1 THEN GOTO MouseWait          'selection must via click and hold
Selection=-1                          'init value to indicate no valid selection
FOR i=0 TO 12 STEP 4     'scan through the array for a valid selection match
IF y>Rect%(i) AND y<Rect%(i+2) THEN Selection=i      'valid match found
NEXT
IF Selection=-1 THEN GOTO MouseWait   'if no valid selection, keep waiting
CALL INVERTRECT(VARPTR(Rect%(Selection))) 'highlight the selected rect
```

Listing 7-12—cont.

```
MouseWait2:            'now wait until the user releases the mouse button :
b=MOUSE(0)
IF b<>1 THEN GOTO MouseWait2
CALL INVERTRECT(VARPTR(Rect%(Selection)))   'un-highlight the selection
LOCATE 12,1                 'show that we know what the user selected :
PRINT "You have selected choice : ";Flavors$(Selection/4)
END
```

The program in Listing 7-12 presents the user with a choice of four different ice cream flavors. Each flavor is listed in a rectangle, as shown in Figure 7-30. The user selects a flavor by moving the mouse pointer to one of the rectangles and clicking. When the user clicks and holds the mouse button, the selected rectangle is highlighted through use of the INVERTRECT call. This condition is maintained as long as the user holds the mouse button down. When the button is released, the rectangle is no longer highlighted (another INVERTRECT call returns it to its original state) and the program ends.

Figure 7-30
The Ice Cream Flavor Choices

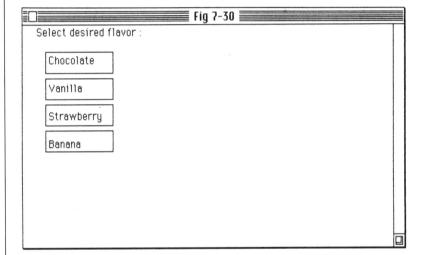

The names of the four flavors are maintained in elements 0 through 3 of array *Flavors$*. Array *Rect%* is dimensioned to hold sixteen elements. As you know, only four elements are needed to define a rectangle. The sixteen elements thus allow four rectangles to be defined. Since all the rectangle definitions are kept in the one array, it is an easy matter to dynamically select any one of them by simply selecting the starting element of the array. The array is filled with the appropriate coordinate values to define the four rectangles so that they enclose the four flavors as they are displayed on the screen. A FOR-NEXT loop then steps through each rectangle definition, and the FRAMERECT routine is used to draw the rectangles. Note the use of the dynamic subscript in the array reference on the FRAMERECT call.

The next step in the program is to wait for the user to make a selection via the mouse. The usual technique is used to wait for mouse button activity. Note that only a single click and hold will be detected by the MouseWait loop. If the mouse x-coordinate is not within the possible range allowed by the rectangles, the click is ignored.

A FOR-NEXT loop is then used to check the mouse y-coordinate against each rectangle definition in *Rect%*. The variable named "Selection" is used to reflect the outcome of this check. It is initialized to −1, and set equal to the starting *Rect%* array element if a match is found. When the loop is completed, the value of Selection is checked. If it is still −1, then no match was found, the user did not click within a rectangle, and the click is ignored.

Otherwise, a valid flavor selection was made, and variable Selection points to the starting element in *Rect%* for the rectangle definition that was selected. It is therefore used in an INVERTRECT call to highlight that rectangle. Now a second loop, beginning with label MouseWait2, is entered. In this loop, the program waits for the user to release the mouse button.

As long as the button is held down, the selected rectangle will remain highlighted on the screen. Note that, while the button is held, the mouse can be moved about but this will not change the selection. When the mouse button is released, a second call to INVERTRECT restores the screen to its original condition. The program then displays the name of the selected flavor and ends.

Execute this program and try experimenting with it. As an exercise, modify the program so that it will beep at the user when the mouse is clicked outside the rectangles.

The final action verb is FILL. This is essentially the same as the PAINTRECT and ERASERECT calls, except you can supply yet another pattern definition to be used in filling the shape. To fill a rectangular area defined by the contents of array *Rect%* with the pattern defined by the contents of array *Pat%*, the following call would be used

```
CALL FILLRECT(VARPTR(Rect%(0)),
VARPTR(Pat%(0)))
```

The pattern definition in *Pat%* is defined in the same fashion as pen and background patterns. Note that, unlike the previous routines, this routine requires that two array parameters be passed to it.

Now that you understand the five basic action verbs that can be applied to graphics shapes, I will describe the more esoteric shapes that are available.

Rounded Rectangles

The ROUNDRECT shape is a basic rectangle with rounded corners. It is defined using three parameters. See Figure 7-31. The first parameter is a four element integer array; it defines the basic rectangle in the usual fashion. The two additional parameters are used to define the curvature of the rounded corners.

These parameters, named *ovalwidth* and *ovalheight*, represent values that are measured relative to the width and height of the defined rectangle. If, for example, the ovalwidth value is made small compared to the width of the rectangle itself, only a small portion of the horizontal lines that make up the top and bottom of the rectangle will be curved.

Figure 7-31
ROUNDRECT Shape Definition

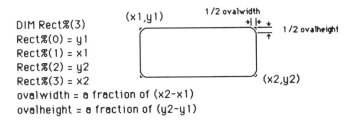

```
DIM Rect%(3)
Rect%(0) = y1
Rect%(1) = x1
Rect%(2) = y2
Rect%(3) = x2
ovalwidth = a fraction of (x2-x1)
ovalheight = a fraction of (y2-y1)
```

e.g. : CALL FRAMEROUNDRECT(VARPTR(Rect%(0)),ovalwidth,ovalheight)

Similarly, if the ovalheight is made small compared to the height of the rectangle, only a small portion of the vertical lines that make up the left and right sides of the rectangle will be curved. This situation is illustrated by the example in Figure 7-32.

In this example, small values for ovalheight and ovalwidth produce a rectangle with slightly rounded corners. As the ovalheight and ovalwidth values are increased towards the actual height and width of the rectangle, more and more of the rectangle corners are curved, as in Figure 7-33.

The maximum values for ovalheight and ovalwidth are the rectangle's height and width, respectively. At this point, however, the figure drawn has no straight lines at all, and is actually an oval that can be inscribed within the rectangle so that its outermost edges would touch the rectangle. This situation is shown in Figure 7-34. In this case, if the rectangle were actually a square (width = height), a circle would be produced.

Figure 7-32
A ROUNDRECT with Slightly Rounded Corners

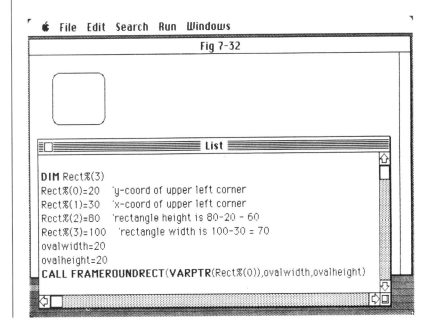

Figure 7-33
A ROUNDRECT with
Very Rounded Corners

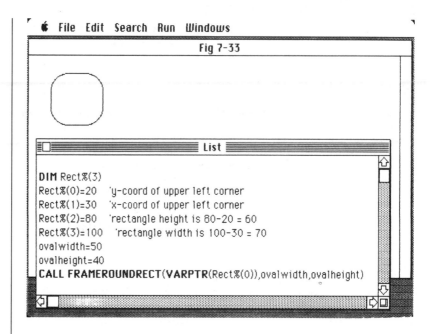

The ROUNDRECT shape is not meant to be used in this fashion, however, since the next shape I discuss (OVAL) is available. For most applications, you will want to use ROUNDRECT to produce rectangles that have slightly rounded corners, so keep the ovalheight and ovalwidth parameters relatively small.

For each of the action verbs FRAME, PAINT, ERASE and INVERT, the ROUNDRECT shape requires the three parameters as shown in the preceding examples. For the FILLROUNDRECT call, four parameters are needed. The first three define the round rectangle, and the fourth defines the fill pattern

```
CALL FILLROUNDRECT(VARPTR(Rect%(0)),
ovalheight, ovalwidth, VARPTR(Pat%(0)))
```

Note that the VARPTR function is used only when passing arrays to the toolbox routines, it is not used when passing simple numeric variables.

Ovals

The OVAL shape is the same as a rounded rectangle where ovalheight and ovalwidth equal the rectangle's height and width, respectively. Since these values are determined by the rectangle definition itself, they do not need to be specified. Thus, the only parameter that needs to be passed to the toolbox routines to define an oval shape is our familar *Rect%* array. This is illustrated by Figure 7-35. If, for example, the elements of array *Rect%* were 20, 30, 80, and 100, then the statement

```
CALL FRAMEOVAL(VARPTR(Rect%(0)))
```

would produce the same image as that shown in Figure 7-34. The OVAL shape can be used to define circles by simply setting the coordinate values in *Rect%* so that the height and width are equal.

Figure 7-34
Maximum Ovalheight and Ovalwidth in a RoundRect

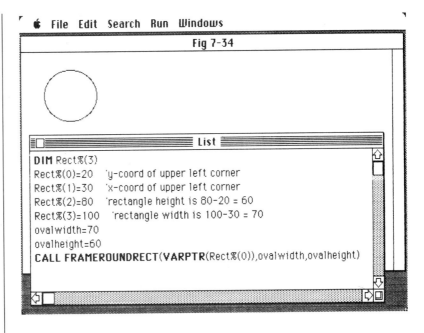

Figure 7-35
OVAL Shape Definition

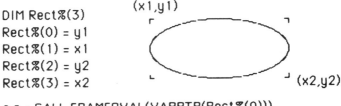

```
DIM Rect%(3)
Rect%(0) = y1
Rect%(1) = x1
Rect%(2) = y2
Rect%(3) = x2
```

e.g. : CALL FRAMEOVAL(VARPTR(Rect%(0)))

Note: if height (y2-y1) equals width (x2-x1), then this will produce a circle.

The radius of the circle thus produced will be half that of the width (or height).

Once again, it is actually much easier to use Microsoft BASIC's CIRCLE command, but this does not provide the ability to do such operations as PAINT, FILL, and INVERT.

An example showing how the OVAL shape can be used to draw a circle with a radius of 50 pixels, and fill it with a diagonally striped pattern, is shown in Figure 7-36.

Arcs

The ARC shape represents a portion of an OVAL shape. It is defined using three parameter values. The first is the rectangle used to define the oval itself. The next two parameters specify a start and duration angle through which the arc should be drawn. The basic idea is very similar to the start and stop angle options on Microsoft BASIC's CIRCLE statement (see Chapter 5).

Unlike the CIRCLE statement, however, the toolbox routines expect the angles to be specified in degrees. Furthermore, the angular coordinate system of the toolbox routines does not conform to the standard mathemetical system, as the CIRCLE statement did. These routines interpret zero degrees as the 12 o'clock position, and they move clockwise as the angle increases. This is shown in Figure 7-37.

Figure 7-36
The FILLOVAL Routine

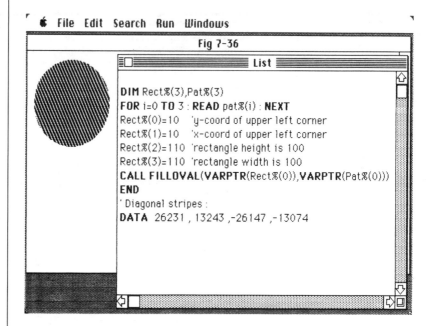

```
 File  Edit  Search  Run  Windows

                        Fig 7-36

                                          List

DIM Rect%(3),Pat%(3)
FOR i=0 TO 3 : READ pat%(i) : NEXT
Rect%(0)=10    'y-coord of upper left corner
Rect%(1)=10    'x-coord of upper left corner
Rect%(2)=110   'rectangle height is 100
Rect%(3)=110   'rectangle width is 100
CALL FILLOVAL(VARPTR(Rect%(0)),VARPTR(Pat%(0)))
END
' Diagonal stripes :
DATA  26231 , 13243 ,-26147 ,-13074
```

Figure 7-37
*Toolbox Routines
Angular Coordinate
System*

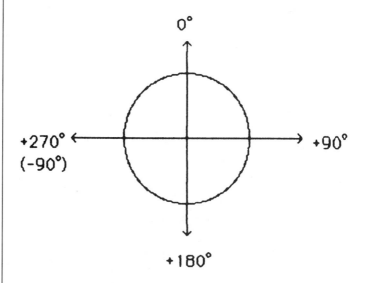

The start angle specifies the starting point for the arc, and the duration angle specifies the number of degrees through which the arc should be drawn, as in Figure 7-38. A negative start angle is measured by moving counterclockwise from the zero position. A negative duration angle represents counterclockwise rotation from the start angle position.

Figure 7-38
ARC Shape Definition

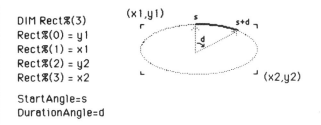

```
DIM Rect%(3)
Rect%(0) = y1
Rect%(1) = x1
Rect%(2) = y2
Rect%(3) = x2

StartAngle=s
DurationAngle=d
```

Note: If d is negative, then rotation is counterclockwise from the StartAngle position.

e.g. : CALL FRAMEARC(VARPTR(Rect%(0)),StartAngle,DurationAngle)

When used with the FRAME action verb, the ARC shape always represents an arc, drawn along the edge of the oval defined by *Rect%*, and running through the angle range specified. An example is shown in Figure 7-39.

Figure 7-39
The FRAMEARC Routine

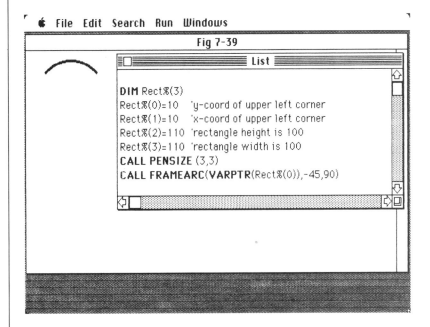

When used with any of the other action verbs, however, the ARC shape represents the pie piece constructed from the arc and a set of lines connecting the endpoints of the arc to the center of the image, as shown in Figure 7-40.

Polygons

The POLY shape is used to specify a wide variety of polygon. This is, in general, a much more complex shape than any of the others. A polygon can have any number of sides, and these sides can be joined together at arbitrary angles. The definition of a polygon is itself a complex matter.

The polygon shape definition is passed to the toolbox routines through a single integer array. The size of the array is variable and depends upon the number of sides in the polygon. Refer to Figure 7-41. The first element of the *poly* array serves to indicate the size of the array. The value in this element must reflect the total number of bytes in the array. Since there are two bytes per element in an integer array, this value must be set to twice the number of elements in the array.

Figure 7-40
*The PAINTARC
Routine*

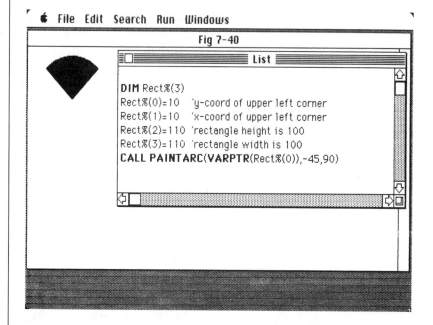

```
DIM Rect%(3)
Rect%(0)=10    'y-coord of upper left corner
Rect%(1)=10    'x-coord of upper left corner
Rect%(2)=110   'rectangle height is 100
Rect%(3)=110   'rectangle width is 100
CALL PAINTARC(VARPTR(Rect%(0)),-45,90)
```

The next four elements of the array are used to define a rectangle that will enclose the defined polygon. The polygon itself is defined by the remaining elements of the array. Each subsequent pair of array elements defines a single endpoint of the polygon.

The polygon is drawn by connecting one endpoint to the next with lines. To close the polygon, the last endpoint specified must be the same as the first endpoint specified. Note that for each endpoint coordinate, the y-coordinate is specified in the array before the x-coordinate. The total number of array elements needed for a polygon with *s* sides is

```
7 + (s * 2)
```

The value to go into the first element of the array (subscript 0), is two times this value. If each endpoint of the polygon is numbered, starting with the number 1, then the coordinates of the endpoint numbered m will be placed in array elements $n-1$ and n, where $n = 4 + (m * 2)$. Or, $m = (n-4)/2$.

Listing 7-13 shows several examples of how to define a POLY type shape. The program code itself has been generalized so that it can produce different images simply by changing the data fed to it. The program expects to receive the data in a particular order, as described in the comments that accompany the listing.

Each polygon definition begins with a value for program variable *s*, the number of sides in the polygon. This is followed by a character string description of the polygon, which will be displayed below the polygon itself on the output window. Based upon the value for s, the program can calculate how much additional data is needed in the $Poly\%$ array.

Figure 7-41
POLY Shape Definition

```
DIM Poly%(n)  (See below to determine value of n)
Poly%(0) = array size in bytes = 2*(n+1)
Poly%(1) = ey1 ⎤
Poly%(2) = ex1 │
Poly%(3) = ey2 ├ Rectangle enclosing the polygon
Poly%(4) = ex2 ⎦
Poly%(5) = y1 ⎤
               ├ First endpoint
Poly%(6) = x1 ⎦
Poly%(7) = y2 ⎤
               ├ Second endpoint
Poly%(8) = x2 ⎦
   ...
   ...
   ...
Poly%(n-1) = ym ⎤
                ├ Last endpoint for a polygon
Poly%(n)   = xm ⎦ with (m-1) sides. This end-
                  point should be equal to the
                  first endpoint.
Note array size, n, can be calculated as :
n = 2*m + 4, where m = 1 + # of sides.

    e.g. : CALL INVERTPOLY(VARPTR(Poly%(0)))
```

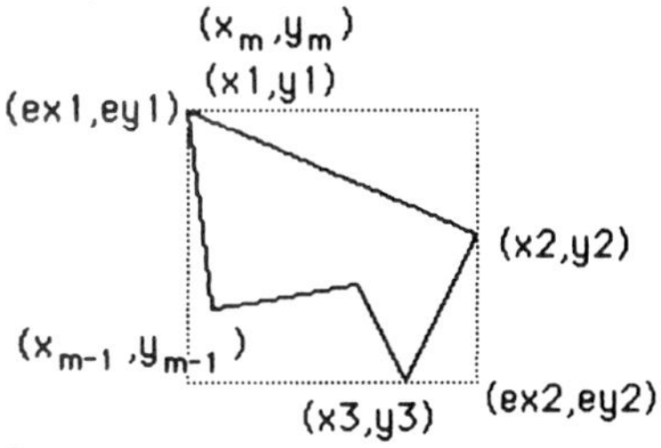

In the figure: (x_m,y_m), (x_1,y_1), (ex_1,ey_1), (x_2,y_2), (x_{m-1},y_{m-1}), (x_3,y_3), (ex_2,ey_2)

Listing 7-13
*Examples of Polygon
Shapes*

```
' This program produces several images of different polygons.
' The program is driven by a stream of data included in the program as
' a set of DATA statements. The general format of this data is as follows:
'       s            = number of sides in the polygon
'    Pname$          = descriptive name of the polygon
'    y1,x1,y2,x2 = coordinates of the rectangle enclosing the polygon
'    [ yi,xi          = coordinates of each polygon endpoint ]
'                      [ the above data repeated for each polygon endpoint,
'                          based upon number of sides in polygon ]
'    xd,yd           = coordinate at which to display the polygon name
'
' The above data structure may be repeated for as many figures as desired.
' The data stream is terminated by a value for s (sides) of 0.
'
DIM Poly%(20)              array to hold the polygon definition.
CALL PENSIZE(2,2)
Again:
READ s                     'get # of sides in polygon
IF s=0 THEN END            'end of data signalled
READ Pname$                'get descriptive name of polygon
Poly%(0)=2* (7 + s*2)      'set size of array based upon # of sides
d=6+s*2                    'calculate amount of data to read based upon # of sides
FOR i=1 TO d               'read in the rest of the polygon definition data
READ p
Poly%(i)=p
NEXT
CALL FRAMEPOLY(VARPTR(Poly%(0)))     'display the polygon
READ x,y          'get 'MOVETO' coords for text description
CALL MOVETO(x,y)
PRINT Pname$;     'display polygon name
GOTO Again
DATA 3,"Isosceles Triangle"
DATA 1,1,50,100
DATA 45,5,5,45,45,85,85,45,5
DATA 2,62
```

Listing 7-13—cont.

```
DATA 3,"Scalene Triangle"
DATA 1,110,50,210
DATA 5,130,20,190,40,160,5,130
DATA 132,62
DATA 4,"Parallelogram"
DATA 1,250,50,350
DATA 5,280,5,340,45,320,45,260,5,280
DATA 252,62
DATA 4,"Trapezoid"
DATA 80,1,130,100
DATA 80,30,80,70,125,90,125,10,80,30
DATA 20,142
DATA 5,"Pentagon"
DATA 80,100,130,200
DATA 80,120,80,150,100,180,120,150,120,120,80,120
DATA 120,142
DATA 6,"Hexagon"
DATA 80,200,130,300
DATA 80,230,80,270,100,290,120,270,120,230,100,210,80,230
DATA 225,142
DATA 0
```

A simple FOR-NEXT loop is then employed to read in this data. The balance of the data consists of the four values that define the enclosing rectangle, as well as a set of values for each polygon endpoint coordinate. Remember that one extra endpoint, equal to the starting endpoint, is needed to "close" the figure. The FRAMEPOLY routine is used to draw the image of the polygon.

Two additional data values accompany each polygon definition. These data values represent the screen coordinate to which the graphics pen should be positioned prior to displaying the polygon's name. This allows each description to be neatly positioned beneath the polygon itself. The output produced by running this program is shown in Figure 7-42. Note that neither the pentagon nor the hexagon produced by this program are regular (i.e., of equal sides and angles).

Figure 7-42
Sample Polygon Images

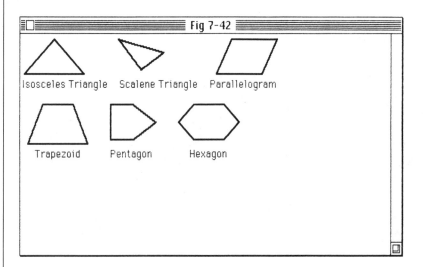

The program provided in Listing 7-14 is a basic Polygon Development Workshop. You can use this program to design your own polygon shapes. Like the other workshop programs, this one also allows you to save a definition of your work as a set of DATA statements on the Clipboard. When you execute this program, it will instruct you to define the polygon endpoints with the mouse. Move the mouse pointer to the desired location for the first endpoint of your shape, and click once. The output of this is shown in Figure 7-43.

Listing 7-14
The Polygon
Development Workshop

```
DIM Poly%(100)          'array holds the polygon definition
StartAgain:
CLS
PRINT "Define polygon endpoints, double-click when done"
i=5          'starting array subscript for 1st endpoint
TryAgain:
GOSUB GetPoint    'get mouse click for endpoint
IF b=2 THEN GOTO TryAgain    'ignore double-clicks at the beginning
Poly%(i)=y                      'set 1st endpoint into array
Poly%(i+1)=x
Miny=y                          'initialize minimum and maximim coords
Minx=x
Maxy=y
Maxx=x
Again:
i=i+2
GOSUB GetPoint                  'get mouse click for next endpoint
IF b=2 THEN GOTO Defined    'double-click means definition complete
Poly%(i)=y              'set polygon endpoint into array
Poly%(i+1)=x
LINE (Poly%(i-1),Poly%(i-2))-(Poly%(i+1),Poly%(i)) 'draw a line of the polygon
GOTO Again
'
Defined:                'get here when the user double-clicks:
i=i-2
Poly%(i)=Poly%(5)    'set final endpoint equal to 1st endpoint to "close" polygon
Poly%(i+1)=Poly%(6)
LINE (Poly%(i-1),Poly%(i-2))-(Poly%(i+1),Poly%(i)) 'draw final side of polygon

s=1+(i-5)/2              'number of sides in the polygon
Poly%(0)=2*(5 + s*2)    'number of bytes in the Poly% array

FOR j=7 TO i STEP 2     'find the coords of the smallest enclosing rectangle:
IF Poly%(j)<Miny THEN Miny=Poly%(j)
IF Poly%(j)>Maxy THEN Maxy=Poly%(j)
IF Poly%(j+1)<Minx THEN Minx=Poly%(j+1)
IF Poly%(j+1)>Maxx THEN Maxx=Poly%(j+1)
NEXT

Poly%(1)=Miny              'place the enclosing rectangle in the Poly% array:
Poly%(2)=Minx
Poly%(3)=Maxy
Poly%(4)=Maxx
CALL PENSIZE(4,4)        'make it a thick line for demo purposes
CALL FRAMEPOLY(VARPTR(Poly%(0)))        'draw the polygon
'
LOCATE 1,1
PRINT "Press 'Y' to save this polygon to clipboard, 'N' to define a new one"
'
WaitKey:                'wait for user response via keyboard:
a$=INKEY$
IF a$="" THEN GOTO WaitKey
IF UCASE$(a$)="Y" THEN GOTO SaveFile
IF UCASE$(a$)="N" THEN GOTO StartAgain
GOTO WaitKey

SaveFile:
```

Listing 7-14—cont.

```
CALL PAINTPOLY(VARPTR(Poly%(0)))    'fill in the shape with solid black

OPEN "O",1,"CLIP:TEXT"          'save the polygon definition to the clipboard
PRINT#1,"DATA ";
FOR j=0 TO 3
PRINT#1,Poly%(j);",";
NEXT
PRINT#1,Poly%(4)
FOR j=5 TO i STEP 2
PRINT#1,"DATA ",Poly%(j);",",Poly%(j+1)
NEXT
CLOSE 1

LOCATE 1,1
PRINT "Polygon definition saved on clipboard.
END

' Subroutine to wait until the user clicks the mouse. Returns b = 1 or 2 to
' indicate a single- or double-click; and (x,y)= coords of mouse pointer at
' time of click.
GetPoint:
b=MOUSE(0)
IF b=2 THEN RETURN
IF b<>1 THEN GOTO GetPoint
x=MOUSE(3)
y=MOUSE(4)
IF x<0 OR y<0 THEN BEEP : GOTO GetPoint
RETURN
```

Figure 7-43
First Polygon Endpoint

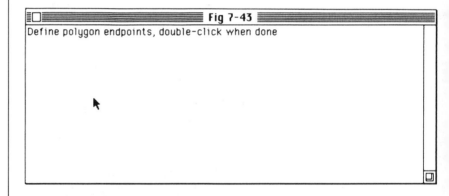

Now move the mouse to the next endpoint location and click again. The result of this is shown in Figure 7-44. A thin line will appear between the two points you selected. In a similar fashion, move the mouse to each additional endpoint and click. As you do

Figure 7-44
First Polygon Side Drawn

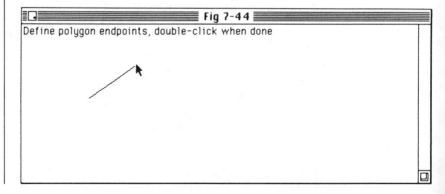

this, the image of your polygon will begin to take shape on the screen. When you have reached the final endpoint (the point that you want joined to the first endpoint), simply double-click the mouse as in Figure 7-45. The polygon shape will be closed and then redrawn in a thicker outline.

Figure 7-45
Polygon Ready for
Double-Click

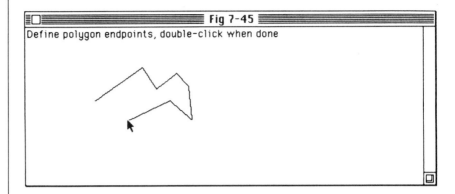

Figure 7-46
Polygon Completed

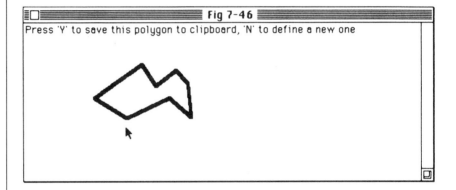

The program now has a complete definition for your shape and will ask if you want to save it. See Figure 7-46. Reply by pressing either the <Y> or <N> keys. If you reply <N> then the program will restart and thus allow you to define a different shape. If you reply <Y> then the program will save the polygon definition on the clipboard. At the same time, the program will use a PAINTPOLY routine to fill in your shape in solid black.

The program obtains the user's mouse clicks in the usual fashion, via a subroutine named GetPoint. Each endpoint of the polygon being defined is obtained as a set of mouse coordinates and saved in the *Poly%* array. A BASIC LINE statement is used to draw the initial outline of the shape, from endpoint to endpoint. When the shape is closed, the program determines the coordinates of the enclosing rectangle (variables *(Minx,Miny)* and *(Maxx,Maxy)*). This is done by searching for the smallest and largest of the x-coordinates and y-coordinates.

The enclosing rectangle definition is placed in the *Poly%* array, as is the total size of the array (calculated as a function of the number of sides in the polygon). This information completes the

Poly% array, and a FRAMEPOLY statement is then used to draw the complete polygon.

The graphics pen size is first set to four pixels by four pixels, so that the polygon will appear with thick lines. At this point the program can be restarted by pressing the <N> key, or the polygon definition can be saved by pressing the <Y> key. The SaveFile code writes the polygon definition to the CLIP:TEXT device as a set of standard DATA statements. Figure 7-47 shows what this data looks like for the sample polygon I drew in Figure 7-46.

Figure 7-47
*Data for Completed
Polygon*

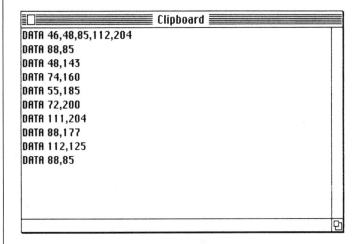

Since the polygon definition carries with it the specific screen location at which the polygon is displayed, it would appear that another polygon definition is necessary if the polygon is to be displayed somewhere else on the screen. Fortunately, however, this is not the case. A very simple procedure can be used to alter the *Poly*% array so that the polygon can be displayed at different points on the screen. The next program illustrates this technique.

In Listing 7-15, the data generated by the polygon development program is read into an array and used to reproduce the polygon image. The polygon definition data is read in two stages. The first five elements of the array are read, since we know they will always be present. The value for the first element is then used to derive the number of sides in the polygon (variable *s*). This value is then used to determine how many more data elements must be read. A FOR-NEXT loop reads these values, and the *Poly*% array is complete and ready for use. The program uses the FRAMEPOLY statement to display the polygon, as per its original definition.

The program now modifies the *Poly*% array so that the image it defines is moved to the upper leftmost position possible within the Output window. This is done by aligning the rectangle enclosing the polygon with the upper left corner of the window. The upper left corner of this rectangle is specified by *Poly*% elements 1 and 2. These values are set into variables *Zy* and *Zx*, respectively. A loop then runs through each x-coordinate and y-coordinate in the

Listing 7-15
*Polygon Repositioning
Techniques*

```
' This program uses the data produced by the Polygon Development Workshop.
DIM Poly%(100)        'array holds the polygon definition
' read the data statements produced by the development workshop program:
FOR i=0 TO 4
READ Poly%(i)        'read in the 1st five elements of the polygon definition
NEXT
s=((Poly%(0)/2) - 7)/2   ' number of sides for this polygon
j=(s+1)*2                'number of elements remaining to be read
FOR i=5 TO (4+j)
READ Poly%(i)            'read in the rest of the polygon definition data
NEXT
' polygon definition read in.

CLS
CALL FRAMEPOLY(VARPTR(Poly%(0))) 'display the original polygon on screen:
LOCATE 1,1
PRINT "Here is the original polygon, press any key to continue."
GOSUB WaitKey

' Now move the polygon to its upper-leftmost position :
Zy=Poly%(1)              'the smallest y-coord in the polygon definition
Zx=Poly%(2)              'the smallest x-coord in the polygon definition
FOR i=1 TO (3+j) STEP 2
Poly%(i)=Poly%(i)-Zy     'adjust each y-coord
Poly%(i+1)=Poly%(i+1)-Zx 'adjust each x-coord
NEXT

CLS
CALL FRAMEPOLY(VARPTR(Poly%(0)))
LOCATE 12,1
PRINT "Here the polygon has been moved as far up and to the left as possible."
PRINT "Press any key to continue."
GOSUB WaitKey

' Now move the polygon a specific number of pixels down and to the right :
Zy=30                    'number of pixels to move down
Zx=150                   'number of pixels to move to the right
FOR i=1 TO (3+j) STEP 2
Poly%(i)=Poly%(i)+Zy     'adjust each y-coord
Poly%(i+1)=Poly%(i+1)+Zx 'adjust each x-coord
NEXT

CLS
CALL FRAMEPOLY(VARPTR(Poly%(0)))
LOCATE 12,1
PRINT "Here the polygon has been moved down and to the right as requested."
PRINT "Press any key to continue."
GOSUB WaitKey
END

' Subroutine to wait until any key is pressed:
WaitKey:
a$=INKEY$
IF a$="" THEN GOTO WaitKey
RETURN

' Polygon image:
DATA 46 , 48 , 85 , 112 , 204
DATA 88 , 85
DATA 48 , 143
DATA 74 , 160
DATA 55 , 185
DATA 72 , 200
DATA 111 , 204
DATA 88 , 177
DATA 112 , 125
DATA 88 , 85
```

polygon definition. The value Zx is subtracted from each x-coordinate and the value Zy is subtracted from each y-coordinate. This effectively moves the polygon to the upper left corner while keeping its original shape intact. The program displays the polygon in its new location, as shown in Figure 7-48.

Figure 7-48
*Polygon Moved to
Upper Left Corner*

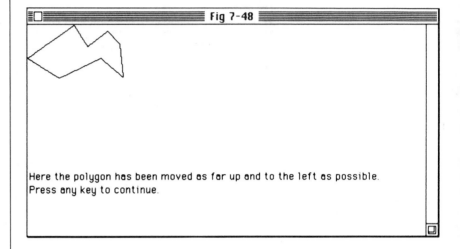

The same technique can be used to move the image anywhere on the screen. In the next part of the program, the image is moved 150 pixels to the right and 30 pixels down on the screen. This is accomplished by setting variable Zx to 150 and variable Zy to 30. Once again, a loop is used to run through each coordinate in the *Poly%* array. Zx is added to each x-coordinate, and Zy is added to each y-coordinate. The resulting image is shown in Figure 7-49.

Figure 7-49
*Polygon Moved Down
and to the Right*

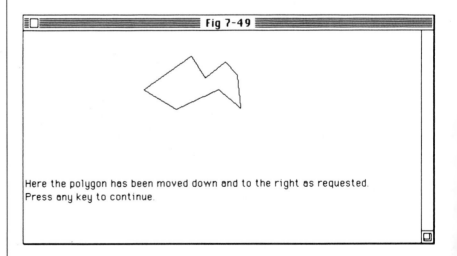

Using these techniques, it will only be necessary to define a specific shape once, regardless of where you intend to display it on the screen. Once the shape is defined, I recommend aligning it to the upper left corner of the Output window, as I did in the example program. From this position, it is an easy matter to move the image to any other area of the screen.

The Scroll Statement

The *SCROLL* statement is a special feature of Microsoft BASIC for the Macintosh. It is a graphics oriented statement in that it treats a section of the display screen as a matrix of individual pixels. The statement operates within a rectangular area of the screen and allows you to shift all of the screen pixels within that area. The pixels may be shifted right or left and/or up and down.

The rectangular area to be affected is specified on the scroll statement by a pair of coordinates. The syntax of the rectangle specification is the same as that used on the LINE statement. The scroll statement looks like this

```
SCROLL (x1,y1)-(x2,y2),Dx,Dy
```

Variable *Dx* specifies the number of pixels the image is to be shifted to the right. If it is negative, the shift will be to the left. If it is zero, no horizontal shifting will take place. Variable *Dy* specifies the number of pixels the image is to be shifted down. If it is negative, the shift will be in the upward direction. If it is zero, no vertical shift will take place.

Listing 7-16 shows a simple example of the SCROLL statement. When run, it displays a small black box in the Output window. A FOR-NEXT loop enclosing a SCROLL statement is used to scroll the box down and to the right. This is done one pixel at a time, by using a value of 1 for both *Dx* and *Dy*. A second loop then scrolls the box up and to the left until it is back in its original position. In this case, a value of –1 is used for both *Dx* and *Dy*.

Listing 7-16
The SCROLL Statement

```
LINE (50,50)-(75,75),,BF        'draw the box
Dx=1
Dy=1
FOR i=1 TO 50
SCROLL (0,0)-(200,200),Dx,Dy    'scroll down and to right
NEXT
Dx=-1
Dy=-1
FOR i=1 TO 50
SCROLL (0,0)-(200,200),Dx,Dy    'scroll up and to left
NEXT
END
```

More rapid scrolling rates can be achieved by using larger values for *Dx* and/or *Dy*. To scroll only horizontally, use a value of 0 for *Dy*. To scroll only vertically, use a value of 0 for *Dx*.

When using the SCROLL statement, it is important that you define the rectangle large enough to enclose the image that you are scrolling, as well as the area that the image will occupy after the scroll is complete. The boundary of the rectangular area on the side(s) vacated by the image will be filled with the current background pattern (all white by default, changeable with the BACKPAT routine).

Unifying Graphics Commands With Picture$

The Macintosh supports a special command structure that can be used to represent every type of command and statement that produces a graphics image on the screen. This powerful facility allows you to bundle any combination of graphics-producing statements into a single entity, a character string variable. That variable can then be manipulated in any way desired—held in storage, saved in a file, transferred to another variable, among others.

By "playing back" the graphics commands stored in the variable, you can at any time reproduce the effects of all of the graphics commands that the variable contains.

To create such a string variable, you must request that BASIC begin recording all of your graphics commands. This is accomplished with the statement

```
PICTURE ON
```

Once this statement is executed, any statements executed that produce an effect on the Output window will be encoded into the special graphics command language and stored in a special area within the computer. It is important that you understand that the statements that will be trapped and encoded in this fashion are only those that would normally have an effect on the display screen (e.g., CLS, PRINT, LINE, CIRCLE, CALL LINETO, and CALL FILLARC).

Statements that affect the way in which the graphics statements function will also be trapped (e.g., CALL MOVETO, CALL TEXTSIZE, and CALL TEXTFONT). When these statements are executed after the PICTURE ON statement, they do not actually affect the screen, as they are directed to the special internal storage area instead.

After you have executed the desired sequence of graphics statements, you must turn off the graphics recording process by executing a

```
PICTURE OFF
```

statement. This restores normal operation of the graphics statements of the BASIC language. All of the graphics statements that were trapped between the execution of the PICTURE ON and PICTURE OFF statements can now be retrieved into a character string variable by referencing the character string function PICTURE$. This function takes no arguments. Thus, the statement

```
P$ = PICTURE$
```

would access the graphics commands sequence previously trapped and place it into variable *P$*. The command sequence held in this variable can be "played back" through use of the PICTURE statement. This statement has several different forms. The simplest form is

```
PICTURE ,P$
```

where *P$* is a string variable containing a sequence of specially encoded graphics commands. Note the comma that must precede the variable specification. This statement will "play back" each of the graphics commands that were trapped earlier (between the PICTURE ON and PICTURE OFF statements).

The effect is as if the graphics statements that were executed at that time are executed now, all at once, in the same order. The screen rapidly fills with the image that those commands define. I will explain how this facility can be used in a moment; first, let me describe the other formats of the PICTURE statement.

The PICTURE statement can also be written as

```
PICTURE (x,y),P$
```

where *(x,y)* represents a screen coordinate. While the first form of the PICTURE statement will reproduce the stored graphics commands exactly as they were originally executed, this form will realign the image produced so that its upper left corner is at the screen coordinate specified. It can thus be used to reproduce the captured image in a different area of the screen.

The final form of the PICTURE statement is as follows

```
PICTURE (x1,y1)-(x2,y2),P$
```

In this case, the pair of coordinates defines an enclosing rectangle, and the image being played back is scaled to fit into that rectangle. This form of the statement can thus be used to grow, shrink, or stretch images that have been previously recorded.

How can this picture recording and playback facility be used? Suppose you have a large and complex image that is created through use of a wide variety of graphics statements. You want to include this picture as part of a program you are writing, but all of those graphics statements take up a lot of room, and may not leave you enough space for the main body of the program. You can write a separate program that only serves to create this special image. This program will record the statements that create the image using the PICTURE ON and PICTURE OFF statements. It will then obtain the character string containing the sequence (use the PICTURE$ function), and save it in a data file.

Now your main program need only open the data file, read in the contents of the character string, and play back the image using the PICTURE statement. This can save an enormous amount of space for the main program.

Sometimes it is necessary to use mathematical functions and calculations to produce a desired image. This often results in an image that appears slowly on the screen (due to the amount of processing time needed for the mathematics). This is another way in which the PICTURE facility can be helpful. The image is created and trapped with PICTURE ON. Then, when you actually want the image to appear on the screen, you use the PICTURE statement to reproduce the image.

Since the calculations have already been made, the image will appear much more rapidly. Listing 7-17 shows an example of this approach. Using the trigonometric functions, this program creates a three-dimensional image of a phonograph record. If you execute

```
PRINT "Please wait a moment"
Pi=3.14159
PICTURE ON
FOR angle=0 TO Pi STEP .025
x1=100 + 50*COS(angle)
y1=100 + 50*SIN(angle+Pi/3)
x2=100 + 50*COS(angle+Pi)
y2=100 + 50*SIN(angle+Pi/3+Pi)
LINE (x1,y1)-(x2,y2)
NEXT
PICTURE OFF
P$=PICTURE$
OPEN "O",1,"PHONO"
PRINT#1,P$
CLOSE 1
PRINT "File 'PHONO' created"
```

this program, you will not actually see this image appear, as it is trapped by the PICTURE ON statement. The purpose of this program is to generate the graphics data, and save it in a sequential disk file named "PHONO." Once this program is run and the file is created, it is a simple matter to rapidly reproduce the image from the data in the file. This is done by Listing 7-18.

```
' This program will read the three-dimensional picture of a phonograph
' record created by the previous program and will display that image on
' the screen in various locations and sizes.
' The sequential data file named "PHONO" must have been previously
' created by running program L7-17.
'
' Read the graphics data in the file :

OPEN "I",1,"PHONO"
P$=INPUT$(LOF(1),1)
CLOSE 1
'
' Display the image as it was recorded :

PICTURE ,P$

LOCATE 1,1
PRINT "Here is the original picture, press any key to continue"
GOSUB WaitKey
'
CLS
'
' Display the image in a different area of the screen :
'
PICTURE (200,0),P$
```

Listing 7-18—cont.

```
LOCATE 1,1
PRINT "Here is the picture at a different location, press any key to continue"
GOSUB WaitKey

CLS

' Display the image in a larger size

PICTURE (0,0)-(400,400),P$

LOCATE 1,1
PRINT "Here is the picture in a larger size, press any key to continue"
GOSUB WaitKey

END

' Subroutine to wait until the user presses a key
WaitKey:
a$=INKEY$
IF a$="" THEN GOTO WaitKey
RETURN
```

This program opens the file and reads its contents into string variable *P$*. The three different forms of the PICTURE statement are then demonstrated. Figure 7-50 shows the picture displayed at its original location. Figure 7-51 shows the picture displayed at a different location. Finally, Figure 7-52 shows how the PICTURE statement can be used to expand the image to a larger size.

Figure 7-50
The Original Phonograph Image

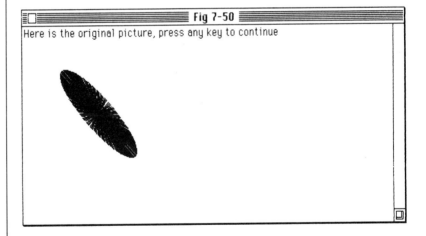

Graphics Images and the Clipboard

Graphics images that have been encoded into the special format used by the PICTURE statement can be cut and pasted to/from the standard Macintosh Clipboard. To access data of this type on the Clipboard from within a BASIC program, you must use the device name "CLIP:PICTURE." There are two ways in which this facility can be used. One would be to create a picture using some other program, such as MacPaint, and include it in your own BASIC program. In this case your BASIC program must read the image data from the Clipboard. The other approach is to create an image using a BASIC program, save that image on the Clipboard, and then incorporate that image into another application/document by pasting.

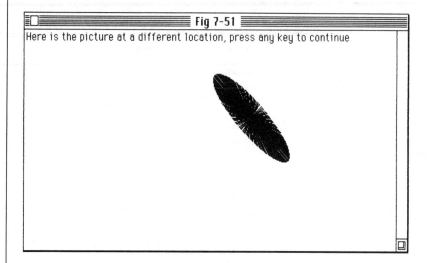

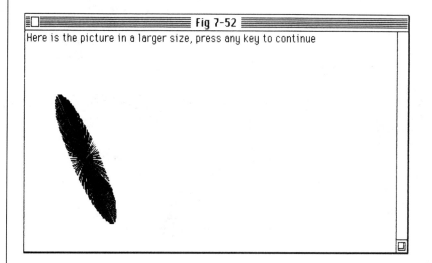

In Figure 7-53 I have drawn a picture of a house, using MacPaint. As you can see, I have used the marquee to select the entire image and copy it to the Clipboard. This image can now be retrieved from the Clipboard by a BASIC program such as the one shown in Listing 7-19. Figure 7-54 shows the results of executing that program. (Before you run the program, you must place a graphics image on the Clipboard, otherwise the program will not work.)

Note that, once you have retrieved the data from the Clipboard, you can save it in an ordinary sequential data file for reuse later. This is a good idea, since it is not easy to maintain the data on the Clipboard for very long. The Clipboard is only meant as a temporary storage area, and is too volatile for long term storage of important data.

Figure 7-53
*Copying an Image out
of MacPaint*

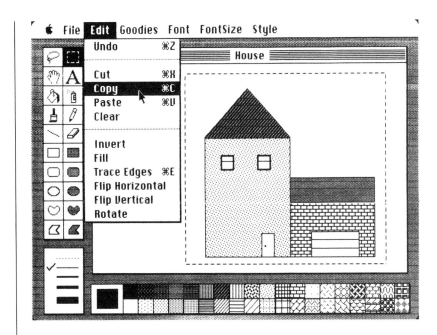

Figure 7-53
*Copying an Image out
of MacPaint*

Listing 7-19
*Retrieving a Graphics
Image from the
Clipboard*

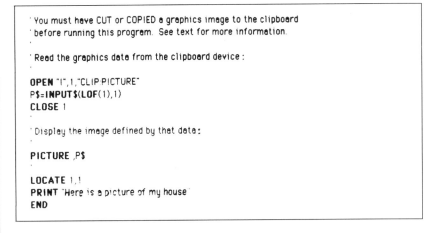

```
' You must have CUT or COPIED a graphics image to the clipboard
' before running this program. See text for more information.
'
' Read the graphics data from the clipboard device:
'
OPEN "I",1,"CLIP:PICTURE"
P$=INPUT$(LOF(1),1)
CLOSE 1

' Display the image defined by that data:
'
PICTURE ,P$

LOCATE 1,1
PRINT "Here is a picture of my house"
END
```

Figure 7-54
Retrieving an Image
from the Clipboard

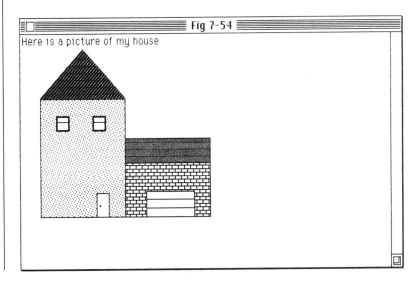

Listing 7-20 contains a program that creates a graph. This graph shows the voltage across a capacitor that is being charged through a resistor, as a function of time. The graph is produced using a simple formula taken from basic electronics theory. The objective, however, is to include this graph in a lab report being written using MacWrite. To this end, the program in Listing 7-20 uses the PICTURE ON statement to capture the image of the graph as a character string. This string is then written to the CLIP:PICTURE device, effectively placing the graph onto the Clipboard.

You can get the graph onto the Clipboard of your system by simply executing the program of Listing 7-20. In Figure 7-55, I have prepared the lab report using MacWrite, and I am about to insert my graph by performing a paste operation. Figure 7-56 shows the completed document with the graph in place.

The Appointment Calendar Program — Version 2

Using the techniques that I have covered in the last few chapters, it is now possible to make some sophisticated enhancements to the

Listing 7-20
Saving a Graphics Image on the Clipboard

```
R=5000000!    ' 5 M ohm resistor
C=.00001      ' 10 uF capacitor
V0=100        ' init voltage
'
PICTURE ON        'start recording graphics data
'
' generate the graph :
'
FOR t=0 TO 200   't = time
V=V0*(1-EXP(-t/(R*C)))        'formula for voltage as a function of time
PSET (t+5,150-V)             'plot a point on the graph
NEXT
'
' Now draw the graph's axis lines :
'
LINE (5,150)-(210,150)    'draw the x-axis (time)
LINE (5,150)-(5,20)       'draw y-axis (voltage)
'
' Now label the graph :
'
LOCATE 10,28
PRINT "t";
LOCATE 1,1
PRINT "v";
LOCATE 11,1
PRINT "Charging voltage of capacitor";
'
PICTURE OFF
'
' Image complete, now save it to clipboard :
'
P$=PICTURE$
OPEN "O",1,"CLIP:PICTURE"
PRINT#1,P$
CLOSE 1
'
LOCATE 1,1
PRINT "Picture written to clipboard"
END
```

appointment calendar program. Recall that the first version of this program was introduced in Chapter 4 as Listing 4-10. That program contained all of the basic features and functions of a general-purpose personal appointment calendar but did not take advantage of the Macintosh user interface. You may want to review the discussion of that program in Chapter 4 at this time.

Figure 7-55
The Lab Report Prior to the Paste

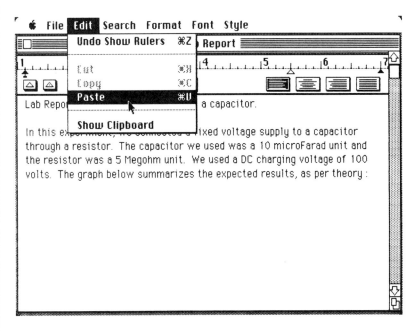

Figure 7-56
The Lab Report with Picture from BASIC in Place

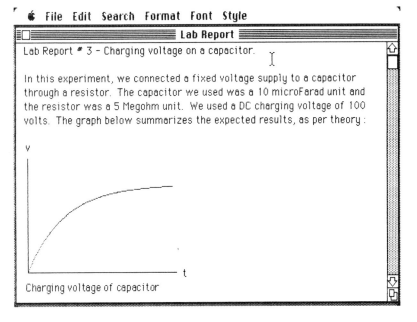

Listing 7-21 gives the second version of this program. In this new version, you need no longer type in the date that you wish to access. Instead, you can use the mouse to select the date from a graphics image of a calendar. Essentially, the only part of the original program that has been changed is the GetDate subroutine.

Listing 7-21
*The Appointment
Calendar Program —
Version 2*

```
' This version of the program displays a graphic image of a monthly
' calendar and allows the user to use the mouse to select a date within
' it. The original version of this program was provided in Listing 4-10.
' Essentially, subroutine GetDate has been changed in this version.
' See the text for more information.
Dmonth%=1      'default display month is Jan
DIM Rect%(3)   'holds rectangle definitions for toolbox calls
Today$=DATE$   'Get date and reformat it to mm/dd/yy format:
Today$=LEFT$(Today$,6)+RIGHT$(Today$,2)  'remove '19' from year
MID$(Today$,3,1)="/"
MID$(Today$,6,1)="/"
Tmonth%=VAL(LEFT$(Today$,2))
Tday%=VAL(MID$(Today$,4,2))
Tyear%=VAL(RIGHT$(Today$,2))
' Initialize array data:
DIM MonthDays%(12)
FOR x%=1 TO 12
READ MonthDays%(x%)
NEXT
DATA 31,28,31,30,31,30,31,31,30,31,30,31

' Determine the starting day of the week for the current year, save
' it in variable NewYearsDay% :
CALL StartDay(1,Tyear%,NewYearsDay%,Days%)
' Set up month of February for the current year :
IF (Tyear%-84) MOD 4 = 0 THEN MonthDays%(2)=29 ELSE MonthDays%(2)=28 'Leap Years
CALL DayofWeek(Tmonth%,Tday%,Tdayw%,Tjday%)

DIM DayNames$(7)
FOR x%=1 TO 7
READ DayNames$(x%)
NEXT
DATA Sunday,Monday,Tuesday,Wednesday,Thursday,Friday,Saturday
DIM MonthNames$(12)
FOR x%=1 TO 12
READ MonthNames$(x%)
NEXT
DATA January, February,March,April,May,June,July,August,September
DATA October,November,December
' Set up a complete textual description of the current date :
Tdate$=DayNames$(Tdayw%)+" "+MonthNames$(Tmonth%)+" "+STR$(Tday%)
Tdate$=Tdate$+", 19"+RIGHT$(Today$,2)+"   (Day #"+STR$(Tjday%)+")"
' Prepare for access to random file CALENDAR :
OPEN "R",1,"CALENDAR",42
FIELD 1, 40 AS Appoint$, 2 AS Link$
HighestRecord%=LOF(1)/42  'current highest record number in the file
Main.Menu:
CLS
LOCATE 1,10
PRINT "Appointment Calendar Program - Version 1"
LOCATE 3,5
PRINT "Today is ";Tdate$
LOCATE 5,1
PRINT "1. Check/Delete Appointments"
PRINT "2. Enter Appointments"
PRINT "3. Exit Program"
LOCATE 9,5
PRINT "Select Choice ==> "
TryAgain:
GOSUB WaitKey
a%=VAL(a$)
IF a%<1 OR a%>3 THEN GOTO TryAgain
ON a% GOTO CheckA,EnterA,Finish

' Check Appointments function :
CheckA:
Prompt$="Check Appointments"
GOSUB GetDate 'get date from user via keyboard
' determine day of week and julian day # for selected date :
```

Listing 7-21—cont.

```
CALL DayofWeek(Month%,Day%,Dayw%,Jday%)
' display the selected date nicely :
PRINT
PRINT DayNames$(Dayw%)+" "+MonthNames$(Month%)+" "+STR$(Day%)
' search CALENDAR file for appointments for selected date :
' ( the initial record number to read is the julian date, Jday% )
GET 1,Jday%
Link%=CVI(Link$)
IF LEFT$(Appoint$,1)="@" AND Link%=0 THEN PRINT "No appointments for this date !" : GOTO NextCheck
heck
' display each appointment in the chain :
Apno=1 'number each appointment starting with 1
Apno.fix=0  'handles case where appoint#1 was deleted but appoint#2 exists
FollowChain:
IF LEFT$(Appoint$,1)<>"@" THEN PRINT Apno;". ";Appoint$ : Apno=Apno+1 ELSE Apno.fix=1
IF Link%=0 THEN GOTO EndofChain
GET 1,Link%
Link%=CVI(Link$)
GOTO FollowChain
EndofChain:
PRINT "---- End of Appointments for selected date ----"
PRINT
PRINT "Do you wish to delete any of these appointments ? (Y/N) "
GOSUB GetYN
IF yn$="N" THEN GOTO NextCheck
RetryApno:
INPUT "Enter appointment number to delete ==> ";Dapno
IF Dapno<1 OR Dapno>=Apno THEN PRINT "Invalid choice" : GOTO RetryApno
Dapno=Dapno+Apno.fix 'handles case where appoint#1 was deleted but appoint#2 exists
' Delete the selected appointment entry from the calendar :
IF Dapno>1 THEN GOTO DeChain 'all entries except the 1st must be returned to the free chain
GET 1,Jday%
LSET Appoint$="@"
PUT 1,Jday%
GOTO DeletedIt
DeChain:  ' find the entry to be deleted and break it out of the chain :
GET 1,Jday%              'start at the head of the chain
Link%=Jday%
Apno=1                  'keep track of the position number (appointment #)
WHILE Apno+1 <> Dapno
Link%=CVI(Link$)
GET 1,Link%              'chain forward and keep looking for it
Apno=Apno+1
WEND
' Now Link% = the record preceding the record to be deleted .
PreLink%=Link%
Link%=CVI(Link$)
GET 1,Link%      'get the record to be deleted
DelLink%=Link%    'the record # to be returned to the free chain
Link%=CVI(Link$)   'Link% = the next entry after the one to be deleted
GET 1,PreLink%    'get the preceding record
LSET Link$=MKI$(Link%)  'connect it to the entry following the deleted one
PUT 1,PreLink%    'this effectively disconnects the deleted entry from the
'                        current appointment chain.
' Now put the deleted entry on the free record chain:
GET 1,367        'get pointer to start of free chain
NextFreeLink%=CVI(Link$)
LSET Link$=MKI$(DelLink%)   'make the deleted entry the first on the free chain
PUT 1,367
GET 1,DelLink%      'get the deleted entry
LSET Link$=MKI$(NextFreeLink%) 'attach the rest of the free chain to it
PUT 1,DelLink%
' Deletion process complete.
DeletedIt:
PRINT "That appointment has been deleted."
NextCheck:
PRINT "Do you wish to check another date ? (Y/N) "
GOSUB GetYN
IF yn$="Y" THEN GOTO CheckA
GOTO Main.Menu
```

Listing 7-21—cont.

```
' Enter Appointments Function :
EnterA:
Prompt$="Add Appointments"
GOSUB GetDate
CALL DayofWeek(Month%,Day%,Dayw%,Jday%)
' display the selected date nicely :
PRINT
PRINT DayNames$(Dayw%)+" "+MonthNames$(Month%)+" "+STR$(Day%)
PRINT
LINE INPUT "Enter the description of the appointment ==> ";Apdesc$
' search CALENDAR file for appointments for selected date :
' ( the initial record number to read is the julian date, Jday% )
GET 1,Jday%
Link%=CVI(Link$)
PrevLink%=Jday%
IF LEFT$(Appoint$,1)="@" AND Link%=0 THEN LSET Appoint$=Apdesc$ : PUT 1,Jday% : GOTO Appoin
tmentMade
WHILE Link%<>0
GET 1,Link%
PrevLink%=Link%
Link%=CVI(Link$)
WEND
' found end of chain, allocate and insert a new record at PrevLink%
GET 1,367   'get start of free record chain
NextFreeLink%=CVI(Link$)
IF NextFreeLink%>HighestRecord% THEN LSET Link$=MKI$(NextFreeLink%+1) : HighestRecord%=High
estRecord%+1 : GOTO AllocateNextFree
GET 1,NextFreeLink%   'get the link to the next free record available
AllocateNextFree:
PUT 1,367   'setup the new start of the free chain
GET 1,PrevLink%   'get previously last record for appointment date chain
LSET Link$=MKI$(NextFreeLink%) 'attach the new record to the end of the chain
PUT 1,PrevLink%
LSET Appoint$=Apdesc$ 'set up the new appointment record
LSET Link$=MKI$(0)   'end of chain indicator for appointment date chain
PUT 1,NextFreeLink% 'write the new appointment record
' the appointment has been added.
AppointmentMade:
PRINT "Do you wish to enter another appointment ? (Y/N) "
GOSUB GetYN
IF yn$="Y" THEN GOTO EnterA
GOTO Main.Menu
'
' End of Program :
Finish:
CLOSE 1
END
'
'
' Subroutine to wait for the user to press any key.
' The keystroke is returned in a$
WaitKey:
a$=INKEY$
WHILE a$=""
a$=INKEY$
WEND
RETURN
'
' Subroutine to obtain the date from the user.
' When called, variable Prompt$= string to display at top of screen
' while waiting for the user to select a date.
' Returns selected month in Month% and day in Day%
' This routine has been rewritten in this version of the program to display
' a graphics image of a calendar and to allow the user to select the date
' via mouse clicks on this graphics image. See text for more information.
GetDate:
CLS
CALL TEXTFONT(1)                'set Geneva font
CALL TEXTSIZE(12)
PRINT Prompt$,"19";RIGHT$(Today$,2)
```

Listing 7-21—cont.

```
'MonthDays%(Month%)
CALL TEXTFONT(0)          'set Chicago font
CALL TEXTSIZE(12)
'
' Display the 12 month selection boxes :
'
Xc%=10                    'starting x-coordinate
FOR i%=1 TO 12
CALL MOVETO(Xc%+2,35)
PRINT LEFT$(MonthNames$(i%),3);
LINE (Xc%,20)-(Xc%+30,40),,B
Xc%=Xc%+40
NEXT
'
' highlight currently selected month box :
'
Xc%=10+40*(Dmonth%-1) 'starting x-coord for box for currently selected month
Rect%(0)=20
Rect%(1)=Xc%
Rect%(2)=41
Rect%(3)=Xc%+31
CALL INVERTRECT(VARPTR(Rect%(0)))
'
' Now display month calendar for selected month, Dmonth%
'
CALL StartDay(Dmonth%,Tyear%,Fday%,Days%) 'get starting day of week, and
'                                number of days for currently selected month
'
Xc%=35
FOR i=1 TO 7                  'display day name titles for calendar
CALL MOVETO(Xc%,80)
PRINT LEFT$(DayNames$(i),3);
Xc%=Xc%+60
NEXT
'
' display day numbers in correct calendar positions for each day on month :
'
Yc%=110                      'starting y-coord for first row in calendar
Cday%=Fday%            'set init current day number (1-7)
FOR Nday%=1 TO Days%
Xc%=35+60*(Cday%-1)     'set x-coord as per current day number
CALL MOVETO(Xc%,Yc%)
PRINT USING "##";Nday%;
Cday%=Cday%+1                 'go on to next day of week (current day number)
IF Cday%>7 THEN Cday%=1 : Yc%=Yc%+30   'wrap from Saturday to Sunday
NEXT
'
FOR x=20 TO 440 STEP 60      'draw vertical lines of calendar
LINE (x,60)-(x,270)
NEXT
FOR y=60 TO 270 STEP 30       'draw horizontal lines of calendar
LINE (20,y)-(440,y)
NEXT
'
' Calendar image complete, now wait for user to make selection via mouse :
'
Swait:
CALL SHOWCURSOR       ' make sure the mouse pointer is visible
GOSUB WaitMouse
CALL OBSCURECURSOR    'turn cursor off when not in use
IF y<20 THEN BEEP : GOTO Swait    'clicked in invalid area
IF y>40 THEN GOTO DayCheck          'check for click in calendar area
'
' click was within month selection area :
'
IF x<10 OR x>480 THEN BEEP : GOTO Swait  'invalid area
Dm%=1+((x-10)\40)  'convert x-coord to month number (1-12)
IF (x-10) MOD 40 > 30 THEN BEEP : GOTO Swait  'between month boxes
IF Dm%=Dmonth% THEN GOTO Swait  'ignore change of month to same month !
Dmonth%=Dm%        'change to newly selected month
```

Listing 7-21—cont.

```
    GOTO GetDate                    'draw new calendar image
    '
    ' click was within day selection area :

    DayCheck:
    IF x<20 OR x>440 THEN BEEP : GOTO Swait      'invalid area
    IF y<90 OR y>270 THEN BEEP : GOTO Swait           'invalid area
    y=1+(y-90)\30     'convert y into calendar row number (1-6)
    x=1+(x-20)\60     'convert x into calendar column number (1-7)
    IF y=1 AND x<Fday% THEN BEEP : GOTO Swait     'before first day on first row
    IF y=1 THEN Day%=1+x-Fday% : GOTO DateSelected
    Day%=1+x-Fday% + (7*(y-1))  'day number for any selection on row 2 or below
    IF Day%>Days% THEN BEEP : GOTO Swait     'after last day on last row

    ' A valid date has been selected :
    '
    DateSelected:
    Rect%(0)=90+(y-1)*30      ' invert selected date rectangle on screen :
    Rect%(1)=20+(x-1)*60
    Rect%(2)=Rect%(0)+30
    Rect%(3)=Rect%(1)+60
    CALL INVERTRECT(VARPTR(Rect%(0)))
    Month%=Dmonth%

    ' restore conditions for original part of the program to continue :

    CALL TEXTFONT(1)                  'set Geneva font
    CALL TEXTSIZE(12)
    LOCATE 18,1
    RETURN


    END
    ' Subroutine to wait until the user clicks the mouse button, returns
    ' the mouse pointer coordinates at the time of the click in variables x and y.
    WaitMouse:
    b=MOUSE(0)
    IF b<>1 THEN GOTO WaitMouse
    x=MOUSE(3)
    y=MOUSE(4)
    RETURN


    ' Subroutine to wait until the user presses either the Y or N keys,
    ' in response to a yes or no question.  Will not return until one of these
    ' keys is pressed.  The keystroke character is returned in yn$.
    GetYN:
    yn$=INKEY$
    WHILE UCASE$(yn$)<>"Y" AND UCASE$(yn$)<>"N"
    yn$=INKEY$
    WEND
    yn$=UCASE$(yn$)
    RETURN
    '
    ' Subprogram StartDay
    ' Finds the starting day of the week for a given month and year.
    ' Call StartDay(Month%,Year%,Day%,Days%)
    ' with Month% = 1(Jan), 2(Feb), ...., 12(Dec)
    ' and Year% = 85, 86, ..., 99 (valid for 1985 thru 1999)
    ' Returns with Day% = 1 (Sun), 2 (Mon), 3 (Tue), ..., 7 (Sat)
    ' and with Days% = number of days in that month.
    SUB StartDay (m%,y%,d%,ds%) STATIC
    SHARED MonthDays%()
    d%=3 'Jan 85 starts with Tuesday
    m1%=1 'start at Jan
    y1%=85 'start at 1985
    StartDayLoop2:
    IF (y1%-84) MOD 4 = 0 THEN MonthDays%(2)=29 ELSE MonthDays%(2)=28 'Leap Years
    StartDayLoop1:
    IF m1%=m% AND y1%=y% THEN GOTO FoundStartDay
    d%=d%+MonthDays%(m1%)
    IF m1%<12 THEN  m1%=m1%+1 : GOTO StartDayLoop1
```

Listing 7-21—cont.

```
m1%=1
y1%=y1%+1
GOTO StartDayLoop2
FoundStartDay:
d%=d% MOD 7
IF d%=0 THEN d%=7
ds%=MonthDays%(m1%)
END SUB

' Subprogram DayofWeek
' Call DayofWeek(month%,day%,dayw%,jday%)
' Variables month% and day% are inputs to this routine.
' Variables dayw% and jday% are outputs from this routine.
' This routine takes a month (1-12) and a day (1-31) and
' returns a day of the week (1(Sun), 2(Mon), ..., 7(Sat)) and
' a julian day (1-366). The current year (Tyear%) is assumed.
SUB DayofWeek(m%,d%,dw%,jd%) STATIC
SHARED MonthDays%(),NewYearsDay%
dw%=NewYearsDay%
jd%=1
m1%=1
WHILE m1%<m%  'Accumulate days for each full month prior to desired month:
dw%=dw%+MonthDays%(m1%)
jd%=jd%+MonthDays%(m1%)
m1%=m1%+1
WEND
' Now in desired month, find desired day :
dw%=dw%+d%-1
jd%=jd%+d%-1
' Adjust day of week to range 1 - 7 :
dw%=dw% MOD 7
IF dw%=0 THEN dw%=7
END SUB
```

This routine is used by both the Check Appointments and Add Appointments functions to obtain a date to process. In the first version, this routine simply input the date from the keyboard. In this new version, the routine uses various graphics functions to draw the image of a calendar. Mouse detection techniques are then employed to allow the user to select the date by positioning and clicking the mouse. Figure 7-57 shows what the display screen will look like when the new GetDate subroutine is active.

The twelve months of the year are displayed across the top of the screen. The month currently being viewed is highlighted. The user can change the currently selected month by moving the mouse pointer to a different month and clicking. Below the month selection row is the image of the calendar for the currently selected month. This image changes automatically when the current month selection is changed.

After selecting the desired month, the user completes the selection by moving the mouse pointer to the desired day within the calendar image, and then clicking the mouse button. The selected day will be highlighted, and then the GetDate subroutine will return to its caller with the appropriate values in variables *Month%* and *Day%*. Note that the rest of the appointment program is basically

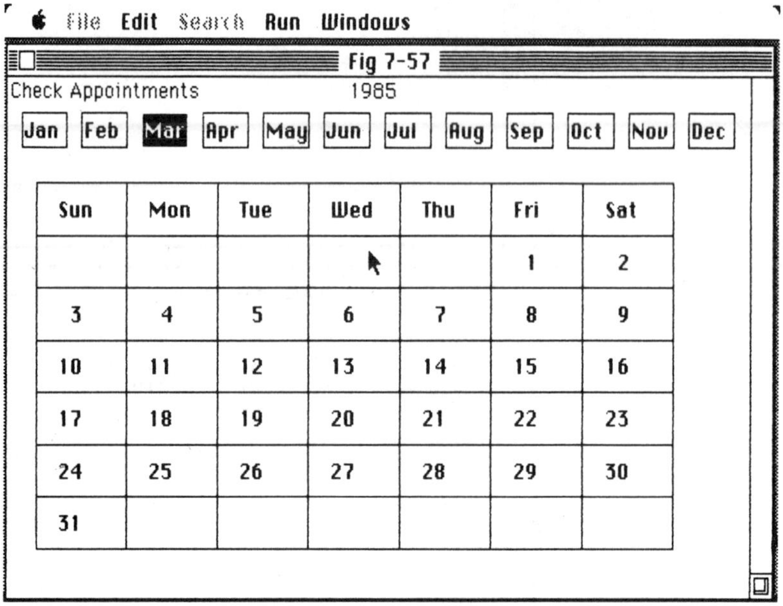

Figure 7-57
*The New GetDate
Routine*

The New GetDate Routine

unchanged; the subroutine mechanism makes it possible to change one part of the program in such a radical way without requiring an entire rewrite. As long as subroutine GetDate maintains the same input and output variables and performs the same basic function, the rest of the program that relies on it can remain unaltered.

At the very beginning of the program, you will notice the addition of two new variables. These are *Dmonth%* and *Rect%*. Variable *Dmonth%* holds the month number for the currently selected month of the GetDate screen. It defaults to 1 for January. Array variable *Rect%* will be used to hold rectangle coordinates for the toolbox routine INVERTRECT. This routine will be used to highlight selections made on the GetDate screen.

One additional change has been made in the calling sequence for the GetDate routine. Its caller must now pass to it a prompt string in variable *Prompt$*. GetDate will display this string at the top of the screen, so that the user can see what function is requesting the date.

The subroutine begins by clearing the screen and setting the Geneva-12 font. The prompt message and the current year is then displayed. The text font is then changed to Chicago-12. In this way, the calendar image will be displayed in a different font, to highlight the fact that it represents a new and enhanced part of the program.

A single FOR-NEXT loop is used to create the row of month names across the top of the screen. The first three letters of each month name are extracted from elements of array *MonthNames$* using the **LEFT$** function. The MOVETO toolbox routine is used to display each name at a precise screen location. Each name is thus equally spaced from its neighbors, and centered in a selection box that is drawn using the LINE statement with the "box" option.

Each selection box is thirty pixels wide and twenty pixels high. The boxes are separated from each other by ten pixels.

The currently selected month is defined by the value of variable *Dmonth%* (1-12). This value is converted into the appropriate screen coordinates for the corresponding selection box, and these coordinates are placed in array *Rect%*. The INVERTRECT toolbox routine is then used to highlight the currently selected month box.

The StartDay subprogram is called to get the starting day of the week and the number of days in the currently selected month. The seven day names (Sun, Mon, Tue, etc.) are displayed across the top row of the calendar area using the same technique that was used to display the month names.

Skip over the next group of statements in the program for a moment, and look at the set of two FOR-NEXT loops that actually draw the grid lines making up the calendar image. The calendar image contains seven rows and seven columns. Each cell in the image is sixty pixels wide and thirty pixels high. The day names are centered within each cell across the top row of the grid.

The remainder of the grid must be filled in with the day numbers that make up the complete set of days in the month. In addition, the numbers must be placed in the proper cells so that each date lands on the proper day of the week. This is accomplished by the section of code that you just skipped over. Study this section of the program now.

It contains a FOR-NEXT loop that runs through each day number for the days in the current month (recall that subprogram StartDay has returned the number of days in the month in variable *Days%*). A MOVETO toolbox call is used to insure that each day number is displayed at the proper location. This location is defined by variable *Xc%* and *Yc%* that contain the x-coordinates and y-coordinates of the screen, respectively.

The days will start, of course, on the first calendar row, so *Yc%* is initialized to 110 before the loop is entered. Throughout the loop, variable *Cday%* will contain the number of the day of the week (1–7) currently being processed. Variable *Cday%* begins with the starting day of the week for the month, which was obtained from subprogram StartDay (variable *Fday%*).

The x-coordinate at which to display is calculated as a simple function of *Cday%*. Each time through the loop, *Cday%* is increased by 1. When *Cday%* exceeds 7, a complete row of the calendar has been filled in. In this case, *Cday%* is reset to 1 (Sunday) and variable *Yc%* is increased to point to the next screen row. In this fashion, the entire calendar image is constructed.

Once the image is complete, a new subroutine, WaitMouse, is invoked to wait until the user makes a selection with the mouse. Since this is currently the only section of the program that relies on mouse activity, the WaitMouse subroutine call is surrounded by mouse cursor toolbox calls that insure the mouse cursor is visible when needed and obscured when not in use.

The WaitMouse subroutine returns the mouse click coordinates in variables *x* and *y*. The next section of the program decodes these values to determine what date the user is selecting. If the mouse is clicked outside a valid selection box, the program beeps and waits for another mouse click.

If the y-coordinate is in the range from 20 to 40, the user could have been making a month selection. The x-coordinate is converted into a month number from 1–12 in variable *Dm%*. The program then checks to be sure that the click was not made between month selection boxes.

If a valid month selection was made, the new month is placed in variable *Dmonth%* and the entire subroutine is restarted. This will redraw the screen with the new month highlighted and with the calendar for that month on display.

If the y-coordinate is in the range from 90 to 270, the user could have been making a day selection. The y-coordinate is converted into a calendar row number from 1 to 6, and the x-coordinate is converted into a calendar column number from 1 to 7.

If the selection was on the first row, and the column number is less than the first day of the month (as returned by StartDay), the user clicked in a cell preceding the first day of the month. This being an invalid selection, the program will beep and wait for another click. Otherwise, the day number selected is derived from the calendar row and column number. This value is checked against the total number of days in the month, to trap possible clicks in cells past the last day of the month.

Assuming a valid day selection, the coordinates of the selected cell are derived from the calendar row and column numbers, and are placed into array *Rect%*. The INVERTRECT toolbox routine is then employed to highlight the selected calendar cell. The subroutine then reverts back to the text font of the main program and returns to its caller with the selected date defined in variable *Month%* and *Day%*. The balance of the program proceeds as in the original version.

Try executing this new version of the program. The advantage of using the mouse to select dates become obvious immediately. It is a much faster and more comfortable way of inputting data. The rest of the program can be improved even further by the addition of more Macintosh user interface techniques. These will be added in the following chapters.

Chapter 8

Windows

The Macintosh is the first successful microcomputer to incorporate the window concept in its underlying architecture. An intrinsic part of any microcomputer system is the display screen. Windows represent a generic technique for partitioning that screen into sections, each of which can be dedicated to an independent function. Any user of the Macintosh expects to be provided with this environment, regardless of the application in use. It is therefore important to be able to incorporate windowing techniques into your own programs. Fortunately, Microsoft BASIC Version 2.0 provides this capability.

When one says "My program can do windows," what does this really mean? Because windows are so fundamental to all Macintosh operations, any BASIC program automatically has some window support. As you already know, the Output window can be repositioned and resized, and other windows can be manipulated while a program is being run (the List window, the Command window).

Doing windows in a Macintosh BASIC program must mean that the program itself exercises some control over the screen windows. The program may move windows about on the screen, alter their size and shape, and possibly even support more than one window at a time. In this chapter, I show you how you can program these activities. In addition, you will learn how to create and use *dialog boxes*. These are specialized windows that really represent a part of the standard Macintosh user interface.

Dialog boxes provide a consistent framework within which the user can enter and receive information. Since all Macintosh users understand how to manipulate the various components that can be placed within dialog boxes (i.e., entry fields and buttons) your program will be easy to learn and use if it also employs these devices.

The Output Window Revisited

By this point, the Output window should be a familiar and comfortable concept. All of our programs have used the Output window to display information while executing and also to accept information. Normally, while a BASIC program is executing we have come to expect the Output window to be active (title bar highlighted). All PRINT and graphics statements have been directed to this window, and all INPUT and mouse activity has also been performed within this window. This default Output window is only one of several Output windows that a BASIC program can maintain. Actually, at any time your program may have up to four individual Output windows in use.

Naturally, when more than one window is in use, many questions arise. Which window will receive the output produced by PRINT statements? Which will echo data that is being entered under control of INPUT statements? To which window will graphics commands be directed? And, finally, relative to which window will the mouse clicks be detected? (This is a very important question, since we know that the mouse coordinates are always returned as relative to the upper left corner of an Output window.)

Current and Active Windows

Regardless of how many windows a program is using, BASIC always denotes a current Output window and an active window. These may or may not be the same at any time. Normally, the default Output window serves as both the current Output window and the active window while a program is running. The active window is always in front of all other windows on the screen and can usually be detected by its highlighted title bar. This is the window that will be used for INPUT statements as well as for mouse activity. The current Output window is the window to which all programmed screen output will be directed (PRINT statements, graphics, etc). In order to use a dialog box, it must be made the active window.

Window Identifiers

Each window is identified by a number. The window numbers range from 1 to 4. Normally, only the single default window is used; it is assigned window number 1. If other windows are added, their numbers should be assigned sequentially (2, 3, 4).

The WINDOW Function

The *WINDOW* function can be used at any time to interrogate the current status of the window environment. Like the MOUSE function, the WINDOW function is passed an argument that determines what type of information is being requested. The type of information that can be accessed is summarized in Table 8-1.

Table 8-1
The WINDOW
Function

WINDOW(0)	Returns the window id number of the currently active window, or 0 if no program output window is currently active.
WINDOW(1)	Returns the window id number of the current output window.
WINDOW(2)	Returns the width, in pixels, of the current output window.
WINDOW(3)	Returns the height, in pixels, of the current output window.
WINDOW(4)	Returns the x-coordinate of the pen location in the current output window.
WINDOW(5)	Returns the y-coordinate of the pen location in the current output window.

Note that the function can be used in a program to determine which window is currently active and which window is the current Output window. In addition, the function can determine the size (in pixels) of any Output window. The default Output window, number 1, is usually both the active and current Output window. Typically it is 490 pixels wide and 255 pixels high. See Figure 8-1 for an example of the WINDOW function.

Figure 8-1
*The WINDOW
Function*

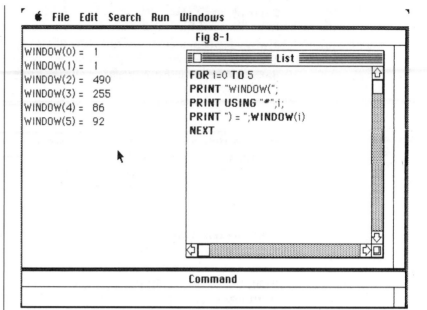

Figure 8-1
*The WINDOW
Function*

The Window Statement

To create additional Output windows from within a program, you use the *WINDOW* statement. This statement also allows you to control the size, shape, and position of the Output window. When a window is created using this statement, it automatically becomes the active and current Output window. The basic format of the WINDOW statement is as follows

```
WINDOW id,title,(x1,y1)-(x2,y2),type
```

The "id" is the window number being created or changed. It can range from 1 to 4. The "title" is a character string that will appear in the title bar of the window (note that some window types will not have title bars). The coordinate pair (x1,y1) and (x2,y2) defines a rectangle that represents the screen area occupied by the window. These values thus define the size, shape, and position of the created window. Note that these coordinates are relative to the *entire screen area* of the Macintosh, with (0,0) being the upper left corner of the screen. The lower right corner of the screen is at coordinate (510,338).

You will not normally want to place a window at coordinate (0,0) since this is above the menu bar that runs across the top edge of the screen. The menu bar is always visible, and so placing a window that far up on the screen will cause the top of the window to be hidden behind it. The default Output window usually has an upper left coordinate of (2,40). Note also that the width and height of the rectangle as defined on the WINDOW statement are not the same as the width and height of the resulting window.

The window width and height represent the number of pixels available for use within the window. The default Output window type has a title bar at the top and (inactive) scroll bar along the right side. These areas are not included in the usable width and height of the window, but they are within the rectangle defined on the WINDOW statement. See Figure 8-2.

Figure 8-2
Window Positioning and Sizing

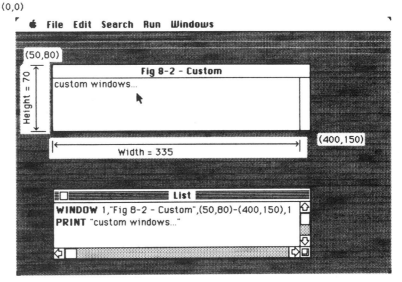

Window Types

The value "type" on the WINDOW statement determines the type, or style, of the window created. There are four possible window types; they are denoted by the values 1 through 4. The types are summarized in Table 8-2. The default Output window is of the default type, type 1. This is a conventional window with a title bar at the top and a size box in the lower right corner. The presence of the size box forces the presence of a scroll bar channel along the right edge of the window. This scroll bar is neither active nor usable.

The remaining three window types have no title bar or size box. This means that these windows cannot be repositioned or resized via mouse activity by the user. Your program can, of course, control these functions for such windows. Type 2 uses a double line border and thus looks similar to the standard system dialog boxes. Type 3

Table 8-2
Window Types

1	Conventional output window with a title bar, size box, and close box. This window type, when active, can be repositioned, resized, and closed by the user. If you want to prevent the user from doing such things, use any other window type.
2	Dialog box window with a double line border surrounding it.
3	Plain window with a single line border.
4	Plain window with a single line border and three-dimensional shadow.

Note: By making the window type value negative, you can prevent any user activity outside the window.

contains a simple one line border, while type 4 contains a border with a shadow which gives it a three-dimensional look.

The demonstration program of Listing 8-1 will allow you to see what each of these window styles looks like. I ran this program to produce the next four figures. Figure 8-3 shows window type 1; note the customized title in the title bar. Figure 8-4 shows window type 2; Figure 8-5 shows window type 3; and Figure 8-6 shows window type 4.

```
' When run, this program displays all four types of output windows
' in succession. Each window is identified by displaying its type within
' the window itself. The program goes on to the next window type when
' the user presses a key.
'
WINDOW 1,"My own title!",(2,40)-(508,290),1
LOCATE 5,5
PRINT "This is window type 1"
GOSUB Uwait
'
WINDOW 1,,(15,40)-(500,280),2
LOCATE 5,5
PRINT "This is window type 2"
GOSUB Uwait
'
WINDOW 1,,(15,40)-(500,280),3
LOCATE 5,5
PRINT "This is window type 3"
GOSUB Uwait
'
WINDOW 1,,(15,40)-(500,280),4
LOCATE 5,5
PRINT "This is window type 4"
GOSUB Uwait
'
END
'
Uwait:
LOCATE 7,5
PRINT "Press any key to continue."
WaitKey:
a$=INKEY$
IF a$="" THEN GOTO WaitKey
RETURN
```

For the last three types, no title specification is used on the WINDOW statement. An extra comma takes the place of the missing parameter in these cases.

Making a Window Active

A program intending to use several Output windows will use multiple WINDOW statements to create those windows. Once this is done, the program can dynamically set the active window by using a different format of the WINDOW statement. In this format, only the window identification is specified, thus

```
WINDOW id
```

This statement causes the window specified to become the active and current Output window. The demonstration program of Listing

8-2 shows how this statement can be used. When executed, it creates two Output windows and displays them side by side on the screen. One window is titled "Even" and the other is titled "Odd." A FOR-NEXT loop is then used to generate the numbers 1 through 10. Numbers that are even are displayed in the "Even" window, while numbers that are odd are displayed in the "Odd" window. Figure 8-7 shows what the screen will look like after this program has been executed. You should execute the program on your own Macintosh, however, so that you can observe the screen appearance while windows are dynamically made active and inactive.

Figure 8-3
Window Type 1

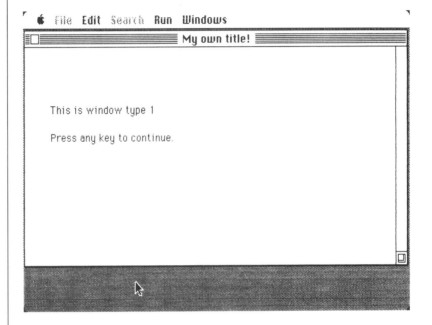

Figure 8-4
Window Type 2

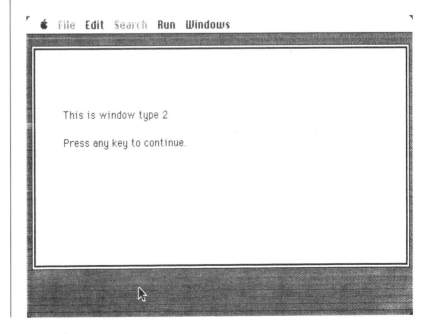

Figure 8-5
Window Type 3

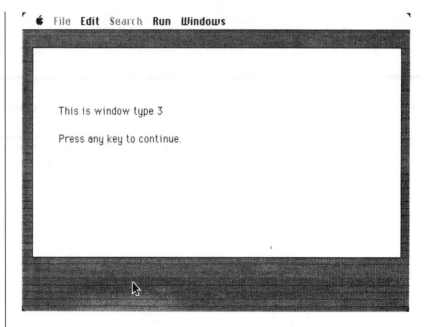

Figure 8-6
Window Type 4

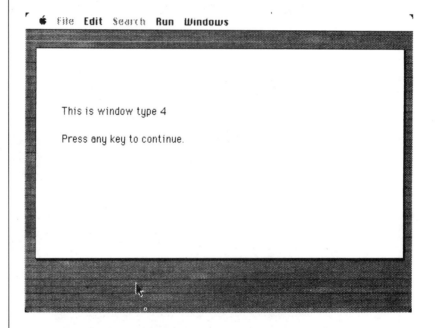

The WINDOW CLOSE Statement

The *WINDOW CLOSE* statement can be used to close a window from within a program. The statement has the following form

```
WINDOW CLOSE id
```

where id is the number of the window to be affected. A closed window disappears from the display screen immediately. It can, of course, be recreated at a later time with the WINDOW statement. If you do recreate the window at a later time, it is not necessary to specify any parameters other than id on the WINDOW statement. Thus,

```
WINDOW id
```

will cause the window to reappear in the same position and size as when it was first created. The window will be empty, however. Any information present in a window when it is closed is lost.

The WINDOW OUTPUT Statement

The *WINDOW OUTPUT* statement is used to designate a particular window as the current Output window. It does not, however, change the designation of the currently active window. This statement thus allows you to have independent active and current Output windows in a multiwindow environment.

The WINDOW OUTPUT statement is specified as follows

```
WINDOW OUTPUT id
```

where id must be the number of a window that is currently displayed on the screen. That window will be made the current Output window immediately. Any subsequent statements that produce screen output will be directed to that window. The active window, however, is not changed. Remember that the active window is the window in which all INPUT statements and mouse activity are processed. If it has a title bar, the active window can be easily identified, as its title bar will be highlighted.

Listing 8-2
Multiple Output Window Demo

```
WINDOW 1,"Even",(2,40)-(250,300),1
WINDOW 2,"Odd",(260,40)-(500,300),1

FOR i=1 TO 10
IF i/2 = i\2 THEN WINDOW 1 : PRINT i : ELSE WINDOW 2 : PRINT i
NEXT
END
```

Figure 8-7
Multiple Output Windows

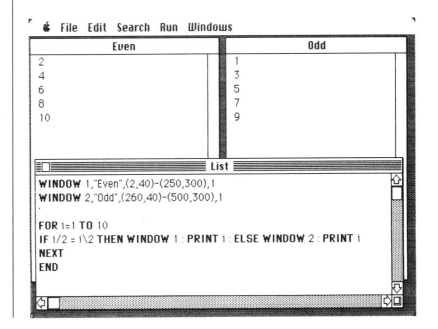

Listing 8-3 shows a program that makes use of independent active and current Output windows. The purpose of this program is to create a connected line graph from data values entered by the user. So that the graph can be constructed as the data is entered, it is displayed in one window, while the user data is input within another window.

Listing 8-3
Creating a Connected Graph

```
' Define the program's windows :
'
WINDOW 1,"Graph",(200,40)-(500,300),1
WINDOW 2,"Input",(2,40)-(150,300),1
'
WINDOW OUTPUT 1          'make "Graph" the current output window
'
LINE (10,10)-(10,250)    'draw graph axis lines
LINE (10,250)-(250,250)
'
x=10                     'init starting point for connected line graph
y=250
'
FOR i=1 TO 10            'obtain ten data points
INPUT y1                 'get data point from user in "Input" window
y1=250-y1                'convert data point to screen coordinate
WINDOW OUTPUT 1          'make "Graph" the current output window again
LINE (x,y)-(x+20,y1)     'plot the connecting line to this data point
y=y1                     'set up for next data point
x=x+20                   'each data point 20 pixels apart on x-axis
NEXT
END
```

The program begins by creating the two windows, appropriately titled Input and Graph. Since the Input window is the last one to be created, it automatically becomes the active and current Output window. A WINDOW OUTPUT statement is then used to change the current Output window to the Graph window. The active window remains the Input window. A pair of LINE statements is used to draw the graph axes.

A connected line graph has a connecting line drawn from a point plotted on the graph to the next point, etc. In this case, the connecting line will begin at the graph origin (where the axis lines cross), and so variables *x* and *y* are initialized to this point. There will be ten data points plotted on the graph, so a FOR-NEXT loop is set up for this many iterations. On each iteration, an INPUT statement is used to obtain from the user the next data point to be plotted. This is input to variable *y1*.

The input takes place in the active window, which is still window Input. Such activity also forces that window to become the current Output window, but this is easily remedied by another WINDOW OUTPUT statement.

A LINE statement draws a line from the previously plotted point to the new data point; each data point is separated from its predecessor by 20 pixels along the horizontal axis. The new point becomes the previous point, and the process is repeated.

In Figure 8-8, I executed this program and have entered the first data point. The second and third data points are entered in Figures 8-9 and 8-10, respectively. Note how the graph is constructed as the data is entered. Figure 8-11 shows the completed graph. The individual data values used can be seen in the Input window. This highlights the advantages of a multiple window environment.

Figure 8-8
First Data Point Plotted

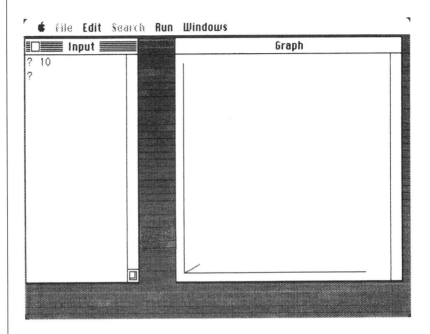

Figure 8-9
Second Data Point Plotted

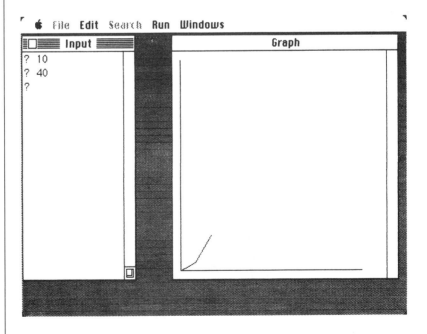

Another example program is shown in Listing 8-4. Here, a secondary window is used to display the time of day while a main program is executing. A timer interrupt is used to periodically (once a second) update the time of day in the Time window. Note how the timer interrupt service subroutine restores the "main" window to active and current output status before returning to the main program.

Figure 8-10
*Third Data Point
Plotted*

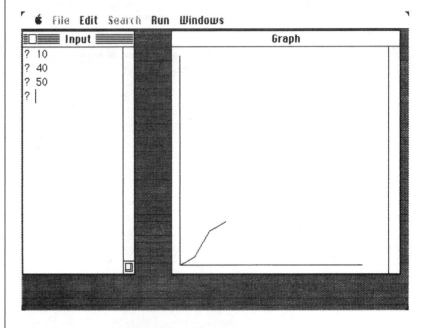

Figure 8-11
*Connected Line Graph
Completed*

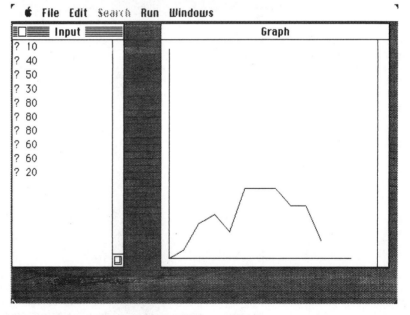

In the listing shown, the main program does nothing particularly interesting; it is just present for illustration purposes. When the program is executed the screen appears as shown in Figure 8-12.

That example may not seem very important, because the same function can be obtained by selecting the Alarm Clock desk

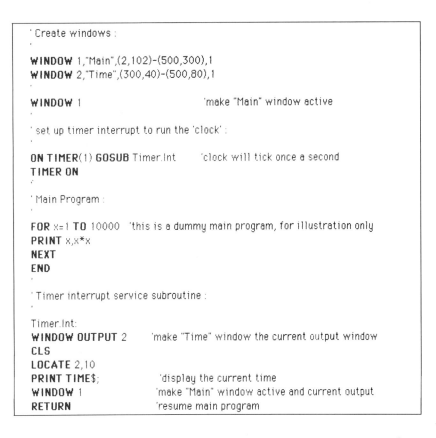

```
' Create windows :
'
WINDOW 1,"Main",(2,102)-(500,300),1
WINDOW 2,"Time",(300,40)-(500,80),1
'
WINDOW 1                          'make "Main" window active
'
' set up timer interrupt to run the 'clock' :
'
ON TIMER(1) GOSUB Timer.Int      'clock will tick once a second
TIMER ON
'
' Main Program :
'
FOR x=1 TO 10000   'this is a dummy main program, for illustration only
PRINT x,x*x
NEXT
END
'
' Timer interrupt service subroutine :
'
Timer.Int:
WINDOW OUTPUT 2      'make "Time" window the current output window
CLS
LOCATE 2,10
PRINT TIME$;            'display the current time
WINDOW 1               'make "Main" window active and current output
RETURN                 'resume main program
```

Figure 8-12
*A Custom Time of Day
Window*

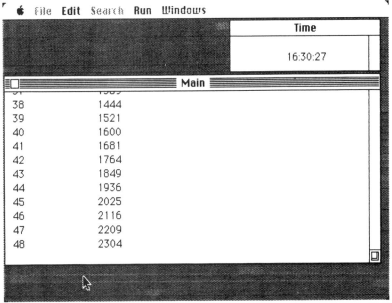

accessory from the standard Apple menu. It is the technique that
is valuable, however. Many programs can benefit from the ability to
periodically update some relevant information in a secondary
Output window. Game programs, for example, could keep track of
player's scores and time remaining to play in this fashion. Programs
that require a great deal of computation time can periodically

report on their progress in this manner. This can help prevent an impatient user from terminating such a program just before it is about to complete.

Creating Custom Dialog Boxes

As I have already mentioned, dialog boxes represent an important element of the standard Macintosh user interface. The ability to create custom dialog boxes and include them in your own BASIC programs is thus of great value when creating applications that conform to the Macintosh standards. To create a custom dialog box, you begin by creating an Output window. Within that window, you then place the various dialog box elements desired.

There are basically two kinds of dialog box elements; they are data entry fields and control buttons. You create data entry fields with the *EDIT FIELD* statement, and you create control buttons with the *BUTTON* statement. Once a dialog box has been set up, other statements are employed to monitor a user's interaction with its elements.

Data Entry Fields

Data entry fields within a dialog box are created with the EDIT FIELD statement. It has the following format

```
EDIT FIELD
id,init,(x1,y1)-(x2,y2),type,justify
```

Each data entry field is identified by a unique number. This is the id specified on the EDIT FIELD statement. Data entry field numbers should be assigned starting with 1 and increasing sequentially as needed. The init value is a string that will be displayed as the initial contents of the entry field. It can be blank if no initial contents are desired.

The coordinate pair specified on the statement defines the rectangular area that the entry field will occupy. Note that the EDIT FIELD statement will create the entry field within the currently active window. Coordinates should thus be specified relative to that window.

The type specified on the EDIT FIELD statement determines the style of entry field to be drawn, and also determines whether or not the <Return> key will be recognized within that field. There are four possible types, denoted by the values 1 through 4. They are summarized in Table 8-3.

Table 8-3
Entry Field Types

Type Value	Field Enclosed in a box	Accept the Return key as data entered in the field.
1	YES	NO
2	YES	YES
3	NO	NO
4	NO	YES

The justify value specified on the EDIT FIELD statement determines how text entered within the field will be justified. It is specified as a value from 1 to 3, described in Table 8-4.

Table 8-4
Entry Field Justify Options

1	Left justify (aligns text with left margin of field)
2	Center justify (centers text within the field)
3	Right justify (aligns text with right margin of field)

When the EDIT FIELD statement is executed, the entry field described is created in the currently active window. Program execution then proceeds with the next statement in the program. Other statements and techniques must be employed to determine if and when the user enters data into the field, and to obtain that data.

Figure 8-13 shows an example of a data entry field and the statement that created it. Note that the rectangle enclosing the field is not visible while the entire field contents are selected. This is because it causes the entire area within the rectangle to be "inverted" (that is, set to a black background). You can, of course, always add your own box surrounding the field, by employing either the LINE statement with the "box" option, or the FRAMERECT routine.

Figure 8-13
Creating a Data Entry Field

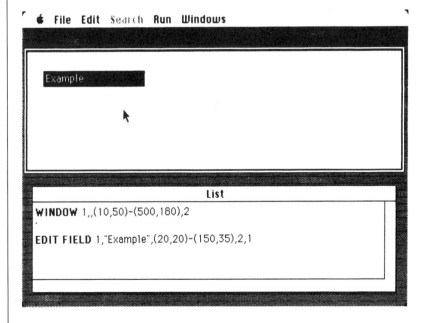

While the window containing the entry field is active, the user of the program can access and modify the contents of the field by using the mouse. Clicking anywhere within the field selects the field as active. At this point, data can be typed into the field from the keyboard. Portions of the data present in the field can be selected by dragging the mouse over them. In addition, the standard Edit menu functions of **Cut, Copy**, and **Paste** will work on the data within these entry fields. This is why it is so desirable to use these fields for data entry in your programs. They automatically increase the user-friendliness of the program.

Control Buttons

Control buttons within a dialog box are created with the *BUTTON* statement. It has the following format

```
BUTTON
id,state,title,(x1,y1)-(x2,y2),type
```

Each control button is identified by a unique number. This is the id specified on the BUTTON statement. Control button numbers should be assigned starting with 1 and increasing sequentially as needed.

The state defines the status of the button at the time it is created. As you know from your experience with other Macintosh applications that use dialog boxes, control buttons are like pull-down menus in that they can be active or inactive. An inactive button appears "dimmed" and cannot be selected. One aspect of control button status is whether or not the button is active.

If the button is active, the other aspect of its status is whether or not the button is currently selected. Some button types appear differently when they are in the "selected" state, but this depends upon the type and will be described below. Table 8-5 shows the values associated with all possible button status conditions.

Table 8-5
Control Button State Options

0	Inactive button (dimmed)
1	Active button, not selected (check boxes and radio buttons are not highlighted)
2	Active button, selected (check boxes and radio buttons are highlighted)

The title field of the BUTTON statement allows you to specify a character string that will appear as a title for the control button. Depending upon the button type, the title field will either appear inside the button, or next to it.

The coordinate pair that follows the title specifies the coordinates of a rectangle that defines the location and size of the button. These coordinates are specified relative to the currently active window, within which the button will be created.

Finally, the "type" field allows you to specify what type of control button is to be created. The three possible types are enumerated in Table 8-6.

Type 1, the so-called "push button," is the most often used type of control button. The title of a type 1 button will appear within the button itself, so you must be sure that you define the button coordinates such that the title will fit within them. When this type of button is clicked with the mouse, it momentarily highlights (the text within is inverted from black letters on a white background to white letters on a black background). When the mouse button is released, the button reverts to its original state.

Table 8-6
Control Button Types

1	Push button (highlights while you hold the mouse button down if you click within the control button)
2	Check box (must be manually highlighted)
3	Radio button (must be manually highlighted)

This type of button is best used for one-time responses. For example, a program that produces a lengthy printed output might prompt the user to click such a button to begin the printing process. A type 1 button does not appear any differently when it is in the selected state.

A type 2 button is called a "check-box." Such a button always appears as a small square, with title displayed immediately to its right. The button coordinates define a rectangular area which must be large enough to enclose the button and its associated title. The size of the button itself cannot be enlarged. When this type of button is in the selected state, an "X" appears within it.

A type 3 button is called a "radio-button." It always appears as a small circle, with the title displayed immediately to the right. Once again, the button coordinates define a rectangular area which must be large enough to enclose the button and its associated title. The size of the button itself also cannot be enlarged. When this type of button is in the selected state, a solid black circle appears in its center.

Listing 8-5 contains a demonstration program that illustrates the various types of control buttons. When run, it produces the screen shown in Figure 8-14. Run this program, and try using the mouse to click each of the buttons. Note that clicking on a button does not automatically change its "selected" status. This must be done by your program! I will show you how in a moment. Press any key to terminate the demonstration program.

Listing 8-5
Control Button Demo

```
' Push-button, inactive :
BUTTON 1,0,"Press Me !",(20,20)-(100,50),1

' Push-button, active :
BUTTON 2,1,"Push to Start",(20,60)-(120,90),1

' Check-box, active, not-selected :
BUTTON 3,1,"Engines",(20,100)-(100,120),2

' Check-box, active, selected :
BUTTON 4,2,"Turbo",(20,130)-(100,150),2
```

Listing 8-5—cont.

```
' Radio-button, active, not-selected :
BUTTON 5,1,"Radar",(20,160)-(100,180),3
'
' Radio-button, active, selected :
BUTTON 6,2,"Windshield Wipers",(20,190)-(170,210),3
'
Pause:                ' wait for user to press a key on keyboard :
a$=INKEY$
IF a$="" THEN GOTO Pause
END
```

Figure 8-14
Sample Control Buttons

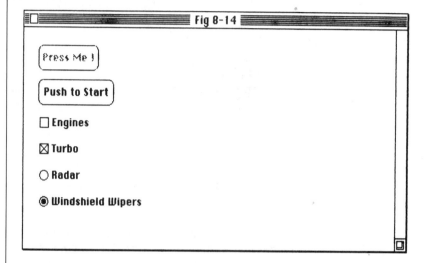

Removing Items from a Dialog Box

Dialog boxes tend to be transitory elements within a program. They appear at a specific moment, the user interacts with them, and then they go away. The buttons and entry fields that appear within dialog boxes take up a considerable amount of memory. They also clutter up the screen and prevent it from being used for general display purposes. It is therefore important to remove these items as soon as the user has completed dealings with them.

One easy way to do this is to use the WINDOW statement to create a custom window for the dialog box, as was done in Figure 8-13. The dialog box items are placed within this window, and the program waits until the user has completed interacting with it. A WINDOW CLOSE statement is then used to remove the window from the screen. This automatically frees up any memory that was used by the dialog box elements.

Often when this approach is used, the type field on the WINDOW statement will be specified as a negative value. Specifying the window type as a negative value forces the user to deal with that window, and that window only. Any attempt to use the mouse to select outside of the currently active window (created with the negative type field) will result in an audible "beep." This allows you to set up a dialog box and wait until the user supplies the required information to that box. Only when this has been done will you allow the program to continue.

In more sophisticated situations, you may want to manually remove certain dialog box items from the active window, without having to close the entire window. This can also be accomplished. The EDIT FIELD CLOSE statement can be used to remove a specific entry field from the currently active window. It is specified as follows

    EDIT FIELD CLOSE id

where id is the number of the entry field to be removed. Similarly, the BUTTON CLOSE statement can be used to remove a specific control button from the currently active window. It is specified as

    BUTTON CLOSE id

where id is the number of the control button to be removed.

Interacting With Custom DIALOG Boxes
At this point, you now know how to create a custom dialog box and place within it the various elements needed by your program. When the dialog box is the active window, the user of your program will be able to enter data into the entry fields, and make selections of the active control buttons.

How does your program detect such user activities? This is accomplished through use of some special purpose built-in functions. These functions are the DIALOG function, the EDIT$ function, and the BUTTON function.

The DIALOG Function
The *DIALOG* function is used to determine what type of window and/or dialog box activity has been performed by the user. In this regard, it is similar to the MOUSE function that tells us what type of mouse activity has been performed by the user.

When you call the DIALOG function, you pass it a single argument to tell it what type of information you are requesting. As with the MOUSE function, you should always begin by calling upon the DIALOG(0) function. Then, depending upon the result you receive from that call, you may call upon other DIALOG functions to obtain further information. The DIALOG function is summarized in Table 8-7.

When you call the DIALOG(0) function, it returns a value indicating what type of window/dialog box activity has occurred since the last call to DIALOG(0). If the value returned is 0, then no activity has taken place. Your program can wait until a nonzero value is returned from this function, if you so desired.

The activities that can be detected in this fashion include the clicking of a control button, selecting a particular entry field, clicking on an inactive window (usually done to request that that window be made the active window), clicking the "close box" of a window (usually done to request that that window be removed from the screen altogether), as well as others.

Note that once the user activity has been detected, it is up to you, as the programmer, to decide how to respond. You may choose not to respond to a certain activity, or you may choose to respond in a nonstandard manner. For example, if you detect that the user has clicked the "close box" of one of your program's Output windows, you may take the standard Macintosh action and execute a WINDOW CLOSE statement. On the other hand, you might want to ignore that request, or possibly print a message to the effect that "user cannot close that window under this application."

DIALOG(0)	Returns a value indicating the dialog event that has occurred, as follows: 0 —No event has occurred. 1 —A control button has been clicked. Use DIALOG(1) to determine the control button id. 2 —A data entry field has been selected. Use DIALOG(2) to determine the selected entry field id. 3 —An inactive output window has been clicked. Use DIALOG(3) to determine the clicked window id. 4 —The close box of an output window has been clicked. Use DIALOG(4) to determine the clicked window id. 5 —An output window that was obscured is now visible and the window requires refreshing. Use DIALOG(5) to determine the window id to refresh. 6 —The Return key has been pressed in an active dialog box containing entry fields, and the current entry field cannot accept it. 7 —The Tab key has been pressed in an active dialog box containing entry fields.
DIALOG(1)	Returns the id number of the clicked control button. Use after DIALOG(0) returns a value of 1 (see above).
DIALOG(2)	Returns the id number of the selected entry field. Use after DIALOG(0) returns a value of 2 (see above).
DIALOG(3)	Returns the id number of the clicked output window. Use after DIALOG(0) returns a value of 3 (see above).
DIALOG(4)	Returns the id number of the output window whose close box was clicked. Use after DIALOG(0) returns a value of 4 (see above).
DIALOG(5)	Returns the id number of the output window requiring refresh. Use after DIALOG(0) returns a value of 5 (see above).

Listing 8-6 contains a program that creates a dialog box with several different control buttons. The program responds to mouse clicks on those buttons in the standard Macintosh fashion, by toggling the clicked button's state between selected and not-selected. Try executing this program. Click the button titled "Done" to terminate the program.

Figure 8-15 shows the dialog box produced by this program. This box allows the user to order an ice cream sundae by specifying one of three possible ice cream flavors and any combination of up to three toppings. The program sets up the three flavor choices as radio buttons, and the three toppings choices as check boxes. Each set of buttons is grouped together on the screen. The program uses the DIALOG(0) function to wait until a control button is clicked, and then calls upon the DIALOG(1) function to determine the number of the button clicked. If button 7 (the "Done" button) is clicked, then the program ends. Otherwise, the program takes two different paths depending upon whether a flavor or topping button was clicked.

Since only one ice cream flavor can be selected at any given time, the program uses variable *flavor* to keep track of the flavor selected. When a flavor button is clicked, the program uses this variable to insure that any previously selected flavor is now unselected. Note the use of the BUTTON function to alter the state of a previously defined button. The new flavor selected is saved in variable *flavor* and its button is made selected.

Since any number of the toppings may be selected at any time, the program uses an array to keep track of the status of each topping button. The array is named *toppings*. Each array element corresponds to a different topping. If the array element is zero, then that topping is currently not selected. If the array element is one, then that topping is selected. When a topping button is clicked, the program simply toggles the value in the appropriate array element (from 0 to 1, or from 1 to 0), and then uses the resulting value to set the button's status to either selected or not-selected. Unfortunately, the Macintosh cannot actually make the sundae for us!

Listing 8-6
Pop's Ice Cream Shoppe

```
' This program sets up a dialog box for selecting an ice cream
' sundae. The user may select from any one of three possible
' flavors, and any combination of up to three different toppings.
WINDOW 1,,(10,45)-(500,300),-2
'
PRINT "Pop's Ice Cream Shoppe"
'
' Set up ice cream flavor selection buttons :
'
BUTTON 1,1,"Vanilla",(10,30)-(100,45),3
BUTTON 2,1,"Chocolate",(10,50)-(100,65),3
BUTTON 3,1,"Strawberry",(10,70)-(120,85),3
'
' Set up topping selection buttons :
'
BUTTON 4,1,"Sprinkles",(10,100)-(100,115),2
BUTTON 5,1,"Whipped Cream",(10,120)-(140,135),2
BUTTON 6,1,"Hot Fudge",(10,140)-(120,155),2
'
BUTTON 7,1,"Done",(10,180)-(50,200),1    ' "Done" push-button
'
' Set up variables to indicate current selection status :
'
flavor = 0       'no ice cream flavor selected as of yet
DIM toppings(3)  'each array element corresponds to one topping choice
FOR i=1 TO 3
toppings(i)=0      'initially, no toppings have been selected
NEXT
'
' Now wait for user to make selections via mouse :
'
```

Listing 8-6—cont.

```
WaitDialog:
d=DIALOG(0)
IF d<>1 THEN GOTO WaitDialog
b=DIALOG(1)                'get number of button that was clicked
IF b=7 THEN END           'button "Done" was pressed
IF b>3 THEN GOTO ToppingSelected

' Handle an ice-cream flavor selection :
' Note: only one flavor may be selected at a time :

IF flavor<>0 THEN BUTTON flavor,1   'de-select previous flavor selection

flavor=b                            'make new selection the selected flavor
BUTTON b,2                           'show the button is selected
GOTO WaitDialog

' Handle a topping selection :
' Note: as many toppings as are desired may be selected at a time :

ToppingSelected:
t=b-3       'convert button number to toppings array index
' toggle state of selected topping :
IF toppings(t)=0 THEN toppings(t)=1 ELSE toppings(t)=0
' make button selection status match :
IF toppings(t)=0 THEN BUTTON b,1 ELSE BUTTON b,2
GOTO WaitDialog
```

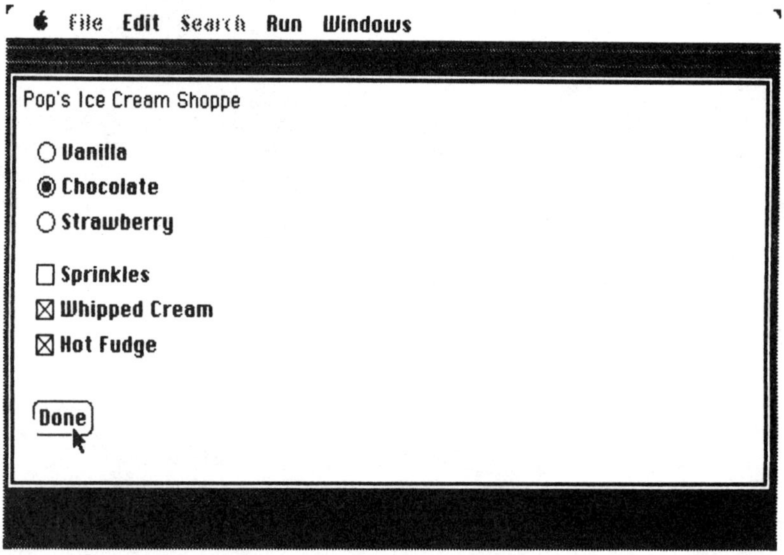

Figure 8-15
Pop's Ice Cream Shoppe

The BUTTON Function

The previous example used program variables to keep track of the status of each control button. Proper programming insured that the program variables always matched the actually visual status of each control button. The built-in function *BUTTON* allows you to interrogate the current status of any button. In some cases, this can eliminate the need for such program variables.

The BUTTON function takes a single argument, which is the number of the button being interrogated. It returns a value between 0 and 2 that indicates that button's current status, as per Table 8-5. For example, the statement

```
x = BUTTON(3)
```

would return the current state of button number 3 to variable *x*.

The EDIT$ Function

The *EDIT$* function is used to retrieve the data placed in data entry
fields. It takes a single argument, which represents the id number of
the data entry field to interrogate. It returns a character string value
equal to the data currently present in that field. Thus, for example,
the statement

```
a$ = EDIT$(1)
```

would return the current contents of data entry field number 1 to
string variable *a$*. It is important to realize that the BUTTON and
EDIT$ function always interrogate the selected items within the
current Output window.

In a multiwindow environment, this can lead to possible errors.
It is therefore best to use only one dialog box at a time, place it in a
custom window, and then close the window when the user has
completed his interaction with that dialog box.

The RETURN and TAB Keys

If you study Table 8-7, you will notice that two of the events that
can be detected via the DIALOG function involve the pressing of
keys on the keyboard. These special keys, the < Return > and
< Tab > keys, represent part of the standard Macintosh user
interface for dialog box activity. As you are no doubt aware, many
dialog boxes that ask for a filename will automatically be exited if
the filename is entered and then the < Return > key is pressed. The
< Return > key as used in a dialog box is generally taken to mean
that the program should accept the data entered and proceed with
its processing.

Your programs can also act in this fashion, by detecting the
< Return > key via the DIALOG function. To do so, however, you
must set up your data entry fields so that they will not accept the
< Return > key. Data entry field values are shown in Table 8-3. If
this is not done, the data entry field accepts the < Return > key as
part of the data being entered, and so it cannot be detected by the
DIALOG function.

For dialog boxes that contain multiple data entry fields, the
< Tab > key is often used to move from one entry field to the next.
This allows the user to fill in each field with data typed on the
keyboard, and he does not have to move his hands off the keyboard
to the mouse to change fields. You can implement this feature in
your programs as well.

Listing 8-7 contains a sample program that sets up a dialog box
to obtain a name and complete mailing address. The program uses
the DIALOG function to implement the special keyboard functions
just described. Figure 8-16 shows the screen produced by executing
this program. Execute the program yourself and try supplying
different data values to the various entry fields.

You can change fields by clicking with the mouse, or by use of
the < Tab > key. The < Tab > key always moves you from one entry

field to the next in a particular order, as determined by the program code.

```
' This program creates a custom dialog box with four data entry fields.
' The user must provide data for each field before exiting from the
' dialog box. The user can go from one field to the other either by
' clicking the desired field with the mouse, or by using the Tab key.
' The user indicates that all data has been supplied either by clicking
' the "Ok" box or by pressing the Return key.
'
WINDOW 1,,(10,45)-(500,300),-2
'
PRINT "Fill out name and mailing address, please"
LOCATE 3,1
PRINT "Name : "
LOCATE 5,1
PRINT "Street : "
LOCATE 7,1
PRINT "City, State : "
LOCATE 7,40
PRINT "Zip :"
'
' Set up data entry fields :
'
EDIT FIELD 1,"",(90,32)-(290,47),1,1        'name field
EDIT FIELD 2,"",(90,64)-(290,79),1,1        'street field
EDIT FIELD 3,"",(90,96)-(290,111),1,1       'city/state field
EDIT FIELD 4,"",(350,96)-(400,111),1,1      'zip field
'
BUTTON 1,1,"Ok",(10,140)-(50,170),1    ' "Ok" push-button
'
EDIT FIELD 1          'make the first entry field the currently active field
f=1                   'variable f shows what field is currently in use
'
' Now wait for user to fill in the dialog box data requested :
'
WaitDialog:
d=DIALOG(0)                      ' wait for a dialog event to occur
IF d=0 THEN GOTO WaitDialog
IF d=1 THEN GOTO ButtonClick
IF d=2 THEN GOTO SelectField
IF d=6 THEN GOTO RetKey
IF d=7 THEN GOTO TabKey
GOTO WaitDialog
'
' A button click dialog event took place :
'
ButtonClick:
b=DIALOG(1)              'get number of button that was clicked
IF b=1 THEN GOTO RetKey          'button "Ok" was pressed
GOTO WaitDialog
'
' A data entry field selection event took place :
'
SelectField:
f=DIALOG(2)    'get entry field number selected
EDIT FIELD f      'make it the currently selected field
GOTO WaitDialog
'
' The Return key was pressed :
'
RetKey:
n$=EDIT$(1)              'obtain the data from each field ;
street$=EDIT$(2)
CityState$=EDIT$(3)
Zip$=EDIT$(4)
' each field must have been filled out properly:
IF n$="" OR street$="" OR CityState$="" OR Zip$="" THEN BEEP : GOTO WaitDialog
'
' data obtained ok, now process it
```

Listing 8-7—cont.

```
  ' ...
  ' ...
  ' ...
  END
  '
  ' The Tab key was pressed :
  '
  TabKey:
  IF f<4 THEN f=f+1 ELSE f=1        'move on to the next field
  EDIT FIELD f
  GOTO WaitDialog
```

The program begins by setting up the dialog window. The use of a negative window type insures that the user cannot exit from this section of the program without going through the specific programmed checks that I will discuss in a moment. Any attempt to select outside the window with the mouse will result in nothing more than a "beep." Try this out for yourself while executing the program.

The program uses PRINT and LOCATE statements to supply prompt text and descriptions of each field. A set of EDIT FIELD statements is then employed to create each data entry field. The default text for each field is initially null. An "Ok" button is created below the entry field area.

The EDIT FIELD statement can be used with just a field id number, as long as that field was previously created with the longer form of the statement. When just the field id is specified, the statement causes that field to become the currently active field. (Once again, remember that the window containing the field must be the current Output window prior to executing this statement.)

In a window with multiple entry fields, only one field can be active at any time. The user can make a specific field active by clicking on it with the mouse (the DIALOG function can be used to detect when this occurs.) Alternatively, the program itself can make a specific field the active field by use of this short form of the EDIT FIELD statement.

My example program uses this short form to make the first entry field the active field when the dialog box is presented to the user. If the active field is not explicitly specified in this manner, the last field created will be the active field. Program variable f keeps track of which field is active at all times. It is initialized to 1.

The program now uses the DIALOG(0) function to wait until specific user activities occur. The only events that the program will be sensitive to at this point are clicking a button with the mouse (DIALOG(0) = 1), clicking an entry field with the mouse (DIALOG(0) = 2), pressing the <Return> key (DIALOG(0) = 6), or pressing the <Tab> key (DIALOG(0) = 7).

It is important to understand that while the program is in the WaitDialog loop, all other user actions are handled automatically by the dialog box devices that have been set up. The user can select an entry field, type some data into it, select another field, or click a button.

While entering data into a field the user might use the <Backspace> key, select some text by clicking and dragging with the mouse, perform a **Cut, Copy,** or **Paste** edit function. All of these activities can take place with no intervention from my program. This is a dramatic example of the power of the Macintosh ROM toolbox (Microsoft BASIC is using toolbox routines to implement these functions).

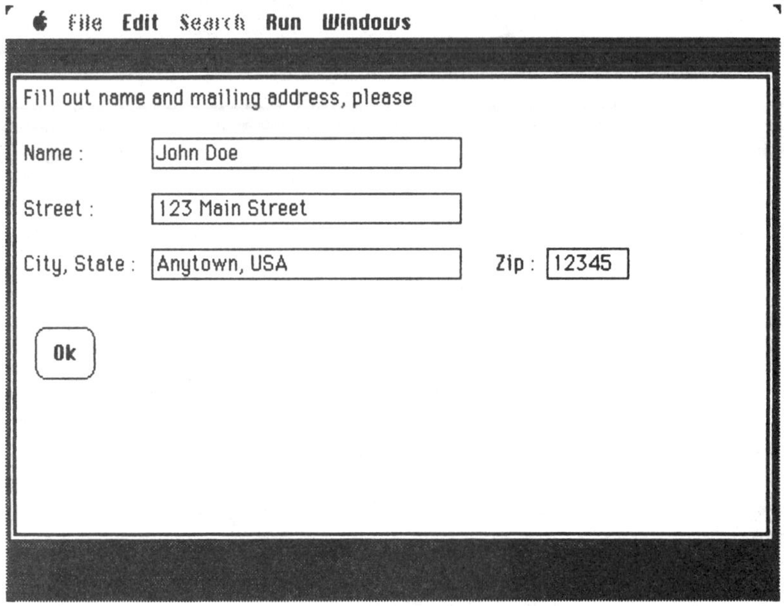

Figure 8-16
*Multiple Data Entry
Fields*

My program does get involved for any of the events mentioned a moment ago, however. If the "Ok" button is clicked, control is transferred to label RetKey. This is the same location that control goes to for the < Return > key event. Either event means that the user is signalling the program that the data requested by the dialog box has been filled in, and that the program should now proceed to process that data. The EDIT$ function is employed to extract the data placed in each field.

For this example, I have stipulated that all fields must be filled in before the dialog box can be exited. This is checked by a single IF-THEN statement. In other programs, you might impose more complex exit requirements. If they are not met, the program issues an audible "beep" and returns to the WaitDialog loop.

Control is transferred to label SelectField when the user uses the mouse to click on an entry field. The DIALOG(2) function is used to obtain the entry field id number of the selected field. The short form of the EDIT FIELD statement is then employed to make that field the active field. The field id is also saved in program variable f.

The only other event that the program has to handle is the < Tab > key being pressed. This is handled at label TabKey. The event is processed by moving the currently active field to the next field. Since the fields were defined and assigned field id numbers in the order that I wanted this sequence to follow, it is a simple matter to implement. I simply increase the contents of variable f by one, unless f is already at the last field number, in which case it is set back to the first field number. The short form of the EDIT FIELD statement is then used to make field f active.

Other DIALOG Events

The DIALOG function will detect three additional events that I have not yet discussed. These correspond to values for DIALOG(0) of 3, 4, and 5 as shown in see Table 8-7. Each of these events occur in a multiple Output window environment. The best way to use the dialog box techniques I have described is to use several Output windows, but not at the same time.

The main program runs in the default Output window, numbered 1. When a dialog box is to be used, it is created as window number 2. Techniques such as those shown in Listings 8-6 and 8-7 are then employed to set up and process the dialog box. When the dialog box is exited, a WINDOW CLOSE statement is used to remove the window from the screen. Processing then resumes in the main Output window.

It is important to realize that when you place window 2 on top of window 1, anything present in that portion of window 1 that is overlaid will be lost. When window 2 is removed, window 1 becomes active again, but its contents cannot be automatically refreshed. It is up to your program to handle this situation.

Usually, the best approach is to use CLS on the window that is being returned to, and then display any information that should appear there. I will show you an example of this approach in a moment.

In general, a multiple Output window environment provides the opportunity for the user to make changes in window positioning and sizing. Active type 1 windows can be repositioned by clicking and dragging on the title bar. They can also be resized via the size box. It is therefore possible for the user to overlay a portion of one Output window with another Output window. This is another way in which the DIALOG(0) event returned as 5 can occur.

This event indicates that part of an Output window needs to be refreshed. Your program can determine which output window by calling DIALOG(5). Your program can choose to ignore this event or process it in any manner desired. Note that, as long as a window is not active, the user cannot reposition or resize it. Through careful programming, it is therefore possible to avoid this event.

The event numbered 4 is returned from DIALOG(0) when the user clicks the "close" box of an active type 1 window. Once again, it is up to you, as the programmer, to decide how you want to handle this event (although the system automatically closes the window when its close box is clicked, you can counteract that effect if desired).

You may wish to counteract the close request, because if your program has made a specific window active, it expects to be communicating with its user via that window. You might interpret this event as a signal that the user wished to end the program. Alternatively, you can conform to Macintosh standards and close the window by use of a WINDOW CLOSE statement. Perhaps you might only respond in this manner under certain other conditions. The choice is up to you. The DIALOG(4) function is used to determine the window id of the window associated with this event.

The event numbered 3 is returned from DIALOG(0) when the

user clicks anywhere on an inactive Output window. The standard Macintosh interpretation of this action is make that window the active window. Of course, you do not have to comply with this request if you do not wish to. The DIALOG(3) function returns the window id of the window that has been clicked.

Listing 8-8 contains a program that creates three Output windows. Each window is filled with a different image. One contains a circle, another a square, and the last one contains a large "X." The program then enters a loop waiting for dialog events.

Listing 8-8
Handling Dialog Events in a Multiple Window Environment

```
' The user can make any window active by clicking on it, can reposition and
' resize active windows, and can close windows. The visible contents of
' each window will always be maintained, even after they have been
' overlaid by other windows. When all three windows are closed, the program
' automatically ends.

WINDOW 1,"Circle",(10,50)-(250,180),1   'create first output window
GOSUB FillW1                             'fill first window with image of a circle
'
WINDOW 2,"Square",(280,50)-(500,180),1   'create second output window
GOSUB FillW2                             'fill second window with image of a square
'
WINDOW 3,"X",(150,220)-(350,330),1       'create third output window
GOSUB FillW3                             'fill third window with image of large "X"
'
WindowsClosed=0 'initialize count of number of windows that have been closed

WaitDialog:        'wait for a dialog event to occur
d=DIALOG(0)
IF d=3 THEN GOTO ActivateWindow
IF d=4 THEN GOTO CloseWindow
IF d=5 THEN GOTO RefreshWindow
GOTO WaitDialog
'
ActivateWindow:    'user clicked on an inactive output window
w=DIALOG(3)               'get window id to be activated
WINDOW w                  'make that window the active window
GOTO WaitDialog
'
CloseWindow:       'user clicked close box of an active output window
w=DIALOG(4)               'get window id to be closed
WINDOW CLOSE w            'close that window
WindowsClosed=WindowsClosed + 1   'keep track of how many windows closed
IF WindowsClosed = 3 THEN END   'if no windows left then all done
GOTO WaitDialog
'
RefreshWindow:     'a portion of an output window needs to be refreshed
w=DIALOG(5)               'get window id to be refreshed
WINDOW OUTPUT w           'make it the current output window
IF w=1 THEN GOSUB FillW1       'draw the proper image for this window:
IF w=2 THEN GOSUB FillW2
IF w=3 THEN GOSUB FillW3
GOTO WaitDialog
'
FillW1:             'window 1 gets a circle
CIRCLE (50,50),25
RETURN
'
FillW2:             'window 2 gets a square
LINE (10,10)-(60,60),,B
RETURN
'
FillW3:             'window 3 gets a large "X"
LINE (10,10)-(60,60)
LINE (60,10)-(10,60)
RETURN
```

The loop is coded to implement the standard Macintosh interpretations of the three events I have just described. Figure 8-17 shows the screen initially produced when the program is run. If you run this program yourself, you will note that you can make any of the three windows active by simply positioning the mouse cursor over the desired window and clicking.

Figure 8-17
Multiple Output Windows — Initial

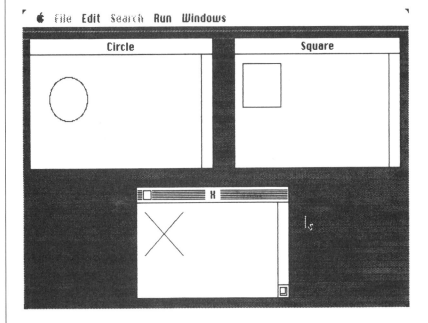

In Figure 8-18, I have clicked the mouse on the title bar of the "X" window and dragged that window over the "Circle" window. This overlays the image that was on display in "Circle." In Figure 8-19, I have dragged the "X" window down and away from the "Circle" window. If you try this yourself, you will see that the image in the "Circle" window is automatically refreshed as soon as the area it occupies becomes visible. The program handles this situation by detecting the refresh dialog event.

Another way that this event can be triggered is illustrated by Figure 8-20. In this figure, I have clicked and dragged the resizing box of the "Circle" window. I resized the window to make it so small that the entire circle image was no longer visible. I then again resized the window, to a larger size.

When more of that portion of the window that contains an image was made visible, as shown in a Figure 8-21, the refresh event was signalled. Once again, the program restored the complete image that belongs in that window.

This program also supports the standard Macintosh "Close Box" function. In Figure 8-22, I have clicked the close box of the "Circle" window and it has disappeared from the screen. The "X" window has become the active window. If you are running this program now, you can follow in a similar fashion and click the close box on the "X" window, and then on the "Square" window. When the last window is closed, the program will automatically end.

Figure 8-18
Obscuring One Window with Another

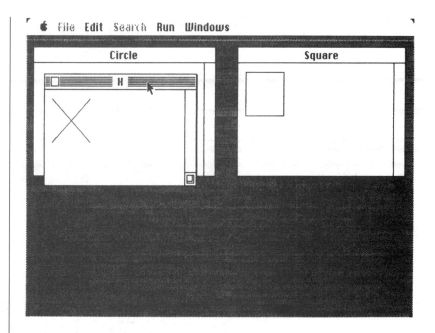

Figure 8-19
Refreshing the Window

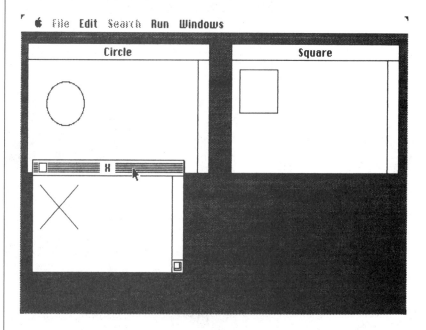

Run this program again, and experiment with moving the windows around. You will find that you can do almost anything with the windows, and they will always retain the proper images, where visible.

Try pulling down the Windows menu and bringing up the List or Command windows. Use them to obscure one or more of the program's Output windows. In all cases, the refresh event is signalled when needed, and the program insures that the proper data is on display.

The program begins by creating each of the Output windows in turn. They are all type 1 windows. The image to be displayed in each window is defined by a unique subroutine. Subroutine FillW1 produces the circle that goes into the "Circle" window, subroutine FillW2 produces the square that goes into the "Square" window, and subroutine FillW3 produces the "X" that goes into the "X" window. Variable *WindowsClosed* is initialized to zero; it will track the number of windows that have been closed.

Figure 8-20
Shrinking a Window to Obscure an Image

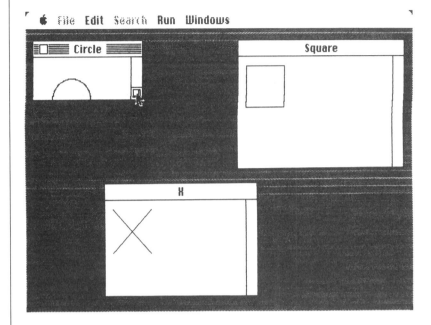

Figure 8-21
Refreshing a Shrunk Window

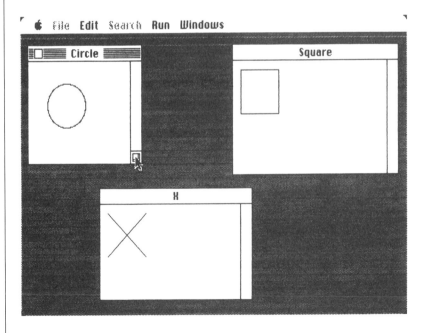

The WaitDialog loop is now entered. The three events that are recognized are number 3, a window activate request; number 4, a close window request; and number 5, a refresh window request. The

activate window request is handled at statement label
ActivateWindow. The id number of the window to be activated is
obtained from the DIALOG(3) function. The WINDOW statement
is then used to make that window active. Remember, this event is
signalled by the user clicking anywhere on the window indicated.

Figure 8-22
Closing Windows

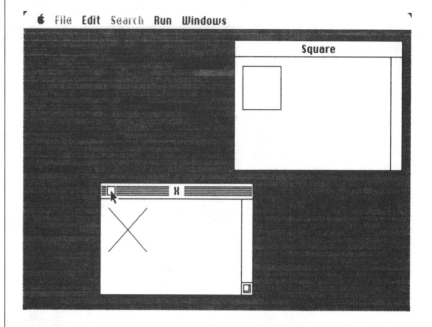

The close window request is handled at statement label
CloseWindow. This event is signalled whenever the user clicks on
the close box of an active window. The DIALOG(4) function is
used to obtain the window that has been so selected. The
WINDOW CLOSE statement performs the requested operation.
Variable *WindowsClosed* is then incremented by one. When it
reaches 3, all of the program windows have been closed, and so the
program ends.

The refresh window request is handled at statement label
RefreshWindow. This event is signalled in many different cases, as
explained above. The DIALOG(5) function is used to obtain the id
of the window that needs to be refreshed.

The WINDOW OUTPUT statement is used to insure that that
window will receive any output that the program produces next.
Note that this does not alter the active window! The proper
subroutine is then called to fill the window with the appropriate
image.

DIALOG Interrupts
The dialog events that I have discussed can also be detected by
means of a program interrupt. The DIALOG interrupt will be
signalled whenever the value of the DIALOG(0) function is not
zero. If you wish to write a program to handle dialog events via the
interrupt mechanism, then you must begin by setting up a dialog
interrupt service subroutine. This is done using a statement such as

```
ON DIALOG GOSUB Dialog.Int
```

The program must then be enabled to receive the dialog interrupts, with the statement

```
DIALOG ON
```

Once these two steps have been taken, every time a dialog event takes place, subroutine Dialog.Int will be called. The subroutine can call the various DIALOG functions to determine what the event was, and which window, button, or edit field was affected. When the subroutine returns, the main program will be resumed at its point of interruption.

The *DIALOG OFF* statement can be used to disable dialog events from interrupting the program. Or, the *DIALOG STOP* statement can be used to temporarily postpone any dialog events from causing interrupts. However, if any dialog events occur while DIALOG STOP is in effect, those events will be signalled by interrupts when the next DIALOG ON statement is encountered.

Listing 8-9 contains a program that demonstrates how dialog interrupts may be used. When you run this program, it will create two windows. The larger window, titled "Main," will slowly be filled with an interesting graphics image. A much smaller window, titled "Time," will display the current time of day, updated once a second.

Listing 8-9
Handling Dialog Events via the Interrupt Mechanism

```
WINDOW 1,"Main",(10,50)-(400,280),1   'create first output window
'
WINDOW 2,"Time",(380,300)-(500,340),1  'create second output window
GOSUB DisplayTime
'
WINDOW 1                 'make Main window active
'
ON DIALOG GOSUB Dialog.Int     'set up a dialog interrupt service subroutine
ON TIMER(1) GOSUB Timer.Int  'set up a timer interrupt service subroutine
DIALOG ON                      'enable dialog interrupts
TIMER ON                       'enable timer interrupts
'
' The main program that follows assumes that output is always being
' directed to the Main window. This condition must be maintained by
' the interrupt service subroutines. This main routine simply draws an
' interesting pattern in the Main window, when the pattern is complete ,
' the window is cleared and the pattern begins again. The main program
' thus runs in an infinite loop.
'
MainProgram:
Pi=3.14159
FOR offset=0 TO 2*Pi STEP .1
FOR angle=0 TO 2*Pi STEP .05
x=110+100*COS(angle)
y=110+100*SIN(angle+offset)
PSET(x,y)
NEXT
NEXT
CLS
GOTO MainProgram
'
' The dialog interrupt service subroutine, entered whenever a dialog
' event takes place:
Dialog.Int:
  TIMER STOP               'temporarily stop all timer interrupts
```

Listing 8-9—cont.

```
d=DIALOG(0)                    'determine dialog event that occurred
IF d=3 THEN GOTO ActivateWindow
IF d=4 THEN GOTO CloseWindow
IF d=5 THEN GOTO RefreshWindow
EndofInt:
TIMER ON                       're-enable timer interrupts
RETURN                         'return to main program
'
ActivateWindow:     'user clicked on an inactive window to make it active
w=DIALOG(3)         'get window to be made active
IF w=1 THEN WINDOW 1   'if Main window then make it active
' if Time window then make it active but maintain Main window as the
' current output window :
IF w=2 THEN WINDOW 2 : WINDOW OUTPUT 1
GOTO EndofInt

CloseWindow:        'user clicked close box of an active output window
w=DIALOG(4)                   'get window id to be closed
' if Main window has been closed, then make it reappear :
IF w=1 THEN WINDOW 1 : GOTO EndofInt
' otherwise, it must be a request to close the Time window, which is ok :
WINDOW CLOSE 2                'close the Time window
GOTO EndofInt

RefreshWindow:     'a portion of an output window needs to be refreshed
w=DIALOG(5)                   'get window id to be refreshed
IF w<> 2 THEN GOTO EndofInt   'only accept refresh request on Time window
WINDOW OUTPUT 2               'make "Time" the current output window
GOSUB DisplayTime
WINDOW OUTPUT 1               'make "Main" the current output window
GOTO EndofInt

' The timer interrupt service subroutine, entered once every second :
Timer.Int:
DIALOG STOP          'temporarily disable any dialog interrupts
WINDOW OUTPUT 2      'make "Time" the current output window
GOSUB DisplayTime    'display the current time
WINDOW OUTPUT 1      'make "Main the current output window
DIALOG ON            're-enable dialog interrupts
RETURN               'return to the main program
'
DisplayTime:                  'display the current clock time
LOCATE 2,2
PRINT TIME$;
RETURN
```

As in the previous program, you can click on either window to make it the active window. Once a window has been made active, you can reposition and resize it. If the Time window is obscured and then made visible, it will automatically be refreshed (although this would happen within one second anyway).

The Main window, however, is not automatically refreshed. The Main window cannot be closed by clicking on the close box, although the Time window can. This program technique can be used to add a time clock to a program, allow the user to move the clock or remove it entirely, and still insure that the main program runs undisturbed.

The program begins by creating the two windows. Subroutine DisplayTime is then called to place the current time within the Time window. Once this has been done, the Main window is made active. It is important to understand that the main program expects the Main window to be the current Output window at all times. I will point out to you how this condition is maintained.

Before the main program loop is entered, interrupt service subroutines are set up for both the dialog and timer events. The timer event is set to occur once every second; it will be used to keep the clock time current in the Time window.

The main program loop uses a pair of nested FOR-NEXT loops and some basic trigonometry to draw an interesting graphics pattern in the Main window. When the pattern is completed, the routine clears the Main window and begins again. For this reason, the program must be terminated manually.

If any dialog event occurs while the main program is running, it will be interrupted and the Dialog.Int subroutine will be entered. This routine immediately disables the timer interrupt, since the program logic cannot handle one interrupt routine being interrupted by another. The DIALOG(0) function is used to determine what event caused the interrupt.

A window activate event is handled at label ActivateWindow. The window to be activated is obtained from the DIALOG(3) function. If it is the Main window (id number 1), then the program complies. If, however, it is the Time window, then the program complies, but it also insures that the Main window remains the current Output window via a special WINDOW OUTPUT statement.

By allowing the user to make the Time window active, the program allows him to reposition, resize, and close that window. At the same time, however, the program insures that the main program can still proceed with its dedicated window.

If the close window event was signalled, then it is handled at label CloseWindow. The DIALOG(4) function is used to determine which window has been closed. Note that the system has actually already performed the close on whatever window is indicated here. If the program determines that this was the Main window, it uses the WINDOW statement to make that window reappear. In this manner, the user is prevented from closing that window. The Time window (id number 2) can be closed without intervention from this routine.

The refresh window event is handled at label RefreshWindow. The DIALOG(5) function is used to determine which window is to be refreshed. Since the program does not support the refreshing of the Main window, such a request is ignored at this point. The Time window is refreshed, however, by calling the DisplayTime routine. Note how the program forces the Time window to be the current Output window before calling DisplayTime, and then insures that the Main window is the current Output window before completing.

Regardless of what dialog event is signalled, and how it is handled, the Dialog.Int subroutine always ends up at label EndofInt. At this label, the timer interrupt is reenabled, and the routine returns to the main program.

The Timer.Int subroutine is entered once every second, as a result of the timer interrupt. This routine begins by disabling any dialog events that might occur while it is executing. It then makes the Time window the current Output window and calls DisplayTime to update its contents. As always, the routine insures that the Main window is the current Output window before returning to the main program. In addition, the routine must reenable the dialog interrupt.

Summary

In this chapter, you have learned how to add the many features and advantages of windows to your own programs. Because of Macintosh's well-defined user interfaces, the addition of windows and dialog box elements can go a long way toward making a program quick to learn and easy to use. This is possible because the experienced Macintosh user already knows how to manipulate windows and interact with control buttons and data entry fields. In the next chapter, I will use these abilities to further enhance some of the sample programs introduced earlier.

Chapter 9

Custom Pull-Down Menus

One of Macintosh's greatest contributions to the microcomputer user is the concept of the *pull-down menu*. For years, users of microcomputer software have been confounded by the many different approaches to implementing program commands. Some software uses a single-keystroke approach, where a special control key is held down in conjunction with a letter key to invoke a specific command. In this case, the user must memorize each command and its associated keystroke. This takes time and discourages new users.

Other software systems use a menu-driven approach. In this case, an easy-to-remember keystroke causes the entire computer screen to be cleared and replaced with a menu of functions. Users can clearly see the various choices and options available, but they can no longer see the data they were working with prior to invoking the menu screen.

In addition, because sophisticated microcomputer software can implement hundreds of commands and functions, users are often forced to chain from one menu screen to another until they find the commands they want. This can be a time-consuming and frustrating process.

The standard Macintosh user interface addresses all of these problems with its *menu bar* and associated pull-down menus. The menu bar lists all major categories of commands that the program supports. Since it is always on display at the top of the screen, the user is always aware of what functions are available.

Even those functions that may not be available, due to the constraints of a current program mode, are visible. This is possible because the menu bar supports both normal and "dimmed" menus, the latter being an indication that the menu is temporarily unavailable.

The various functions that appear below any menu can be seen simply by "pulling down" that menu. This process does not destroy the information being displayed on the rest of the screen. Although it does hide some of this information, most of the screen is still visible. This is the most important feature of pull-down menus and is the main reason why they go so far to improve user friendliness and comfort.

The seasoned Macintosh user is going to expect to be able to use pull-down menus when working with any program on the Mac. It is thus important to be able to add pull-down menu support to your own BASIC programs. Once again, Microsoft has come through for us, providing a powerful set of BASIC statements that support the Macintosh menu system. In this chapter, I show you how to use these statements to add pull-down menus to your own programs.

The Menu Statement

The *MENU* statement allows you to construct your own custom pull-down menus. You may also use it to remove any or all of the standard menu items that appear when running Microsoft BASIC. The basic format of the MENU statement is as follows

```
MENU menu-id,item-id,status,title
```

Each menu that appears in the menu bar is assigned a unique menu id number. These numbers are assigned from left to right, starting with the number 0. Thus, for the normal Microsoft BASIC menu, the Apple menu will be identified as number 0, the File menu as number 1, the Edit menu as number 2, and so on. The menu-id shown in the above statement refers to the menu identification number of the menu being defined/redefined. It may be specified as any number from 1 to 10 (you may not redefine the Apple menu, numbered 0). As you know, when a menu is pulled down, several *menu items* are listed within it. Each of these items is identified by a unique item id number.

Within each menu, the items are numbered from top to bottom, starting with item id number 1. The item-id shown in the model statement above refers to the item id number of the item being defined/redefined. Alternatively, the item-id can be specified as 0, in which case the statement refers to the entire menu, and not just a single item within that menu.

The status field allows you to specify whether you want a menu or menu item to be dimmed; it can also be used to place a check mark next to a specific menu item. This is often done to indicate that the function represented by that menu item has been selected and is "on." Table 9-1 lists the values that can be specified in the status field of the MENU statement. Finally, the title field contains a character string that represents the text of the menu or the menu item itself.

Table 9-1
MENU Statement Status Field

0	Menu or menu item is dimmed and unavailable for selection.
1	Menu or menu item is available for selection.
2	Menu item is available for selection and is displayed with a check mark.

Defining a Complete Menu

To completely define a custom menu requires the execution of several MENU statements. The first MENU statement should define the menu title itself; its item-id field should be 0. Subsequent MENU statements should define each menu item within that menu.

To replace one of the standard Microsoft BASIC menus, simply choose a menu id number that corresponds to an existing menu (ids 1 through 5). For example, to replace the standard BASIC menu titled "Windows," you would use a menu id of 5. In Figure 9-1, I have used this technique to replace the Windows menu with my own custom menu, titled "My Menu." The menu contains four items, "Sleep," "Wake Up," "Eat Breakfast," and "Use Mac." Study the sequence of MENU statements that were used to create this menu. This is the recommended sequence for defining menus.

Note that when a program using custom menus ends, the system does not automatically restore the menu bar to its standard state. Figure 9-2 illustrates how menu items can be either dimmed or checked by proper status field values. In that example, the "Sleep" item has been dimmed, and the "Eat Breakfast" item has been checked.

Figure 9-1
Creating a Custom Pull-Down Menu

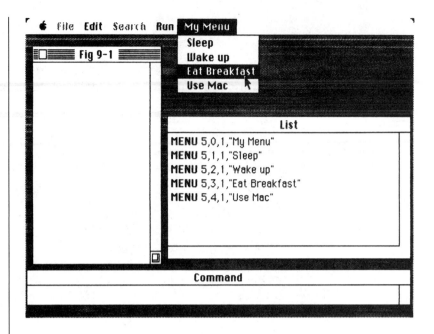

To add a custom menu to the menu bar without removing any of the standard system menus, simply choose a menu id number greater than 5.

Removing Standard Menus

The MENU statement can also be used to remove standard menus from the menu bar without replacing them with custom menus. To do this, you use the following form of the MENU statement

```
MENU id,0,0,""
```

where id represents the number of the standard menu to be removed. Note that you cannot remove the standard Apple menu, as it has id number 0 and Microsoft only allows id numbers from 1 to 10 on the MENU statement. In Figure 9-3 I have used this technique to remove the standard Search menu from the menu bar.

Removing system menus from the menu bar while your program is running helps to give your program that "finished" look. Certainly once your program is fully debugged and "out in the field," you will not want the user to be tinkering with it. You can therefore use this technique to remove the system menus that allow the user to manipulate the program.

Typically you will want to remove the "Search," "Run," and "Windows" menus. You may replace the "File" menu with your own custom menu that can be used to "Quit" your program but cannot be used for any other purpose. You may combine this approach with the technique introduced in Chapter 3 for making a program unbreakable.

In most cases, however, I do not recommend removing the standard "Edit" menu. The functions of this menu are accessible to the user when supplying data to Dialog Box data entry fields, so you will want them to be present.

Figure 9-2
*Dimmed and Checked
Menu Items*

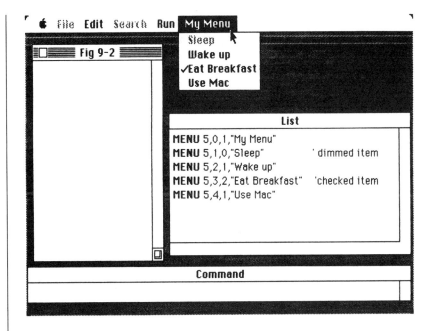

The MENU RESET Statement

If at any point in your program you wish to remove all of your custom menus and restore the standard system menus, you can do so. This is accomplished by a special form of the *MENU* statement, which is coded as

    MENU RESET

The statement simply restores the entire menu bar to its default state.

The Menu Function

The *MENU* function is used to detect user activity within custom pull-down menus. It cannot be used to detect selection of the standard system menus. The MENU function accepts an input argument of either 0 or 1 and should always be called in a specific sequence.

First, make a call to MENU(0). Follow this immediately with a call to MENU(1). The first call will return a value indicating the menu id number of the custom menu last selected by the user. If there have been no custom menu selections since the previous call to MENU(0), then the call will return a value of 0. Assuming a custom menu was selected, the second call (to MENU(1)) will return the item id number of the selected item within that menu.

Figure 9-4 shows the basic technique for detecting user selections of custom menu items. The program first sets up the custom menus as needed. The wait loop starting at label MenuWait is then entered. Each time through this loop, the MENU(0) and MENU(1) functions are interrogated. If the value of MENU(0) is zero, then no custom menu activity has occurred, and so the program stays in the wait loop. If MENU(0) is not zero, then it indicates the id number of the selected menu, and variable *mi* contains the selected item id number.

Figure 9-3
Removing a Standard Menu

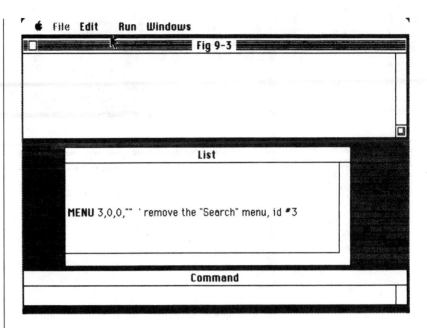

Figure 9-4
Detecting Menu Activity

```
' Set up custom menus :
'
MENU 6,0,1,"..."
MENU 6,1,1,"..."
MENU 6,2,1,"..."
'   ...
'   ...
'   .... (etc.)
'
' Wait for menu activity :
'
MenuWait:
m=MENU(0)
mi=MENU(1)
IF m=0 THEN GOTO MenuWait
'
' Item 'mi' within menu 'm' has been selected.
'
'   ...
'   ... (perform function requested)
'   ...
'
' Un-highlight the selected menu in the menu bar :
'
MENU
'
GOTO MenuWait     'go wait for more menu activity
```

The program proceeds to process the function thus defined. When processing is complete, a short form of the MENU statement is executed. This short form has no parameters, just the keyword MENU. Its function is to unhighlight the selected menu title from the menu bar. The menu title became highlighted as soon as the user pulled down that menu, and it remained in that state once the user selected an item (even though the rest of the menu disappeared).

Using this technique, the menu bar remains highlighted while the requested function is performed and then unhighlights when the function is complete. This allows the user to visually observe when a function is being executed and when it is completed. (For functions implemented by a few simple statements, this feature will not be noticed. However, if you program a function that takes some time to execute, such as reading or writing a disk file, then the menu title within the menu bar will be noticeable as it remains highlighted for the duration of the function.)

Listing 9-1 contains a program that demonstrates the use of the MENU statement and function. For this example, I have taken the very simple program of Listing 3-7 and modified it so that it supports the Macintosh user interface. As you will recall, the original program was designed to roll dice for fantasy role playing games. To this end, it allows the user to specify how many dice to roll, and how many sides each die should have.

Listing 9-1
Fantasy Game Dice Rolling Program — Version 2

```
' The original version of this program can be found in Listing 3-6.
' Simulates the rolling of any number of dice, with any number of sides per die.
' In this version, the user specifies the number of sides per die and number
' of dice to roll in a dialog box. The dice rolls are displayed in a seperate
' "Display" window. Dice rolling is accomplished by selecting "Roll" from the
' custom pull-down menu titled "File." Other functions that can be selected
' from the menu are "Clear Display," "Standard Dice," and "Quit."
DEF FNrand(l,u)=CINT(1+RND(1)*(u-1))
RANDOMIZE TIMER
'
' set up the custom pull-down menu titled "File" :
'
MENU 1,0,1,"File"
MENU 1,1,1,"Standard Dice"
MENU 1,2,1,"Roll Dice"
MENU 1,3,1,"Clear Display"
MENU 1,4,1,"Quit"
'
' remove all other standard menus :
'
MENU 2,0,0,""
MENU 3,0,0,""
MENU 4,0,0,""
MENU 5,0,0,""
'
' define each of the program's output windows :
'        window 1 = "Display" = usually current output window = displays rolls.
'        window 2 = "untitled" = dialog box for specifying roll parameters =
'                                always active window.
'
WINDOW 1,"Display",(10,170)-(500,330),1
WINDOW 2,,(100,40)-(400,140),2
'
' display field descriptions for dialog box :
'
PRINT "Specify Dice Rolling Parameters"
LOCATE 3,1
PRINT "Number of Dice :"
LOCATE 5,1
PRINT "Sides per Die :"
'
' create data entry fields for dialog box :
'
EDIT FIELD 1,"2",(125,32)-(150,47),1,1
EDIT FIELD 2,"6",(125,64)-(150,79),1,1
```

Listing 9-1—cont.

```
EDIT FIELD 1

' set up data entry field tracking variables :

f=1                'currently active field id
field.number%=2    'number of dice to roll
field.sides%=6     'sides per die

' make the Display window the current output window :

WINDOW OUTPUT 1

' set up to receive dialog interrupts :

ON DIALOG GOSUB Dialog.Int
DIALOG ON

' wait for user menu activity :

MenuWait:
m=MENU(0)
mi=MENU(1)
IF m=0 THEN GOTO MenuWait

' branch to appropriate routine based upon menu item selected :

ON mi GOSUB Standard,RollDice,ClearD,Quit

MENU              'un-highlight the menu in the menu bar
GOTO MenuWait

' Function = Standard : reset Roll Parameters for standard dice (2 x 6) :

Standard:
WINDOW OUTPUT 2       'access the dialog box window
' restore the default settings for the entry fields :
EDIT FIELD CLOSE 1
EDIT FIELD CLOSE 2
EDIT FIELD 1,"2",(125,32)-(150,47),1,1
EDIT FIELD 2,"6",(125,64)-(150,79),1,1
EDIT FIELD 1
f=1                'currently active field id
field.number%=2    'number of dice to roll
field.sides%=6     'sides per die
WINDOW OUTPUT 1       'make the Display window the current output window
RETURN

' Function = Roll Dice : roll dice as per parameters and display results :

RollDice:
DIALOG STOP                  'temporarily disable dialog event interrupts
number%=field.number%        'capture current entry field settings
sides%=field.sides%
DIALOG ON                    'reenable dialog event interrupts
' Note that any changes in the entry field data at this point will not affect
' this run of the "Roll Dice" function.

' actually do the roll of the dice :

total%=0
FOR x%=1 TO number%
die%=FNrand(1,sides%)
total%=total%+die%
PRINT " ";die%;
NEXT
PRINT
PRINT "Total = ";total%
PRINT
RETURN
```

Listing 9-1—cont.

```
' Function = Clear Display : clears display window :
'
ClearD:
CLS
RETURN
'
' Function = Quit : terminates program :
'
Quit:
END
'
'
' Dialog event interrupt service subroutine :
'
Dialog.Int:
d=DIALOG(0)        'determine what dialog event took place
IF d=2 OR d=6 OR d=7 THEN GOTO FieldEvent
RETURN                   'ignore all other dialog events
'
' come here if user tried to select alternate edit field or if he pressed
' the tab or return key :
'
FieldEvent:
WINDOW OUTPUT 2
x$=EDIT$(f)            'get data for field the user is trying to exit from
x=VAL(x$)                'convert to numeric
IF x<=0 OR x>99 THEN GOTO EntryError
'
' accept new entry field data into program variable :
'
IF f=1 THEN field.number%=x
IF f=2 THEN field.sides%=x
'
' switch to the other entry field :
'
IF f=1 THEN f=2 ELSE f=1
EDIT FIELD f
WINDOW OUTPUT 1
RETURN
'
' come here if user attempts to enter invalid data into an entry field :
' (f = entry field id number in question)
'
EntryError:
BEEP
IF f=1 THEN x=field.number%        'get previous data for this field
IF f=2 THEN x=field.sides%
x$=STR$(x)                              'convert it to character string
x$=RIGHT$(x$,LEN(x$)-1)        'remove leading blank character from string
'
' restore previous (valid) data to that field :
'
EDIT FIELD CLOSE f
IF f=1 THEN EDIT FIELD 1,x$,(125,32)-(150,47),1,1
IF f=2 THEN EDIT FIELD 2,x$,(125,64)-(150,79),1,1
WINDOW OUTPUT 1
RETURN
```

In this new version of the program, these inputs are supplied by the user via Dialog Box data entry fields. The user starts the dice rolling process by selecting a custom pull-down menu item. It is interesting to note how the very basic and simple program of Listing 3-7 is transformed into a much larger and more complex program, simply as a result of the addition of fancy user interfaces. While this is true, the essence of the program—what it actually does—is not changed at all!

Figure 9-5 shows the screen produced by running this program. As you can see, the program uses two windows and a single, custom pull-down menu. In Figure 9-6, I have pulled down the custom File menu so that you can see the items within. The Dialog Box window, at the top of the screen, allows the user to specify the number of dice to roll as well as the number of sides per die. It also serves to display the current setting of these parameters at all times.

Figure 9-5
Fantasy Game Dice Rolling Program — Version 2

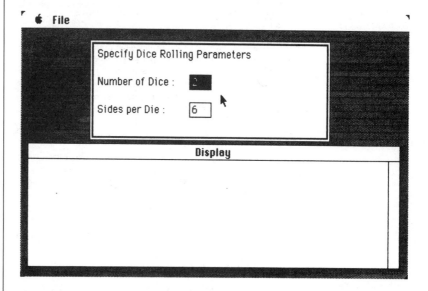

Figure 9-6
Dice Rolling Program Menu

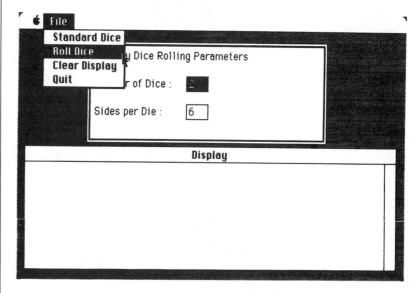

The user can select either entry field in the Dialog Box by clicking on it with the mouse. In addition, the user can press either the <Tab> or the <Return> key to move from one entry field to the other. The Display window below the Dialog Box will display the actual results of each roll.

The File menu provides the user with four functions. These are

Standard Dice, Roll Dice, Clear Display, and Quit. Each time the user selects the Roll Dice function, the dice are rolled as per the current roll parameter settings, and the results appear in the Display window. The user can clear the Display window at any time by selecting the Clear Display function. The roll parameters can be automatically reset to the standard 2 dice, 6 sides per die, by selecting the Standard Dice function. Finally, the Quit function allows the user to terminate the program.

Give this program a try. As you can see, it performs the same basic function as Listing 3-7. Because of the user interface, however, it is much easier for a new user to figure out what the program does and how to use it.

The program begins by defining the random number function that will be used to produce the dice rolls. It then provides a starting seed for the random function. The custom pull-down menu titled File is then defined. Next, the rest of the standard system menus are removed.

The two Output windows are created, and the Dialog Box window is left active. PRINT and LOCATE statements are used to provide prompts and entry field definitions within this window. Then the two data entry fields are created with EDIT FIELD statements. Variable *f* will keep track of which entry field is currently active. Variables *field.number%* and *field.sides%* are set to the current (default) parameters for each field. The Display window is made the current Output window, as it will be used by the main program function, Roll Dice.

Subroutine Dialog.Int is set up to receive control for any dialog events. It will be used to detect user activity in the data entry fields. The program then enters a menu wait loop. During the time spent in this loop, any Dialog Box activity will be handled by the interrupt service subroutine. The menu wait loop is exited as soon as the user selects a menu item. An ON-GOSUB statement is used to direct program flow to the appropriate routine based upon the menu item selected.

Each routine is responsible for handling a specific menu function, and is written as a subroutine. In this fashion, each function completes by returning to the point following the ON-GOSUB statement. Here a MENU statement is used to unhighlight the File menu, and the menu wait loop is reentered.

The Standard Dice function is handled by the subroutine named Standard. Its purpose is to reset the roll parameters. Because the reset values must also be displayed in the entry fields of the Dialog Box window, it will be necessary to close and then recreate those fields. Since the EDIT FIELD statement only acts on the current Output window, the program must explicitly set the Dialog Box window (id number 2) to the current Output window with a WINDOW OUTPUT statement. (The user, on the other hand, can only interact with entry fields within the active window).

The EDIT FIELD CLOSE statement is then used to remove the two entry fields. They are then recreated, assuring that they contain the proper (default) values. The program variables *f*, *field.number%*, and *field.sides%* are also reset at this time. Before returning, the routine restores the Display window to the current output window.

The Roll Dice function is handled by the subroutine named RollDice. This routine is responsible for actually simulating the dice rolls and displaying the results. Since the roll parameters might change at any time as a result of a dialog event interrupt, this routine uses a different set of variables for these parameters. At the beginning of the routine, the variables that track the Dialog Box parameters (*field.number%* and *field.sides%*) are copied into the routine's version of those variables (*number%* and *sides%*). For just that moment, dialog event interrupts are disabled. This insures that if the user tries to change the roll parameters at the exact moment that the roll is about to begin, the previous roll parameters will be used. Note also that the user can change the parameters in the Dialog Box while the dice are being rolled, but this will not affect the current roll.

The next time the roll function is used, the new parameters will be in force. The balance of the RollDice routine is identical to the code contained in the earlier program (Listing 3-7) and requires no further explanation.

The Clear Display function is handled in a very simple manner by subroutine ClearD. The Quit function requires even less discussion; it can be found at program label Quit.

The rest of the program consists of the dialog event interrupt service subroutine. This routine uses the DIALOG(0) function to determine precisely what dialog event took place. Most of these events are ignored by this program. The only events that are handled are the user selecting an entry field, pressing the <Tab> key, or pressing the <Return> key. Each of these events is processed in the same manner, at label FieldEvent.

These events indicate that the user has entered some data into a data entry field and is trying to exit from that field. At this point the program must obtain the data in the field, verify its validity, and enter it into the program's variables. Since the **EDIT$** function acts only on the current Output window, the Dialog Box window (id number 2) is made the current Output window.

The **EDIT$** function is then employed to obtain the data within the current data entry field. This is, of course, character string data. The **VAL** function is used to convert it to numeric. The data is then checked for validity (numeric value in range 1 to 99). If the data is acceptable, it is placed within the appropriate field parameter variable, the Display window is made the current Output window, and the program returns from the interrupt.

If the user has entered invalid data into a data entry field, the program branches to label EntryError. This can occur if nonnumeric characters are placed in the entry fields, because the **VAL** function will return a value of 0. The purpose of this section of code is to inform the user that invalid data has been entered and, since the program must always have valid parameters available for a roll, then replace the invalid data with the previous data for that field. The BEEP statement is used to inform the user of the entry error.

The previous (valid) data is obtained from the appropriate field variable and converted to character string format via the **STR$** function. Since the data must represent a positive number, the leading blank produced by the **STR$** function is removed at this time. The EDIT FIELD CLOSE statement is used to remove the offending data entry field, and then the field is recreated with the previous valid data. The "Display" window is made the current Output window, and the routine returns.

If you have used this program for a while, you may find it annoying to have to pull down the menu each time you want to roll the dice. An excellent enhancement to the program would be a "push-button" in the Dialog Box window. This button could be labelled "Roll" and could be clicked by the user to initiate a dice roll. I have left this enhancement as an exercise for you to do on your own. I caution that it is not a trivial modification. Bear in mind that the button click will be detected by the Dialog.Int routine and, as an interrupt event, can occur at almost any time during the execution of the program. It could occur even while the dice are being rolled due to a previous dice-roll request. You will have to take this into account when writing the code to support this feature.

The Menu Interrupt

User activity in custom pull-down menus can be detected via the interrupt mechanism. To set up a menu interrupt service subroutine, use the statement

ON MENU GOSUB Menu.Int

This statement sets up the subroutine named Menu.Int to handle the event that occurs whenever a user makes a menu selection from a custom menu defined earlier in the program. To enable the program to receive menu interrupts, the statement *MENU ON* must be executed. To disable menu interrupts, you use the *MENU OFF* statement. Alternatively, the *MENU STOP* statement can be used. This statement will disable menu interrupts but will keep track of any that do occur. These will be signalled to the program as soon as the next MENU ON statement is executed.

The program contained in Listing 9-2 illustrates how the menu interrupt can be used. When executed, this program adds one custom menu to the menu bar. It is titled "Fontsize." The main body of the program is a simple loop that repeatedly displays the letters of the alphabet in a single line across the Output window.

Listing 9-2
Menu Interrupt Demo

```
' This program adds a custom pull-down menu titled "Fontsize"
' It runs in an infinite loop, continually displaying the letters
' of the alphabet. The user can pull down the Fontsize menu at
' any time and use it to change the size of the text being produced.
' The current font size is always indicated within the custom menu
' by a check mark alongside the appropriate menu item.

DIM sizes(5)        ' array to hold the font sizes listed in the menu
FOR i=1 TO 5        ' initialize the array contents
READ sizes(i)
NEXT
DATA 9,12,18,24,36
'
```

Listing 9-2—cont.

```
' set up the custom menu :

MENU 6,0,1,"Fontsize"
MENU 6,1,1," 9"
MENU 6,2,2," 12"      'note: by default, fontsize is 12, so check mark is here
MENU 6,3,1," 18"
MENU 6,4,1," 24"
MENU 6,5,1," 36"
'
size=2       'variable tracks current font size setting, as index of sizes array

' set up the menu interrupt service subroutine :

ON MENU GOSUB Menu.Int
MENU ON                          'enable menu interrupts
'
MainLoop:          'the extremely simplistic main loop of the program :
PRINT "abcdefghijklmnopqrstuvwxyz"
GOTO MainLoop

' The menu interrupt service subroutine :

Menu.Int:
m=MENU(0)         'get menu id number (it must be 6 in this program)
mi=MENU(1)        'get menu item id number
CALL TEXTSIZE(sizes(mi))      'set text display size to selected value
MENU 6,size,1         'remove check mark from previously active size
MENU 6,mi,2          'place check mark alongside new size
size=mi             'keep the variable up to date
MENU                'reset the menu highlight
RETURN              'return to main program
```

At any time while the program is executing the user can pull down the Fontsize menu and select a different text font size. The newly selected font size will be put into effect immediately and will be used on the subsequent display line. Try executing this program and experimenting by selecting various different font sizes from the custom menu. Note that the menu always indicates the currently selected font size by a check mark next to the appropriate menu item. This is a commonly used and important technique; I explain how to implement it below.

The program begins by dimensioning an array named sizes. This array holds the five different font sizes that will be made available via the custom menu. It is initialized from a DATA statement with a simple FOR-NEXT loop. The custom menu is then set up. Note that the normal default font size, 12, is defined to contain a check mark (status field value of 2). Program variable *size* keeps track of the current font size setting at all times.

The value in *size* represents the index of array *sizes* and not the actual font size itself. This value corresponds to the item id number for the font size within the custom menu. The program now sets up subroutine Menu.Int to handle any menu interrupts, and then enables such interrupts. The main body of the program, consisting of a simple and infinite loop, is then entered. If at any time while this loop is being executed the user selects an item from the custom menu, the program will be interrupted and subroutine Menu.Int will be called.

This subroutine determines the menu activity by calling upon the MENU(0) and MENU(1) functions. Note that, although there is only one possible value for MENU(0), this routine is called anyway. The important value is provided by MENU(1), this supplies the item id number that was selected. This number is used to extract the appropriate font size from the *sizes* array.

The toolbox routine *TEXTSIZE* is then employed to actually set the desired font size. The MENU statement is used to remove the check mark from the previously selected item (indicated by variable *size*). Another MENU statement is used to place a check mark alongside the newly selected menu item. Variable *size* is updated to indicate the new current font size, and the MENU statement is used to unhighlight the menu itself.

The subroutine then returns to the main program. Figure 9-7 shows the screen while this program is executing. At the moment when I created this screen snapshot, I had tried out font sizes 9, 12 and 18, and was about to select font size 24.

Figure 9-7
Menu Interrupt Demo

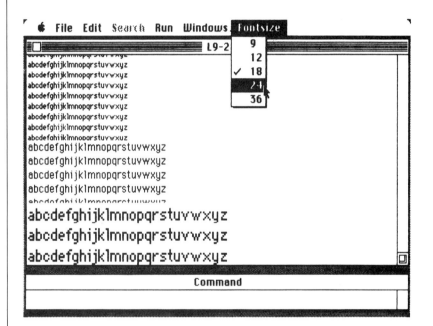

The Terminal Program Revisited

At this point you know enough about Microsoft BASIC to be able to write complete applications programs that conform to Apple's standards for the Macintosh user interface. These programs will be easy to learn, easy to use, and more fun to use than programs using more conventional user interfaces. I will now bring three of the more interesting programs in this book up to date by adding the new features with which you are now familiar.

We begin with the terminal communications program orginally introduced in Chapter 4 as Listing 4-7. As you will recall, this program turns the Macintosh into a general-purpose terminal, useful for communicating with other computers and communications devices. Chapter 4 contained detailed information about the hardware considerations pertinent to this application.

New Program Features

A new and much more sophisticated version of the terminal program can be found in Listing 9-3. This version uses custom pull-down menus and windows to provide a friendly user interface. In addition, I have added several important new features. The program now supports a wider variety of communications parameters, and these can be selected via control buttons within a dialog box.

Since many users find the 9-point font necessary for 80-column operation hard to read, the program supports a 40-column mode. In this mode, larger characters can be used, making the screen easier to read. The program automatically inserts carriage returns when the current text line is filled in either column width. This prevents a loss of data to the right edge of the screen.

Listing 9-3
The Terminal Communications Program — Version 2

```
' The original version of this program can be found in Listing 4-7.
' This version of the program is much more sophisticated and includes
' custom pull-down menus, a dialog box for setting serial communications
' parameters, selectable text display width, multiple terminal windows,
' and a capture buffer. See text for complete information on how to use
' this program, as well as details about how it works.

' array "Parms$" holds the device name modifiers for all possible
' serial parameter choices :
DIM Parms$(10)
FOR i=1 TO 10
READ Parms$(i)
NEXT
DATA "300","1200","2400","7","8","E","O","N","1","2"

Button.BR=1       'default baud rate selection = 300
Button.WL=4       'default word length selection = 7
Button.Par=6      'default parity selection = even
Button.StB=9      'default stop bits selection = 1
Button.DW=12      'default display width selection = 80

ComOpen=0      'this variable set to 1 to indicate the com port is open
BufferOpen=0   'this variable set to 1 to indicate the capture buffer is open
MT=0           'this variable set to 1 to indicate the transmit monitor is on

' set up custom pull down menus :

MENU 1,0,1,"File"
MENU 1,1,1,"Set Parameters"
MENU 1,2,1,"Quit"

MENU 2,0,1,"Capture Buffer"
MENU 2,1,1,"Display"
MENU 2,2,1,"Open"
MENU 2,3,2,"Close"          'currently checked
MENU 2,4,1,"Clear"
MENU 2,5,1,"Save"

MENU 3,0,1,"Windows"
MENU 3,1,2,"Standard"         'currently checked
MENU 3,2,1,"Monitor Transmit"

MENU 4,0,0,""          'remove unused system menus
MENU 5,0,0,""

' define each of the program's output windows as per :
'   window 1 = standard terminal display screen
'   window 2 = transmit monitor screen
'   window 3 = parameter setting dialog box
'   window 4 = buffer display screen
```

Listing 9-3—cont.

```
WINDOW 1,,(2,30)-(506,300),4        'create standard terminal display screen

GOSUB GetParameters        'get communications parameters via dialog box

' begin communications session, also keep checking for menu activity :
'
linesize=0        'count of characters displayed on current line
CLS
PRINT CHR$(95);        'display cursor in terminal window

Again:
'
' check for any user menu activity .
'
m=MENU(0)
mi=MENU(1)
IF m<>0 THEN GOSUB MenuFunction   'handle any user menu activity
'
' process any received characters :
'
WHILE LOC(1)>0
a$=INPUT$(1,#1)
a$=CHR$(ASC(a$) AND 127)  'force all incoming data to be pure ASCII
IF a$=CHR$(10) THEN GOTO SkipChar   'ignore all line feed characters
IF linesize=w AND a$<>CHR$(13) THEN PRINT CHR$(8);" " : linesize=0
PRINT CHR$(8),a$,CHR$(95);
IF a$=CHR$(13) THEN linesize=0 ELSE linesize=linesize+1
IF BufferOpen=1 AND LEN(Buf$)<32767 THEN Buf$=Buf$+a$
SkipChar:
WEND
'
' check for any characters to transmit :
'
a$=INKEY$
IF a$="" THEN GOTO Again            'nothing to transmit
PRINT #1,a$;                         'transmit the typed character
IF MT=0 THEN GOTO Again
'
' display the typed character in the special Transmit Monitor Window :
'
WINDOW OUTPUT 2
IF TMsize=w AND a$<>CHR$(13) THEN PRINT CHR$(8);" " : TMsize=0
PRINT CHR$(8);a$;CHR$(95);
IF a$=CHR$(13) THEN TMsize=0 ELSE TMsize=TMsize+1
WINDOW OUTPUT 1
GOTO Again
'
' Come here to process any user menu selections :
'
MenuFunction:
ON m GOSUB FMenu,CMenu,WMenu  'branch to appropriate menu handling routine
' all routines return to here :
MENU                'unhighlight the menu selection
RETURN              'return to main loop
'
' The File Menu was used :
'
FMenu:
IF mi=1 THEN GOSUB GetParameters : RETURN   'set comm parameters
' the only other File menu option is "Quit" so do so :
MENU RESET
END
'
' The Capture Buffer Menu was used :
'
CMenu:
ON mi GOSUB DispBuf,OpenBuf,CloseBuf,ClearBuf,SaveBuf
RETURN              'return to menu function handler

OpenBuf:            'open the capture buffer :
BufferOpen=1        'show that capture buffer is open
```

Listing 9-3—cont.

```
MENU 2,2,2              'put check mark next to "open" in the menu
MENU 2,3,1              'remove check mark from "close" in the menu
RETURN
'
CloseBuf:               'close the capture buffer :
BufferOpen=0            'show that capture buffer is closed
MENU 2,3,2             'put check mark next to "close" in the menu
MENU 2,2,1             'remove check mark from "open" in the menu
RETURN
'
ClearBuf:               'clear the capture buffer :
Buf$=""
RETURN
'
DispBuf:                    'display the capture buffer :
IF LEN(Buf$)=0 THEN RETURN      'capture buffer empty, bypass function
WINDOW 4,,(8,60)-(500,280),4     'create capture buffer display screen
CALL TEXTFONT(0)
CALL TEXTSIZE(12)
PRINT "CAPTURE BUFFER DISPLAY"
PRINT "Press any key to pause, press key again to resume"
CALL TEXTFONT(4)
IF Button.DW=11 THEN CALL TEXTSIZE(12) ELSE CALL TEXTSIZE(9)
lsize=0
FOR i=1 TO LEN(Buf$)
a$=MID$(Buf$,i,1)
IF lsize=w AND a$<>CHR$(13) THEN PRINT : lsize=0
PRINT a$;
IF a$=CHR$(13) THEN lsize=0 ELSE lsize=lsize+1
p$=INKEY$                      'does user want to pause ?
IF p$<>"" THEN GOSUB WaitKey      'yes - pause until another key is pressed
NEXT
PRINT
CALL TEXTFONT(0)
CALL TEXTSIZE(12)
PRINT "END OF CAPTURE BUFFER, press any key to continue"
GOSUB WaitKey
WINDOW CLOSE 4
CALL TEXTFONT(4)
IF Button.DW=11 THEN CALL TEXTSIZE(12) ELSE CALL TEXTSIZE(9)
RETURN
'
WaitKey:                   'subroutine to wait until any key is pressed
p$=INKEY$
IF p$="" THEN GOTO WaitKey
RETURN
'
SaveBuf:                   'save the capture buffer in a disk file :
IF LEN(Buf$)=0 THEN RETURN    'capture buffer empty, bypass function
'get filename from user via standard dialog box :
f$=FILES$(0,"Filename for Save Buffer")
IF f$="" THEN RETURN          'user "Cancelled" the save request
OPEN "O",2,f$                   'write the buffer contents to the named file :
PRINT#2,Buf$
CLOSE 2
RETURN
'
' The Windows menu was used :
'
WMenu:
IF mi=1 AND MT=0 THEN RETURN     'no change requested
IF mi=2 AND MT=1 THEN RETURN      'no change requested
IF mi=2 THEN GOTO MonitorOn        'go turn on the Transmit Monitor
' turn off the transmit monitor :
MT=0                    'show monitor has been turned off
WINDOW CLOSE 2          'remove the monitor window
MENU 3,1,2             'put check mark alongside "Standard" in menu
MENU 3,2,1             'remove check mark from "Monitor" in menu
RETURN
' turn on the transmit monitor :
MonitorOn:
```

Listing 9-3—cont.

```
MT=1                        'show monitor is on
WINDOW 2,,(2,305)-(506,340),4       'create transmit monitor display screen
CALL TEXTFONT(4)
IF Button.DW=11 THEN CALL TEXTSIZE(12) ELSE CALL TEXTSIZE(9)
MENU 3,2,2                   'put check mark alongside "Monitor" in menu
MENU 3,1,1                   'remove check mark from "Standard" in menu
RETURN
'
GetParameters:
WINDOW 3,,(50,60)-(460,290),-2   'create dialog box
CALL TEXTFONT(0)            'set font to match button titles
CALL TEXTSIZE(12)
CALL MOVETO(100,12)
PRINT "Set Communications Parameters"
CALL MOVETO(20,40)
PRINT " Baud Rate       Word Length      Parity       Stop Bits"
BUTTON 1,1,"300",(25,60)-(80,75),3
BUTTON 2,1,"1200",(25,80)-(80,95),3
BUTTON 3,1,"2400",(25,100)-(80,115),3
'
BUTTON 4,1,"7",(130,60)-(180,75),3
BUTTON 5,1,"8",(130,80)-(180,95),3
'
BUTTON 6,1,"Even",(250,60)-(300,75),3
BUTTON 7,1,"Odd",(250,80)-(300,95),3
BUTTON 8,1,"None",(250,100)-(300,115),3
'
BUTTON 9,1,"1",(330,60)-(380,75),3
BUTTON 10,1,"2",(330,80)-(380,95),3
'
CALL MOVETO(20,160)
PRINT " Display Width"
BUTTON 11,1,"40 Characters",(25,180)-(150,195),3
BUTTON 12,1,"80 Characters",(25,200)-(150,215),3
'
BUTTON 13,1,"Ok",(250,180)-(280,210),1
'
' dialog box set up, now set button states to show current settings :
'
ShowSettings:
BUTTON Button.BR,2          'current baud rate selection
BUTTON Button.WL,2          'current word length selection
BUTTON Button.Par,2         'current parity selection
BUTTON Button.StB,2         'current stop bits selection
BUTTON Button.DW,2          'current display width selection
'
' now wait for user activity within the dialog box, note that since the
' window type is negative, the user cannot do anything outside of this
' dialog box until it is exited :
'
DialogWait:                 'wait for a dialog event :
d=DIALOG(0)
IF d<>1 THEN GOTO DialogWait    'ignore all events but button clicks
b=DIALOG(1)                     'get id number of button that was clicked
'
' if any radio button, then deselect the previously selected button in that
' button group, set the appropriate parameter variable to the new selection,
' and branch back to "ShowSettings" so that the new button choice will appear
' selected :
'
IF b>=1 AND b<=3 THEN BUTTON Button.BR,1 : Button.BR=b : GOTO ShowSettings
IF b=4 OR b=5 THEN BUTTON Button.WL,1 : Button.WL=b : GOTO ShowSettings
IF b>=6 AND b<=8 THEN BUTTON Button.Par,1 : Button.Par=b : GOTO ShowSettings
IF b=9 OR b=10 THEN BUTTON Button.StB,1 : Button.StB=b : GOTO ShowSettings
IF b=11 OR b=12 THEN BUTTON Button.DW,1 : Button.DW=b : GOTO ShowSettings
'
' if program reaches this point, then button #13 ("Ok") must have been pushed :
'
' construct device name from parameters selected :
Dev$="COM1:"+Parms$(Button.BR)+","+Parms$(Button.Par)+","+Parms$(Button.WL)+","+Parms$(Button.S
tB)
```

Listing 9-3—cont.

```
' if com port already open and parms havent changed then dont reopen it :
IF ComOpen=1 AND Device$=Dev$ THEN GOTO SkipOpen
IF ComOpen=1 THEN CLOSE 1        'close port if it is already open

' Open the serial communications port :
Device$=Dev$
OPEN Device$ AS 1 LEN=5000
ComOpen=1                                'show that port is now open

SkipOpen:
WINDOW CLOSE 3       'remove the dialog box
WINDOW 1             'make the main terminal display screen active

CALL TEXTFONT(4)     'set Monaco font (a non-proportionally spaced font)
' set text size as per display width requested, also variable "w" :
IF Button.DW=11 THEN CALL TEXTSIZE(12) : w=40 : ELSE CALL TEXTSIZE(9) : w=80

RETURN
```

The Capture Buffer

When communicating with dial-up services, many users find a *Capture Buffer* facility helpful. The Capture Buffer may be used to retain any portion of the communications session, so that it can be redisplayed at leisure after the session is ended. Since most dial-up services charge by the minute for connect time, it is nice to be able to get online, obtain the information desired, and then log off as quickly as possible. With the Capture Buffer facility, the information obtained from the service can be perused at your convenience, without incurring additional service charges.

The Transmit Monitor

Many dial-up services now provide a feature called *teleconferencing*. This feature allows many users to call in to one central service and then communicate among themselves. Each user logged in to the conferencing service will receive the messages sent by any other users on the service. Any message that the user transmits to the service will be seen by each of the other users. The concept is not unlike that of the old-fashioned telephone party line. Use of this type of service can be complicated by a problem known as *text interleaving*.

Since users cannot control the transmission of text to their own terminal (which occurs whenever anyone else on the service enters a message), it often becomes interspersed with the characters of their own message as they enter it. This makes both the incoming and outgoing messages hard to read.

The new version of the terminal program solves this problem by providing an optional "Transmit Monitor" window. This window displays the text being transmitted by the user. Since that is all that it displays, the text cannot become interspersed with incoming data.

Another way that this feature can be used is to monitor the transmission of passwords. Many services do not echo passwords when they are supplied by the user. This is for the user's protection. But, since the text being typed is not echoed on the screen, typing errors can easily go unnoticed. The Transmit Monitor window alleviates this problem by directly displaying any text being typed by the user.

How To Use the Program

Figure 9-8 shows the initial screen produced when the terminal program is run. As you can see, the program provides three custom pull-down menus; they are titled File, Capture Buffer, and Windows. The main terminal display screen can be seen behind the currently active Dialog Box. This Dialog Box is used to set the communications parameters. A complete discussion of the terminal parameters can be found in Chapter 4.

The parameters are easily set by clicking the desired control buttons with the mouse. One additional parameter available in the Dialog Box is Display Width. This determines the size of the displayed text within the terminal display screen. It can be set to either 40 or 80 characters per line. Once the parameters are set, the "Ok" button is clicked. Communications may then begin.

Figure 9-8
*Terminal Program —
Initial Screen*

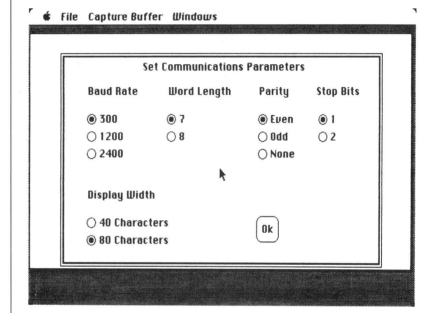

Figure 9-9 shows the program with the File menu pulled down. As you can see, this menu contains two items. The Set Parameters item can be selected at any time to bring back the parameter setting Dialog Box. The other option in this menu is used to terminate the program.

Figure 9-10 shows the Capture Buffer menu. This menu allows the user to manipulate the Capture Buffer. At any time during the communications session, the buffer may be open or closed. When the buffer is opened, it will capture (retain) any text received from the communications port. When closed, text received will not be captured, but the buffer will retain any previous contents. You can alternately open and close the buffer by selecting the appropriate item from the menu. A checkmark in the menu itself indicates the current status of the buffer.

The Display option creates a new window in which the current contents of the buffer may be viewed. If the buffer is very large, its contents will scroll through this window as they are displayed. You can pause the scrolling at any point by pressing any key on the

Figure 9-9
*Terminal Program File
Menu*

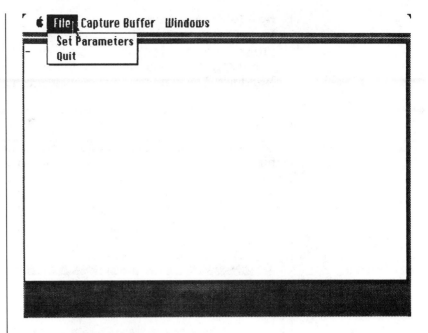

Figure 9-10
*Terminal Program
Capture Buffer Menu*

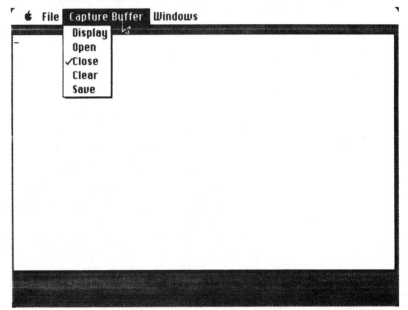

keyboard. Once paused, press any key to resume the scrolling. Figure 9-11 shows what the Capture Buffer display window looks like.

Other options in the Capture Buffer menu allow you to clear the Capture Buffer and save it to a disk file. Clear the Capture Buffer in preparation for receiving new data. The buffer can be cleared when it is open or closed. When the save option is selected, the program uses a standard FILES$ Dialog Box to prompt for a filename. The buffer contents are saved in a standard format text file. This file can be read at a later time by the program of Listing 4-11. It can also be processed by word processing programs, if desired.

Figure 9-12 shows the options in the Windows menu. At any time, the terminal windows can be set to either "Standard" or "Monitor Transmit." The current setting is indicated by a checkmark within the menu itself. In Figure 9-12, the standard window configuration is shown. Figure 9-13 shows the program screen with the Monitor Transmit option turned on. Notice the narrow window near the bottom of the screen. This window will monitor all characters transmitted from the terminal.

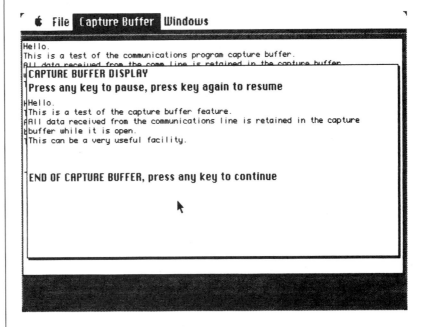

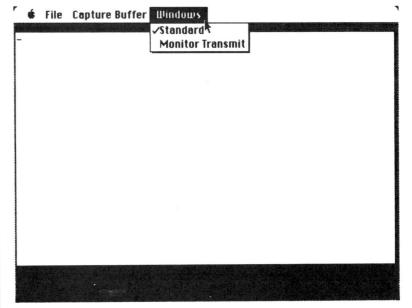

How It Works

The program begins by defining and initializing array *Parms$*. This array holds the character strings that represent each serial parameter choice available in the Set Parameters Dialog Box, shown in Figure 9-8. Its contents will be used to construct the device name modifier for the OPEN statement that accesses the serial port.

The current choices for each parameter group in the dialog box are indicated by saving the corresponding button number in a specific variable. These variables are named *Button.BR*, *Button.WL*, *Button.Par*, *Button.StB*, and *Button.DW*. They are initialized to the default settings.

Three more variables are also initialized at this time. They are *ComOpen*, which indicates whether the serial port has been opened, *BufferOpen*, which indicates the current status of the Capture Buffer, and *MT*, which indicates the current status of the Transmit Monitor window.

Figure 9-13
The Transmit Monitor Window

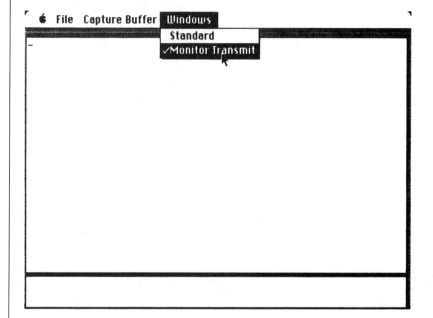

The program now proceeds to define the custom menus. Note that the default settings for Capture Buffer Open/Close and Transmit Monitor On/Off are indicated by the appropriate checkmark settings in the menu definitions. The program will use all four of the available Output windows. The main terminal display screen will be window 1; it is created at this time.

Subroutine GetParameters is now called to display and process the Set Parameters Dialog Box. This routine creates the Dialog Box as window 3. Note that a negative window type is used. This forces the user to interact with the Dialog Box before doing anything else with or to the program. The text format is set to Chicago-12 to match the format used automatically when titling the control buttons. This gives the Dialog Box a nice uniform appearance.

A series of BUTTON statements creates each of the control buttons. At program label ShowSettings, the appropriate buttons are set to the selected state, to show the current settings as per the *Button.xxx* variables. A dialog wait loop is then employed to wait until the user makes a button selection. A group of IF-THEN statements segregates each possible button selection into its proper button group, and sets the appropriate *Button.xxx* variable. In this way, only one selection within each group is possible at any time. The code at label ShowSettings always highlights the buttons corresponding to the current settings.

When the "Ok" button is clicked, the complete serial port device name is constructed from the current settings and strings extracted from the *Parms$* array. An OPEN statement prepares the port for use. The Dialog Box window is closed, and the main terminal window is made active. The Monaco font is set (necessary because it is nonproportional) so backspace over characters will work. The font size is set to 9 or 12, depending upon the display width parameter selection. Variable *w* is set to the prevailing display width. It will be used elsewhere in the program to insure that text does not extend past the right screen margin.

The program now prepares to enter its main loop. Variable *linesize* is initialized to 0; it will keep track of the total number of characters on the current line. The main program loop starts at label Again. Each time through the loop, the program checks for any user activity within the pull-down menus. Such activity is handled at label MenuFunction. I will cover that section of code in a moment. First, let us look at the code that handles the actual transmission and reception of data.

As in the previous version of this program, a WHILE-WEND loop is used to process all data received from the serial port. The incoming characters are processed one at a time, in variable *a$*. Each character is stripped of its high order bit, to insure that the program will only have to deal with pure ASCII characters. The line feed character is bypassed altogether, if and when it is received. All other characters are displayed on the main terminal screen (window number 1).

Note that the program checks to see if the current line size has reached the maximum screen width (variable *w*) before printing any character. If it has, and the character to be printed is not a carriage return, then the program forces a carriage return. This insures that text will not appear beyond the right margin of the screen, regardless of the display text size. This section of code also maintains the linesize variable as an indicator of the current number of characters on the line at all times.

A single IF-THEN statement is used to implement the capture buffer at this time. If the Capture Buffer is open (*BufferOpen* = 1), the incoming data is appended to the Capture Buffer. The Capture Buffer itself is a simple character string variable named *Buf$*; it can hold a maximum of 32767 characters.

When all incoming characters have been processed (for the current moment), the program proceeds to see if there is any data to transmit. The keyboard is checked with an INKEY$ function. Any characters typed on the keyboard are sent out over the serial port. In addition, if the Monitor Transmit window is active (*MT* = 1), these characters are displayed in that window (id number 2).

Note that the same code is employed here to insure that the right margin of the transmit monitor window is not exceeded. Variable *TMsize* is used to track the number of characters on the current line of that window. This concludes the code of the main program loop.

User activity in the pull-down menus is handled at label MenuFunction. Program flow is directed to one of three subroutines, based upon which menu was selected (variable *m*). Within each of these subroutines, a separate subroutine is called to handle each individual menu item. All menu function handlers thus return to the same point, where the menu selection in the menu bar is unhighlighted, and the program returns to the main program loop.

The File menu is used to either change the serial parameters, or quit. The serial parameter change is accomplished by simply calling upon subroutine GetParameters, which has already been described. The Quit function is handled by restoring the standard system menu bar, and terminating the program.

The Capture Buffer menu is used to perform many different functions affecting the Capture Buffer. The Open Buffer function simply sets variable BufferOpen to indicate that the buffer is open. It then sets the appropriate check marks in the menu, and returns.

The Close Buffer function operates in a similar fashion. The Clear Buffer function empties the Capture Buffer by setting it (variable *Buf$*) to a null string. The Display Buffer function is more complicated. If there is no data in the Capture Buffer, the function is ignored. Otherwise, the Capture Buffer display window (number 4) is created. The characters are extracted from *Buf$* one at a time and displayed within this window.

Once again, the code is written to insure that the specified display width is not exceeded. As each character is displayed, the program checks for a key press from the keyboard. This event is used to momentarily pause the display loop. Another key press (any key) resumes the loop. When the entire Capture Buffer has been displayed, the program waits for a key press. The Capture Buffer display window is then closed, and the main program loop is resumed.

The Save Buffer function is bypassed if invoked when the Capture Buffer is empty. Otherwise, the FILES$ function is used to present the user with a standard Macintosh file specification window. The file so specified is opened for sequential output, and the Capture Buffer contents are written to it in a single statement.

The Windows menu has only two items within it, and they represent turning the Transmit Monitor function on and off. This is reflected in status variable *MT*, as well as by check marks within the menu itself. In addition, the supporting code either creates or closes the transmit monitor window, which has id number 2.

The Check-Writing Program Revisited

Listing 9-4 contains the second version of the check-writing program, the original of which can be found in Listing 4-8. This new version utilizes a single pull-down menu for all program functions. In addition, Dialog Boxes are employed to obtain input data from the operator.

Listing 9-4
The Check Writing
Program — Version 2

```
' The previous version of this program can be found in Listing 4-8.
' This program will help you to maintain your personal check-book.
' The program allows you to add entries that represent deposits.
' You can also add entries that represent payments (checks).
' In this case, the subroutine Check.Print will be used to actually
' fill out the fields in a check on the Imagewriter printer.
' Continuous forms checks can be ordered from many sources with
' your name, your bank name and your account number pre-printed.
' You will probably have to modify the print field locations in
' subroutine Check.Print to match the specific format of the checks
' that you order.
' The check register is maintained on disk in a file named CHECKS.
' The program maintains a constantly updated balance and can produce
' a printed copy of the register at any time.
' The program allows you to set up a list of predefined accounts to which
' you often write checks. This saves time when actually using the program
' to write checks to the same payees each month. Define your payees in
' the data statements indicated below:
' You may have up to 10 predefined payee accounts:
DIM Account$(10),Accountno$(10)
Predefined=0
GetPredefined:
READ a$ 'get a predefined account name
IF a$="END" THEN GOTO EndPredefData
Predefined=Predefined+1
Account$(Predefined)=a$
READ Accountno$(Predefined)
GOTO GetPredefined
EndPredefData:
' Predefined data has been setup, variable Predefined = # of Predefined accounts
' Place your predefined account names here, two strings per account:
' The first string will be the payee name for the check, the second will be
' placed on the comment line of the check and usually set to your account
' number with that payee. Sample data follows:
DATA "ABC Telephone Company","555-1212"
DATA "HTD Power and Light","123-456789-01"
DATA "XYZ Heating Oil Co.","001-58726724"
DATA "SUPERCARD Credit Company","5123-456-7890"
DATA "Book of the Hour Club","0012233445566"
' --------end of predefined accounts data.
DATA "END"
'
DIM Numbers$(19), Numbers10$(9)
FOR i=1 TO 19
READ Numbers$(i)
NEXT
FOR i=2 TO 9
READ Numbers10$(i)
NEXT
DATA ONE,TWO,THREE,FOUR,FIVE,SIX,SEVEN,EIGHT,NINE,TEN,ELEVEN
DATA TWELVE,THIRTEEN,FOURTEEN,FIFTEEN,SIXTEEN,SEVENTEEN
DATA EIGHTEEN,NINETEEN,TWENTY,THIRTY,FOURTY,FIFTY,SIXTY
DATA SEVENTY,EIGHTY,NINETY
BalanceKnown=0 'set flag to show current balance not known yet
FileOpen=0 'set flag to show CHECKS file not open
Today$=DATE$   'Get date and reformat it to mm/dd/yy format:
Today$=LEFT$(Today$,6)+RIGHT$(Today$,2) 'remove '19' from year
MID$(Today$,3,1)="/"
MID$(Today$,6,1)="/"
'
' set up custom pull-down menu, note that this replaces the
' "main-menu" of the previous version of this program :
'
MENU 1,0,1,"Checkbook"
MENU 1,1,1,"Display Register"
MENU 1,2,1,"Print Register"
MENU 1,3,1,"Write Checks"
```

Listing 9-4—cont.

```
MENU 1,4,1,"Add Deposits"
MENU 1,5,1,"Initialize New Register"
MENU 1,6,1,"End Program"

MENU 2,0,0,""              'remove all other system menus from the menu bar
MENU 3,0,0,""
MENU 4,0,0,""
MENU 5,0,0,""
'
' define main program window :

WINDOW 1,,(2,30)-(510,330),3
CLS
PRINT "Today is ";Today$
'
Main:       'wait for the user to select a function from the pull-down menu :
m=MENU(0)
m1=MENU(1)
IF m<>1 THEN GOTO Main   'there is only one menu in this program

' branch to proper subroutine based upon menu item selected :
'
ON m1 GOSUB Rdisp,Rprint,Cwrite,Deposit,Rinit,Finish

' return to here when requested menu function is complete :
MENU                'unhighlight the menu bar
GOTO Main
'
' Display Register Function:
Rdisp:
CLS
LOCATE 1,10
PRINT "DISPLAY REGISTER"
OPEN "O",2,"SCRN:"
MergeDispPrint: 'both disp and print functions are the same from this point on
GOSUB GetStartDate
GOSUB ScanFile
IF Cdate$="" THEN PRINT "No records found for that start date" :CLOSE 2: RETURN
' display the register info:
DispAgain:
PRINT#2, STRINGS$(70,"-")
PRINT#2, TAB(35);"Balance",TAB(45);
PRINT#2, USING "$$####.##";Bal
PRINT#2, MID$(Cdate$,3,2)+"/"+MID$(Cdate$,5,2)+"/"+MID$(Cdate$,1,2),"   ";
IF Camt>0 THEN PRINT#2, "** DEPOSIT ** ";
PRINT#2, Cdesc$
IF Camt<0 THEN PRINT#2, TAB(10);"Check # ";Cno%,
PRINT#2, TAB(45);
IF Camt>0 THEN PRINT#2, USING "$$####.##";Camt ELSE PRINT#2, USING "$$####.##";-Camt
' get next record :
IF EOF(1) THEN GOTO DispEnd
INPUT#1,Cdate$,Cdesc$,Cno%,Camt,Bal
GOTO DispAgain

' End of file reached on display/print function :
DispEnd:
CLOSE 1
PRINT#2, STRINGS$(70,"-")
PRINT#2, TAB(29);"Closing Balance",TAB(45);
PRINT#2, USING "$$####.##";Bal+Camt
Balance=Bal+Camt
BalanceKnown=1 'set flag to show that the current balance is known
CLOSE 2
RETURN

' Print Register Function :
Rprint:
CLS
LOCATE 1,10
```

Listing 9-4—cont.

```
PRINT "PRINT REGISTER"
OPEN "O",2,"LPT1:"
GOTO MergeDispPrint 'both Disp and Print functions are the same
                                from this point on.
'
' Check Write Function :
Cwrite:
CLS
LOCATE 1,10
PRINT "CHECK WRITING"
IF BalanceKnown = 0 THEN GOSUB GetBalance
LOCATE 3,1
PRINT "Today is ";Today$
LOCATE 3,20
PRINT "Your current balance is ";
PRINT USING "$$#### ##";Balance
'
' create a dialog box to allow the user to select the payee account :
'
WINDOW 2,,(20,90)-(490,300),-2
'
' fill the dialog box with buttons corresponding to the predefined accounts :
'
y=20
FOR i=1 TO Predefined   'show all predefined account codes :
BUTTON i+1,1,Account$(i),(10,y)-(200,y+15),3
y=y+20
NEXT
BUTTON 1,1,"Other Account",(10,y)-(200,y+15),3
'
' wait for the user to make an account selection :
'
GOSUB DialogWait
WINDOW CLOSE 2            'remove the dialog box
IF b=1 THEN GOTO GetPayee       'must obtain payee info manually
' use a predefined account name and number for check payee :
payee$=Account$(b-1)
payee2$=Accountno$(b-1)
GOTO GetDesc
'
' create another dialog window to manually obtain the payee info :
'
GetPayee:
WINDOW 2,,(20,90)-(490,300),-2
LOCATE 2,5
PRINT "Make check payable to : "
LOCATE 5,5
PRINT "Additional text on check to read : "
EDIT FIELD 1,"",(35,33)-(250,48),1,1
EDIT FIELD 2,"",(35,83)-(250,98),1,1
EDIT FIELD 1          'start out with field 1 as the active field
BUTTON 1,1,"Ok",(300,150)-(330,180),1
'
' wait for user to fill out the requested info and click the "Ok" button :
'
GetPayee:
GOSUB DialogWait
' (no need to check return values from DialogWait, as there is only one
' button in the dialog box!)
'
payee$=EDIT$(1)
payee2$=EDIT$(2)
IF payee$="" THEN BEEP : GOTO GetPayee   'user must supply a payee name
WINDOW CLOSE 2      'remove this dialog box
'
' get any additional info to be stored with this check entry :
'
GetDesc:
WINDOW 2,,(20,90)-(490,300),-2
```

Listing 9-4—cont.

```
PRINT "Check will be made out to : ",payee$
PRINT "Additional text on check will read : ",payee2$
LOCATE 5,5
PRINT "Additional text to go in register : "
LOCATE 8,5
PRINT "Amount of check : "
EDIT FIELD 1,"",(35,83)-(250,98),1,1
EDIT FIELD 2,"",(35,133)-(250,148),1,1
EDIT FIELD 1           'start out with field 1 as the active field
BUTTON 1,1,"Ok",(300,150)-(330,180),1

GetAmt:
GOSUB DialogWait

' obtain data supplied by user in dialog box :
desc$=EDIT$(1)
Ckamt$=EDIT$(2)
CKamt=VAL(CKamt$)          'convert check amount to numeric
IF CKamt<=0 THEN BEEP : GOSUB GetAmt    'dont let user exit this dialog box
'                                until a valid check amount is supplied.

' close dialog box :
WINDOW CLOSE 2

' process check writing request :

IF Ckamt<=Balance THEN GOTO AmtOK
Question$="That will cause an overdraft, proceed anyway ?"
GOSUB GetYN
IF yn$="N" THEN PRINT "Check NOT Written" : RETURN
PRINT yn$
AmtOK:
CLS
LOCATE 1,10
PRINT "PLEASE CONFIRM"
LOCATE 3,1
PRINT Today$;" Check #";
PRINT USING "###";Cno%+1;
PRINT " to ";payee$;"   ";
PRINT USING "$$####.##";CKamt
PRINT TAB(20);payee2$;"   ";
PRINT TAB(20);desc$
PRINT
Question$="Proceed to write this check ?"
GOSUB GetYN
IF yn$="N" THEN PRINT "Check NOT Written" : RETURN

Cno%=Cno%+1
Camt=-CKamt   ' show amount as negative to indicate check and not deposit
GOSUB TextAmount  'convert CKamt to TextCKamt$

' print the check on the Imagewriter printer. the following LPRINT
' statements must be modified to conform to the specific check forms
' that you use.
LPRINT TAB(60);"No. "; 'column location for check number, upper right corner
LPRINT USING "###"; Cno%
LPRINT TAB(60);   'column location for date, beneath check number
LPRINT Today$
LPRINT
LPRINT                   'number of blank lines before payee line is reached
LPRINT TAB(5);payee$ 'column location for payee
LPRINT TAB(5);          'column location for text of amount of check
LPRINT TextCKamt$       'print out amount of check in text
LPRINT TAB(60);         'column location for check amount in numeric form
LPRINT USING "$$####.##";-Camt
LPRINT
LPRINT                   'number of blank lines before comment line is reached
LPRINT TAB(5);payee2$  'column location for comment on check
LPRINT
```

Listing 9-4—cont.

```
LPRINT
LPRINT                        'number of blank lines to top of next check form
'--------end of check printing statements that need custom modification.
'
' Now add entry to the CHECKS file for this check:
IF FileOpen=0 THEN OPEN "A",1,"CHECKS" : FileOpen=1
GOSUB SetCdate
Cdesc$=payee$+"/"+desc$
' Cno% is already set
' Camt is already set
Bal=Balance 'balance prior to this check
Balance=Balance+Camt  'keep program's balance current
WRITE#1,Cdate$,Cdesc$,Cno%,Camt,Bal 'write register record to file
'
CLOSE 1 'close CHECKS file
FileOpen=0 ' show that file not open
PRINT
PRINT "Check Written."
RETURN
'-------------End of Check Write Function.
'
' Deposit Function :
Deposit:
CLS
LOCATE 1,10
PRINT "MAKE DEPOSITS     ",Today$
WINDOW 2,,(20,90)-(490,300),-2
LOCATE 2,5
PRINT "Deposit Description : "
LOCATE 5,5
PRINT "Deposit Amount : "
EDIT FIELD 1,"",(35,33)-(250,48),1,1
EDIT FIELD 2,"",(35,83)-(250,98),1,1
EDIT FIELD 1        'start out with field 1 as the active field
BUTTON 1,1,"Ok",(300,150)-(330,180),1
'
' wait for user to fill out the requested info and click the "Ok" button :
'
GetDep:
GOSUB DialogWait
' (no need to check return values from DialogWait, as there is only one
' button in the dialog box!)
'
desc$=EDIT$(1)
DPamt$=EDIT$(2)
DPamt=VAL(DPamt$)
IF DPamt<=0 THEN BEEP : GOTO GetDep    'user must supply a valid deposit amount
WINDOW CLOSE 2        'remove this dialog box
'
PRINT
PRINT Today$;" DEPOSIT from ";desc$;"  ";
PRINT USING "$$####.##";DPamt
PRINT
Question$="Proceed to register this deposit ?"
GOSUB GetYN
IF yn$="N" THEN PRINT "DEPOSIT ABORTED" : RETURN
IF BalanceKnown=0 THEN GOSUB GetBalance
' Now add entry to the CHECKS file for this deposit:
IF FileOpen=0 THEN OPEN "A",1,"CHECKS" : FileOpen=1
GOSUB SetCdate
Cdesc$=desc$
' Cno% is already set - it remains same as last check number for deposit entries
Camt=DPamt
Bal=Balance 'balance prior to this check
Balance=Balance+Camt  'keep program's balance current
WRITE#1,Cdate$,Cdesc$,Cno%,Camt,Bal 'write register record to file
'
PRINT "Deposit Processed"
CLOSE 1 'close CHECKS file
```

Listing 9-4—cont.

```
FileOpen=0 ' show that file not open
RETURN
'--------------End of Deposit Function.
'
' Initialize CHECKS file function :
Rinit:
CLS
LOCATE 1,10
PRINT "INITIALIZE CHECK REGISTER"
LOCATE 2,1
PRINT "WARNING! - This function will destroy any previous register contents!"
PRINT "Be sure to rename the CHECKS file and obtain a printout of the current"
PRINT "register before proceeding  !!!"
PRINT
'
WINDOW 2,,(20,120)-(490,300),-2    'create dialog box window
LOCATE 2,5
PRINT "Starting Balance : "
LOCATE 5,5
PRINT "Starting Check Number : "
EDIT FIELD 1,"",(35,33)-(250,48),1,1
EDIT FIELD 2,"",(35,83)-(250,98),1,1
EDIT FIELD 1         'start out with field 1 as the active field
BUTTON 1,1,"Ok",(300,150)-(330,180),1
'
' wait for user to fill out the requested info and click the "Ok" button :
'
GetIdata:
GOSUB DialogWait
' (no need to check return values from DialogWait, as there is only one
' button in the dialog box!)
'
Camt$=EDIT$(1)
Cno$=EDIT$(2)
Camt=VAL(Camt$)
Cno%=VAL(Cno$)
IF Camt<=0 OR Cno%<=0 THEN BEEP : GOTO GetIdata   'user must supply valid data
WINDOW CLOSE 2     'remove this dialog box
'
PRINT
PRINT Today$;" Opening Balance = ";
PRINT USING "$$####.##";Camt;
PRINT "  Next Check Number will be ",Cno%
PRINT
Question$="Proceed to initialize new register ? "
GOSUB GetYN
IF yn$="N" THEN PRINT "INIT ABORTED" : RETURN
GOSUB SetCdate
Cdesc$="OPENING BALANCE"
Cno%=Cno%-1 'adjust so next check written will be correct number
' Camt is already set up
Bal=0
Balance=Camt
BalanceKnown=1
OPEN "O",1,"CHECKS"
WRITE#1,Cdate$,Cdesc$,Cno%,Camt,Bal 'write register record to file
CLOSE 1
PRINT
PRINT "INIT COMPLETED."
RETURN
'-------------------End of INIT Function.
'
' End of Program:
Finish:
MENU RESET
END
'
' Subroutine to wait for the user to press any key.
' The keystroke is returned in a$
WaitKey:
```

Listing 9-4—cont.

```
a$=INKEY$
WHILE a$=""
a$=INKEY$
WEND
RETURN
'
' Subroutine to obtain starting date for display or print functions:
' Returns value in format yymmdd in variable d$
GetStartDate:
LOCATE 3,1
GSDretry:
LINE INPUT "Enter start date as mm/dd/yy ==> ";d$
' Verify valid input:
IF LEN(d$)<>8 THEN GOTO GSDerr
IF MID$(d$,3,1)<>"/" OR MID$(d$,6,1)<>"/" THEN GOTO GSDerr
d$=MID$(d$,7,2)+MID$(d$,1,2)+MID$(d$,4,2)
RETURN
GSDerr:
PRINT "Invalid input, try again please"
GOTO GSDretry
'
' Subroutine to open the CHECKS file and scan until the date in d$
' is reached, returning with the first file record at or beyond that
' date in variables Cdate$,Cdesc$,Cno%,Camt,Bal and the file left opened
' to that position. If the date could not be found, then the file is closed
' and Cdate$ is returned as null.
ScanFile:
OPEN "I",1,"CHECKS"
ScanAgain:
IF EOF(1) THEN CLOSE 1 : Cdate$="" : RETURN
INPUT #1,Cdate$,Cdesc$,Cno%,Camt,Bal
IF Cdate$<d$ THEN GOTO ScanAgain
RETURN
'
' Subroutine to read the CHECKS file completely for the purposes of
' obtaining a current balance. The file is closed when the
' operation is complete, and the current balance is returned
' in variable Balance. In addition, the variable BalanceKnown is set
' to 1 to indicate that the current balance is now available.
GetBalance:
OPEN "I",1,"CHECKS"
WHILE NOT EOF(1)
INPUT #1,Cdate$,Cdesc$,Cno%,Camt,Bal
WEND
CLOSE 1
Balance=Bal+Camt
BalanceKnown=1
RETURN
'
' Subroutine to ask a yes or no question via a dialog box.
' The question prompt is passed to this routine in variable Question$.
' The routine returns the reply via variable yn$, which contains
' either "Y" for yes or "N" for no upon return.
GetYN:
WINDOW 2,,(130,200)-(370,300),-2
LOCATE 2,1
PRINT Question$
BUTTON 1,1,"Yes",(50,50)-(80,80),1
BUTTON 2,1,"No",(120,50)-(150,80),1
GOSUB DialogWait
IF b=1 THEN yn$="Y" ELSE yn$="N"
WINDOW CLOSE 2
RETURN
'
' Subroutine to wait for activity within a dialog box. This routine always
' waits until a control button is clicked within the active dialog box
' window, and returns the control button id in variable "b".
' While this routine is active, the user can press either the Tab or Return
' keys to switch between the two entry fields in the dialog box (if they
```

Listing 9-4—cont.

```
' are present).

DialogWait:
f=1                 'keeps track of currently selected entry field
DWait:
d=DIALOG(0)
IF d=1 THEN GOTO GetButton        'a button was clicked
IF d=6 OR d=7 THEN GOTO SwapFields 'the Tab or Return key was pressed
GOTO DWait                        'ignore all other dialog events

GetButton:
b=DIALOG(1)                       'get button id number
RETURN
'
SwapFields:               'swap active entry fields .
IF f=1 THEN f=2 ELSE f=1
EDIT FIELD f
GOTO DWait

' Subroutine to convert Today$, in the format mm/dd/yy into
' Cdate$, in the format yymmdd :
SetCdate:
Cdate$=RIGHT$(Today$,2)+LEFT$(Today$,2)+MID$(Today$,4,2)
RETURN
'
' Subroutine to convert a numeric dollar amount to a textual description
' as used on a bank check. The amount is input in variable CKamt and the
' result is returned in string variable TextCKamt$.
TextAmount:
TextCKamt$=""
IF CKamt>.99 THEN GOTO NotNoDollars
TextCKamt$="NO DOLLARS AND "+STR$(CKamt*100)+" CENTS"
RETURN
NotNoDollars:
IF CKamt<1000 THEN GOTO NoThousands
amt=FIX(CKamt/1000)
CKamt=Ckamt-amt*1000
GOSUB Textamt
TextCKamt$=Textamt$+" THOUSAND "
NoThousands:
IF CKamt<100 THEN GOTO NoHundreds
amt=FIX(CKamt/100)
CKamt=CKamt-amt*100
GOSUB Textamt
TextCKamt$=TextCKamt$+Textamt$+" HUNDRED "
NoHundreds:
amt=FIX(CKamt) 'remove any cents
CKamt=Ckamt-amt 'isolate just the cents
GOSUB Textamt
TextCKamt$=TextCKamt$+Textamt$+" DOLLARS "
IF CKamt=0 THEN TextCKamt$=TextCKamt$+"AND NO CENTS" : RETURN
TextCKamt$=TextCKamt$+" AND "+STR$(CINT(Ckamt*100))+" CENTS"
RETURN
'
' Subroutine to convert a value from 0-99 in variable amt into a textual
' description of that amount in variable Textamt$
Textamt:
IF amt=0 THEN Textamt$="" : RETURN
IF amt<20 THEN Textamt$=Numbers$(amt) : RETURN
amt10=FIX(amt/10) 'get tens digit of number
amt=amt-amt10*10
Textamt$=Numbers10$(amt10) 'tens digit in text
IF amt=0 THEN RETURN
Textamt$=Textamt$+" "+Numbers$(amt) 'append ones digit in text
RETURN
```

When executed, this program displays a predominantly blank
screen on which the current date is displayed. The single menu on

display in the menu bar is titled "Checkbook" (Figure 9-14). Compare this pull-down menu to the full screen program menu shown in Figure 4-11. This program is an excellent example of how a program with conventional user interfaces may be modified to support the Macintosh user interface.

Figure 9-14
Check Writing Program
Menu

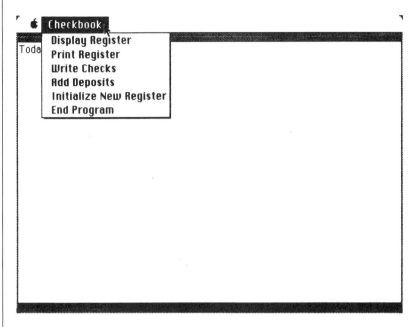

The program uses an interesting approach to window management. The activites of each function are displayed in the Main window, seen behind the menu in Figure 9-14. Whenever input is needed from the operator, however, a Dialog Box window is displayed in front of the Main window. Through careful placement of this secondary Dialog Box window, the information in the Main window pertaining to the function in progress is never obscured. In this way, we avoid the need to program a complex and unwieldy Window Refresh function.

You may begin using the new program by selecting the Initialize New Register function. See Figure 9-15. A Dialog Box allows you to supply a starting balance and check number. Click the "Ok" button when the data has been supplied. Figure 9-16 shows the result if we supply a starting balance of $1000 and a starting check number of 100. Note the way the Dialog Box is always displayed below the pertinent information in the Main window.

At this point, we are being asked to confirm the function. Figure 9-17 shows the display after you click the "Yes" button. Note that the Main window still displays the information relating to the last function performed, but the Checkbook menu is now available. Thus, we can go on to a different program function while still viewing the results of the last function performed.

In a similar fashion, a display or printout of the checkbook register can be requested. These functions work much as they did in the original version of the program. In Figure 9-18, the Check Writing function has been requested. The Main window displays the date and current balance. The Dialog Box displays my

Figure 9-15
The Initialize Function

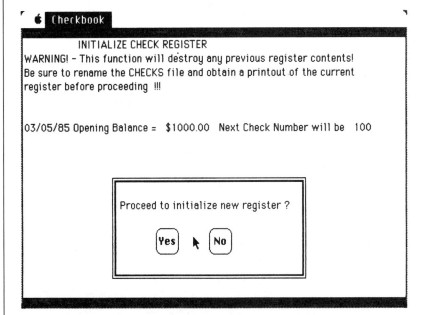

Figure 9-16
*Initialize Function
Confirmation*

predefined payee accounts. To select an account, simply click the appropriate control button. The "Other Account" button allows you to manually enter a payee.

In Figure 9-19, the SUPERCARD payee account has been selected, and we are being asked for additional descriptive text for the register, as well as a check amount. Enter this information and press the "Ok" button. The screen results are shown in Figure 9-20. By clicking the "Yes" button, a request is made that the check be written (printed on the Imagewriter) and entered into my register. The "Add Deposits" function works in a similar fashion.

Much of this program is unchanged from its original version, so I will only concentrate on those portions that are new. After the bulk of the program is initialized, a set of MENU statements is employed

Figure 9-17
*Initialize Function
Completed*

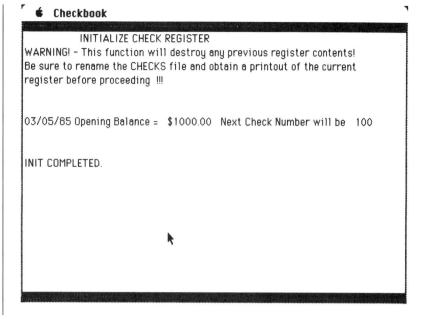

```
🍎  Checkbook

              INITIALIZE CHECK REGISTER
WARNING! – This function will destroy any previous register contents!
Be sure to rename the CHECKS file and obtain a printout of the current
register before proceeding  !!!


03/05/85 Opening Balance =   $1000.00   Next Check Number will be   100


INIT COMPLETED.
```

Figure 9-18
*Selecting a Payee
Account*

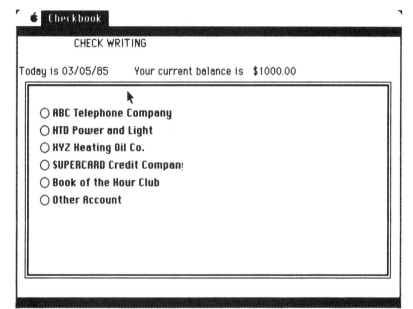

```
🍎  Checkbook

              CHECK WRITING

Today is 03/05/85       Your current balance is   $1000.00

    ┌─────────────────────────────────────────────┐
    │                                              │
    │   ○ ABC Telephone Company                    │
    │   ○ HTD Power and Light                      │
    │   ○ XYZ Heating Oil Co.                       │
    │   ○ SUPERCARD Credit Compan¦                 │
    │   ○ Book of the Hour Club                    │
    │   ○ Other Account                            │
    │                                              │
    └─────────────────────────────────────────────┘
```

to create the Checkbook menu and to remove the other standard menus from the menu bar. The Main Display window, id number 1, is then created.

The main program loop consists of a menu wait loop. The program remains in this wait loop until the user selects a function from the pull-down menu. Since there is only one menu, it is a simple matter to transfer control to the appropriate routine based upon the item selection (variable *mi*).

Each function handler is written as a subroutine, so that they will all return to the same point in the code. This is where the menu bar selection is unhighlighted, and the main menu wait loop is resumed. The display and print functions are essentially unchanged from the original version.

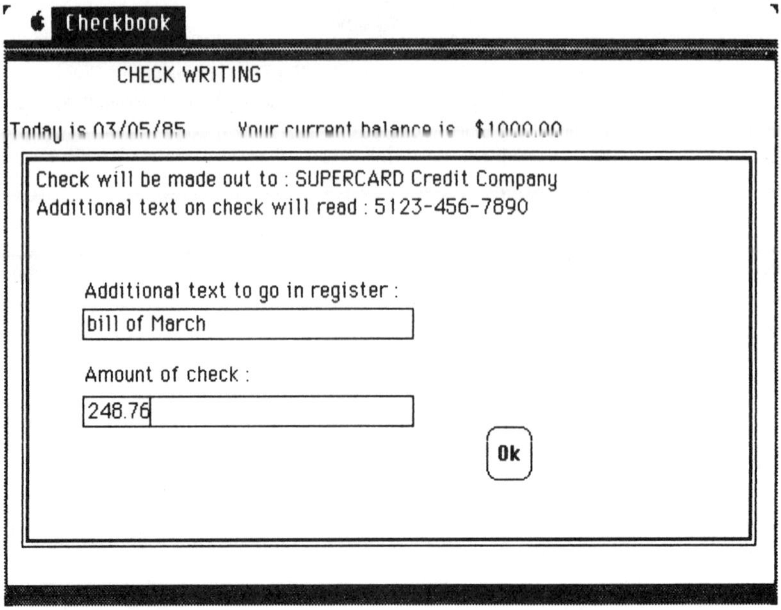

Figure 9-19
*Supplying the Check
Amount*

Figure 9-19 caption (left margin): *Supplying the Check Amount*

```
 ┌ ⚫ Checkbook ──────────────────────────────────────────┐

          CHECK WRITING

 Today is 03/05/85     Your current balance is  $1000.00

   ┌──────────────────────────────────────────────────┐
   │ Check will be made out to : SUPERCARD Credit Company │
   │ Additional text on check will read : 5123-456-7890  │
   │                                                      │
   │                                                      │
   │     Additional text to go in register :              │
   │     ┌──────────────────────────────────┐            │
   │     │ bill of March                    │            │
   │     └──────────────────────────────────┘            │
   │     Amount of check :                                │
   │     ┌──────────────────────────────────┐    ┌────┐  │
   │     │ 248.76                           │    │ Ok │  │
   │     └──────────────────────────────────┘    └────┘  │
   │                                                      │
   └──────────────────────────────────────────────────┘
```

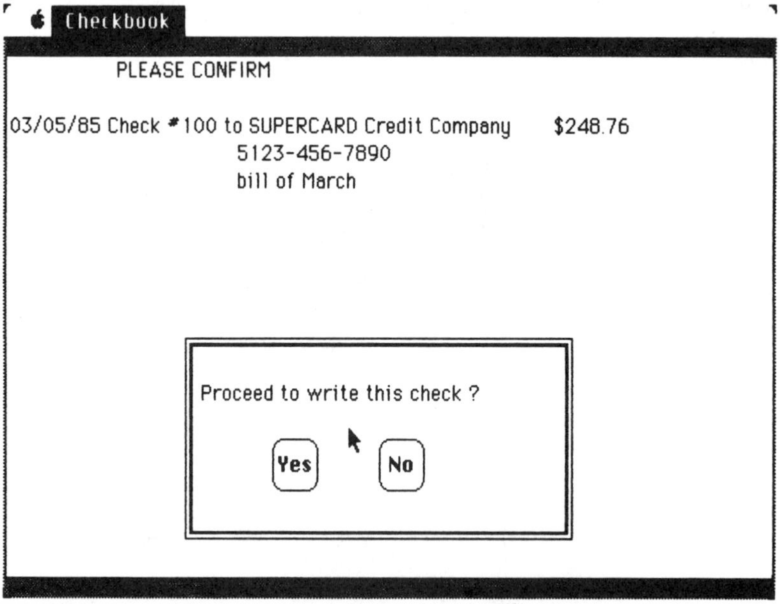

Figure 9-20
*Check Writing
Confirmation*

Figure 9-20 caption (left margin): *Check Writing Confirmation*

```
 ┌ ⚫ Checkbook ──────────────────────────────────────────┐

          PLEASE CONFIRM

 03/05/85 Check #100 to SUPERCARD Credit Company    $248.76
                    5123-456-7890
                    bill of March


              ┌─────────────────────────────┐
              │ Proceed to write this check ?│
              │                              │
              │  ┌─────┐        ┌─────┐      │
              │  │ Yes │        │ No  │      │
              │  └─────┘        └─────┘      │
              └─────────────────────────────┘
```

The Check Write function obtains the current balance and
displays it along with the current date in the Main window. A
secondary Dialog Box window is then created on top of the Main
window. A FOR-NEXT loop is used to go through each predefined
payee account in the *Account$* array. For each account, a control
button is created in the Dialog Box. The control button id numbers
are one greater than the actual *Account$* array subscript. This is
because button id 1 is being reserved for the "Other Account"
selection.

Subroutine DialogWait is called to wait for the user to make a
control button selection. This is a general purpose routine that will
be described in more detail later. For now, it is sufficient to note
that it will return with variable *b* containing the button id number

that was selected. The dialog box is removed as soon as the routine returns.

For button ids greater than 1, the appropriate payee name and account number are extracted from the *Account$* and *Acountno$* arrays. Otherwise, the program creates another Dialog Box, used to manually obtain the payee data. There are two data entry fields in this Dialog Box, and a single "Ok" control button.

Once again, routine DialogWait is used to wait until the control button is clicked. Take a moment and study the DialogWait routine. Note that it assumes there are two entry fields in the active window, and it allows the user to switch between these two fields by pressing either the <Tab> or <Return> keys.

This routine can be called from many places within this program, because all Dialog Boxes with entry fields always have exactly two such fields. When the routine returns, the EDIT$ function is used to obtain the data supplied by the user in the entry fields. In this case, the program checks to be sure that the user entered some data for the payee field, otherwise it beeps and waits once again. When acceptable data has been supplied, the Dialog Box window is closed (removed from the screen), and the program continues.

The Check Write function now puts up yet another Dialog Box, this time to obtain additional register data and a check amount. The same technique is employed to obtain this data. Once again, the program does not allow the user to proceed until valid data has been supplied. The program code that follows is essentially unchanged from the original version.

As you may recall, in the original version the prompt for "Proceed to write this check" was processed by a subroutine called GetYN. This routine waited until the user pressed either the <Y> or the <N> keys. In this version of the program, I have rewritten the routine to present the Yes/No Dialog Box seen in Figures 9-16 and 9-20.

By keeping the input and output requirements of the routine similar to the original version, the amount of code that needs to be rewritten has been minimized. The routine still returns the user's answer in character string *yn$*, as either "Y" or "N."

The way the user supplies a response is quite different and more in keeping with the Macintosh philosophy. The routine now also accepts an input variable, *Question$*. This variable contains the prompt to be displayed within the Yes/No Dialog Box.

In a similar fashion, the Add Deposits and Initialize New Register functions have been modified to use Dialog Boxes to obtain user input. Note that the general-purpose subroutine DialogWait can be used by each of these functions because they all create Dialog Boxes with exactly two data entry fields. If the number of data entry fields were variable, the program would be considerably more complex. In this case, the DialogWait loop would have to be custom coded each time it was used.

I recommend that you study this program carefully and compare it to the original on which it is based. This will give you many insights into how to convert conventional software so that it conforms to the Macintosh standards for user interfaces.

The Appointment Calendar Program — Version 3

Finally, I would like to introduce yet another version of the appointment calendar program. In this final version, the program can be operated completely by mouse action and is a lot of fun to use. Previous versions of this program can be found in Listings 4-10 and 7-21.

The latest version, introduced in Chapter 7, used the mouse to make date selections. This was done without Dialog Box techniques. In the new version, I have added such Dialog Boxes to manipulate the actual appointments made for a specific date.

The new version of the program can be found in Listing 9-5. If this is the first time you are using this program, you must first create the CALENDAR file by running the program shown in Listing 4-9. When executed, the program produces a screen display similar to that in Figure 9-21.

Listing 9-5
The Appointment Calendar Program — Version 3

```
' Previous versions of this program can be found in Listings 4-10 and 7-21.
' This version of the program displays a graphic image of a monthly
' calendar and allows the user to use the mouse to select a date within
' it. The user can delete appointments easily by simply clicking
' control buttons. Dialog box entry fields are employed to help the
' user enter new appointments.
'
DIM Deletions(20)   'array identifies appointment numbers to be deleted
Dmonth%=1       'default display month is Jan
DIM Rect%(3)    'holds rectangle definitions for toolbox calls
Today$=DATE$  'Get date and reformat it to mm/dd/yy format:
Today$=LEFT$(Today$,6)+RIGHT$(Today$,2) 'remove '19' from year
MID$(Today$,3,1)="/"
MID$(Today$,6,1)="/"
Tmonth%=VAL(LEFT$(Today$,2))
Tday%=VAL(MID$(Today$,4,2))
Tyear%=VAL(RIGHT$(Today$,2))
' Initialize array data:
DIM MonthDays%(12)
FOR x%=1 TO 12
READ MonthDays%(x%)
NEXT
DATA 31,28,31,30,31,30,31,31,30,31,30,31
'
' Determine the starting day of the week for the current year, save
' it in variable NewYearsDay% :
CALL StartDay(1,Tyear%,NewYearsDay%,Days%)
' Set up month of February for the current year :
IF (Tyear%-84) MOD 4 = 0 THEN MonthDays%(2)=29 ELSE MonthDays%(2)=28 'Leap Years
CALL DayofWeek(Tmonth%,Tday%,Tdayw%,Tjday%)
'
DIM DayNames$(7)
FOR x%=1 TO 7
READ DayNames$(x%)
NEXT
DATA Sunday,Monday,Tuesday,Wednesday,Thursday,Friday,Saturday
DIM MonthNames$(12)
FOR x%=1 TO 12
READ MonthNames$(x%)
NEXT
DATA January, February,March,April,May,June,July,August,September
DATA October,November,December
' Set up a complete textual description of the current date :
Tdate$=DayNames$(Tdayw%)+" "+MonthNames$(Tmonth%)+" "+STR$(Tday%)
Tdate$=Tdate$+", 19"+RIGHT$(Today$,2)+"   (Day #"+STR$(Tjday%)+")"
'
' set up program menu bar :
```

Listing 9-5—cont.

```
         MENU 1,0,1,"File"          'the file menu is used simply to terminate
         MENU 1,1,1,"Quit"
         MENU 2,0,0,""              'all other system menus are not used
         MENU 3,0,0,""
         MENU 4,0,0,""
         MENU 5,0,0,""

         ' set up main program window :

         WINDOW 1,,(2,24)-(508,334),4

         ' set up to handle the Quit menu selection as an interrupt :
         ' (this way, the user can exit the program at any time)

         ON MENU GOSUB Menu.Int
         MENU ON

         ' Prepare for access to random file CALENDAR :
         OPEN "R",1,"CALENDAR",42
         FIELD 1, 40 AS Appoint$, 2 AS Link$
         HighestRecord%=LOF(1)/42   'current highest record number in the file

         ' let the user select a date from the calendar image :

         MainScreen:
         GOSUB GetDate  'get date from user via mouse selection

         CLS
         ' determine day of week and julian day # for selected date :
         CALL DayofWeek(Month%,Day%,Dayw%,Jday%)
         ' display the selected date nicely :
         PRINT DayNames$(Dayw%)+" "+MonthNames$(Month%)+" "+STR$(Day%)
         ' search CALENDAR file for appointments for selected date :
         ' ( the initial record number to read is the julian date, Jday% )
         GET 1,Jday%
         Link%=CVI(Link$)
         IF LEFT$(Appoint$,1)="@" AND Link%=0 THEN HighButton=2: GOTO PushButton

         ' display each appointment in the chain as a control button :
         ' (the control button id number is two more than the "appointment number")
         Apno=1 'number each appointment starting with 1
         Apno.fix=0  'handles case where appoint#1 was deleted but appoint#2 exists
         y=20        'starting y-coord for control button
         FollowChain:
         IF LEFT$(Appoint$,1)<>"@" THEN BUTTON Apno+2,1,Appoint$,(10,y)-(280,y+15),2 : Apno=Apno+1 : y
         =y+20 ELSE Apno.fix=1 '
         IF Link%=0 THEN GOTO EndofChain
         GET 1,Link%
         Link%=CVI(Link$)
         GOTO FollowChain
         EndofChain:
         HighButton=Apno+1    'highest button number used

         ' display the rest of the dialog box control buttons :

         PushButton:
         BUTTON 1,1,"Delete Checked Items/Exit",(300,20)-(490,35),1
         BUTTON 2,1,"Add Appointment",(300,40)-(490,55),1

         ' create the dialog box entry field for any new appointments to be added :

         CALL MOVETO(300,75)
         PRINT "New Appointment text : "
         EDIT FIELD 1,"",(300,80)-(490,95),1,1

         ' the Deletions array will indicate which control buttons have been
         ' checked indicating appointments to be deleted. It is initialized
         ' at this point to show that, at the outset, no appointments are scheduled
```

365 *Custom Pull-Down Menus*

Listing 9-5—cont.

```
' for deletion.
FOR i=1 TO 20
Deletions(i)=0
NEXT

' wait for the user to make a button selection :

DialogWait:
d=DIALOG(0)
IF d<>1 THEN GOTO DialogWait   'ignore all but button click events
b=DIALOG(1)                    'get button id that was clicked
IF b<3 THEN GOTO FunctionRequest   'branch if an action is to be taken
' an appointment button was clicked :
' toggle the selected state of the clicked button, and track its state in the
' Deletions array :
IF Deletions(b-2)=0 THEN Deletions(b-2)=1 ELSE Deletions(b-2)=0
IF Deletions(b-2)=0 THEN BUTTON b,1 ELSE BUTTON b,2
GOTO DialogWait   'wait for an action request

' a button was clicked indicating an action is to be taken :
FunctionRequest:
IF b=2 THEN GOTO AddAppoint
' come here if the "Delete" button was clicked .
' delete all appointments indicated in the Deletions array .
FOR i=20 TO 1 STEP -1
IF Deletions(i)=1 THEN Dapno=i : GOSUB AppointDelete
NEXT

' function completed : remove the dialog box items and redraw the main
' calendar screen :

RemoveDialog:
FOR i=1 TO HighButton   'remove all control buttons
BUTTON CLOSE i
NEXT
EDIT FIELD CLOSE 1          'remove the entry field
GOTO MainScreen

' user requested the add appointment function :

AddAppoint:
Apdesc$=EDIT$(1)         'get the data supplied to the entry field
IF Apdesc$="" THEN BEEP : GOTO DialogWait   'no appointment supplied yet
' search CALENDAR file for appointments for selected date :
' ( the initial record number to read is the julian date, Jday% )
GET 1,Jday%
Link%=CVI(Link$)
PrevLink%=Jday%
IF LEFT$(Appoint$,1)="@" AND Link%=0 THEN LSET Appoint$=Apdesc$ : PUT 1,Jday% : GOTO Appoin
tmentMade
WHILE Link%<>0
GET 1,Link%
PrevLink%=Link%
Link%=CVI(Link$)
WEND
' found end of chain, allocate and insert a new record at PrevLink%
GET 1,367   'get start of free record chain
NextFreeLink%=CVI(Link$)
IF NextFreeLink%>HighestRecord% THEN LSET Link$=MKI$(NextFreeLink%+1) : HighestRecord%=High
estRecord%+1 : GOTO AllocateNextFree
GET 1,NextFreeLink%   'get the link to the next free record available
AllocateNextFree:
PUT 1,367   'setup the new start of the free chain
GET 1,PrevLink%   'get previously last record for appointment date chain
LSET Link$=MKI$(NextFreeLink%) 'attach the new record to the end of the chain
PUT 1,PrevLink%
LSET Appoint$=Apdesc$ 'set up the new appointment record
LSET Link$=MKI$(0)   'end of chain indicator for appointment date chain
PUT 1,NextFreeLink%  'write the new appointment record
```

Listing 9-5—cont.

```
' the appointment has been added.
AppointmentMade:
GOTO RemoveDialog

' End of Program : (come here when the custom pull-down menu item,
' there is only one, is selected) :

Menu.Int:
CLOSE 1              'close the CALENDAR file
WINDOW CLOSE 1    'remove the output window
MENU RESET         'restore the standard menu bar
END                'terminate the program

' Subroutine to delete the appointment number defined by Dapno :
AppointDelete:
Dapno=Dapno+Apno.fix 'handles case where appoint#1 was deleted but appoint#2 exists
' Delete the selected appointment entry from the calendar :
IF Dapno>1 THEN GOTO DeChain 'all entries except the 1st must be returned to the free chain
GET 1,Jday%
LSET Appoint$="@"
PUT 1,Jday%
GOTO DeletedIt
DeChain:   'find the entry to be deleted and break it out of the chain :
GET 1,Jday%            'start at the head of the chain
Link%=Jday%
Apno=1                 'keep track of the position number (appointment #)
WHILE Apno+1 <> Dapno
Link%=CVI(Link$)
GET 1,Link%            'chain forward and keep looking for it
Apno=Apno+1
WEND
' Now Link% = the record preceding the record to be deleted :
PreLink%=Link%
Link%=CVI(Link$)
GET 1,Link%      'get the record to be deleted
DelLink%=Link%   'the record # to be returned to the free chain
Link%=CVI(Link$)   'Link% = the next entry after the one to be deleted
GET 1,PreLink%   'get the preceding record
LSET Link$=MKI$(Link%) 'connect it to the entry following the deleted one
PUT 1,PreLink%   'this effectively disconnects the deleted entry from the
                      current appointment chain.
' Now put the deleted entry on the free record chain:
GET 1,367        'get pointer to start of free chain
NextFreeLink%=CVI(Link$)
LSET Link$=MKI$(DelLink%)   'make the deleted entry the first on the free chain
PUT 1,367
GET 1,DelLink%    'get the deleted entry
LSET Link$=MKI$(NextFreeLink%) 'attach the rest of the free chain to it
PUT 1,DelLink%
' Deletion process complete.
DeletedIt:
RETURN

' Subroutine to obtain the date from the user.
' Returns selected month in Month% and day in Day%
' In this version of the program, this routine displays
' a graphics image of a calendar and to allows the user to select the date
' via mouse clicks on this graphics image.
GetDate:
CLS
CALL TEXTFONT(1)            'set Geneva font
CALL TEXTSIZE(12)
LOCATE 1,27
PRINT "19",RIGHT$(Today$,2)
'MonthDays%(Month%)
CALL TEXTFONT(0)         'set Chicago font
CALL TEXTSIZE(12)

' Display the 12 month selection boxes :
```

Listing 9-5—cont.

```
    Xc%=10                          'starting x-coordinate
    FOR i%=1 TO 12
    CALL MOVETO(Xc%+2,35)
    PRINT LEFT$(MonthNames$(i%),3);
    LINE (Xc%,20)-(Xc%+30,40),,B
    Xc%=Xc%+40
    NEXT

    ' highlight currently selected month box :

    Xc%=10+40*(Dmonth%-1) 'starting x-coord for box for currently selected month
    Rect%(0)=20
    Rect%(1)=Xc%
    Rect%(2)=41
    Rect%(3)=Xc%+31
    CALL INVERTRECT(VARPTR(Rect%(0)))

    ' Now display month calendar for selected month, Dmonth%

    CALL StartDay(Dmonth%,Tyear%,Fday%,Days%) 'get starting day of week, and
    '                               number of days for currently selected month

    Xc%=35
    FOR i=1 TO 7                     'display day name titles for calendar
    CALL MOVETO(Xc%,80)
    PRINT LEFT$(DayNames$(i),3);
    Xc%=Xc%+60
    NEXT

    ' display day numbers in correct calendar positions for each day on month :
    '
    Yc%=110                         'starting y-coord for first row in calendar
    Cday%=Fday%                     'set init current day number (1-7)
    FOR Nday%=1 TO Days%
    Xc%=35+60*(Cday%-1)             'set x-coord as per current day number
    CALL MOVETO(Xc%,Yc%)
    PRINT USING "##";Nday%;
    Cday%=Cday%+1                   'go on to next day of week (current day number)
    IF Cday%>7 THEN Cday%=1 : Yc%=Yc%+30   'wrap from Saturday to Sunday
    NEXT

    FOR x=20 TO 440 STEP 60         'draw vertical lines of calendar
    LINE (x,60)-(x,270)
    NEXT
    FOR y=60 TO 270 STEP 30         'draw horizontal lines of calendar
    LINE (20,y)-(440,y)
    NEXT

    ' Calendar image complete, now wait for user to make selection via mouse :

    Swait:
    CALL SHOWCURSOR              ' make sure the mouse pointer is visible
    GOSUB WaitMouse
    IF y<20 THEN BEEP : GOTO Swait       'clicked in invalid area
    IF y>40 THEN GOTO DayCheck           'check for click in calendar area

    ' click was within month selection area :

    IF x<10 OR x>480 THEN BEEP : GOTO Swait   'invalid area
    Dm%=1+((x-10)\40)   'convert x-coord to month number (1-12)
    IF (x-10) MOD 40 > 30 THEN BEEP : GOTO Swait   'between month boxes
    IF Dm%=Dmonth% THEN GOTO Swait 'ignore change of month to same month !
    Dmonth%=Dm%             'change to newly selected month
    GOTO GetDate                    'draw new calendar image

    ' click was within day selection area :

    DayCheck:
```

Listing 9-5—cont.

```
IF x<20 OR x>440 THEN BEEP : GOTO Swait        'invalid area
IF y<90 OR y>270 THEN BEEP : GOTO Swait         'invalid area
y=1+(y-90)\30    'convert y into calendar row number (1-6)
x=1+(x-20)\60    'convert x into calendar column number (1-7)
IF y=1 AND x<Fday% THEN BEEP : GOTO Swait 'before first day on first row
IF y=1 THEN Day%=1+x-Fday% : GOTO DateSelected
Day%=1+x-Fday% + (7*(y-1))  'day number for any selection on row 2 or below
IF Day%>Days% THEN BEEP : GOTO Swait     'after last day on last row
'
' A valid date has been selected :
'
DateSelected:
Rect%(0)=90+(y-1)*30    ' invert selected date rectangle on screen :
Rect%(1)=20+(x-1)*60
Rect%(2)=Rect%(0)+30
Rect%(3)=Rect%(1)+60
CALL INVERTRECT(VARPTR(Rect%(0)))
Month%=Dmonth%
'
' restore conditions for original part of the program to continue :
'
CALL TEXTFONT(1)              'set Geneva font
CALL TEXTSIZE(12)
LOCATE 18,1
RETURN

END
' Subroutine to wait until the user clicks the mouse button, returns
' the mouse pointer coordinates at the time of the click in variables x and y.
WaitMouse:
b=MOUSE(0)
IF b<>1 THEN GOTO WaitMouse
x=MOUSE(3)
y=MOUSE(4)
RETURN
'
' Subprogram StartDay
' Finds the starting day of the week for a given month and year.
' Call StartDay(Month%,Year%,Day%,Days%)
' with Month% = 1(Jan), 2(Feb), ..., 12(Dec)
' and Year% = 85, 86, ..., 99 (valid for 1985 thru 1999)
' Returns with Day% = 1 (Sun), 2 (Mon), 3 (Tue), ..., 7 (Sat)
' and with Days% = number of days in that month.
SUB StartDay (m%,y%,d%,ds%) STATIC
SHARED MonthDays%()
d%=3 'Jan 85 starts with Tuesday
m1%=1 'start at Jan
y1%=85 'start at 1985
StartDayLoop2:
IF (y1%-84) MOD 4 = 0 THEN MonthDays%(2)=29 ELSE MonthDays%(2)=28 'Leap Years
StartDayLoop1:
IF m1%=m% AND y1%=y% THEN GOTO FoundStartDay
d%=d%+MonthDays%(m1%)
IF m1%<12 THEN  m1%=m1%+1 : GOTO StartDayLoop1
m1%=1
y1%=y1%+1
GOTO StartDayLoop2
FoundStartDay:
d%=d% MOD 7
IF d%=0 THEN d%=7
ds%=MonthDays%(m1%)
END SUB
'
' Subprogram DayofWeek
' Call DayofWeek(month%,day%,dayw%,jday%)
' Variables month% and day% are inputs to this routine.
' Variables dayw% and jday% are outputs from this routine.
' This routine takes a month (1-12) and a day (1-31) and
```

Listing 9-5—cont.

```
' returns a day of the week (1(Sun), 2(Mon), ..., 7(Sat)) and
' a julian day (1-366). The current year (Tyear%) is assumed.
SUB DayofWeek(m%,d%,dw%,jd%) STATIC
SHARED MonthDays%(),NewYearsDay%
dw%=NewYearsDay%
jd%=1
m1%=1
WHILE m1%<m%  'Accumulate days for each full month prior to desired month :
dw%=dw%+MonthDays%(m1%)
jd%=jd%+MonthDays%(m1%)
m1%=m1%+1
WEND
' Now in desired month, find desired day :
dw%=dw%+d%-1
jd%=jd%+d%-1
' Adjust day of week to range 1 - 7 :
dw%=dw% MOD 7
IF dw%=0 THEN dw%=7
END SUB
```

Figure 9-21
*Appointment Calendar
Program Initial Screen*

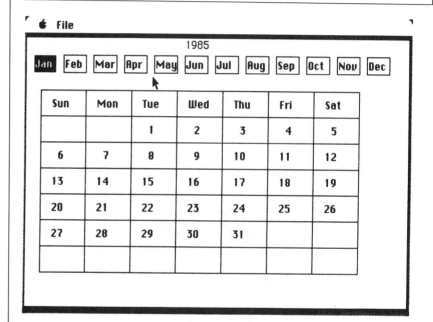

The File menu shown in the menu bar has only one function within it, the Quit function, which is used to terminate the program. All other program activities are initiated by selecting a date from the calendar with the mouse. In Figure 9-22, I have selected the date June 2nd from the calendar. The calendar image has been replaced by a new screen showing all appointments for that date. Each appointment has a control button associated with it.

You can delete any scheduled appointments by clicking on the corresponding control buttons. In Figure 9-23, the second and third appointments are marked for deletion. They can be deleted by clicking the "Delete Checked Items/Exit" control button on the right side of the screen. If no appointments are marked for deletion, then clicking this control button simply returns you to the calendar display screen.

This same appointment display screen can be used to add additional appointments to the indicated date. To do so, fill in the "New Appointment Text" entry field with the desired information, and then click the "Add Appointment" control button.

Figure 9-22
Appointment Display

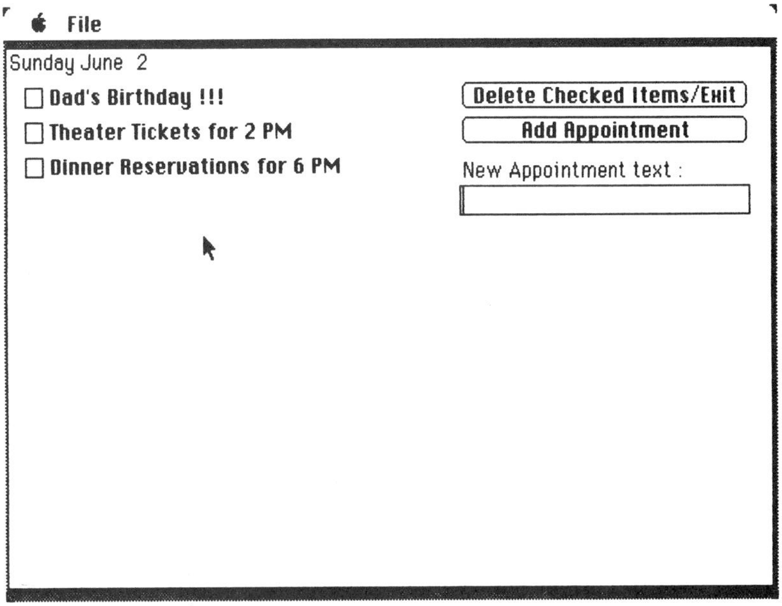

Figure 9-23
Marking Appointments for Deletion

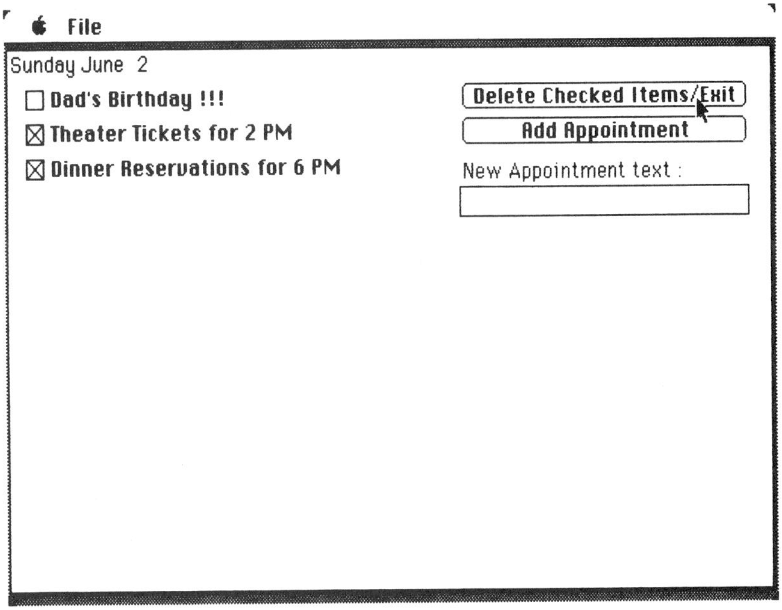

In Figure 9-24, this feature has been used to supply an additional appointment for this date, and can be executed by clicking the "Add Appointments" button. When either the Add or the Delete button is clicked, the program always returns to the main calendar display screen. To return to that screen without making any changes, simply insure that no existing appointments are marked for deletion, and then click the Delete/Exit button. To terminate the program, select Quit from the File menu.

Figure 9-24
Adding Appointments

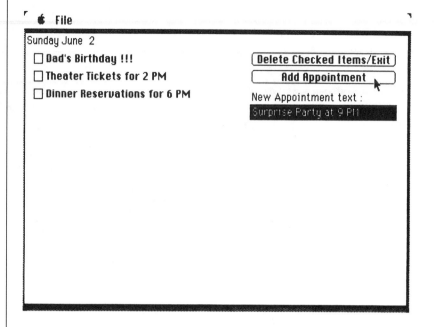

Much of this program is unchanged from the previous version. I will cover only the new and changed portions at this time. The program uses only one window and simply creates and removes dialog box items from that window as needed.

At the very beginning of the program, a new array, named *Deletions*, is defined. This array keeps track of any appointments marked for deletion on the appointment display screen, as in Figure 9-23. The rest of the program initialization code is unchanged. The simple File menu is set up and all other standard menus are removed.

The Main window is created using a WINDOW statement. A Menu Interrupt service subroutine is set up. In this way, the user can select Quit from the File menu at any time to exit from the program. The interrupt is serviced by subroutine Menu.Int.

The random file CALENDAR is opened and fielded. The main program loop begins at label MainScreen. Here, subroutine GetDate is used to present the graphic image of the calendar and let the user select a month and day. This routine was discussed in detail in Chapter 7. The routine returns when the user has clicked in a day square of the calendar, and variables *Month%* and *Day%* indicate the selected date.

At this point, the screen is cleared. The entire Main window is now turned into a Dialog Box that performs the functions of the appointment display screen. Id numbers 1 and 2 are assigned to the Delete/Exit and Add control buttons, respectively.

The loop that tracks the appointment chain in the calendar file displays each appointment as a type 2 control button. These are assigned button id numbers starting with 2. Variable *HighButton* keeps track of the highest button id number used; it will be needed when the buttons are removed later.

The new appointment data entry field is set up at this time. Each element in the Deletions array is initialized to 0. These elements will correspond to the checked or unchecked state of the appointment control buttons.

A DialogWait loop is now entered. Only button selection events are recognized. If either button 1 or button 2 is clicked, then the program must perform the requested action, and control is transferred to label FunctionRequest. Any other button click represents an appointment selection. This is handled by checking the corresponding entry in Deletions to determine the current state of the button (initially, they are all in the unchecked state). The state of the button that was clicked is toggled from checked to unchecked, or vice versa. This fact is reflected on the screen by changing the affected button's status, as well as in the Deletions array. Note that the Deletion array subscript is two less than the actual button id number; button ids 1 and 2 were specially reserved.

The program remains in this basic loop until either button 1 or button 2 is clicked. At label FunctionRequest, the two cases are separated. The Add button is handled by branching to label AddAppoint. The Delete button is handled by running through each element of Deletions in a simple FOR-NEXT loop.

For each element that contains a 1 (indicating that the corresponding button was checked), the AppointDelete subroutine is called. This routine performs the appointment deletion function and was extracted essentially unchanged from the previous version of the program. It accepts as input the variable *Dapno* as an indication of which appointment to delete. Note that the appointments are deleted in reverse order, with the highest appointment number deleted first.

The program must work in this order. If it started with the lower numbered appointments, then each deletion action would cause the remaining appointments to be renumbered. Thus the remaining appointment numbers scheduled for deletion would no longer correspond to the appropriate appointments in the chain. When all the appointments scheduled to be deleted are deleted, the program reaches label RemoveDialog. Here, all of the control buttons are removed from the screen, as well as the entry field. The screen can now be cleared, and the program can redraw the main calendar display.

The Add Appointments function is handled at label AddAppoint. The appointment text to be added is obtained from the data entry field via an EDIT$ statement. Note that the program checks for some valid data here, and beeps if it is not present. The rest of the add function is essentially unchanged from the previous version of the program. When the function is complete, a branch to label RemoveDialog cleans up the screen and allows an orderly return to the main calendar display screen.

Summary

The example programs in this chapter employ many of the techniques introduced earlier for producing Macintosh applications. They are intended to give you a head start toward developing your own programs. You can combine different techniques in different ways and also develop your own. The mouse, windows, Dialog Boxes, and pull-down menus go a long way toward providing a user-friendly environment. But never forget that other users may be unfamiliar with many standard Macintosh operations. Try to design your programs to be understandable to them as well.

Index

☐ INTRODUCING THE APPLE MACINTOSH™

Introduces you to the design philosophy and physical structure of the Macintosh, and explores its displays, keyboard, mouse, software, and accessories. Covers graphics, word processing, spreadsheets, BASIC, and windowing. Contains a complete glossary plus 4 appendices. Learn how the Mac can fit into an office environment, educational setting, or your home. Connolly and Lieberman.
ISBN 0-672-22361-9 . . . .$12.95

☐ MACINTOSH USER'S GUIDE

Is the Macintosh right for you? The introductory section of this complete user's guide contains a comparison with 5 other best-selling micros. What follows is an extremely well-written, well-illustrated, and attractively presented explanation of fundamental and advanced applications of the Macintosh. You'll want it right next to your Mac. Gordon McComb.
ISBN 0-672-22328-7 . . . .$16.95

☐ PREPARING YOUR BUSINESS PLAN WITH JAZZ™

Discover how to use the Jazz program to create a successful business plan. This "mini-MBA course" walks you step-by-step through marketing and competition, organizing operations and management, forecasting sales and expenses, and a host of other valuable information. Each chapter includes "tips" about solving unusual problems that may occur either with the software or in preparing a business plan. Dennis P. Curtin.
ISBN 0-672-22465-8 . . . .$24.95

☐ BUSINESS PROBLEM SOLVING WITH JAZZ

Use Jazz to identify and solve business problems. Credit and collections, pricing, inventory, and sales and marketing are examined in light of problems that can occur and how to use Jazz to solve them. This book highlights problems such as breakeven analysis, fixed or variable costs, sales and sales expenses, and much more. Dennis P. Curtin.
ISBN 0-672-22467-4 . . . .$24.95

☐ PLANNING AND BUDGETING WITH JAZZ

Use this powerful integrated software package to build spreadsheets, graphs, windows, macros, and menus to help you plan your budget and control sales and expenses. This concise, well-written text takes you step-by-step through Jazz's five modules so you can get a better handle on your business. Dennis P. Curtin.
ISBN 0-672-22466-6 . . . .$24.95

☐ AI ON THE MAC

A hands-on introduction to the hottest topic in microcomputers. Ten complete programs are written in the easy-to-learn Logo language for the Macintosh which demonstrate the look and feel of "artificially intelligent" programs. Listings are completely annotated according to the purpose of the code and the relationship between the code and the AI concepts being discussed. Programs begin simply and progress to more complex projects. Parallel BASIC listings are included for the introductory programs. Dan Shafer.
ISBN 0-672-22447-X $24.95

☐ C ON THE MACINTOSH

This intermediate level programming book provides a thorough understanding of the C programming language as it is uniquely designed for the Macintosh. Allows you to access over 500 ROM tool kit routines, and shows you how to use the routines to develop a programming application in C. Eyes and Medneiks.
ISBN 0-672-22461-5 . . . .$18.95

☐ USING MAC PASCAL

An excellent book for beginning and intermediate Pascal programmers. Guides you in using the innovative Pascal language developed by Think Technologies for the Macintosh. Discusses in detail how to access the ROM tool kit, and how to create applications and programs in Pascal. Cassidy and Steinberg.
ISBN 0-672-22440-2 . . . .$15.95